D0403993

# Overcoming Trumpery

# Overcoming Trumpery

## How to Restore Ethics, the Rule of Law, and Democracy

EDITED BY

## NORMAN EISEN

BROOKINGS INSTITUTION PRESS

*Washington, D.C.*

The Brookings Institution is a private nonprofit organization devoted to research, education, and publication on important issues of domestic and foreign policy. Its principal purpose is to bring the highest quality independent research and analysis to bear on current and emerging policy problems. Interpretations or conclusions in Brookings publications should be understood to be solely those of the authors.

Library of Congress Control Number: 2021953036

ISBN 9780815739678 (pbk)
ISBN 9780815739685 (ebook)

9 8 7 6 5 4 3 2 1

Typeset in Freight Text Pro

Composition by Elliott Beard

**Trumpery, n.\***

Pronunciation: /ˈtrʌmpəri/

1. Deceit, fraud, imposture, trickery.

a1578 R. Lindsay Hist. & Cron. Scotl. (1899) I. 141 "They concordit alltogither in trumperie and fallsit."

1677 T. Gale Court of Gentiles: Pt. III iii. 78 "Their Ethics were but false or..imperfect ideas of Vertues..their politics were but carnal and so false reasons of State..and therefore stiled in the Scripture tromperie, deceit, and lies."

2. 'Something of less value than it seems'; hence, 'something of no value; trifles' (Johnson); worthless stuff, trash, rubbish. (Usually collective singular; also, now rarely, plural.)

1789 H. L. Piozzi Observ. Journey France II. 353 "A heap of trumpery fit to furnish out the shop of a Westminster pawnbroker."

1807 Salmagundi 20 Mar. 111 "An abundance of trumpery and rubbish, with which the house is incumbered,..every room, and closet, and corner, is crammed with three legged chairs, clocks without hands, swords without scabbards [etc.]."

---

\*_Oxford English Dictionary Online_, Oxford University Press, 2021.

# Contents

# Acknowledgments

The editor and authors of this book are grateful to Daniel Berger for his steadfast support in so many different ways, as well as to Brookings' president John Allen and vice president of Governance Studies at Brookings Darrell West for making this volume possible. We would like to thank our wonderful publisher, Bill Finan, and his colleagues at the Brookings Institution Press, including Cecilia González, Kristen Harrison, Elliott Beard, and many others, for their always stellar efforts. Norman Ornstein also offered insightful comments and analysis on the draft manuscript, for which we are deeply appreciative.

We are indebted to several colleagues at Brookings who were part of the book's inception, research, and production, as well as an earlier Brookings report that this book is based on. Catherine Conrow was a project and research assistant in the Governance Studies program at Brookings. Edison Forman, Madison Gee, Elias Kaul, Alivia Kiefer, Ishita Krishan, Rakhi Kundra, Cyndi Lai, Luis Neuner, Taylor Redd, Sue Ryu, and Kate Tandberg were interns in the Governance Studies program. They conducted essential fact-checking and proofreading of the text, standardized the citations, and managed the book's production by coordinating with the authors and editor.

A number of chapters in this book were adapted from a Brookings report released under the name "If It's Broke, Fix It: Restoring Federal Government Ethics and Rule of Law," which was published in February 2021. The authors greatly expanded upon their contributions to that report in writing their longer chapters for this volume. The views of the authors of each chapter are solely their own and not that of the editor, the Brookings Institution Press, or the Brookings Institution.

# Editor's Note

## Trumpery Nevermore

**NORMAN EISEN**

"If it ain't broke, don't fix it." So goes the old adage. Its corollary, however, is equally important, particularly to U.S. governance and its constant reinventions over the past almost 250 years: if it is broken, do fix it. That principle has guided the American experiment from the earliest days of the republic through the Civil War and its aftermath, cycles of depression and recovery, grievous domestic and foreign policy blunders and atrocities, and alternating progress and triumphs.

When it comes to federal government ethics, rule of law, and democracy, a great deal was broken by President Donald J. Trump and his administration that must now be repaired. In this book, a group of distinguished scholars and practitioners has come together to provide an independent assessment of that problem and its solutions. The mission that these accomplished individuals undertake is to think broadly and deeply about what went awry, the profound weaknesses that were exposed, and how to fix these weaknesses moving forward in the authors' particular domains of expertise. Trump shook and damaged the pillars of U.S. governance. The authors consider how to shore them back up so that what happened under Trump can never happen again.

The authors catalog for posterity the startling details of Trump's federal governance misconduct—what may be termed "Trumpery." As you will read in these pages, it is characterized by a disdain for ethics, the rule of law, and the structures and values of democracy itself that rises to the level of abuse of power. Trumpery is brazen, justifying itself through transparent lies and disinformation with an utter lack of shame. It corruptly advances the personal and political interests of its leader and his cronies and galvanizes its cult-like populist base through fear and paranoia, often accompanied by racist subtext or, indeed, text. It does so without regard for the harm to the public interest or the pain caused to innocent targets. Indeed, sadism is part of the spectacle. As we discuss in the pages that follow, these features can be found from the initial minute of Trump's presidency to its last, from his very first transgressions of the Constitution by taking foreign emoluments and banning Muslim immigrants (though not from any nation that was a source of payments to him) to his final and still ongoing assault upon democracy itself by promoting the Big Lie that the 2020 election was purloined.[1]

Trumpery also transcends Trump. Some of the ills cataloged here have been set up or practiced by predecessors of both parties, as you will read. The more fundamental danger, however, lies in our future. From senators and House members to governors and party leaders, acolytes of Trumpery have learned its lessons and may seek to apply them in their current federal offices and in future ones. If major structural reform is not undertaken to shore up federal ethics, rule of law, and democratic functionality, Trumpery could recur in even worse forms. Accordingly, the authors focus not just on the symptoms but also on the cure: the changes that are needed to prevent the recurrence of Trumpery. The issues that the authors address range from reconstructing federal ethics, conflicts of interest rules, and transparency to restoring independence and enforcement at the Department of Justice (DOJ); from rebuilding how elections are conducted to reconsidering how campaigns are financed; and from reviving congressional oversight powers to reforming the filibuster that stands in the way of many of the legislative changes that are necessary to prevent a reversion of Trumpery in governance. Throughout the authors also look beyond domestic concerns to consider national security and international aspects of these issues, concluding the volume with a chapter on how to restore U.S. leadership internationally

## THE SEVEN DEADLY SINS OF TRUMPERY

Disdain for ethics

Assault on the rule of law

Incessant lying and disinformation

Shamelessness

Pursuit of personal and political interest, not the public interest

Exploitation and exacerbation of division

Attack on democracy itself

on ethics and the rule of law that Trump so badly undermined. Trumpery is a U.S.-flavored example of a style of governance that is all too familiar to many nations that have fought for democracy, and our allies are no less interested in solutions than are Americans.

Because these issues are interwoven and the authors have dealt with all of them in their long professional careers, virtually any one of them could have written any of the chapters. Topics were ultimately chosen based on areas of preeminent expertise among the group. My only other request of them was to balance describing the problem with offering the solution: imagine what would be the best policies to prevent the repeat of the governance offenses of the Trump administration, without regard for any other consideration. Each chapter and the views therein are entirely the authors' own. The authors and I certainly recognize that many compromises will be necessary to translate these ideas into law and practice. Indeed, we welcome that as part of the normal policy process in which, collectively, we have all worked for well over a century. But compromise must not come at the expense of comprehensiveness. As the broad and interlocking scope of this book demonstrates, the challenges are interconnected and so any solution must address each of these areas.

We have followed the Brookings practice of not endorsing particular proposed legislation, including H.R. 1 and S. 1, the comprehensive reform bills known collectively as the For the People Act, which passed in the House in March 2021 and were introduced twice in the Senate in June and August 2021. (As this volume goes to press in November 2021, the Freedom to Vote Act, S. 2747, a compromise version of S. 1 agreed upon by the Senate Democratic caucus, has stalled in the Senate after initial attempts to pass both it and S. 1, its predecessor, fell short of the sixty votes currently needed to open debate, splitting fifty-fifty along party lines.) Instead we focus on what we think are the best solutions; the extent to which the recommendations may track with the proposed legislation or with other bills is not intended as an endorsement of this legislation, although it merits and receives close attention.

As for the executive branch of government, the Biden administration has commenced the reconstruction that is needed after the ethics, rule of law, and democracy devastation of the Trump era. Pending the legislative fixes that are the main focus of this volume, the administration has essayed executive action to the extent possible in all three areas. For example, President Biden announced his own ethics plan through an executive order (EO) on January 20, Inauguration Day.[2] Many of the legislative solutions discussed in this book are addressed by the Biden executive order. Because EOs can be swept away by a successor president, they are no substitute for more permanent legislative fixes. Still, the significance of Biden's executive action is not to be minimized. A number of the authors and I had the privilege of implementing President Barack Obama's demanding ethics vision for his administration, including its centerpiece, his "day one" executive order setting tough new rules on conflicts of interest.[3] It may seem like a very long time ago after four years of Donald Trump, but Obama had arguably the most scandal-free presidency in memory, owing to those clear ethics rules backed by strong transparency about their application.[4]

Biden's new executive order on ethics restores the fundamentals of the Obama plan by closing loopholes Trump opened—but going further, it also includes new crackdowns on special interest influence. If implemented rigorously (always a big if), Biden's plan promises to go further to "drain the swamp" than either of his predecessors.[5] Is the new Biden ethics plan perfect? Of course not. Even more restrictions could have been loaded on prior relationships coming into government, and even longer exclusions onto officials leaving the administration. Corporate lobbyists could have been barred altogether, and public interest lobbyists automatically waived in. But all of those strictures would have come at a cost of finding the right people to do the urgent work of government in a time of pandemic, economic crisis, domestic unrest, and continued foreign war.

Government by EO is, however, ephemeral, as the previous administration proved when it revoked the Obama ethics order. Legislative changes are necessary for permanence. That is true both in ethics and in parallel reform fields affecting democracy and rule of law: DOJ independence, voting regulation, congressional oversight, and on and on. As you will read in the pages that follow, the administration has taken important steps in a number of these areas on its own, but its powers are limited absent congressional action. Leaders in both the House and the Senate seem to recognize that. As of this writing, they remain committed to moving forward with the Freedom to Vote Act (discussed throughout along with H.R. 1 and S. 1) and companion legislation such as the John Lewis Voting Rights Act (chapter 5) and the Protecting Our Democracy Act (chapter 8). Readers can learn a great deal more about the policy concerns these and many other proposed bills address in the pages that follow.

The authors and I are proud to contribute these insights about reconstructing ethics, the rule of law, and democracy to the vibrant discussions in which Washington and the United States are now engaged. They offer hope that the very dark period of Trumpery through which we have passed can be prevented from recurring ever again.

Notes

1. Norman Eisen and Richard Painter, "Contempt for Ethics Hobbles Trump: Painter and Eisen," *USA Today*, April 26, 2017, www.usatoday.com/story/opinion/2017/04/26/contempt-ethics-hobbles-trump-painter-and-eisen/100891776/.

2. Joseph R. Biden Jr., "Executive Order on Ethics Commitments by Executive Branch Personnel," White House, January 20, 2021, www.whitehouse.gov/briefing-room/presidential-actions/2021/01/20/executive-order-ethics-commitments-by-executive-branch-personnel/.

3. The following paragraphs are heavily adapted from an op-ed written by the editor. See Norman Eisen, "I Wrote President Obama's Ethics Plan—Biden's Is Better," *Politico*, January 19, 2021, www.politico.com/news/magazine/2021/01/19/biden-white -house-ethics-plan-460472.

4. For a detailed comparison of the executive orders on ethics issued by past administrations from Clinton to Biden, see "Comparing Ethics Orders: Biden's Is on Top, But It Could Be Stronger," Project on Government Oversight, January 28, 2021, www.pogo.org/resource/2021/01/comparing-ethics-orders-bidens-is-on-top-but-it -could-be-stronger/?utm_source=pogofacebook&utm_medium=social&utm_ campaign=governance&utm_term=link&utm_content=live.

5. Biden's ethics EO, as good as it is, has not insulated his administration from facing ethics issues. All administrations do, and this one has been no exception. As of this writing, questions have been raised about a series of issues largely outside the scope of the EO, principally focused on activities of family members of administration officials. The press and experts, including some of those who have contributed to this volume, have raised important inquiries about lobbying by the brother of a senior White House official; about family members of senior administration officials obtaining administration jobs; and about art created by the president's son being sold for large sums. There are also concerns about outside institutions, including consulting and defense firms, sending relatively large numbers of personnel into the administration. See Michael Scherer and Sean Sullivan, "Lobbyist Brother of Top Biden Adviser Poses Challenge to President's Ethics Promises," *Washington Post*, June 15, 2021, www .washingtonpost.com/politics/biden-lobbying-ethics-ricchetti/2021/06/13/1f2f0826 -c864-11eb-81b1-34796c7393af_story.html; Sean Sullivan and Michael Scherer, "A Family Affair: Children and Other Relatives of Biden Aides Get Administration Jobs," *Washington Post*, June 19, 2021, www.washingtonpost.com/politics/biden-aides -relatives-jobs/2021/06/17/ab504a22-cea4-11eb-8cd2-4e95230cfac2_story.html; Matt Viser, "Deal of the Art: White House Grapples with Ethics of Hunter Biden's Pricey Paintings," *Washington Post*, July 8, 2021, www.washingtonpost.com/politics/deal-of -the-art-white-house-grapples-with-ethics-of-hunter-bidens-pricey-paintings/2021/ 07/07/97e0528c-da72-11eb-9bbb-37c30dcf9363_story.html; and Eric Lipton and Kenneth P. Vogel, "Progressives Press Biden to Limit Corporate Influence in Administration," *New York Times*, November 12, 2020, www.nytimes.com/2020/11/12/us/politics/ biden-administration-corporate-influence.html. In some of these instances, the White House or the individuals involved have responded by curtailing the activity. For example, the lobbyist has stated that he will no longer lobby the White House Office, where his brother works. See Scherer and Sullivan, "Lobbyist Brother of Top Biden Adviser Poses Challenge to President's Ethics Promises." In the case of the art sales, the White House has helped craft a remedy in which the names of the buyers will be withheld even from the artist to avoid the appearance of influence peddling. While sharply criticized by some experts (including authors in this volume) for a lack of transparency, it is an attempt to balance the legally permitted economic activity of an

adult presidential child with ethics concerns. See Viser, "Deal of the Art": "'Because we don't know who is paying for this art and we don't know for sure that [Hunter Biden] knows, we have no way of monitoring whether people are buying access to the White House,' said Walter Shaub, who headed the Office of Government Ethics from 2013 to 2017. 'What these people are paying for is Hunter Biden's last name.' Hunter Biden, through his attorney Chris Clark, did not respond to an interview request for this article. When asked about the artwork—including terms of sale and potential ethics concerns—Clark referred questions to the White House. Andrew Bates, the deputy White House press secretary, suggested that the buyers' confidentiality would ensure the process is ethical. 'The president has established the highest ethical standards of any administration in American history, and his family's commitment to rigorous processes like this is a prime example,' Bates said." In other cases, such as the hiring of family members, the administration has strongly defended the selections as based on merit. Addressing public controversy regarding alleged nepotism among senior Biden administration officials, White House Press Secretary Jen Psaki tweeted: "can confirm my job over the last 5 months did not retroactively get my brilliant sister a master's degree from Harvard, a PhD in public health from Johns Hopkins and decades of published work and respect in the field. She is more qualified than I am to be here." See Jen Psaki (@jrpsaki), Twitter, June 18, 2021, 7:43 AM, https://twitter.com/jrpsaki/status/1405898946841563139. With respect to the institutions originating substantial numbers of administration members, the answer has been that all rules have been complied with, which appears to be the case. For further discussion of this, see also Aaron Schaffer, "Analysis—The Technology 202: Biden Administration Full of Officials Who Worked for Prominent Tech Companies," *Washington Post*, June 22, 2021, www.washingtonpost.com/politics/2021/06/22/technology-202-biden-administration-full-officials-who-worked-prominent-tech-companies/. The world will be watching to see how these issues evolve and are dealt with, whether new ones arise, and whether the ethics laws and best practices are scrupulously followed. The hallmark of excellence in ethics is not just avoiding problems, but also how they are addressed when they inevitably occur, whether governed by the ethics EO or otherwise.

# Overcoming Trumpery

# Introduction

# From Nixon to Trump and Beyond

## ANNE WEISMANN | NORMAN EISEN

Corruption in America, both perceived and real, has plagued the body politic since the government's inception. The Constitution's drafters added the Foreign Emoluments clause after Benjamin Franklin received a jeweled snuffbox and a portrait from the French king. The framers feared government influence could be bought by lavish foreign gifts.[1] Nineteenth-century administrations were riddled with corruption, with the Grant presidency representing one, but by no means the only, low point. That continued in the twentieth century with such outrages as the Teapot Dome scandal, which reached into the administration of President Warren G. Harding when it became known that a cabinet head had accepted bribes for oil leases.[2] But until the presidency of Donald Trump, it was Watergate—a scandal of such proportions that it brought down a president—that loomed the largest in terms of pure corruption and violation of the rule of law. That honor now goes to President Trump and his asymmetrical exploitation of the loopholes and weaknesses in U.S. democracy, a conclusion reinforced by Trump's conduct during his last few weeks in office.[3] We term that dangerously dysfunctional governance style "Trumpery."[4]

The lawlessness of Trumpery taught Americans that the traditions of U.S. government are not as sturdy as many had thought. Restoring democracy to its full strength will take more than renewing laws (and norms) alone; it will require sober leadership that sets high expectations for ethical conduct. But legal reforms can raise the floor for ethics and close gaps in the current rule of law and democratic framework.

This introduction proceeds in three parts. First, it examines many of the reforms Congress enacted to address the problems that surfaced during the Nixon presidency. Second, it describes how, broadly speaking, the post-Watergate checks failed to hold President Trump and his associates back from repeated transgressions, setting Trumpery on a course to run amok across the foundations of American governance. Third, it outlines the chapters that follow and details how to prevent the recurrence of Trumpery—that is, the corrections that must be made to do better when a future president seeks to test the gaps that Trump exposed.

## The Post-Watergate Reforms

Watergate, widely perceived as an inflection point, motivated Congress to enact major reforms strengthening the ethics framework and accountability measures governing public officials.[5] Those reforms started with the 1974 amendments to the 1971 Federal Election Campaign Act (FECA).[6] Congress amended FECA to address the campaign finance improprieties that the Watergate scandal brought to light: use of slush funds, money laundering, and undisclosed campaign contributions.[7] The 1974 amendments imposed dollar limitations on individual contributions to candidates and political action committees (PACs), as well as expenditure limits that were later deemed unconstitutional in *Buckley* v. *Valeo*, 424 U.S. 1 (1976). The 1974 statute imposed reporting and disclosure requirements on campaigns and political committees, and established a six-member bipartisan Federal Election Commission (FEC).[8] The amendments also established a process for presidential candidates to receive federal matching funds.[9] President Gerald Ford, in his signing statement, noted, "There are certain periods in our Nation's history when it becomes necessary to face up to certain unpleasant truths. We have passed through one of those periods. The unpleasant truth is that big money influence has come to play an unseem[ly] role in our electoral process."[10]

Four years later, in 1978, Congress responded to both the Watergate scandal and the Saturday Night Massacre—Nixon's firing of Special Prosecutor Archibald Cox—by enacting the Ethics in Government Act.[11] The new law created mandatory disclosure requirements including the financial and employment histories of public officials and their immediate families; tightened restrictions on lobbying by public officials after leaving office; and established the Office of Government Ethics (OGE).[12] Answering the need to restore public confidence in government by guaranteeing the independence of a special counsel, Congress created the Office of Special Counsel (OSC) within the Department of Justice (DOJ) and empowered it, at the recommendation of the attorney general and upon appointment by a special court, to investigate and prosecute certain government officials for violating criminal laws.[13] As then codified, the Ethics in Government Act granted the special counsel "full power and independent authority to exercise all investigative and prosecutorial functions and powers of the Department of Justice, the attorney general, and any other officer or employee of the Department of Justice."[14] (The special counsel statute has since been allowed to lapse, and the function has become a creature of DOJ-promulgated regulations, not statutes.)

In response to evidence of government fraud, waste, and mismanagement of agency programs and operations that emerged in congressional hearings, Congress passed the Inspector General Act of 1978.[15] This act established independent inspectors general within every major agency, reporting directly to their agency heads and authorized to conduct audits and investigations of agency programs and operations, and to help develop policies to detect and fight government abuse and fraud.[16] In his signing statement, President Jimmy Carter described the new inspectors general that the act created as "perhaps the most important new tools in the fight against fraud."[17]

Post-Watergate reforms also codified specific transparency measures designed to bring greater accountability by shedding light on the actions of federal agencies and officials. These include the 1974 amendments to the Freedom of Information Act (FOIA),[18] which were enacted over President Ford's veto and motivated in part by disputes over access to President Nixon's White House tape recordings as well as the failure of the executive branch to implement the FOIA as written.[19] The legislative history reflects Congress's concern that "most of the Federal bureaucracy, already set in its ways, never got the message" that Congress intended to send when it first enacted the FOIA in 1962: "a rule of government that all information with some valid exceptions was to be made available to the American people—no questions asked."[20] Instead, agencies had hindered "the efficient operation of the Freedom of Information Act . . . by 5 years of foot-dragging," displaying a "widespread reluctance . . . to honor the public's legal right to know."[21]

To remedy these problems, the 1974 amendments clarified the meaning and reach of several of the FOIA's exemptions; made explicit the obligation for agencies to produce all reasonably segregable, nonexempt material; required agencies to publish indexes of certain agency materials; created a public interest waiver of fees charged to requesters to process their requests; added a provision authorizing the disciplining of agency personnel found to have acted arbitrarily and capriciously in the withholding of agency records; broadened the definition of *agency* to include the Executive Office of the President (EOP) and other executive and government-controlled entities; provided that FOIA complaints take precedence over other litigation on federal court dockets; and established administrative processing deadlines of ten working days for requests and twenty working days for administrative appeals.[22]

Other post-Watergate reforms include the 1976 Government in the Sunshine Act, which mandated that agencies conduct open meetings unless subject to one of the act's exemptions, and prohibited *ex parte* communications to and from agency decisionmakers with respect to a pending proceeding.[23] Intended to increase public understanding of agency decisionmaking processes, the act was premised on the concept that, "in the words of *Federalist* No. 49, 'the people are the only legitimate fountain of power, and it is from them that the constitutional charter . . . is derived.' Government is and should be the servant of the people, and it should be fully accountable to them for the actions which it supposedly takes on their behalf."[24]

In response to President Nixon's ownership claim over his presidential papers, Congress passed the Presidential Recordings and Materials Preservation Act of 1974, which applied only to Nixon's presidential materials and placed them in the custody of the National Archives, to be processed and released to the public.[25] Four years later, Congress passed the Presidential Records Act (PRA) governing all presidential records post-Nixon. The PRA imposes record-keeping obligations on the president and vice president, including the mandate to document all activities, deliberations, decisions, and policies reflecting the performance of their duties, and establishes a multistep process they must complete before destroying presidential records during their time in office.[26] With this legislation, Congress had three goals in mind: (1) promoting "the creation of the fullest possible documentary record" of a presidency; (2) ensuring "the preservation of that record"; and (3) providing eventual public access to that record.[27] The PRA stems from the foundational principle that "essential to understanding the past is access to the historical record, to the documents, and other materials that were produced in the course of governing and which shed light on the decisions, and the decisionmaking processes of earlier years."[28]

The Watergate hearings that Congress had conducted in 1973 and 1974 exposed how politicized the Department of Justice had become under President Nixon, who lamented while in office, "We have never used (our power). We haven't used the (Federal) Bureau (of Investigation) and we haven't used the Justice Department, but things are going to change now. And they're going to change, and, and they're going to get it right."[29] In the aftermath of the Watergate scandal, Attorney General Edward Levi, appointed by President Gerald Ford, instituted reforms within the Justice Department. They included guidelines for FBI surveillance and other activities, reinforced the ideal of professionalism and adherence to separation of powers and the rule of law, and imposed new rules and structures to assure the integrity of DOJ actions.[30]

Attorney General Griffin Bell continued those reforms during the Carter administration.[31] He also imposed strict limits on FBI investigations[32] and protocols for communication between the White House and the DOJ that, in revised form, remained in place when President Trump took office.[33] These protocols sharply limit who on the White House staff may communicate with the DOJ about particular investigations and prosecutions.[34] Bell played a critical role in designing the Foreign Intelligence Surveillance Act of 1978,[35] which set limits on government wiretaps of U.S. persons by establishing a special court and other safeguards in cases of importance for national security.[36]

Following the Watergate scandal, which contributed to the public's distrust of government and the bureaucracy, Jimmy Carter made civil service reform a central promise of his election campaign. In 1978, Congress passed

the Civil Service Reform Act. It established three new federal agencies—
the Office of Personnel Management, the Merit Systems Protection Board,
and the Federal Labor Relations Authority—that would oversee federal civil
servants and strengthen the merit system. The act also established stronger
protections for whistleblowers who revealed government misconduct, providing them with the right to appeal to the Merit Systems Protection Board
if they were retaliated against for their disclosures.[37]

With these reforms, Congress believed it was remedying the problems
that Watergate had exposed. Even if not comprehensive, these reforms were
expected to prevent other American presidents from putting their interests
above those of the country.[38] And for decades it appeared that Congress had
more or less succeeded.

## Trumpery: A Failure of Accountability

The post-Watergate reforms sought to restore ethics and the rule of law and
to shore up the foundations of U.S. democracy. Since their passage, Congress has tweaked and amended them in response to specific perceived
flaws or loopholes, but by and large they stood the test of time—until they
ran headlong into the presidency of Donald Trump. From the moment he
descended that golden escalator to announce his candidacy for president,
Donald Trump signaled that he was a rule breaker intent on blowing up the
U.S. government and remaking it in his own image. His conduct while in
office lived up to that promise, and the post-Watergate reforms often proved
inadequate to hold him in check. Moreover, loopholes those reforms failed
to close also allowed President Trump to flout long-established norms with
impunity. Four words sum up the Trump presidency: a failure of accountability.[39]

President Trump's initial decision not to divest ownership or control of
the 500-plus companies that comprise his vast business empire constitutes
the "original sin" that put him on a collision course with ethics rules and
principles.[40] By one calculation, his failure to divest his financial interests
in the Trump Organization gave rise to more than 3,400 conflicts of interest.[41] His retention of his financial interest in these businesses through a
revocable trust that gave him the right of control and enjoyment over the
trust assets, including the right to withdraw money at any time,[42] did little to

assuage concerns about continuing conflicts of interest that could threaten the security of the United States.[43] Those concerns were heightened by the over $400 million Trump reportedly owes to his lenders that must be paid over the next few years.[44] While estimates of the size of his debt vary,[45] the debt made him particularly susceptible to foreign influence. Given the growing number of banks that cut ties with Trump in light of his role in the January 6, 2021, insurrection against the nation's Capitol, we must ask whether he looked abroad for help bailing him out of his financial problems.[46]

The federal conflicts of interest statute, 18 U.S.C. § 208, generally prohibits executive branch employees from participating in a matter in which they have a financial interest. But Congress exempted the president from the statute's reach.[47] Separation of powers considerations suggest restraint in legislating presidential conduct. Until Trump, Congress and the public could also rely upon the unbroken precedent that presidents had set since the 1970s, namely, the custom of placing their assets in blind trusts administered by independent trustees, in U.S. Treasuries, or in publicly held diversified mutual funds.[48] As a voluntary practice, it proved no match for a president like Trump, who did not share the institutional interest of his predecessors in maintaining both the legitimacy and the appearance of legitimacy of the presidency. His foreign entanglements and self-dealing quickly fueled a concern that he was elevating his personal and business interests over the interests of the United States,[49] with Congress and the courts powerless to act in the absence of a law banning this conduct by a president.[50]

Nor did the disclosure requirements to which the president was subject provide a sufficient brake against Trumpery, as they exclude liabilities of nonpublicly traded businesses like those of President Trump and require the reporting only of assets that are unrelated to the operations of the business, and of the value of assets only in broad ranges.[51] Had President Trump followed the course of all previous presidents and released his taxes, the public may have had a clearer picture of the extent of his foreign entanglements and the degree to which his business holdings posed conflicts of interest and national security risks.[52] But by also flouting this norm, the former president was able to keep the public and congressional overseers in the dark.

The foreign dignitaries that flocked to President Trump's Washington, D.C., hotel raised the specter of emoluments paid by governments seeking to win favor with the American president, as did the sixty-six or more foreign trademarks the Trump Organization received during his presidency, mostly from China.[53] Emoluments as potential sources of transnational corruption concerned the Constitution's framers, who responded with a prohibition on accepting foreign emoluments that is one of the "more strongly worded prohibitions in the Constitution."[54] The former president's financial stake in his Washington hotel, which he leases from the federal government, and the federal government's agreement to forbear from enforcing the default and termination provisions of the lease themselves suggest a violation of the Constitution's Domestic Emoluments Clause (as well as a violation of the terms of the lease).[55] A subservient General Services Administration (GSA) and a Republican majority in the Senate allowed the former president to skate right by the constitutional prohibition against accepting emoluments,[56] while individual lawsuits challenging his acceptance of emoluments got tied up in the courts and failed to yield a final result while the former president was in office.[57]

Trump's emoluments—violations that sprang into existence the moment he took his oath of office, because of his business holdings—were the original sin of the Trump administration. They set the pattern for the many other violations that followed and that this volume chronicles and terms Trumpery. The emoluments violated laws and norms alike; they were shrouded in opacity and mired in controversy; they served Trump's personal interest; they were facilitated by subservient officials throughout his administration, who enabled Trump instead of enforcing the law; and they challenged and strained the existing legal structures. The identical pattern can be seen throughout the four years of Trump's misconduct that this book recounts, up to and including his closing acts of granting corrupt pardons, assaulting the election, and inciting an insurrection.

## Preventing the Recurrence of Trumpery
### Chapters 1 and 2: Conflicts and Other Ethics Issues

Trump's presidency highlights the need to not only revise existing conflicts of interest laws to include the president and vice president, but also to toughen the laws for all executive branch officials; to enact legislation clarifying the meaning of key terms in the Domestic and Foreign Emoluments Clauses and their reach; to legislatively mandate that presidential candidates release their tax forms; and to enhance public financial disclosure requirements to create much more transparency, including preventing a president's financial debts and obligations from implicating national security concerns. Chapter 1 covers the specific weaknesses in presidential and White House ethics that Trump exposed. It analyzes them in depth and sets out proposals for addressing them. The chapter also focuses on corruption in Trump's immediate circle of family members and advisors. As to the former, laws against nepotism presented no obstacle for Trump, who brought both his daughter and son-in-law to the White House as top advisors.[58] A Department of Justice memorandum from the Office of Legal Counsel, released on the day President Trump assumed office, concluded that the White House was exempt from 5 U.S.C. § 3110, the anti-nepotism statute, which forbids a public official from appointing a relative "to a civilian position in the agency . . . over which [the official] exercises jurisdiction or control."[59] This paved the way for Ivanka Trump and Jared Kushner to join the president in the White House, where, once ensconced, they used the levers of power at their disposal to exert significant influence over U.S. domestic and foreign policies and, allegedly, to advance their financial interests.[60] To address this egregious nepotism, chapter 1 discusses how Congress must clarify that the anti-nepotism statute does not exempt the president.

Moving beyond Trump and his family, the actions of others in the Trump White House also exposed deficiencies in the Hatch Act. Enacted in 1939 in reaction to a scandal in the Roosevelt administration,[61] the Hatch Act prohibits federal employees from using their public office for partisan political purposes.[62] Despite this statutory prohibition, the White House refused to enforce the law against senior political appointees. For example, senior White House official Kellyanne Conway, counselor to the president, violated the law repeatedly by using her official Twitter account more than fifty times to bolster the president's political interests and by engaging in partisan efforts during television interviews.[63] Her pattern of conduct led the U.S. Office of Special Counsel, which is charged with enforcing the Hatch Act, to recommend that Ms. Conway be barred from public service.[64] President Trump refused to act on that recommendation.[65] That pattern was repeated over and over again during the Trump years. As chapter 1 discusses, reforms are needed to strengthen OSC's ability to investigate Hatch Act violations, clarify that EOP employees can be investigated for Hatch Act violations, and authorize OSC to issue civil fines for violations committed by political appointees.[66]

Chapter 2 builds on the primary (but not exclusive) White House focus of chapter 1 to mainly consider detailed ethics reforms impacting the remainder of the executive branch and, indeed, the federal government as a whole. President Trump exposed some of the problems with the government's ethics programs, but he did not create them. The Trump administration was a stress test for the executive branch's ethics program across government, and the program failed in many regards in going well beyond the president, his immediate family, and his closest White House aides. The lesson Congress should draw from Trump's presidency is that the systems for ethics in government need to be strengthened. Just as the Watergate scandal prompted a wave of government reforms, the ethical failure of the Trump administration should prompt significant reforms. Chapter 2 offers remedies for these insufficiencies by proposing laws that would require broad divestiture by top administration officials, additional post-employment restrictions, expansion of golden parachute payment constraints, and much more.

Nor does the problem stop with the executive branch of government. The ethics program in Congress is even weaker than the executive branch ethics program, and the Supreme Court has no formal ethics program at all. When a possible conflict or other ethics situation arises for a justice, each is left to decide what she or he thinks ethics require. If Trumpery has taught us anything, it is the danger of that lack of rules. Because both Congress and the Supreme Court require substantial ethics upgrades for the twenty-first century, chapter 2 also proposes legislative solutions that address deficiencies in those branches of the federal government as well.

A note to the reader: Aspects of the recommendations in chapter 2 are necessarily technical and in depth. That is because this volume seeks to provide a roadmap for legislators on deeper structural flaws in U.S. federal ethics programs and how to repair them. But the editor also hopes that the basic thrust of each recommendation and its aim is easy enough to understand.

## Chapters 3 and 4: Rule of Law Reforms

Turning back to the executive, the post-Watergate reforms not only met resistance in the White House. They also proved to be no match for an attorney general intent on expanding the scope and strength of the president's executive powers. Attorney General William Barr catapulted the Justice Department in a radical direction, to both expand the president's executive powers and protect his personal interests. Chapter 3 addresses change that is needed at the DOJ if the rule of law is to be restored and protected against further incursions. At Barr's direction, the department took extraordinary steps in two politically charged prosecutions: that of former national security advisor and Trump campaign official Michael Flynn, and that of political operative and Trump friend and supporter Roger Stone.[67] In testimony before the House Judiciary Committee, Aaron Zelinsky, one of four prosecutors who withdrew from the prosecution team in *United States v. Roger Stone*, described the Department of Justice as "exerting significant pressure on the line prosecutors in the case to obscure the correct Sentencing Guidelines calculation to which Roger Stone was subject—and to water down and in some cases outright distort the events that gave rise to his conviction."[68] By breaching the wall between the White House and DOJ that historically had protected federal criminal prosecutions from undue political interference—a wall that existed only as a matter of practice, policy, and comity—Barr signaled that there was little he would not do to protect the president's political fortunes.[69] An equally startling DOJ reversal in the Flynn case occasioned an eruption of controversy and a substantial inquiry by the concerned federal judge who was overseeing the matter, until the case was resolved by Trump's pardon of Flynn.[70] Stone, too, ultimately received clemency.[71]

Those are only two of many examples that chapter 3 discusses in its focus on reforming the DOJ. Like President Nixon, President Trump viewed the Justice Department and the FBI as directly under his control and answerable to him alone, telling the *New York Times*, "I have the absolute right to do what I want to with the Justice Department."[72] Trump's politicization of the DOJ came to a head in the 2020 campaign for president, when the attorney general lent his pre-election support to the discredited view that mail-in voting would produce a fraudulent result, helping to pave the way for the president's post-election assault on the integrity of the election.[73] Shocking revelations about the Trump-era DOJ have continued in his post-presidency. For example, the public has learned that in 2017 and 2018, the DOJ subpoenaed Apple for data from the accounts of Democrats on the House Intelligence Committee, their aides, and their family members in an attempt to identify who was behind leaks of classified information early in the Trump administration.[74]

These abuses highlight the need to restore the DOJ's independence, protect it from partisan politics, and assure its commitment to the rule of law through changes in DOJ policies, executive orders, and legislation. Chapter 3 proposes specific recommendations toward those ends, with ideas that range from giving other governmental entities a role in monitoring and reporting to Congress what is happening at the DOJ, to strengthening the independence of the special counsel. The latter mechanism in its existing form deserves particular attention. The 2017 decision to appoint Special Counsel Robert Mueller to investigate links between the Russian government and the Trump campaign was a promising step by the Department of Justice.[75] President Trump, however, sought to undermine the legitimacy and efficacy of the special counsel investigation from its inception.[76] He asked his then White House counsel Donald McGahn to have Mueller fired, and pressured then attorney general Jeff Sessions to unrecuse from the Russia investigation to stop the special counsel investigation into the president's conduct.[77] But Barr was ultimately able to thwart the special counsel process and insulate the president from accountability for what appear to be repeated acts of obstruction of justice. As the chapter details, he did so by a variety of means, including misrepresenting the contents of the Mueller report and refusing to take any action on it. Two federal judges have since sharply criticized Barr's "lack of candor" in his handling of the matter.[78] The special counsel regulations must be strengthened to prevent the recurrence of these and other abuses of the Trump era, and to shore up the independence of that office, as detailed in chapter 3. The chapter also offers some thoughts on what the current department should do to expose and prosecute the wrongs of the Trump era.

Under President Trump, the nation also faced an increased threat to the basic institutions of democratic governance from foreign adversaries. The 2016 and 2020 presidential elections revealed the true threat from malign foreign actors intent on interfering in the United States' democratic institutions.[79] The country can expect much more foreign activity, including through the actions of foreign agents here on American shores. But one tool to combat foreign influence—the Foreign Agent Registration Act (FARA)[80]— has been largely ineffective. Implemented in 1938, FARA was intended to promote transparency in regard to foreign influence by mandating that the information of foreign agents who operate in the United States, and that may influence American public opinion, policy, and laws, be publicized.[81] Impeding its efficacy are fairly minimal enforcement efforts by the DOJ, likely due to the statute's poor design and reliance on voluntary disclosure of foreign lobbying efforts.[82] As chapter 4 explains, reforms are needed to transform FARA from a blunt instrument to a more effective tool by amending its media exemption, giving the DOJ civil investigative demand authority (CID), reconciling FARA with the Lobbying Disclosure Act, and enhancing FARA's transparency and notification provisions.

### Chapters 5 and 6: Democracy Reforms: Elections and Voting

No discussion of reform would be complete without addressing challenges to the nation's voting and the integrity of elections. This, too, is a legacy of Trump: his Big Lie that the election was stolen from him, which resulted in the January 6, 2021, insurrection, has endured and metastasized in devastating fashion since he left office (in part because he continues to repeat it to anyone who will listen). Chapter 5 addresses the phenomenon of accelerated voter suppression across the country following the 2020 presidential election. Trump may be out of office, but Trumpery is going strong. That includes a worrisome subset of bills at the state level that go beyond voter suppression (as bad as that is) to constitute what some have termed "election subversion": partisan state legislatures seizing the power to decide elections and otherwise undermining the current election administration system that worked so well in 2020.

Chapter 5 discusses how a number of these bills threaten to throw the U.S. election system into chaos and concludes that if these laws had been in effect in 2020, partisan state legislatures may have illegitimately altered the outcome of the 2020 election contrary to the will of voters. These bills needlessly criminalize the work of election officials, interfere in the minutia of their jobs, and even seize from them the power to decide elections. The chapter further analyzes how federal legislation could address many of the worst provisions of these bills and concludes that federal legislation establishing a uniform, national standard for basic federal elections processes will be essential to ensuring that Americans have the opportunity to exercise the right to vote.

Money in politics, the topic of chapter 6, also remains a threat to American democracy—one that deepened under Donald Trump. Campaign cash influences who wins U.S. elections and controls decisions that elected officials make once in office. Trump began his presidential campaign railing against the corrosive effect of money in politics and promised his supporters "to inoculate himself from the influence of donors."[83] The reality was far different. Trump campaign donors wielded enormous influence at all levels of his administration, laying the groundwork for one of the most corrupt presidencies in history.[84] A completely dysfunctional FEC enabled dark money to continue its unrestrained impact on democratic processes.[85] Chapter 6 proposes a three-step plan that minimizes big money in politics, provides for robust disclosure to expose the role of persons and entities that pour large sums into political campaigns, and provides a counterbalance by bringing more small donors into the picture.

### Chapters 7 to 10: Other Democracy Reforms, Domestic and International

The actions of the Trump administration also revealed the critical role that an open government plays generally in countering attacks on the foundations of the U.S. government. President Trump was able to exploit legislative loopholes and shortcomings in government accountability mechanisms by pulling a blanket of secrecy over his administration and its actions. As chapter 7 discusses, he set the tone early in his presidency when the White House announced it would no longer continue the Obama administration practice of making White House visitor logs public.[86] When Trump administration officials refused outright to cooperate with congressional oversight efforts, the Freedom of Information Act proved to be no replacement. Leaks became a principal source of reports on internal goings-on, bedeviling an administration committed to secrecy.[87] But leaks are inherently selective and uncertain, and hardly a substitute for the usual flow of information.

That lack was felt keenly when the public needed access to critical information about a raging pandemic, and the Trump administration was able to rely on FOIA exemptions to prevent that access.[88] To protect U.S. democracy, as chapter 7 explains, Congress must arm citizens with the necessary tools for transparency: a FOIA law that works, providing access to a wealth of data ranging from accurate and current ethics information on public officials to reliable scientific data. The new administration must also commit to a radically changed view of transparency in government, beginning with providing public access to details of what happened in the Trump administration and why. Only by understanding its past can the nation hope to not repeat its failures and mistakes.

Chapter 7 explains that Congress must address the loopholes and limitations in the Federal Records Act, and expand private rights of action to ensure the public can act when an agency refuses to do so. While separation of powers principles place constitutional limits on how far Congress can go with the PRA, they would not prevent Congress from imposing disclosure and reporting requirements that would provide the public with more timely information about a president's record-keeping failures. Congress should also provide the archivist of the United States with more effective enforcement tools and greater access to the record-keeping practices of an incumbent president.

The Trump administration's wholesale disregard for powers conferred on Congress by the Constitution, including oversight, investigation, and the power of the purse, accelerated a pattern of executive aggrandizement in the federal government that chapter 8 describes. Congressional subpoenas for documents and testimony related to potential wrongdoing were openly flouted by Trump, his counsel, and his administration. The ex-president also rerouted congressional funds to unrelated projects including the wall on the southern border. Trump exploited the emergency powers of the executive to augment his own influence and weaken that of Congress. What resulted was an executive branch too often operating unburdened by the constraints the framers of the Constitution devised to ensure that American presidents could not govern unilaterally.

These examples of executive overreach predated the Trump administration but were taken to new extremes in the Trump era. Together they have diluted Congress's constitutional prerogatives and intensified that of the executive, throwing the balance of powers between those two government branches out of whack. Luckily, Congress has recourse to restore this balance. Chapter 8 explains how Congress can claw back some of the power taken by the executive branch and restore Congress's full constitutional role as a coequal branch. It explores the solutions contained in the Protecting Our Democracy Act (PODA), which passed the House in 2021, was transmitted for consideration in the Senate, and would address many of the problems of executive overreach analyzed in the chapter. The chapter also ventures beyond the bill to consider other solutions not yet codified in pending legislation.

Because some of the reforms discussed in this book may need the support of sixty members of the Senate to overcome the filibuster and advance to debate under current Senate rules, there has been significant discussion of amending the filibuster so that these reforms have an opportunity to be passed in this Congress. Chapter 9 surveys the principal changes to the filibuster rules that are under discussion. They include requiring senators to "stand there and talk" during a filibuster, keeping the filibuster in place but requiring forty-one senators to be present to vote to sustain a filibuster, and creating a diminishing threshold for cloture with each successive vote on a piece of legislation. Other proposals would establish the threshold for cloture as the number of senators in the majority of any given Congress or would restrict the filibuster to votes on substantive policy rather than motions to proceed (open debate).

The chapter weighs the pros and cons of each proposed change, and also delves into a solution that would allow Congress to pass much-needed democracy reforms without completely overhauling the filibuster. Just as budget reconciliation allows the Senate to pass budgetary legislation with a simple majority without needing to overcome the filibuster, chapter 9 proposes that the same threshold should be applied to legislation relating to an even more core area of the government's functioning: the right to vote. The authors refer to this proposal as democracy reconciliation. As they explain, creating a democracy-focused exception to the filibuster is crucial to thwarting state-based efforts to restrict the vote and subvert elections (which are discussed at length in chapter 5). Doing so would help to restore the fundamental premise of representative democracy and could reduce abuse of the filibuster in an era of hyper-partisanship and government gridlock.

Finally, chapter 10 explains that the ethics and rule of law issues of the past four years were not limited to domestic concerns, nor to domestic impacts. The Trump administration also neglected or backpedaled on a multitude of international partnerships and alliances created for nations to work collectively toward more ethical, transparent, and just governance. As a result, the Biden administration has an array of opportunities to reengage on international ethics and rule of law issues. Two of the best opportunities for the renewal of meaningful U.S. participation are the Open Government Partnership (OGP) and the Extractive Industries Transparency Initiative (EITI). Both efforts were founded with U.S. leadership and revolve around national and international collaboration on improving governance and instituting reforms that bolster ethics, transparency, and the rule of law in both the public and private sectors. Another opportunity for the Biden administration to demonstrate its commitment to multilateralism and U.S. leadership is the Summit for Democracy, a gathering described by President Biden as part of his foreign policy platform. Concerted U.S. engagement on these and other international collaborations will begin to undo the damage to American credibility on ethics and rule of law issues around the world.

---

Taken together, these ten chapters offer a survey of some of the principal ways that the United States can fix what was broken in ethics, the rule of law, and democracy during the Trump years, and assure that those ills do not occur again. As the chapter authors repeatedly note, the former president and his administration often exploited or worsened preexisting weaknesses. The post-Watergate order was already showing its age; Trump and his cronies shone a bright light on and worsened its cracks, while opening some new ones. The damage was not done in a day, and neither will be the work of repair and of assuring that Trumpery does not recur. But we must begin somewhere, and the editor and authors hope the essays that follow are part of that effort.

## Notes

1. Zephyr Teachout, *Corruption in America* (Harvard University Press, 2014), pp. 25–27.

2. Ibid., p. 187. See also Bryan Craig, "Making the Teapot Dome Scandal Relevant Again!" *Miller Center*, April 11, 2017, https://millercenter.org/issues-policy/us-domestic -policy/making-teapot-dome-scandal-relevant-again; "Historical Highlights: Senate Investigates the 'Teapot Dome' Scandal, April 15, 1922," Art & History, U.S. Senate, www.senate.gov/about/powers-procedures/investigations/senate-investigates-the -teapot-dome-scandal.htm.

3. See Ashley Collman, "Carl Bernstein Says Trump's Call Asking a Georgia Official to Help Him Overturn Biden's Win Is 'Far Worse' Than Watergate," *Business Insider*, January 4, 2021, www.businessinsider.com/carl-bernstein-trump-call-with -georgia-official-worse-than-watergate-2021-1.

4. For our definition of "Trumpery," see the "Editor's Note," this volume.

5. Matt Ford, "Donald Trump and the Absolute Power Presidency," *New Republic*, November 18, 2019, https://newrepublic.com/article/155762/donald-trump-absolute -power-presidency.

6. Federal Election Campaign Act Amendments of 1974, Pub. L. No. 93–443, 88 Stat. 1263.

7. See, e.g., "Mission and History," Federal Election Commission, www.fec.gov/ about/mission-and-history/; Mark Stencel, "Watergate 25: The Reforms," *Washington Post*, June 13, 1997, www.washingtonpost.com/wp-srv/national/longterm/watergate/ legacy.htm.

8. Ibid. See also Anthony J. Gaughan, "The Forty-Year War on Money in Politics: Watergate, FECA, and the Future of Campaign Finance Reform," *Ohio State Law Journal* 77, no. 4 (2016), pp. 791–837, https://kb.osu.edu/bitstream/handle/1811/79605/5/ OSLJ_V77N4_0791.pdf.

9. John Dunbar, "A Modern History of Campaign Finance: From Watergate to 'Citizens United,'" Center for Public Integrity, November 15, 2017, https:// publicintegrity.org/politics/a-modern-history-of-campaign-finance-from-watergate -to-citizens-united/.

10. Presidential Statement on the Federal Election Campaign Act Amendments of 1974, Pub. Papers 303 (October 15, 1974), www.fordlibrarymuseum.gov/library/ document/0248/whpr19741015-011.pdf.

11. Sam Berger and Alex Tausanovitch, "Lessons from Watergate," Center for American Progress, July 30, 2018, www.americanprogress.org/issues/democracy/ reports/2018/07/30/454058/lessons-from-watergate/.

12. Ethics in Government Act of 1978, Pub. L. No. 95–521, 92 Stat. 1824.

13. Ibid. See also Jim Mokhiber, "A Brief History of the Independent Counsel Law," *Frontline*, May 1998, www.pbs.org/wgbh/pages/frontline/shows/counsel/office/ history.html; Jared P. Cole, Cong. Rsch. Serv., R44857, *Special Counsel Investigations: History, Authority, Appointment, and Removal* (2019), https://fas.org/sgp/crs/misc/

R44857.pdf. The independent counsel provisions of the Ethics in Government Act expired in 1999.

14. Those provisions are codified at 28 U.S.C. § 594(a).

15. Ben Wilhelm, Cong. Rsch. Serv., R45450, *Statutory Inspectors General in the Federal Government: A Primer* (2019).

16. See generally 5 U.S.C. App. 2.

17. See, e.g., Council of the Inspectors General on Integrity and Efficiency, "IG Act History," www.ignet.gov/content/ig-act-history.

18. Freedom of Information Act, Pub. L. No. 93–502, H.R. 12471, 93rd Cong. § 1 (1975).

19. "Historical Highlights: The Freedom of Information Act, November 20, 1974," History, Art & Archives, U.S. House of Representatives History, https://history.house.gov/HistoricalHighlight/Detail/35741; Berger and Tausanovitch, "Lessons from Watergate."

20. Freedom of Information Act and Amendments of 1974, Pub. L. No. 93–502, 7, 94th Cong. (Comm. Print 1975), www.loc.gov/rr/frd/Military_Law/pdf/FOIA-1974.pdf.

21. Ibid., 15.

22. "1974 Amendments to the Freedom of Information Act," Pub. L. No. 93-502, H.R. 12471, 93rd Cong., U.S. Department of Justice, www.justice.gov/oip/1974-amendments-freedom-information-act.

23. Government in the Sunshine Act, Pub. L. No. 94–409, 90 Stat. 124 (1976).

24. Harold Relyea, United States Congress Senate Committee on Government Operations, and United States Congress House Committee on Government Operations, *Government in the Sunshine Act, S. 5 (Public Law 94-409): Source Book, Legislative History, Texts, and Other Documents* (U.S. Government Printing Office, 1977).

25. Presidential Recordings and Materials Preservation Act of 1974, Pub. L. No. 93-526, 88 Stat. 1695 (44 U.S.C. § 2111 note); see also Presidential Records Act of 1978: Hearings on H.R. 10998 and Related Bills, 95th Cong. (1978), hereinafter PRA Hearings.

26. Management and Custody of Presidential Records, 44 U.S.C. § 2203. See also Congressional Record vol. 124, pt. 26, 34895-34896, 95th Cong. (1978), www.congress.gov/bound-congressional-record/1978/10/10/house-section?q=%7B%22search%22%3A%5B%22Presidential+records+act%22%5D%7D&s=4&r=5.

27. PRA Hearings, 70–73, statement of Rep. John Brademas, PRA cosponsor.

28. Ibid., 70.

29. Richard Nixon, "Private White House Tape, September 15, 1972," in Marshall Cohen, Annie Grayer, and Tal Yellin, "In Their Own Words: Nixon on Watergate, Trump on the Russia Investigation," CNN, April 12, 2019, www.cnn.com/interactive/2019/politics/trump-nixon-comparison/index.html.

30. Edward H. Levi, *Restoring Justice: The Speeches of Attorney General Edward H. Levi*, edited by Jack Fuller (University of Chicago Press, 2013).

31. See Griffin B. Bell and Ronald J. Ostrow, *Taking Care of the Law* (Mercer University Press, 1982).

32. See Griffin B. Bell, Attorney General of the United States, address at the Yale Law Journal Banquet, April 20, 1978, www.justice.gov/sites/default/files/ag/legacy/2011/08/23/04-20-1978.pdf.

33. "Internal Memorandum from Donald F. McGahn II, Counsel to the President, to all White House Staff," Politico, January 27, 2017, www.politico.com/f/?id=0000015a-dde8-d23c-a7ff-dfef4d530000; Jane Chong, "White House Interference with Justice Department Investigations? That 2009 Holder Memo," *Lawfare*, February 22, 2020, www.lawfareblog.com/white-house-interference-justice-department-investigations-2009-holder-memo. Protocols limiting DOJ and White House contact have been renewed under the Biden administration. See also Josh Gerstein, "Justice Department Issues Policy Limiting White House Contact," Politico, July 21, 2021, www.politico.com/news/2021/07/21/justice-white-house-contact-biden-trump-500476.

34. Ibid.

35. Bell, address at Yale banquet.

36. 50 U.S.C. §§ 1801–1811.

37. Berger and Tausanovitch, "Lessons From Watergate."

38. Kathryn Olmsted, "Watergate Led to Sweeping Reforms. Here's What We'll Need After Trump," *Washington Post*, November 15, 2019, www.washingtonpost.com/outlook/2019/11/15/watergate-led-sweeping-reforms-heres-what-well-need-after-trump/?arc404=true.

39. Linnaea Honl-Stuenkel and Lauren White, "Trump's War on Accountability Started with His Tax Returns. It's Gotten Worse Ever Since," Citizens for Responsibility and Ethics in Washington (CREW), April 22, 2020, www.citizensforethics.org/reports-investigations/crew-investigations/trump-war-accountability-timeline/; Edward J. Larson, "Trump Isn't First President to Abuse the Constitution, But He's Gone So Far We Need a Reckoning," *USA Today*, September 17, 2020, www.usatoday.com/story/opinion/2020/09/17/constitution-day-trump-era-abuses-failures-require-reckoning-column/5817963002/; Sam Berger, "How a Future President Can Hold the Trump Administration Accountable," Center for American Progress, August 5, 2020, www.americanprogress.org/issues/democracy/reports/2020/08/05/488773/future-president-can-hold-trump-administration-accountable/.

40. Andy Sullivan, Emily Stephenson, and Steve Holland, "Trump Says Won't Divest from His Business While President," Reuters, January 11, 2017, www.reuters.com/article/us-usa-trump-finance/trump-says-wont-divest-from-his-business-while-president-idUSKBN14V21I. See also Donald J. Trump, 2016 "Executive Branch Personnel Public Financial Disclosure Report," June 14, 2017, https://oge.app.box.com/s/kz4qvbdsbcfrzq16msuo4zmth6rerh1c; Donald J. Trump, 2017 "Executive Branch Personnel Public Financial Disclosure Report," May 15, 2018, https://cryptome.org/2018/06/trump-278e-2017.pdf; Donald J. Trump, 2018 "Executive Branch Personnel Public Financial Disclosure Report," May 15, 2019, http://pfds.opensecrets.org/N00023864_2018.pdf; Donald J. Trump, 2019 "Executive Branch Personnel Public Financial Disclosure Report," July 31, 2020, https://extapps2.oge.gov/201/Presiden.nsf/PAS+Index/

181BAF52E298FD70852585B70027E054/$FILE/Trump,%20Donald%20J.%202020 Annual%20278.pdf.; Donald J. Trump, 2020 "Executive Branch Personnel Public Financial Disclosure Report," January 15, 2021, https://extapps2.oge.gov/201/Presiden. nsf/PAS+Index/6E78B163F816EF6A852586630075291D/$FILE/Trump,%20Donald% 20J.%202021Termination%20278.pdf.

41. "President Trump's 3,400 Conflicts of Interest," CREW, September 24, 2020, www.citizensforethics.org/reports-investigations/crew-reports/president-trumps -3400-conflicts-of-interest/.

42. Letter from Kevin M. Terry, GSA Contracting Officer, to Trump Old Post Office LLC c/o the Trump Organization, March 23, 2017, www.gsa.gov/cdnstatic/Con tracting_Officer_Letter_March_23__2017_Redacted_Version.pdf; Donald J. Trump Jr. is the trustee, Allen Weisselberg is the business trustee, and Eric F. Trump is the chairman of the advisory board for the trust. Its terms give Trump Sr. the right of control and enjoyment over the trust and its underlying assets, including the right to withdraw money from any business at any time: "President Trump is the Donor of the Trust; President Trump is believed to be the sole beneficiary of the Trust; the purpose of the Trust is to 'hold assets for the exclusive benefit of Donald J. Trump'; the Trustees are required to distribute net income or principal 'at [President Trump's] request as the Trustees deem necessary for his maintenance, support or uninsured medical expenses or as the Trustees otherwise deem appropriate'; the Trustees consist of a close family member and close business associate rather than independent and unaffiliated persons; and President Trump retains the power to revoke the Trust." See also letter from Noah Bookbinder, Executive Director, CREW, to Sen. John Barrasso and Sen. Tom Carper, April 25, 2017, p. 5, www.epw.senate.gov/public/_cache/files/c84b06 95-3504-4ed7-b3d7-e4817a4444e3/citizens-for-responsibility-and-ethics-in-washing ton.pdf; Drew Harwell, "Trump Can Quietly Draw Money from Trust Whenever He Wants, New Documents Show," *Washington Post,* April 3, 2017, www.washingtonpost .com/politics/trump-can-quietly-draw-money-from-trust-whenever-he-wants-new -documents-show/2017/04/03/7f4c0002-187c-11e7-9887-1a5314b56a08_story.html? utm_term=.b2e41134181.

43. Russ Buettner, Susanne Craig, and Mike McIntire, "Long-Concealed Records Show Trump's Chronic Losses and Years of Tax Avoidance," *New York Times,* September 27, 2020, www.nytimes.com/interactive/2020/09/27/us/donald-trump-taxes.html.

44. Dan Alexander, "Donald Trump Has at Least $1 Billion in Debt, More Than Twice the Amount He Suggested," *Forbes,* October 16, 2020, www.forbes.com/sites/ danalexander/2020/10/16/donald-trump-has-at-least-1-billion-in-debt-more-than -twice-the-amount-he-suggested/?sh=6c450fc43306.

45. According to the *New York Times,* Trump has personally guaranteed $421 million in debt. Russ Buettner and Susanne Craig, "$421 Million in Debt: Trump Calls It 'a Peanut,' But Challenges Lie Ahead," *New York Times,* October 16, 2020, www.ny times.com/2020/10/16/us/trump-taxes.html.

46. See, e.g., Rob Wile, "Professional Bank and BankUnited Sever Trump Ties,"

*Miami Herald*, January 22, 2021, www.miamiherald.com/news/business/article248690 290.html.

47. 18 U.S.C. § 202(c).

48. Matt O'Brien, "Donald Trump Won't Do What Ronald Reagan, George H.W. Bush, Bill Clinton and George W. Bush Did," *Washington Post*, November 15, 2016, www.washingtonpost.com/news/wonk/wp/2016/11/15/ronald-reagan-did-it-george-h -w-bush-did-it-bill-clinton-did-it-george-w-bush-did-it-donald-trump-wont-do-it/.

49. See, e.g., Sheelah Kolhatkar, "Trump's Conflict-of-Interest Problem," *New Yorker*, November 14, 2016, www.newyorker.com/business/currency/trumps-conflict -of-interest-problem.

50. 18 U.S.C. § 208 bars most executive branch employees, but not the president, from participating in any matter that would have a direct and predictable effect on their financial interests or those imputed to them, unless they receive a waiver or a regulatory exemption applies.

51. U.S. Office of Government Ethics (OGE), *Public Financial Disclosure Guide*, 268, May 2018, https://oge.gov/Web/278eGuide.nsf/Public%20Fin%20Disc%20Guide_ PrintMay2018.pdf; OGE Form 278e, Part 2, July 2020, www.oge.gov/Web/OGE.nsf/ OGE%20Forms/FE904FADB163B45A852585B6005A23E8/$FILE/OGE%20Form% 20278e%20July%202020_accessible.pdf?open.

52. Katie Rogers, "Trump on Releasing His Tax Returns: From 'Absolutely' to 'Political Prosecution,'" *New York Times*, July 9, 2020, www.nytimes.com/2020/07/09/us/ politics/trump-taxes.html.

53. Rebecca Jacobs, "Trump Company Received New Trademark from Argentina," CREW, September 4, 2020, www.citizensforethics.org/reports-investigations/crew-in vestigations/trump-company-received-new-trademark-from-argentina/; "President Trump's 3,400 Conflicts of Interest," CREW, September 24, 2020.

54. Teachout, *Corruption in America*, pp. 26–28; See also Norman L. Eisen, Richard Painter, and Laurence H. Tribe, "The Emoluments Clause: Its Text, Meaning, and Application to Donald J. Trump," Brookings Institution, December 16, 2016, http://brook .gs/2hGIMbW.

55. See Second Complaint, *Citizens for Responsibility and Ethics in Washington, et al.* v. *Trump*, No. 1:17-cv-00458-RA ¶ 145 (S.D.N.Y. May 10, 2017), E.C.F. No. 28. See also Amended Complaint, *District of Columbia, et al.* v. *Trump*, No. 17-01596 (D. Md. Feb. 23, 2018) E.C.F No. 90-2.

56. See Office of Inspections, Office of Inspector General, and U.S. General Services Administration, *Evaluation of GSA's Management and Administration of the Old Post Office Building Lease* 5, JE19-002, January 16, 2019, www.gsaig.gov/sites/default/ files/ipa-reports/JE19-002%20OIG%20EVALUATION%20REPORT-GSA%27s%20 Management%20%26%20Administration%20of%20OPO%20Building%20Lease_ January%2016%202019_Redacted.pdf. "OGC decided to ignore the constitutional issues without preparing a formal decision memorandum to document the rationale for the position they were taking"; pp. 17–18 fault GSA for ignoring existing precedent

and instructions; pp. 18–19 fault GSA for ignoring precedent from the DOJ's Office of Legal Counsel.

57. At the end of the Trump administration, two lawsuits challenging the president's unconstitutional acceptance of emoluments were pending: *Trump v. Citizens for Responsibility and Ethics in Washington, et al.*, No. 20-330, a Trump petition for certiorari before the Supreme Court, and *District of Columbia, et al. v. Trump*, No. 20-1839 (4th Cir.), an appeal by Trump. They were dismissed by the Supreme Court as moot on January 25, 2021 (Supreme Court Order List 592 U.S. 20-331). Disclosure: The editor was counsel in both of those actions when they were filed and for much of their pendency, and the authors of this chapter as well as a number of the other authors were or are associated with CREW, which was involved in both cases.

58. "Ivanka Trump's and Jared Kushner's Roles in the Administration," American Oversight, July 24, 2020, www.americanoversight.org/investigation/ivanka-trumps -role-in-the-administration.

59. Memorandum opinion from Daniel L. Koffsky, Deputy Assistant Attorney General, Office of Legal Counsel, to the Counsel to the President, January 20, 2017, www.justice.gov/olc/opinion/application-anti-nepotism-statute-presidential -appointment-white-house-office. See also Josh Gerstein, "DOJ Releases Overruled Memos Finding It Illegal for Presidents to Appoint Relatives," Politico, October 3, 2017, www.politico.com/story/2017/10/03/justice-department-legal-memos-presidents -appoint-relatives-243395; Michael S. Schmidt, "Jared Kushner, Trump's Son-in-Law, Is Cleared to Serve as Adviser," *New York Times*, January 21, 2017, www.nytimes.com/ 2017/01/21/us/politics/donald-trump-jared-kushner-justice-department.html.

60. "Nepotism and Conflicts of Interest—Jared Kushner and Ivanka Trump," CREW, April 25, 2017, www.citizensforethics.org/reports-investigations/crew-reports /nepotism-and-conflicts-of-interest-jared-kushner-and-ivanka-trump/. See also letter from Noah Bookbinder, Executive Director, CREW, to Rod J. Rosenstein, Deputy Attorney General, January 4, 2019, www.citizensforethics.org/wp-content/uploads/ legacy/2019/01/Complaint-concerning-Assistant-to-the-President-Ivanka-Trump.pdf; Jesse Drucker, Kate Kelly, and Ben Protess, "Kushner's Family Business Received Loans After White House Meetings," *New York Times*, February 28, 2018, www.ny times.com/2018/02/28/business/jared-kushner-apollo-citigroup-loans.html?referer= https://www.google.com/.

61. Lesley Kennedy, "What Is the Hatch Act, and Why Was Established in 1939?" History, September 22, 2020, www.history.com/news/hatch-act-fdr-politics.

62. See generally Cong. Rsch. Serv., IF11512, *The Hatch Act: A Primer* (2020), https: //fas.org/sgp/crs/misc/IF11512.pdf.

63. See *Citizens for Responsibility and Ethics in Washington v. U.S. Office of Special Counsel*, Civil Action No. 19-3157 (D.D.C. Aug. 6, 2020); Donald K. Sherman, "Kellyanne Conway Eclipses 50 Hatch Act Violations on Twitter," CREW, October 21, 2019, www.citizensforethics.org/reports-investigations/crew-reports/kellyanne-conway -eclipses-50-hatch-act-violations-on-twitter/.

64. Letter from Henry J. Kerner, Special Counsel, U.S. Office of Special Counsel, to President Trump, June 13, 2019, www.citizensforethics.org/wp-content/uploads/legacy/2019/06/Report-to-the-President-re-Kellyanne-Conway-Hatch-Act.pdf.

65. John Wagner and Michelle Ye Hee Lee, "Trump Says He Won't Fire Kellyanne Conway over Hatch Act Violations," *Washington Post*, June 14, 2019, www.washington post.com/politics/trump-says-he-wont-fire-kellyanne-conway-over-hatch-act-violations/2019/06/14/76f31a94-8e9f-11e9-adf3-f70f78c156e8_story.html.

66. For a summary of the bill's provisions, see H. Comm. on Intelligence, 116th Cong., "The Protecting Our Democracy Act," fact sheet, https://intelligence.house.gov/uploadedfiles/fact_sheet.pdf.

67. See *United States* v. *Michael Flynn*, No. 17-cr-232-EGS (D.D.C. 2020), brief for court-appointed *amicus curiae*. In a 72-page brief, *amicus curiae* John Gleeson outlines "gross abuse of prosecutorial power"; Center for Ethics and the Rule of Law (CERL) and CREW, *Report on the Department of Justice and the Rule of Law Under the Tenure of Attorney General William Barr* (2020), www.law.upenn.edu/live/files/10900-report-on-the-doj-and-the-rule-of-law.

68. Hearings on Political Interference and Threats to Prosecutorial Independence, statement of Aaron S. J. Zelinsky, Assistant U.S. Attorney, H. Comm on the Judiciary, 116th Cong. (2020), https://judiciary.house.gov/uploadedfiles/zelinsky_opening_statement_hjc.pdf?utm_campaign=4024-519.

69. Devlin Barrett and Matt Zapotosky, "Barr Accuses Justice Department of Headhunting and Meddling with Politics," *Washington Post*, September 16, 2020, www.washingtonpost.com/national-security/william-barr-hillsdale-college/2020/09/16/0986dac4-f887-11ea-a275-1a2c2d36e1f1_story.html. See also CERL and CREW, *Report on the Department of Justice*.

70. Charlie Savage and Adam Goldman, "Outsider Tapped in Flynn Case Calls Justice Dept. Reversal a 'Gross Abuse' of Power," *New York Times*, June 10, 2020, www.nytimes.com/2020/06/10/us/politics/john-gleeson-michael-flynn.html; Josh Gerstein and Kyle Cheney, "'Any and All Possible Offenses': Trump Pardon Grants Flynn a Sweeping Reprieve," Politico, November 30, 2020, www.politico.com/news/2020/11/30/trump-flynn-pardon-reprieve-441527.

71. Peter Baker, Maggie Haberman, and Sharon LaFraniere, "Trump Commutes Sentence of Roger Stone in Case He Long Denounced," *New York Times*, July 10, 2020, www.nytimes.com/2020/07/10/us/politics/trump-roger-stone-clemency.html.

72. "Excerpts from Trump's Interview with The Times," *New York Times*, December 28, 2017, www.nytimes.com/2017/12/28/us/politics/trump-interview-excerpts.html; Peter Baker, "'Very Frustrated' Trump Becomes Top Critic of Law Enforcement," *New York Times*, November 3, 2017, www.nytimes.com/2017/11/03/us/politics/trump-says-justice-dept-and-fbi-must-do-what-is-right-and-investigate-democrats.html.

73. See, e.g., Bob Christie, "U.S. Attorney General Barr Attacks Voting by Mail While in Arizona," *PBS News Hour*, September 10, 2020, www.pbs.org/newshour/nation/u-s-attorney-general-barr-attacks-voting-by-mail-while-in-arizona.

74. Katie Benner and others, "Hunting Leaks, Trump Officials Focused on Democrats in Congress," *New York Times*, June 10, 2021, www.nytimes.com/2021/06/10/us/politics/justice-department-leaks-trump-administration.html.

75. Office of the Deputy Attorney General, U.S. Department of Justice, *Appointment of Special Counsel to Investigate Russian Interference with the 2016 Presidential Election and Related Matters*, Order No. 3915-2017 (May 2017), www.justice.gov/archives/opa/press-release/file/967231/download.

76. Artin Afkhami, "Timeline of Trump and Obstruction of Justice: Key Dates and Events," Just Security, January 25, 2018, www.justsecurity.org/45987/timeline-trump-obstruction-justice-key-dates-events/.

77. See Barbara McQuade, "Did Trump and His Team Successfully Obstruct Mueller's Investigation?" Just Security, June 25, 2019, www.justsecurity.org/64679/did-trump-and-his-team-successfully-obstruct-muellers-investigation/.

78. As quoted in *EPIC v. DOJ*, No. 19-810, 145 (D.D.C. 2020) and *Leopold v. DOJ*, 487 F. Supp. 3d 1 (D.D.C. 2020), https://int.nyt.com/data/documenthelper/6805-judge-walton-ruling-on-barr-cr/2df9b5c6d7de0fef1e35/optimized/full.pdf#page=1; *Citizens for Resp. & Ethics in Wash. v. DOJ*, No. 19-1552, 2021 WL 1749763 (D.D.C. May 3, 2021), https://context-cdn.washingtonpost.com/notes/prod/default/documents/40591227-65b2-461d-8245-5e5778f88996/note/6823b0c7-bb17-4a01-b555-f4049936f7a6.#page=1.

79. James Lamond and Jeremy Venook, "Blunting Foreign Interference Efforts by Learning the Lessons of the Past," Center for American Progress, September 2, 2020, www.americanprogress.org/issues/security/reports/2020/09/02/489865/blunting-foreign-interference-efforts-learning-lessons-past/.

80. 22 U.S.C. §§ 611 et seq.

81. U.S. Department of Justice, "FARA Frequently Asked Questions," December 3, 2020, www.justice.gov/nsd-fara/frequently-asked-questions.

82. Office of the Inspector General, *Audit of the National Security Division's Enforcement and Administration of the Foreign Agents Registration Act*, U.S. Department of Justice, Audit Report 16-24, September 2016, www.oversight.gov/sites/default/files/oig-reports/a1624.pdf. See also "Recent FARA Cases," U.S. Department of Justice, www.justice.gov/nsd-fara/recent-cases.

83. See Peter Overby, "Presidential Candidates Pledge to Undo Citizens United. But Can They?" NPR, February 14, 2016, www.npr.org/2016/02/14/466668949/presidential-candidates-pledge-to-undo-citizens-united-but-can-they.

84. Isaac Arnsdorf, "Trump Rewards Big Donors with Jobs and Access," Politico, December 27, 2016, www.politico.com/story/2016/12/donald-trump-donors-rewards-232974; "Presidential Profiteering: Trump's Conflicts Got Worse in Year Two," CREW, January 16, 2019, www.citizensforethics.org/reports-investigations/crew-reports/presidential-profiteering-trumps-conflicts-got-worse-in-year-two/.

85. Brendan Fischer and Maggie Christ, "How the FEC Is Still Allowing Dark Money Groups to Remain Dark," Campaign Legal Center, October 17, 2018, https://campaignlegal.org/update/how-fec-still-allowing-dark-money-groups-remain-dark.

86. Ayesha Rascoe, "Trump White House Will Not Make Visitor Logs Public, Break from Obama Policy," Reuters, April 14, 2017, www.reuters.com/article/us-usa -trump-visitors/trump-white-house-will-not-make-visitor-logs-public-break-from -obama-policy-idUSKBN17G1GF.

87. "The Limits of Transparency and the Freedom of Information Act," First Amendment Watch, https://firstamendmentwatch.org/deep-dive/the-limits-of -transparency-and-foia-under-trump/. See also Liz Hempowicz and Anne Tindall, "Trump Won't Cooperate with Congressional Oversight. Here Are Congress's Options," Washington Post, September 15, 2020, www.washingtonpost.com/politics/2020 /09/15/trump-wont-cooperate-with-congressional-oversight-here-are-congresss -options/.

88. Nate Jones, "Public Records Requests Fall Victim to the Coronavirus Pandemic," Washington Post, October 1, 2020, www.washingtonpost.com/investigations/ public-records-requests-fall-victim-to-the-coronavirus-pandemic/2020/10/01/ cba2500c-b7a5-11ea-a8da-693df3d7674a_story.html; Khahalia Shaw, Christine Monahan, and Amanda Teuscher, "A Pandemic Is No Time for Secrecy," American Oversight, March 28, 2020, www.americanoversight.org/a-pandemic-is-no-time-for -secrecy.

**Part I**

# Conflicts and Other Ethics Issues

# 1

# President Trump's Abuse of Office

## VIRGINIA CANTER

President Trump's decision to retain the 500-plus companies that comprise the Trump Organization gave rise to unprecedented presidential profiteering and conflicts of interest.[1] From the outset of his administration, Trump is alleged to have violated the Constitution by profiting from foreign and domestic governments who patronized his hotels and other companies.[2] Trump's businesses served as vehicles for Trump's own personal enrichment leading to literally thousands of conflicts of interest.[3] His debt-laden businesses made him particularly susceptible to foreign influence and a possible national security risk.[4] Trump's appointment of his son-in-law and daughter paved the way for them to advance their own financial interests.[5] That woeful lack of "tone at the top" was complemented by a callous indifference to serious ethics violations by Trump's administration cronies, particularly of the Hatch Act.

True, Trump is gone and, as this book has already noted, a new tone has been set by the current administration. With the ex-president's departure, the most outrageous misconduct has ceased. But the weaknesses and gaps in ethics law that Trump and those around him exposed remain.[6] Those issues must be addressed to ensure that Trumpery never returns—that no future administration can abuse public office to further the president's and senior officials' personal financial or political interests as Trump and his cronies did. To address these deficiencies, this chapter itemizes some of the worst misconduct of the prior administration, accompanying it with specific recommendations that are intended to prevent misconduct. While the chapter takes no position on pending legislation, it notes that a number of these issues of presidential ethics are addressed by the For the People Act, which passed the House in March 2021. The bill's Senate counterpart has been the subject of hearings and considerable other activity in that body, though it is now pending disposition after attempts to open floor debate failed fifty-fifty along party lines.[7] (Sixty votes are currently required to open debate; that impasse is one of the principal drivers for filibuster reform of the kind discussed in chapter 9.) Other issues, such as emoluments, presidential tax transparency, and Hatch Act reform, are the subject of the Protecting Our Democracy Act, which as of this writing passed the House in 2021 as H.R. 5314 and has been transmitted to the Senate.[8]

## Trump's Foreign and Domestic Emoluments Clause Violations

Until Trump took office, the Foreign and Domestic Emoluments Clauses were among the lesser-known provisions of the U.S. Constitution. Public awareness of the two clauses grew significantly shortly after he took office, when Trump was sued for violating these provisions through a trust arrangement that allowed him to profit from his companies' business with foreign and domestic governments.[9]

Unlike most modern presidents who placed their assets in independently managed blind trusts, U.S. Treasuries, or publicly held diversified mutual funds, all of which are widely viewed as acceptable means for addressing presidential conflicts of interest,[10] President Trump retained his financial interests in the over 500 companies[11] that comprise the Trump Organization. He did so through a revocable trust, managed by his two adult sons and a former business associate, which gave Trump the right of control and enjoyment over the trust and its underlying assets, including the right to withdraw money from any business at any time.[12]

Because the Trump Organization profits from business dealings with foreign and domestic governments, it posed the risk of corrupt influences like those feared by the constitutional framers.[13] The Foreign Emoluments Clause was the framers' response to the tactics deployed by foreign sovereigns and their agents to acquire influence over officials by giving them gifts, money, and other things of value.[14] One of the "more strongly worded" prohibitions in the Constitution,[15] the Foreign Emoluments Clause states:

> No Title of Nobility shall be granted by the United States: And no Person holding any Office of Profit or Trust under them, shall, without the Consent of the Congress, accept of any present, Emolument, Office, or Title, of any kind whatever, from any King, Prince, or foreign State.[16]

Expressly limited to the president, the prohibition in the Domestic Emoluments Clause is narrower than the Foreign Emoluments Clause. But, like the Foreign Emoluments Clause, it also was intended to protect the government from corruption.[17] The Domestic Emoluments Clause provides:

> The President shall, at stated Times, receive for his Services, a Compensation, which shall neither be encreased nor diminished during the Period for which he shall have been elected, and he shall not receive within that Period any other Emolument from the United States, or any of them.[18]

After Trump took office, the Trump Organization continued to profit from business with foreign and domestic governments.[19] For example, one Trump company, the Trump Tower Commercial LLC, is estimated to have collected at least $5.4 million in payments from the Industrial and Commercial Bank of China (ICBC), a largely state-owned Chinese enterprise.[20] Foreign diplomats have held numerous national day celebrations at Trump hotels, including the Philippine and Kuwaiti embassy events at the Trump Old Post Office Hotel in Washington, D.C., and the Romanian consulate event at Trump's Chicago hotel.[21] These events resulted in multiple payments to the Trump Organization from foreign governments for services provided in connection with the celebrations.[22] In addition, the Trump Organization has received at least sixty-six foreign trademarks, the majority from China.[23]

Trump attempted to deflect concerns about his companies' dealings with foreign governments by announcing he would donate profits from foreign governments to the U.S. Treasury,[24] but the amounts he paid to the Treasury, totaling $448,473 for 2017 through 2019, only raised more questions.[25] There is no public accounting that independently verifies the accuracy of the amounts reported, and other unknowns abound.[26]

In addition to the foreign government payments received since Trump took office, his companies were paid at least $2.5 million by the U.S. government in apparent violation of the Domestic Emoluments Clause.[27] Some of these payments resulted from official White House and State Department events hosted by President Trump for foreign leaders, such as Chinese president Xi Jinping and Japan's then-prime minister Shinzo Abe, at Trump's Mar-a-Lago resort in Palm Beach, Florida.[28] Other payments derived from personal visits Trump made to his resorts, where the Secret Service was charged for room and board.[29] For example, Trump's two-week visit to Mar-a-Lago for Christmas in 2019 cost the Secret Service $32,400 for guest rooms, and his visits to his Bedminster, New Jersey, club cost the Secret Service $17,000 per month to rent a cottage there from May to November of each year.[30] Trump also benefited from his lease with the federal government for the Trump Old Post Office Hotel in Washington, D.C.[31]

## Emoluments Recommendation

To ensure that future presidents do not retain business interests that could run afoul of the Foreign and Domestic Emoluments Clauses, Congress should adopt legislation as follows:[32]

- Define *emolument* for the purposes of both Emoluments Clauses to include "any profit, gain, or advantage, of more than *de minimis* value, received, directly or indirectly, from foreign, the federal, or domestic governments, including profits from private or commercial transactions, even those involving services given at fair market value."

- Clarify that the president and vice president hold an "Office of Profit or Trust" for purposes of the Foreign Emoluments Clause.

- Bar the president, vice president, and other covered officials from accepting an emolument from foreign governments without congressional approval.

- Bar the president from accepting an emolument from the federal government or any domestic government under any circumstances.

- Define *de minimus value* for purposes of the Foreign Emoluments Clause.

- Bar the president and vice president (including any entity owned or controlled by them) from being party to any federal government contract, lease, or grant, and from deriving any monetary benefit from any federal government contract, lease, or grant regardless of when the contract, lease, or grant was awarded.

- Establish a statutory framework for an incoming president to disclose and divest within thirty days of taking office any business interests that present a credible risk of violating the Emoluments Clauses.

- Confirm Congress's ability to sue the president and obtain declaratory and injunctive relief, including forfeiture relief, for violating the Emoluments Clauses.

- Establish civil penalty and forfeiture provisions for violations of the Emoluments Clauses.

- Give the Office of Government Ethics (OGE) the responsibility to issue regulations that establish reporting as well as congressional notification and divestiture requirements and procedures.

- Give agency inspectors general explicit authority to investigate and refer violations to the Department of Justice to pursue civil penalties and forfeiture actions. Because there is no agency inspector general for the White House[33] for possible violations involving the president, vice president, and White House officials, Congress should establish a statutory framework for OGE to investigate (including authority to subpoena documents and appoint an agency inspector general or contract with external parties to assist with the investigation) and refer violations to the DOJ. Should the department decline to pursue civil penalties and/or forfeiture action within ninety days of a referral, the DOJ should be required to notify Congress and OGE of the basis for that determination. In such cases, OGE should be directed to review the DOJ's determination and separately submit its own findings and recommendations in a report to Congress. Should any covered official fail to cooperate with an Emoluments Clause investigation, OGE, the DOJ, or an agency inspector general overseeing the investigation should be required to report promptly to Congress.[34]

## Trump's Conflicts of Interest

By one calculation, President Trump's failure to divest his financial interests in the Trump Organization gave rise to more than 3,700 conflicts of interest during his time in office.[35] In addition to Emoluments Clause concerns, President Trump received more than $13 million from special interest groups seeking to gain favor with the administration, which have hosted or sponsored 137 events at Trump properties.[36] Political groups hosted 88 events at Trump properties, bringing in $9.7 million after Trump took office.[37] By using the office of the presidency to enrich Trump's businesses, the Trump Organization has profited from customers seeking to influence policy, who were often able to obtain personal access to the president or other members of the administration by frequenting the president's properties.[38]

Although the criminal conflict of interest statute, 18 U.S.C. § 208, bars most executive branch employees from participating in any particular matter that would have a direct and predictable effect on their financial interests or those imputed to them (e.g., those of their spouse or minor children), unless they receive a waiver or a regulatory exemption applies, the president and vice president are not subject to the statute.[39] Thus there was no statutory basis to hold President Trump accountable for abusing his office by partaking in official decisions that could further his own financial interests.[40] As well as making section 208 applicable to the president as recommended below, additional measures should be adopted to prevent foreign, domestic, and special interests from successfully undertaking influence-type campaigns that personally enrich the president at the expense of the public interest.

## Conflicts of Interest Recommendation

To ensure that future presidents do not retain business interests that can result in actual or apparent conflicts of interest, Congress should adopt legislation as follows:

- Make the president and vice president subject to the prohibitions of 18 U.S.C. § 208(a) with respect to their "business interests," unless the president (or vice president) agrees to divest all business interests not later than thirty days after taking office.

- Define *business interest* to include investments in any business enterprise, whether publicly or privately owned, but not to include U.S. Treasuries, diversified mutual funds that qualify for a regulatory exemption, residential property that is not held for the production of rental, or other income or family-owned and operated farms.

- Stipulate that divestiture of a business interest would be satisfied by placing business interests into an OGE-qualified blind or diversified trust with a commitment for those assets to be sold.[41]

## Trump's $400 Million–Plus Debt Obligations Coming Due

President Trump's precarious financial situation made him a possible national security risk susceptible to foreign influence while in office.[42] Concerns about his financial situation have come into sharp focus based on recent reports that Trump incurred $47.4 million in business losses for tax year 2018.[43] Had he been reelected with more than $400 million in loans expected to come due over the next four years,[44] President Trump's outstanding debt could have presented an untenable national security risk,[45] especially if his businesses continued to incur large losses and reputable sources of funding, which present their own conflicts of interest,[46] continued to dry up.

If Trump's reported tax losses are accurate,[47] they appear to be part of a Trump pattern of business failures, including six bankruptcies.[48] Except for Deutsche Bank's private banking unit,[49] many reputable Wall Street financial institutions have been reluctant to lend Trump money due to his history of bankruptcies and propensity for litigation.[50] Making his financial situation even more uncertain, reporting indicates that Deutsche Bank, which holds approximately $340 million of the loans that will come due over the next four years,[51] has ended its relationship with the former president in the wake of the deadly January 6 insurrection at the Capitol.[52]

Trump's indebtedness and bankruptcies raised national security concerns based on the criteria listed in the National Security Adjudicative

Guidelines.[53] Among disqualifying financial conditions listed in the adjudicative guidelines used to assess federal employees' security risks are "inability to satisfy debts," "unwillingness to satisfy debts regardless of the ability to do so," and "a history of not meeting financial obligations."[54] While the president is not subject to the same adjudication procedures as other executive branch officials, the national security risk he presents based on these criteria is nonetheless real. If a president does not have sufficient income and financing available to cover his or her debt obligations, it could make that president vulnerable to pressure or coercion by a foreign interest.

## Financial Disclosure Recommendation

To address current deficiencies in public financial disclosure reporting requirements, legislation should be enacted as follows:

- Enhance disclosure requirements for privately held businesses owned or controlled by a presidential candidate, the president, and other covered filers.

- For covered business interests, require the filer to disclose the source and amount of all business debts (including any amounts that have been personally guaranteed by the filer) that exceed $10,000, along with the identity and financial interests of any major investors, creditors, and customers.[55]

- Require a newly elected president and vice president to file their initial public financial disclosure report (OGE 278) with OGE not later than May 15 in the year they first take office and thereafter annually.[56]

## Trump's Nepotistic Appointments

If Trump's failure to divest his business interests was his original sin, appointing his son-in-law and daughter to serve as senior White House advisors runs a very close second.[57] A Department of Justice memo from the Office of Legal Counsel, released on the day President Trump assumed office, concluded that the White House was exempt from 5 U.S.C. § 3110, the anti-nepotism statute, which forbids a public official from appointing a relative "to a civilian position in the agency . . . over which [the official] exercises jurisdiction or control."[58] This opinion overturned more than forty years of precedent, paving the way for Ivanka Trump and Jared Kushner to use their White House positions allegedly to advance their financial interests and exert significant influence over U.S. domestic and foreign policies.[59]

Trump's appointment of Jared and Ivanka as senior White House advisors was an early suggestion that Trump expected his appointees' personal loyalty to take precedence over their oath of allegiance to the U.S. Constitution.[60] Ultimately, his White House position and close family ties to Trump made Kushner tantamount to a second chief of staff.[61] As former Trump campaign manager Brad Parscale noted, "Nobody has more influence in the White House than Jared. Nobody has more influence outside the White House than Jared. He's No. 2 after Trump."[62] Kushner's influence was made abundantly clear when Trump reportedly put aside national security concerns and ordered then chief of staff John Kelly to grant a top-secret security clearance to Kushner against the recommendations of career White House security specialists and then White House counsel Donald McGahn, who had reportedly objected due to Kushner's foreign business entanglements and potential susceptibility to foreign influence.[63]

## Anti-Nepotism Recommendation

To ensure that all persons appointed to serve future presidents owe their primary allegiance to the U.S. Constitution, legislation should be enacted as follows:

- Clarify that the anti-nepotism statute, 5 U.S.C. § 3110, supersedes the presidential and vice-presidential appointment authority, at 3 U.S.C. § 105(a) and 106(a), thereby barring the president and vice president from appointing a relative to any position in the executive branch, including a position in the White House Office or the Office of the Vice President.

- Prohibit relatives of the president and vice president from being granted an official security clearance except through normal security clearance processes.[64]

However, nothing in this proposal should be construed to prevent the spouses of a president and vice president from being able to carry out their traditional role consistent with that of their predecessors and with the appropriate professional staff provided to support them in that role.

## Trump's Tax Returns: Missing from Public View

Although President Trump indicated in 2016 that he would release his tax returns once his "routine" tax audit was over, he did not publicly disclose them in the four years of his term, even though there was no legal bar that prevented it.[65] Moreover, his excuse of a pending audit was specious. All presidential tax returns are subject to mandatory audits,[66] but this has not kept any modern president from releasing them.[67]

Following a tax scandal involving Richard Nixon, all U.S. presidents since Jimmy Carter have voluntarily released their tax returns.[68] By publicly releasing their returns, presidents show their willingness and ability to comply with their tax obligations, and reveal that they have nothing to hide in terms of personal enrichment and secret sources of income. Thus, public disclosure not only serves as a window into the president's trustworthiness and honesty, but can also help identify possible conflicts of interests.[69]

If President Trump had released his tax returns like every other modern American president, the American people would not have needed to rely on investigative reporting by the New York Times to learn about allegedly "questionable measures" employed by Trump to avoid tax payments in ten of the previous fifteen years—or that he paid only $750 in federal income taxes in both 2016 and 2017,[70] significantly less than the average American paid in taxes in 2016.[71] For example, questions have been raised about the legitimacy of an "abandoned" interest Trump claimed with respect to his Atlantic City, New Jersey, casinos so as to obtain a $72.9 million tax refund.[72] There are indications that he may not have legally "abandoned" that interest.[73] If the abandonment claim was not legitimate, Trump could owe the U.S. government more than $100 million in taxes and penalties. Many more issues have been alleged.[74]

The reporting also revealed potential conflicts of interest involving the Trump Organization's business dealings overseas, based on reports of a previously undisclosed bank account in China and $188,561 paid to China in income tax between 2013 and 2015,[75] more than he or his companies paid to the U.S. government.[76] Similar income tax payments were made by President Trump or his companies in 2017 to Panama ($15,598), India ($145,400), and the Philippines ($156,824).[77]

## Tax Transparency Recommendation

To ensure transparency into future presidents' compliance with their tax obligations and to enhance transparency into potential conflicts of interests, Congress should introduce legislation that mandates disclosure of presidential tax returns as follows:

- Require all candidates of a major party for the office of president or vice president to release their three most recent federal income tax returns for public disclosure by submitting them to the Federal Election Commission (FEC) on or before May 15 of the current filing year.

- Require all presidents to release their annual federal income tax returns for public disclosure by submitting them to the Office of Government Ethics on or before May 15 of the filing year.

- Require the FEC and OGE to redact personal information (e.g., contact information such as street addresses, email addresses, and phone numbers; dates of birth; names of immediate family members; social security numbers; and account numbers).

- Require the federal income tax returns to be made available by the FEC and OGE to the public online in a searchable, sortable, and download-able format.[78]

## The Trump Administration's Pervasive Hatch Act Violations

Enacted in 1939 to address widespread political party corruption and coercion,[79] the Hatch Act restricts federal employees from using their public office for partisan political purposes.[80] Although White House political appointees and presidential appointees confirmed by the Senate have greater flexibility to engage in political activity than other federal employees, they, like all government employees, are barred from using their official authority or influence to interfere with or affect elections.[81]

While the law has been strictly enforced against career employees found to have violated the Hatch Act,[82] at least thirteen of President Trump's senior political appointees violated the Hatch Act with little to no repercussions. That included most notably Kellyanne Conway, counselor to the president, who received no disciplinary action even though the U.S. Office of Special Counsel (OSC) referred her repeated and willful violations to Trump.[83]

Not only did Trump fail to enforce the Hatch Act against Conway and others,[84] but he also exploited the White House, the very emblem of the presidency, by authorizing it to be used as the central backdrop for the Republican National Convention.[85] Vice President Mike Pence and others in the Trump administration engaged in similar abuses of national parks and official government resources during the convention. Pence gave his acceptance speech at Fort McHenry, which served as the inspiration for Francis Scott Key when he composed the national anthem during the War of 1812.[86] Secretary of State Mike Pompeo used a diplomatic trip to Israel as the venue for his convention speech,[87] while the acting secretary of the Department of Homeland Security (DHS), Chad Wolf, presided over a naturalization ceremony for five new U.S. citizens in a swearing-in held at the White House, which was prominently featured in a film clip aired during the convention.[88]

Although the Hatch Act has been amended several times,[89] the Trump administration's abysmal enforcement record and unprecedented abuses mandate further reform. Enforcement problems during the Trump administration stemmed primarily from two concerns. First, OSC, which is responsible for enforcing the Hatch Act,[90] took the position that the Merit Systems Protection Board (MSPB) lacks the authority to pursue disciplinary action against non-Senate confirmed presidential appointees, leaving it to the president. In Trump's case, he declined to hold senior White House officials accountable for their flagrant violations.[91] The second problem stemmed from the president and the vice president not being subject to most Hatch Act prohibitions and therefore being left largely unaccountable for abuses of their offices for partisan political purposes.[92]

As of this writing, a series of reforms are being considered in the 117th Congress to address the Hatch Act's deficiencies exposed by the Trump administration.[93] These include strengthening OSC's ability to investigate violations of the Hatch Act, authorizing MSPB to issue civil fines for Hatch Act violations committed by political appointees, and increasing the maximum fine for Hatch Act violations by political appointees to $50,000.[94] But additional reforms are also necessary to prevent national parks, like the White House and Fort McHenry, and other government resources from being exploited by future presidents or vice presidents for partisan political purposes to promote their own candidacy or political party. By enhancing reporting requirements, Congress will be able to conduct more meaningful oversight to ensure that U.S. aircraft, personnel, and other federal government resources are properly accounted for and reimbursed whenever they are deployed for partisan political purposes.

### Failure to Take Disciplinary Action Against Trump Political Appointees for Hatch Act Violations

Based on multiple complaints filed by government watchdog organizations,[95] OSC found that more than a dozen Trump administration officials violated the Hatch Act using their official authority or influence for partisan political purposes, including by influencing elections.[96] In addition to Kellyanne Conway,[97] violators included Secretary of Agriculture Sonny Perdue;[98] the director of the White House Office for Trade and Manufacturing Policy, Peter Navarro;[99] Dan Scavino, director of social media for the White House;[100] former U.S. ambassador to the United Nations Nikki Haley;[101] Stephanie Grisham, the communications director for the Office of the First Lady;[102] former principal deputy White House press secretary Raj Shah;[103] Lynne Patton, the regional administrator for the U.S. Department of Housing and Urban Development (HUD);[104] and several lesser-known White House officials—Jessica Ditto, Madeleine Westerhout, Helen Aguirre Ferre, Alyssa Farah, and Jacob Wood—who misused their official White House Twitter accounts for political activity.[105] Dozens of additional allegations are pending investigation.[106] One watchdog group alleged that in October 2020 alone, during the peak of the election cycle, "at least 16 Trump administration officials . . . violated the Hatch Act a total of more than 60 times."[107]

OSC issued two reports documenting numerous violations of the Hatch Act by Kellyanne Conway in television interviews and on her social media account, which she used for official purposes.[108] In the first report, OSC found that the White House Communications Office arranged two separate television interviews for Conway, preparing her with official talking points.[109] In both television interviews, Conway stood on the White House grounds with the White House visible in the background and was introduced as the counselor to the president of the United States with the chyron at the bottom of the interview describing her as "Counselor to President Trump." In both, she discussed why voters should not support the Democratic candidate in a special election for the Alabama U.S. Senate seat. In the second interview, she also explained why voters should support the Republican Senate candidate. OSC found that Conway's statements during the interviews impermissibly mixed official government business with political views about candidates in the Alabama special election for U.S. Senate, in violation of the Hatch Act.[110] While political appointees may engage in some political activity, OSC explained they are still barred from using their official authority or influence to interfere with or affect elections.[111]

OSC issued a second report that detailed numerous additional violations by Conway, which they determined would almost certainly result in her removal from a federal position if she were in any other class of federal employee.[112] In the report, OSC determined that Conway engaged in a pattern of partisan attacks on several Democratic Party presidential candidates during at least ten official media appearances and in both official and political activity on her Twitter account.[113] Since she used her "@KellyannePolls" Twitter account to execute her official duties, OSC found that Conway engaged in significant political activity to endorse Trump's reelection and to advocate against Democratic candidates for the Senate and presidency.[114] Citing her substantial knowledge of the Hatch Act and her escalation of partisan critiques even after receiving warnings, OSC recommended Conway's removal. Noting that Conway was a "repeat offender" and that it has never before had to issue multiple reports to the president concerning Hatch Act violations by the same individual, OSC characterized Conway's Hatch Act violations as "persistent, notorious, and deliberate," creating an "unprecedented challenge to this office's ability to enforce the Act."[115]

However, instead of pursuing Conway's violations with the Merit Systems Protection Board, a "quasi-judicial agency with original jurisdiction over Hatch Act complaints," which has authority to impose fines and disciplinary action ranging from reprimand to removal,[116] OSC referred the violations to Trump. He failed to take any disciplinary action.[117] OSC explained that in consideration of the president's constitutional authority to appoint senior officers of the United States, it believed the proper course of action for violations of the Hatch Act by such officers is to refer the violations to the president.[118] A subsequent lawsuit brought by the watchdog group Citizens for Responsibility and Ethics in Washington (CREW) challenged this premise. On the basis that Conway did not qualify for the exemption applicable to presidential appointees confirmed by the Senate, CREW sought injunctive and declarative relief to compel OSC to commence MSPB proceedings against Conway for repeatedly violating the Hatch Act. The case was dismissed for lack of standing—that is, that an outside group did not have the legal authority to initiate the case.[119] As a result, the court did not address the merits of whether the statutory enforcement scheme set forth in 5 U.S.C. § 1215(a)(1) compelled OSC to file a complaint with the MSPB.[120]

As egregious as OSC found Conway's violations, Conway failed to take them seriously. When asked about her Hatch Act violations, she responded, "Blah blah blah" and "Let me know when the jail sentence starts."[121] It was a signal moment of Trumpery. Conway's reaction and Trump's failure to hold her accountable stand in stark contrast to past administrations' handling of similar violations. For example, President Obama's Secretary of Health and Human Services Kathleen Sebelius and Secretary of Housing and Urban Development Julian Castro both made amends when they were found by OSC to have violated the Hatch Act. Castro's violation occurred during a television interview when, asked about the 2016 election, he unsuccessfully attempted to give a disclaimer to separate his personal views from his official responses to questions about HUD programs.[122] Sibelius reimbursed the U.S. Treasury for all costs and expenses associated with her travel to North Carolina after she went off script to extemporaneously endorse a candidate in an upcoming gubernatorial election and Obama's reelection effort during a speech.[123]

As with Conway, OSC also found that Peter Navarro repeatedly violated the Hatch Act by attacking presidential candidate Joe Biden and vice presidential candidate Kamala Harris during official media appearances and on his official Twitter account.[124] Like Conway's violations, Navarro's attacks occurred in at least six media interviews in which he appeared in his official capacity and on his "@PeterNavarro45" Twitter account, which he often used for official purposes. OSC determined that Navarro's violations were "knowing and willful" since most of them occurred after Navarro received training on the Hatch Act and after OSC had informed him he was being investigated for similar prohibited political activity.[125]

## Hatch Act Enforcement Recommendation

To ensure that future White House officials and presidential appointees confirmed by the Senate can be held duly accountable for Hatch Act violations, Congress should clarify OSC's authority to investigate and assess administrative fines against political appointees.[126] To take one example, under the Protecting Our Democracy Act of 2021, the current $1,000 fine would be increased to $50,000 to meaningfully deter future political appointees from engaging in Hatch Act violations. Fines would only be pursued against political appointees if the president fails to take disciplinary action within ninety days of OSC finding a Hatch Act violation. Appropriate due process protections, including an administrative hearing and judicial review, would necessarily be included in the legislation.[127] Because the president retains sole authority to remove any political appointee found to have engaged in a Hatch Act violation, these measures should not reasonably be viewed as interfering with the president's appointment authority under the Constitution.[128]

## The Trump Administration's Unprecedented Abuse of Federal Resources During the 2020 Republican Convention

Trump engaged in unprecedented abuse of the White House[129]—the official residence of the U.S. president—for partisan political purposes when he used the grounds as the centerpiece for the Republican National Convention, including delivering his acceptance speech from the South Lawn beneath the Truman Balcony.[130] Trump similarly authorized his daughter and senior White House advisor, Ivanka Trump, to use the same podium to give her convention speech that introduced him.[131] First Lady Melania Trump also used the White House Rose Garden as the venue for her convention speech earlier in the week.[132]

Several other Trump administration officials likewise exploited official government resources during the convention for partisan political purposes. For Pence's aforementioned convention speech,[133] the Maryland Republican Party submitted a special permit request approved by the National Park Service to allow a political event to be conducted on the grounds of Fort McHenry.[134]

Apparently not wanting to be outdone, Secretary of State Mike Pompeo delivered his pretaped convention speech from the hills overlooking Jerusalem while on an official diplomatic trip to the Middle East and North Africa.[135] Not only was Pompeo criticized for giving the speech while on an official trip, but also it was the first time in at least seventy-five years that a sitting secretary of state addressed a national nominating convention. In doing so, Pompeo defied the long-standing norm that secretaries of state should keep domestic politics at the water's edge.[136] While no government funds were reportedly used to "film" the speech, it is not known at the time of this writing whether Pompeo reimbursed the U.S. Treasury for the travel costs incurred in order to use the city of Jerusalem as the backdrop for the speech.[137] "With the lights of the Old City and its Jewish, Muslim, and Christian shrines visible over his shoulder," the staging of the speech reportedly gave Pompeo a nationally televised platform to appeal to a core segment of Trump supporters—white evangelical voters—whom Pompeo himself is believed to be "courting" for his own possible presidential campaign in the future.[138]

Pompeo was not the only cabinet member prominently featured at the convention. Acting DHS secretary Wolf took center stage with Trump in a naturalization ceremony held in the Great Hall of the White House.[139] Apparently, the ceremony was taped on a Monday and aired the next evening during the convention's prime-time television slot, but none of the five newly sworn-in citizens knew they would be included in the convention.[140] Nor did the White House make the event or film clip publicly available until it was posted on YouTube just a few short hours before being aired during the convention, raising concerns that it was filmed for partisan political purposes rather than official purposes.[141]

These convention appearances by the sitting president, first lady, vice president, secretary of state, acting DHS secretary, and a senior White House advisor mix the authority and influence of their official positions with the president's and vice president's reelection efforts. These events moreover likely required extensive logistical support from a plethora of federal employees, including staff from the White House residence, National Park Service, State Department, and DHS.

The president and vice president are exempt from most provisions of the Hatch Act,[142] even though all other government employees, including political appointees, are barred from using their official authority or influence for purposes of interfering with or affecting the result of an election.[143] Furthermore, certain parts of the White House that are reserved for the president's personal use, as well as the exterior of the White House, have been viewed by OSC as exempt from the Hatch Act.[144] Thus, unless there is evidence to establish a violation of the criminal anti-intimidation statute, 18 U.S.C. § 610, which bars any person, including the president or vice president, from coercing employees of the federal government to engage in or not to engage in any political activity, it is difficult to hold Trump or Pence legally accountable for using federal resources, including government personnel, to support the Republican National Convention.

Establishing a section 610 violation, however, can be challenging. The Department of Justice has reported no section 610 convictions.[145] In one Justice Department investigation into the then secretary of labor for leaving a voice mail on a subordinate's government phone soliciting donations for President Obama's reelection, no criminal charges were ever brought.[146]

There are several practical challenges to establishing the element of coercion. While most federal employees are prohibited from engaging in political activity while on duty or in any room or building occupied in the discharge of official duties by an individual employed or holding office in the federal government,[147] White House officials and presidential appointees subject to Senate confirmation are excluded from that prohibition.[148] That gives them greater flexibility to engage in political activity during normal working hours and in their respective offices. Furthermore, even federal employees subject to the restrictions barring them from political activity on duty and in federal rooms or buildings can attend White House political events in their off-duty hours, provided the activity is not held in the West Wing or in another area of the White House regarded as a federal room or building for purposes of the Hatch Act.[149]

## Recommendations to Prevent Abuse of the
## White House and National Parks[150]

The Trump administration's unprecedented level of abuse of the White House and other federal resources during the 2020 Republican National Convention can only be averted in the future by strengthening the Hatch Act.

- To prevent future presidents from exploiting the White House and national parks, like Fort McHenry, for partisan political purposes, the Hatch Act should be amended to prohibit the White House and other national parks from being used for political party nominating conventions or for political fundraisers to support any political candidate or party.[151]

- To prevent domestic politics from interfering with U.S. foreign policy interests, the Hatch Act should be amended to bar government officials, including the secretary of state and other political appointees, from engaging in political activity while overseas when any part of the overseas trip is being carried out for official purposes.

- To ensure that Congress can more fully account for proper reimbursement of costs incurred in connection with political activity conducted by executive branch officials using government aircraft or while on mixed political-official travel, the Hatch Act should be amended to require detailed reports to be filed with the Department of the Treasury whenever noncommercial aircraft (i.e., federal, military, or government-leased aircraft) is used to transport executive branch officials, including the president or vice president, to or from a political event, and whenever commercial aircraft is used by executive branch officials or employees for mixed political-official travel. Reports should be filed quarterly by the Executive Office of the President and all government agencies with the Treasury Department, including the name of the executive branch traveler and any executive branch employees who accompanied the principal traveler to the political activity (excluding security personnel); travel departure and destination locations; total costs incurred by the government for the trip; and the date, source, and amount reimbursed to the Department of the Treasury. Reports should be made publicly available on the official Treasury website within thirty days of being filed with the department.[152]

───────────

The volume and magnitude of ethical transgressions that arose during the Trump administration were some of the earliest and ugliest manifestations of Trumpery. They are clear evidence that the existing presidential ethics framework is too weak and full of gaps to be meaningful or enforceable. To ensure that the integrity of the presidency is maintained for future generations, legislative reforms are necessary. They must address foreign and domestic emoluments, presidential conflicts of interest, and nepotistic appointments. Congress must enact transparency requirements for presidential tax returns and private business interests, as well as amend the Hatch Act to ensure that violators are held accountable regardless of rank and position and to prevent federal resources from being misused for political conventions and other political purposes. Only then can we be assured that no future president will exploit inadequate federal ethics rules to commit these wrongs—or even worse ones.

## Notes

1. Donald J. Trump, 2016 "Executive Branch Personnel Public Financial Disclosure Report," June 14, 2017, https://oge.app.box.com/s/kz4qvbdsbcfrzq16msuo4zmth6rerh1 c; Donald J. Trump, 2017 "Executive Branch Personnel Public Financial Disclosure Report," May 15, 2018, https://cryptome.org/2018/06/trump-278e-2017.pdf; Donald J. Trump, 2018 "Executive Branch Personnel Public Financial Disclosure Report," May 15, 2019, http://pfds.opensecrets.org/N00023864_2018.pdf; Donald J. Trump, 2019 "Executive Branch Personnel Public Financial Disclosure Report," July 31, 2020, https://extapps2.oge.gov/201/Presiden.nsf/PAS+Index/181BAF52E298FD70852585B70027 E054/$FILE/Trump,%20Donald%20J.%202020Annual%20278.pdf; Donald J. Trump, 2020 "Executive Branch Personnel Public Financial Disclosure Report," January 15, 2021, https://extapps2.oge.gov/201/Presiden.nsf/PAS+Index/6E78B163F816EF6A85258 6630075291D/$FILE/Trump,%20Donald%20J.%202021Termination%20278.pdf.

2. Jan Wolfe, "U.S. Appeals Court to Revisit Trump Win in Hotel 'Emoluments' Case," Reuters, October 15, 2019, www.reuters.com/article/us-usa-trump-emolu ments/u-s-appeals-court-to-revisit-trump-win-in-hotel-emoluments-case-idUSKBN1 WU2WI.

3. "President Trump's Legacy of Corruption, Four Years and 3,700 Conflicts of Interest Later," Citizens for Responsibility and Ethics in Washington (CREW), January 15, 2021, www.citizensforethics.org/reports-investigations/crew-reports/president -trump-legacy-corruption-3700-conflicts-interest/.

4. Joe Cirincione, "Why Donald Trump's Debt Is a National Security Risk," Defense One, October 18, 2020, www.defenseone.com/ideas/2020/10/why-donald-trumps-debt-national-security-risk/169330/.

5. Andrea Bernstein and others, "The Winners of Trump's Washington—Fifty-one Insiders Who Profited Off the Presidency," *New York Magazine*, October 28, 2020, https://nymag.com/intelligencer/article/trump-presidency-insider-profits.html.

6. As we discuss in this book, federal law establishes the basic rules for government officials to avoid conflicts of interest and other behavior that is corrupt or appears corrupt by benefiting themselves, their families, or associates. As president, Obama went further, ordering each of his appointees to sign a pledge committing to additional safeguards on their behavior. Trump greatly watered down the standards, with scandalous results. And that was before he abrogated his plan entirely on the last night of his presidency, wiping away post-employment restrictions for his officials, including restrictions on serving as foreign agents. Biden has done the opposite, restoring the Obama rules and expanding them, including when it comes to lobbying and working for foreign governments. For example, take one of the centerpieces of the Obama plan: "reverse" revolving door restrictions. Most ethics plans focus on officials leaving government, but the Obama administration also imposed limits on those coming into government, with even tougher restrictions on ex-lobbyists. Trump's executive order loosened those lobbying rules, lifting the limitation on ex-lobbyists serving at an agency they previously lobbied. It is little wonder a flood of lobbyists inundated Trump's administration—more than four times the number in just one Trump term than served under Obama during his two terms. There is much more about these issues in the pages that follow. The Biden plan puts that core Obama restriction for lobbyists back in place, barring them from jobs in agencies they previously sought to influence. This makes sense—letting the fox into the henhouse it just stalked is simply too dangerous, as proved by the numerous controversies involving Trump officials who led agencies they once lobbied. The Biden plan not only fixes what Trump got wrong, it also does the same for Obama's ethics regime. For example, the Biden executive order adds a restriction on so-called golden parachutes—cash bonuses granted to executives as they leave a business to join the government. These windfalls create the perception that an ex-employee may favor her or his benefactor, and it is about time they ended. The Biden plan does that, restricting exit bonuses and requiring newly appointed officials to certify that they have not accepted other benefits (such as deferred ones) in lieu of such packages. It goes well beyond existing law and is a strong step forward. The plan also builds on Obama's in closing the revolving door on the other side of government employment: when employees leave. Federal law imposes a one-year limit on a departing senior official communicating on behalf of clients with the agency where the official worked. The Obama administration extended that to two years, on the theory that an employer might pay an ex-official to do nothing for twelve months, but twenty-four months is a long time for cold storage.

Trump eliminated the Obama extension, farcically declaring that his officials must follow the applicable statute—which they already had to do. Here too Biden not only restores the Obama restriction of two years, he goes further. Now officials are restricted from representing clients to their former agencies and are also cordoned off from their peers in the White House itself. This recognizes the reality that senior agency officials engage with the White House constantly and have ties there too, not just at their former agencies. This rule restricts officials from using the special access and influence for private gain. A number of other post-employment restrictions are added as well, including a ban on materially assisting others in making communications or appearances that ex-officials are prohibited from undertaking themselves under the pledge. Here the Biden plan improves on the Obama ethics rules by closing a loophole for "shadow lobbying"—when former officials who might not be able to meet with an agency themselves prepare and strategize with their colleagues to do so instead. There is no reason that a former official should be able to do indirectly what they cannot do directly. The Biden plan also carries over one of the few good aspects of the otherwise spurious Trump plan: restricting former officials from working as an agent for a foreign country after leaving government. But Biden also goes further, not allowing any former lobbyists for foreign countries from entering his administration. The Obama plan gets another upgrade when it comes to one of its most controversial aspects: waivers. These are written authorizations that make an exception to the rules when doing so is in the public interest. While working for Obama, controversy erupted when the author of this chapter and the book's editor started authorizing waivers. I learned they need to be tightly regulated and highly transparent. That is why I am glad to see the waiver provision of the Obama plan improved. Biden's plan includes a new provision that waivers be made public within ten days and imposes much more detailed rules guiding when waivers are appropriate. Above all, the new policy makes explicit that service as a public interest lobbyist may be taken into account in deciding whether a waiver shall be issued. There is no reason why someone who advocates on behalf of charitable causes should be on the same footing as a corporate lobbyist. For the three executive orders discussed above—President Obama's, Trump's, and Biden's—see, respectively: Exec. Order No. 13490, 74 Fed. Reg. 4673-4678 (January 26, 2009); Exec. Order No. 13770, 82 Fed. Reg. 9333-9338 (January 28, 2017); Exec. Order No. 13989, 86 Fed. Reg. 7029-7035 (January 20, 2021).

7. H.R. 1, 117th Cong. 1st Sess. (2021); S. 2093, 117th Cong. 1st Sess. (2021); S.2671, 117th Cong. 1st Sess. (2021); S.2670, 117th Cong. 1st Sess. (2021).

8. H.R. 5314, 117th Cong. 1st Sess. (2021); S. 2921, 117th Cong. 1st Sess. (2021). Charlie Savage, "Proponents of Post-Trump Curbs on Executive Power Prepare New Push," *New York Times*, September 9, 2021, www.nytimes.com/2021/09/09/us/politics/executive-orders-trump.html.

9. *Citizens for Responsibility and Ethics in Washington* v. *Trump*, 971 F.3d 102 (2d Cir. Aug. 17, 2020), vacated and remanded with instructions to dismiss as moot, Supreme Court Order List 592 U.S. 20-330 (2021); in re Trump, 958 F.3d 274 (4th Cir. 2020),

vacated and remanded with instructions to dismiss as moot, Supreme Court Order List 592 U.S. 20-331 (2021); see also *Blumenthal* v. *Trump*, 949 F.3d 14 (D.C. Cir. 2020). The editor was formally counsel of record in the first two matters.

10. "The [Trump] plan does not comport with the tradition of our Presidents over the past 40 years. This isn't the way the Presidency has worked since Congress passed the Ethics in Government Act in 1978 in the immediate aftermath of the Watergate scandal. Since then, Presidents Jimmy Carter, Ronald Reagan, George H.W. Bush, Bill Clinton, George W. Bush, and Barack Obama all either established blind trusts or limited their investments to nonconflicting assets like diversified mutual funds, which are exempt under the conflict of interest law." See Walter M. Shaub Jr., U.S. Office of Government Ethics Director, Remarks at the Brookings Institution, January 11, 2017, www.brookings.edu/wp-content/uploads/2017/01/20170111_oge_shaub_remarks.pdf.

11. See note 1.

12. Letter from Kevin M. Terry to Trump Old Post Office LLC, March 23, 2017; Donald J. Trump Jr. is the trustee, Allen Weisselberg is the business trustee, and Eric F. Trump is the chairman of the Advisory Board of the trust. The trust's terms give Trump the right of control and enjoyment over the trust and its underlying assets, including the right to withdraw money from any business at any time:

> President Trump is the Donor of the Trust; President Trump is believed to be the sole beneficiary of the Trust; the purpose of the Trust is to 'hold assets for the exclusive benefit of Donald J. Trump'; the Trustees are required to distribute net income or principal 'at [President Trump's] request as the Trustees deem necessary for his maintenance, support or uninsured medical expenses or as the Trustees otherwise deem appropriate'; the Trustees consist of a close family member and close business associate rather than independent and unaffiliated persons; and President Trump retains the power to revoke the Trust.

See letter from Noah Bookbinder to Sen. John Barrasso and Sen. Tom Carper, April 25, 2017, p. 5; Drew Harwell, "Trump Can Quietly Draw Money from Trust Whenever He Wants, New Documents Show," *Washington Post*, April 3, 2017, www.washingtonpost.com/politics/trump-can-quietly-draw-money-from-trust-whenever-he-wants-new-documents-show/2017/04/03/7f4c0002-187c-11e7-9887-1a5314b56a08_story.html?utm_term=.b2e41134181.

13. Zephyr Teachout, *Corruption in America* (Harvard University Press, 2014); Norman L. Eisen, Richard Painter, and Laurence H. Tribe, "The Emoluments Clause: Its Text, Meaning, and Application to Donald J. Trump," Brookings Institution, December 16, 2016, www.brookings.edu/wp-content/uploads/2016/12/gs_121616_emoluments-clause1.pdf.

14. Eisen, Painter, and Tribe, "The Emoluments Clause."

15. Teachout, *Corruption in America,* pp. 26–27.

16. See U.S. Const. art. I, § 9, cl. 8.

17. "The legislature, on the appointment of a President, is once for all to declare what shall be the compensation for his services during the time for which he shall have been elected. This done, they will have no power to alter it, either by increase or diminution, till a new period of service by a new election commences. They can neither weaken his fortitude by operating on his necessities, nor corrupt his integrity by appealing to his avarice. Neither the Union, nor any of its members, will be at liberty to give, nor will he be at liberty to receive, any other emolument than that which may have been determined by act. He can, of course, have no pecuniary inducement to renounce or desert the independence intended for him by the Constitution." See Alexander Hamilton, James Madison, and John Jay, *The Federalist, on the New Constitution, Written in the Year 1788* (Philadelphia: R. Wilson Desilver, 1847).

18. See U.S. Const. art. II, § 1, cl. 7.

19. Dan Alexander, "Trump's Businesses Raked in $1.9 Billion of Revenue During His First Three Years in Office," *Forbes,* September 11, 2020, www.forbes.com/sites/danalexander/2020/09/11/trumps-businesses-raked-in-19-billion-of-revenue-during-his-first-three-years-in-office/.

20. Dan Alexander, "Forbes Estimates China Paid Trump at Least $5.4 Million Since He Took Office, Via Mysterious Trump Tower Lease," *Forbes*, October 23, 2020, www.forbes.com/sites/danalexander/2020/10/23/forbes-estimates-china-paid-trump-at-least-54-million-since-he-took-office-via-mysterious-trump-tower-lease/#106bd06eed11.

21. "President Trump's Legacy of Corruption, Four Years and 3,700 Conflicts of Interest Later," CREW, January 15, 2021, www.citizensforethics.org/reports-investigations/crew-reports/president-trump-legacy-corruption-3700-conflicts-interest/.

22. Ibid.

23. Ibid.

24. See Ben Protess and Steve Eder, "It's Complicated, Trump Group Says of Donating Profit from Foreign Officials," *New York Times*, May 24, 2017, www.nytimes.com/2017/05/24/business/its-complicated-trump-group-says-of-donating-profit-from-foreign-officials.html/.

25. See Jonathan O'Connell and David A. Fahrenthold, "Trump Organization's Donation to U.S. Treasury Shows Drops in Foreign Government Profits," *Washington Post,* March 9, 2020, www.washingtonpost.com/business/2020/03/09/trump-foreign-profits/; Jonathan O'Connell, "Trump Organization Reports Small Bump in Foreign Government Profits in 2018," *Washington Post*, February 25, 2019, www.washingtonpost.com/business/economy/trump-organization-reports-small-bump-in-foreign-government-profits-in-2018/2019/02/24/b49f3b6c-3872-11e9-a2cd-307b06d0257b_story.html.

26. Alexander, "Forbes Estimates China Paid Trump at Least $5.4 Million."

27. David A. Fahrenthold and others, "During Trump's Term, Millions of Government and GOP Dollars Have Flowed to His Properties," *Washington Post*, October 27, 2020, www.washingtonpost.com/politics/ballrooms-candles-and-luxury-cottages

-during-trumps-term-millions-of-government-and-gop-dollars-have-flowed-to-his
-propertiesmar-a-lago-charged-the-government-3-apiece-for-glasses-of-water-for
-trump-and-the-japanese-leader/2020/10/27/186f20a2-1469-11eb-bc10-40b25382f1be_
story.html.

28. Ibid.

29. Ibid.

30. Ibid.

31. See Isaac Arnsdorf, "Trump Picks Leader for Federal Agency Overseeing His D.C. Hotel," Politico, January 26, 2017, http://politi.co/2psgMfU.

32. The author's recommendations as to emoluments are in line with similar provisions in the Protecting Our Democracy Act, including recommendations to clarify that emoluments include payments arising from commercial transactions, to allow Congress to sue the president for running afoul of the Emoluments Clause, and to establish civil penalties for emoluments violations.

33. See "OIG Public Affairs Point of Contact," Council of the Inspectors General on Integrity and Efficiency, www.ignet.gov/content/inspectors-general-directory.

34. See Protecting Our Democracy Act, H.R. 8363, 116th Cong. § 2 (2020). Most provisions remain unchanged in the 117th Congress's version of the Protecting Our Democracy Act. See U.S. Congress, House of Representatives, H.R. 5314, 117th Congress, 1st Sess. (2021–2022), § 2, www.congress.gov/bill/117th-congress/house-bill/5314; Bob Bauer and Jack Goldsmith, After Trump: Reconstructing the Presidency (Washington: Lawfare Press, 2020).

35. "President Trump's Legacy of Corruption, Four Years and 3,700 Conflicts of Interest Later," CREW.

36. Rebecca Jacobs and Walker Davis, "Special Interest Groups Likely Spent More Than $13 Million at Trump Properties. They Got What They Paid For," CREW, October 30, 2020, www.citizensforethics.org/reports-investigations/crew-investigations/special-interest-groups-spent-13-million-trump-properties/.

37. Ibid.

38. "President Trump's Legacy of Corruption, Four Years and 3,700 Conflicts of Interest Later," CREW.

39. 5 C.F.R. § 2640.202; Congressional Research Service, "Conflicts of Interest and the Presidency" (2016), https://fas.org/sgp/crs/misc/conflicts.pdf.

40. Glenn Kessler and Michelle Ye Hee Lee, "Trump's Claim That 'The President Can't Have a Conflict of Interest,'" Washington Post, November 23, 2016, www.washingtonpost.com/news/fact-checker/wp/2016/11/23/trumps-claim-that-the-president-cant-have-a-conflict-of-interest/.

41. See For the People Act, H.R. 1, 116th Cong. § 1 (2019); CREW and Public Citizen, Trump-Proofing the Presidency: A Plan for Executive Branch Ethics Reform, October 2, 2018, www.citizensforethics.org/wp-content/uploads/legacy/2018/10/Trump-Proofing-the-Presidency.pdf. Title VIII, Subtitle B, § 8012 of H.R. 1 calls for the president and vice president to divest from all financial interests that pose a conflict of in-

terest within thirty days of assuming office. In addition to placing these investments in blind trusts, as this recommendation calls for, H.R. 1 would accept converting these assets into cash or another OGE certified investment. Sen. Joe Manchin has also indicated that he would support this divestment proposal and timeline. See also U.S Congress, Senate, S. 1, 117th Congress, 1st sess., Title VIII, Subtitle B, § 8012, www.congress.gov/bill/117th-congress/senate-bill/1/text. However, the Freedom to Vote Act, its successor bill, does not contain these provisions. See U.S. Congress, Senate, S. 2747, 117th Congress, 1st Sess. (2021–2022), www.congress.gov/bill/117th-congress/senate-bill/2747/text.

42. Michael Morell and David Kris, "Trump Is in Debt. We Can't Ignore the National Security Risks That Come with That," *Washington Post*, October 11, 2020, www.washingtonpost.com/opinions/2020/10/11/trump-is-debt-we-cant-ignore-national-security-risks-that-come-with-that/.

43. Russ Buettner, Susanne Craig, and Mike McIntire, "Long-Concealed Records Show Trump's Chronic Losses and Years of Tax Avoidance," *New York Times*, September 27, 2020, www.nytimes.com/interactive/2020/09/27/us/donald-trump-taxes.html.

44. Dan Alexander, "Donald Trump Has At Least $1 Billion in Debt, More Than Twice the Amount He Suggested," *Forbes*, October 16, 2020, www.forbes.com/sites/danalexander/2020/10/16/donald-trump-has-at-least-1-billion-in-debt-more-than-twice-the-amount-he-suggested/?sh=6c450fc43306.

45. U.S. Office of the Director of National Intelligence, *National Security Adjudicative Guidelines*, Security Executive Agent Directive 4, December 2016, www.dni.gov/files/NCSC/documents/Regulations/SEAD-4-Adjudicative-Guidelines-U.pdf; Morell and Kris, "Trump Is in Debt."

46. Jesse Eisinger, "Deutsche Bank Remains Trump's Biggest Conflict of Interest Despite Settlements," ProPublica, February 9, 2017, www.propublica.org/article/deutsche-bank-trump-conflict-of-interest-despite-settlements; David Enrich, "The Money Behind Trump's Money," *New York Times*, February 4, 2020, www.nytimes.com/2020/02/04/magazine/deutsche-bank-trump.html.

47. Trump's reported 2018 tax losses appear to be inconsistent with income of $434.9 million reported on his 2018 public financial disclosure report (Donald J. Trump, 2018 "Executive Branch Personnel Public Financial Disclosure Report"). In President Trump's case, the reported income on his 2018 public financial disclosure report reflects his revenue, which appears to give a distorted view of his financial status. Traditionally, OGE has given filers discretion when they report business income on their public financial disclosure reports. See 5 C.F.R. § 2634.105(j). (Generally, income means "gross income" as determined in conformity with the Internal Revenue Service principles at 26 C.F.R. §§ 1.61-1 to 1.61-15, 1.61-21.) For losses, filers need only report "none" for income rather than the actual losses.

48. Michelle Lee, "Fact Check: Has Trump Declared Bankruptcy Four or Six Times?" *Washington Post*, September 6, 2016, www.washingtonpost.com/politics/2016

/live-updates/general-election/real-time-fact-checking-and-analysis-of-the-first-pres
idential-debate/fact-check-has-trump-declared-bankruptcy-four-or-six-times/.

49. Suzanne Craig, "Trump Boasts of Rapport with Wall St., But the Feeling Is Not Quite Mutual," *New York Times*, May 23, 2016, www.nytimes.com/2016/05/24/business /dealbook/donald-trump-relationship-bankers.html.

50. Ibid.

51. Alexander, "Trump Debt."

52. Luke Harding and Kalyeena Makortoff, "Deutsche Bank Joins Companies Cutting Ties with Donald Trump," *Guardian*, January 13, 2021, www.theguardian.com/ business/2021/jan/12/deutsche-bank-severs-ties-with-donald-trump. Furthermore, documents released by the House Oversight Committee in October 2021 showed that Trump's Washington, D.C., hotel incurred $70 million in losses during his presidency. The same documents detail $3.7 million paid to the hotel by foreign governments. See Katelyn Polantz, Veronica Stracqualursi, and Kristen Holmes, "Trump DC Hotel Incurred More Than $70 Million in Losses while Trump Was President, Documents Show," CNN, October 8, 2021, www.cnn.com/2021/10/08/politics/trump-hotel-dc/ index.html.

53. Director of National Intelligence, *Adjudicative Guidelines*, Appendix A.

54. Ibid., paragraph 19, at line 15.

55. Title VIII, Subtitle B, § 8012 of H.R. 1 would also enhance disclosure filings by requiring filers to report the value, identity, and category of each liability over $10,000 and the name of each other person who holds a significant financial interest in the entity in question. The bill goes further to require a description of the nature and value of any assets with a value of $10,000 or more. Sen. Joe Manchin has also indicated that he would support this divestment proposal and timeline. See also U.S. Congress, Senate, S. 1, 117th Congress, 1st sess., Title VIII, Subtitle B, § 8012, www.congress.gov/ bill/117th-congress/senate-bill/1/text. However, the Freedom to Vote Act (2021– 2022), has dropped these proposed provisions. See U.S. Congress, Senate, S. 2747.

56. See For the People Act, H.R. 1, 116th Cong. § 1 (2019); Provisions regarding the president's and the vice president's public financial disclosure reports are dropped in the Freedom to Vote Act. See U.S. Congress, Senate, S. 2747, § 1; CREW, Public Citizen, *Trump-Proofing the Presidency*.

57. "Nepotism and Conflicts of Interest: Jared Kushner and Ivanka Trump," CREW, April 25, 2017, www.citizensforethics.org/reports-investigations/crew-reports /nepotism-and-conflicts-of-interest-jared-kushner-and-ivanka-trump/.

58. See *Application of the Anti-Nepotism Statute to a Presidential Appointment in the White House Office*, 41 Op. O.L.C. __ 14 (2017), www.justice.gov/opinion/file/930116/down load.

59. Ibid., p. 8; Jill Abramson, "Nepotism and Corruption: The Handmaidens of Trump's Presidency," *Guardian*, March 6, 2018, www.theguardian.com/commentisfree /2018/mar/06/nepotism-corruption-handmaiden-trump-presidency.

60. See 5 U.S.C. § 3331. "An individual, except the President, elected or appointed to an office of honor or profit in the civil service or uniformed services, shall take the following oath: 'I, AB, do solemnly swear (or affirm) that I will support and defend the Constitution of the United States against all enemies, foreign and domestic; that I will bear true faith and allegiance to the same; that I take this obligation freely, without any mental reservation or purpose of evasion; and that I will well and faithfully discharge the duties of the office on which I am about to enter. So help me God.'"

61. In the case of Kushner and Ivanka, their close family ties to Trump made a personal loyalty pledge like the one Trump sought from then FBI director James Comey and other officials unnecessary. Michael S. Schmidt, "In a Private Dinner, Trump Demanded Loyalty. Comey Demurred," *New York Times*, May 11, 2017, www.ny times.com/2017/05/11/us/politics/trump-comey-firing.html; Jonathan Swan, "Trump Offered FBI Director Job to John Kelly, Asked for Loyalty," Axios, August 30, 2020, www.axios.com/trump-john-kelly-fbi-41678290-167a-44c2-a20a-377955485bc8.html.

62. Brian Bennett, "Inside Jared Kushner's Unusual White House Role," *Time*, January 16, 2020, https://time.com/5766186/jared-kushner-interview/.

63. Ibid. See Maggie Haberman and others, "Trump Ordered Officials to Give Jared Kushner a Security Clearance," *New York Times*, February 28, 2019, www.ny times.com/2019/02/28/us/politics/jared-kushner-security-clearance.html; Josh Dawsey, Seung Min Kim, and Shane Harris, "Trump Demanded Top-Secret Security Clearance for Jared Kushner Last Year Despite Concerns of John Kelly and Intelligence Officials," *Washington Post*, February 28, 2019, www.washingtonpost.com/ politics/trump-sought-top-secret-security-clearance-for-jared-kushner-last-year -despite-concerns-of-john-kelly-and-intelligence-officials/2019/02/28/2eacc72e-3bae -11e9-aaae-69364b2ed137_story.html.

64. See "Trump-Proofing the Presidency," CREW, October 2, 2018, www.citizens forethics.org/reports-investigations/crew-reports/trump-proofing-the-presidency/.

65. Katie Rogers, "Trump on Releasing His Tax Returns: From 'Absolutely' to 'Political Prosecution,'" *New York Times*, July 9, 2020, www.nytimes.com/2020/07/09/us/ politics/trump-taxes.html.

66. "Internal Revenue Manual: Processing Returns and Accounts of the President and Vice President, 4.2.1.15," Internal Revenue Service, May 29, 2019, www.irs.gov/irm /part4/irm_04-002-001#idm140647862743984.

67. "Presidential Tax Returns," TaxNotes, www.taxnotes.com/presidential-tax -returns.

68. The Protecting Our Democracy Act would codify tax transparency for presidential and vice presidential candidates, as well as for sitting presidents and vice presidents. Title XII of the act would require presidents and vice presidents, as well as candidates for those offices, to supply the Federal Election Commission with income tax returns for the preceding ten taxable years. These forms would then be made publicly accessible after necessary redactions. The act orders the Treasury secretary to make the returns available if the president, vice president, or candidates fail to provide

the forms themselves. See Protecting Our Democracy Act, H.R. 5314, 117th Cong. 1st Sess., Title XII, § 1201, www.congress.gov/117/bills/hr5314/BILLS-117hr5314ih.pdf. Ibid.

69. See "Trump-Proofing the Presidency," CREW.

70. See David Leonhardt, "18 Revelations from a Trove of Trump Tax Records," *New York Times*, September 27, 2020, www.nytimes.com/2020/09/27/us/trump-taxes -takeaways.html; Buettner, Craig, and McIntire, "Long-Concealed Records."

71. See Alicia Adamczyk, "Trump Reportedly Paid $750 in Taxes in 2016 and 2017. Here's How Much the Average American Pays," CNBC, September 28, 2020, https:// cnb.cx/2SNu6c2. The tax estimate for the average American is based on an adjusted gross income of between $20,000 and $24,900.

72. Buettner, Craig, and McIntire, "Long-Concealed Records."

73. Ibid.

74. Ibid.

75. Mike McIntire, Russ Buettner, and Susanne Craig, "Trump Records Shed New Light on Chinese Business Pursuits," *New York Times*, October 20, 2020, www.ny times.com/2020/10/20/us/trump-taxes-china.html.

76. Buettner, Craig, and McIntire, "Long-Concealed Records."

77. Ibid.

78. See For the People Act, H.R. 1, 116th Cong. § 1 (2019); "Trump-Proofing the Presidency," CREW. Title X, §10001 of H.R. 1 also calls for candidates of major parties for the offices of president and vice president, as well as elected presidents, to submit their annual federal income tax returns to the FEC. As in the recommendation, H.R. 1 would require the chairman of the FEC to make these filings publicly available in accordance with IRS disclosure laws. However, the bill goes further than the recommendation by requiring candidates to submit their ten most recent tax returns no later than fifteen days after they become covered candidates. For presidents, the bills require submission of the nine most recent tax filings and the tax filing of the current year, all due no later than the tax filing deadline of each year. Sen. Joe Manchin has indicated support for requiring disclosure of individual and business tax returns by sitting presidents and vice presidents, as well as candidates for those offices. See also Protecting Our Democracy Act, H.R. 5314, 117th Cong. 1st. Sess. (2021); S. 2921, 117th Cong. 1st Sess. (2021).

79. "Hatch Act Overview," U.S. Office of Special Counsel, https://osc.gov/Services /Pages/HatchAct.aspx; Nikhel Sus, "Yes We Can . . . Fire You for Sending Political E-mails: A Proposal to Update the Hatch Act for the Twenty-First Century," *George Washington Law Review* 78, no. 1 (2009): p. 171, www.gwlr.org/wp-content/uploads/ 2012/08/78-1-Sus.pdf.

80. 5 U.S.C. §§ 7321–7326.

81. 5 U.S.C. § 7323(a)(1).

82. Sus, "Yes We Can," p. 172; Lisa Rein, "As Trump Appointees Flout the Hatch Act, Civil Servants Who Get Caught Get Punished," *Washington Post*, August 28, 2020,

www.washingtonpost.com/politics/hatch-act-trump-convention/2020/08/28/dce68a
7e-e877-11ea-bc79-834454439a44_story.html.

83. "The Hatch Act," CREW, October 2, 2018, www.citizensforethics.org/reports
-investigations/crew-reports/the-hatch-act/; "Peter Navarro Referred for Disciplinary
Action for Hatch Act Violations," CREW, December 7, 2020, www.citizensforethics.
org/news/press-releases/peter-navarro-hatch-act-violation/; Peter Stone, "Top Trump
Administration Figures Flout Law Banning Partisan Campaigning," *Guardian*, October 15, 2020, www.theguardian.com/us-news/2020/oct/15/trump-administration-par
tisan-campaigning-hatch-act. As referenced in the preceding chapter, a November
2021 report by the U.S. Office of Special Counsel found that thirteen top Trump administration officials had violated the Hatch Act in the lead-up to the 2020 elections,
with the report stating that some officials "intentionally ignored the law's requirements and tacitly or expressly approved of senior administration officials violating the
law." The list includes Trump's former Secretary of State Mike Pompeo, Chief of Staff
Mark Meadows, and Press Secretary Kayleigh McEnany, and the report found that
some of the thirteen officials violated the Hatch Act multiple times. See Nick Niedzwi-
adek, "Watchdog: 13 Trump Officials Violated Hatch Act During 2020 Campaign,"
Politico, November 9, 2021, www.politico.com/news/2021/11/09/trump-officials-hatch
-act-violated-520420.

84. Letter from Pat A. Cipollone, Counsel to the President, White House, to Henry
Kerner, Special Counsel, U.S. Office of Special Counsel, June 11, 2019, https://int.nyt
.com/data/documenthelper/1168-pac-osc-06-11-2019-letter/11f2a2d73d1e14d197f3/opti
mized/full.pdf.

85. Michael D. Shear, "The President Turns the White House into a Partisan
Prop," *New York Times*, September 1, 2020, www.nytimes.com/live/2020/08/27/us/rnc
-convention-election/the-president-turns-the-white-house-into-a-partisan-prop.

86. Reid J. Epstein, "Full Transcript: Mike Pence's R.N.C. Speech," *New York
Times*, August 26, 2020, www.nytimes.com/2020/08/26/us/politics/mike-pence-rnc
-speech.html.

87. Lara Jakes, "Pompeo Delivers R.N.C. Speech from Israel, with Eye Toward
2024," *New York Times*, August 25, 2020, www.nytimes.com/2020/08/25/us/politics/
pompeo-trump-jerusalem-republican-convention.html.

88. Anne Gearan and others, "Trump Uses Powers of Government in Service of
Reelection, with Pardoning and Naturalization Ceremonies," *Washington Post*, August
26, 2020, www.washingtonpost.com/elections/2020/08/25/republican-national
-convention-live-updates/.

89. See Whitney K. Novak, Cong. Rsch. Serv., IF11512, *The Hatch Act: A Primer*
(2020), https://crsreports.congress.gov/product/pdf/IF/IF11512.

90. "About OSC," U.S. Office of Special Counsel, https://osc.gov/Agency.

91. See *Citizens for Responsibility and Ethics in Washington* v. *U.S. Office of Special
Counsel, et al.*, Civil Action No. 19-3757 (JEB) (D.D.C. Aug. 6, 2020), www.scribd.com/
document/473308874/CREW-v-OSC-19-3757.

92. 5 U.S.C. § 7322(1).

93. See Protecting Our Democracy Act, H.R. 5314, 117th Cong. 1st Sess. (2021); S. 2921, 117th Cong. 1st Sess. (2021).

94. Ibid.

95. See "The Hatch Act," CREW; letter from Walter M. Shaub Jr., Senior Director, Ethics, and Brendan M. Fischer, Director, Federal and FEC Reform Program, to Ana Galindo-Marrone, Chief, Hatch Act Unit, U.S. Office of Special Counsel, November 29, 2017, https://campaignlegal.org/sites/default/files/AMENDED%20CONWAY%20COMPLAINT.pdf; letter from Walter M. Shaub, Jr., Senior Director, Ethics, and Brendan M. Fischer, Director, Federal and FEC Reform Program, to Ana Galindo-Marrone, Chief, Hatch Act Unit, U.S. Office of Special Counsel, December 7, 2017, https://campaignlegal.org/sites/default/files/12-07-17%20CLC%20Conway%20Hatch%20Act%20complaint.pdf.

96. See "The Hatch Act," CREW; Donald K. Sherman and Linnaea Honl-Stuenkel, "Sixteen Trump Administration Officials Violated the Law to Boost Trump Campaign in October," CREW, November 2, 2020, www.citizensforethics.org/reports-investigations/crew-reports/sixteen-trump-administration-officials-violated-the-law-to-boost-trump-campaign-in-october/.

97. Letter from Henry J. Kerner, Special Counsel, U.S. Office of Special Counsel, to President Trump, March 5, 2018, http://cdn.cnn.com/cnn/2018/images/03/06/conway.ha-18-0966.final.report.pdf; letter from Henry J. Kerner to President Trump, June 13, 2019.

98. Letter from Ana Galindo-Marrone, Chief, Hatch Act Unit, U.S. Office of Special Counsel, to Donald K. Sherman, Deputy Director, CREW, October 8, 2020, www.citizensforethics.org/wp-content/uploads/2020/10/HA-20-000394-Closure-Letter-to-CREW.pdf.

99. Letter from Henry J. Kerner, Special Counsel, U.S. Office of Special Counsel, to President Trump, December 7, 2020, www.citizensforethics.org/wp-content/uploads/2020/12/Report-of-Prohibited-Political-Activity-Dr.-Peter-Navarro-HA-20-000279.pdf.

100. Letter from Ana Galindo-Marrone, Chief, Hatch Act Unit, U.S. Office of Special Counsel, to Adam J. Rappaport, Chief Counsel and Assistant Director, CREW, June 5, 2017, www.citizensforethics.org/wp-content/uploads/legacy/2017/06/DOC060817-06082017170020.pdf.

101. Letter from Erica S. Hamrick, Deputy Chief, Hatch Act Unit, U.S. Office of Special Counsel, to Noah Bookbinder, Executive Director, CREW, September 28, 2017, www.citizensforethics.org/wp-content/uploads/legacy/2017/10/DOC100217-10022017112049-1.pdf.

102. Letter from Erica S. Hamrick, Deputy Chief, Hatch Act Unit, U.S. Office of Special Counsel, to Noah Bookbinder, Executive Director, CREW, September 20, 2018, https://s3.amazonaws.com/storage.citizensforethics.org/wp-content/uploads/2018/09/21140938/GrishamHatchLetter.pdf; "CREW Files Hatch Act Complaint against

Stephanie Grisham," CREW, July 16, 2018, www.citizensforethics.org/news/press -releases/crew-files-hatch-act-complaint-against-stephanie-grisham/.

103. Letter from Erica S. Hamrick, Deputy Chief, Hatch Act Unit, U.S. Office of Special Counsel, to Noah Bookbinder, Executive Director, CREW, November 30, 2018, www.citizensforethics.org/wp-content/uploads/legacy/2018/11/CREW-ltr-re-10 -complaints.pdf; "Six Officials Reprimanded for Hatch Act Violations Following CREW Complaints," CREW, November 30, 2018, www.citizensforethics.org/news/ press-releases/six-officials-reprimanded-for-hatch-act-violations-following-crew -complaints/.

104. Letter from Erica S. Hamrick, Deputy Chief, Hatch Act Unit, U.S. Office of Special Counsel, to Noah Bookbinder, Executive Director, CREW, September 18, 2019, www.citizensforethics.org/wp-content/uploads/legacy/2019/09/Ltr-to-CREW-re -Patton.pdf.

105. Letter from Hamrick to CREW, November 30, 2018.

106. Sherman and Honl-Stuenkel, "Sixteen Trump Administration Officials Violated the Law."

107. Ibid. The Hatch Act violations of eleven additional senior Trump administration officials along with repeat offenders Alyssa Farah and Kellyanne Conway were documented in the November 2021 Office of Special Counsel report. Among the new offenders were then Press Secretary Kayleigh McEnany, Chief of Staff Mark Meadows, Secretary of State Mike Pompeo, and acting Secretary of State Chad Wolf. The report also found that many of the officials listed violated the Hatch Act on multiple occasions. See U.S. Office of Special Counsel, "Investigation of Political Activities by Senior Trump Administration Officials During the 2020 Presidential Election," November 9, 2021, https://osc.gov/Documents/Hatch%20Act/Reports/Investigation%20 of%20Political%20Activities%20by%20Senior%20Trump%20Administration%20Of ficials%20During%20the%202020%20Presidential%20Election.pdf.

108. Letter from Henry J. Kerner to President Trump, March 5, 2018; letter from Henry J. Kerner to President Trump, June 13, 2019.

109. Letter from Henry J. Kerner to President Trump, March 5, 2018.

110. Ibid.

111. Ibid.

112. Letter from Henry J. Kerner to President Trump, June 13, 2019.

113. Ibid.

114. Ibid.

115. Ibid.

116. CREW v. Special Counsel.

117. Letter from Henry J. Kerner to President Trump, March 5, 2018; letter from Henry J. Kerner to President Trump, June 13, 2019.

118. Letter from Henry J. Kerner to President Trump, March 5, 2018, p. 10.

119. Complaint for Injunctive and Declaratory Relief, Citizens for Responsibility and Ethics in Washington v. U.S. Office of Special Counsel, Civil Action No. 1:19-cv-03757

(D.D.C. Dec. 17, 2019) ECF No. 1, www.citizensforethics.org/wp-content/uploads/legacy/2019/12/CREW-v.-OSC-Complaint-as-filed.pdf.

120. See 5 U.S.C. § 1215(a)(1).

121. Aaron Blake, "'Blah, Blah, Blah': This 2-Week-Old Kellyanne Conway Clip Looks a Lot Worse Today," *Washington Post*, June 13, 2019, www.washingtonpost.com/politics/2019/06/13/blah-blah-blah-this-week-old-kellyanne-conway-clip-looks-exceedingly-painful-today/.

122. Josh Gerstein, "Ethics Agency Says HUD Chief Castro Violated Hatch Act," Politico, July 18, 2016, www.politico.com/story/2016/07/julian-castro-ethics-hud-hatch-225732.

123. See letter from Carolyn Lerner, Special Counsel, U.S. Office of Special Counsel, to President Barack H. Obama, September 12, 2012, https://osc.gov/Documents/Hatch%20Act/Reports/Report%20of%20Prohibited%20Political%20Activity,%20Kathleen%20Sebelius%20(HA-12-1989).pdf.

124. Letter from Henry J. Kerner to President Trump, December 7, 2020.

125. Ibid.

126. Protecting Our Democracy Act, H.R. 5314, 117th Cong. 1st Sess. (2021); S. 2021, 117th Cong. 1st Sess. (2021).

127. Ibid.

128. U.S. Const. art. II, § 2, cl. 2.

129. Although President Franklin D. Roosevelt delivered his 1940 acceptance speech for an unprecedented third term from the White House via radio, the 1940 Democratic convention itself was held in Chicago, which was where Eleanor Roosevelt gave her convention speech noting that it was "no ordinary time." Savannah Behrmann, "RNC: Trump Criticized for Using White House as a Backdrop for the Convention," *USA Today*, August 25, 2020, www.usatoday.com/story/news/politics/elections/2020/08/25/rnc-white-house-convention-speeches-ethics-hatch-act-trump/5628864002/; Diane M. Blair, "No Ordinary Time: Eleanor Roosevelt's Address to the 1940 Democratic National Convention," *Rhetoric and Public Affairs* 4, no. 2 (2001), pp. 203–222, www.jstor.org/stable/41939669.

130. Shear, "Partisan Prop."

131. "Full Text: Ivanka Trump's 2020 Republican National Convention Speech," ABC News, August 27, 2020, https://abcnews.go.com/Politics/full-text-ivanka-trumps-2020-republican-national-convention/story?id=72668294.

132. Gearan and others, "Pardoning and Naturalization Ceremonies."

133. Epstein, "Pence's R.N.C. Speech."

134. Jeff Barker, "Maryland GOP Got 'Special Use' Permit Allowing Pence to Give Convention Speech on National Park Land," *Baltimore Sun*, August 21, 2020, www.baltimoresun.com/politics/bs-md-pence-fort-mchenry-permit-20200822-fy5r4auk3ne7zpyssl7qiywaky-story.html.

135. Jakes, "Pompeo Delivers R.N.C. Speech."

136. Ibid.

137. Ibid.

138. Ibid.

139. Gearan and others, "Pardoning and Naturalization Ceremonies."

140. Philip Bump, "Why Chad Wolf's Awareness of the Republican Convention Naturalization Event Matters," *Washington Post*, August 31, 2020, www.washington post.com/politics/2020/08/31/why-chad-wolfs-awareness-republican-convention -naturalization-event-matters/.

141. Ibid.

142. 5 U.S.C. § 7322(1).

143. 5 U.S.C. § 7323.

144. Letter from Erica S. Hamrick, Deputy Chief, Hatch Act Unit, U.S. Office of Special Counsel, to Carolyn Maloney, Chairwoman, H. Comm. on Oversight and Reform, August 12, 2020, https://republicans-oversight.house.gov/wp-content/ uploads/2020/08/AO-re-Convention-speech-at-WH.pdf.

145. Letter from Claire O. Finkelstein and Richard Painter to Corey R. Armundson, Chief, Public Integrity Section, U.S. Department of Justice, October 26, 2020, www.law .upenn.edu/live/files/10951-trump-criminal-hatch-act-complaint.

146. See Paul Pringle and Abby Sewell, "Complaint over Obama Fundraiser Triggered Solis Probe," *LA Times*, May 9, 2014, www.latimes.com/local/la-me-solis -investigation-20140510-story.html.

147. 5 U.S.C. § 7324(a)(1)–(2).

148. 5 U.S.C. § 7324(b).

149. See letter from Erica S. Hamrick to Carolyn Maloney, August 12, 2020.

150. Regarding the Hatch Act, the Protecting Our Democracy Act would, in line with the author's recommendations, institute stricter enforcement and penalties for violations of the Hatch Act. These provisions remain unchanged in the 117th Congress's version of the Protecting Our Democracy Act. See U.S. Congress, House of Representatives, H.R. 5314. The author goes further, however, in regulating political activity by public officials, including by barring political appointees such as the secretary of state from engaging in partisan activity while on official business overseas, and by prohibiting the use of the White House or other national parks from being used for nominating conventions or other activities in support of a particular party or candidate.

151. See 18 U.S.C. § 60: "It shall be unlawful for any person to solicit or receive a donation of money or other thing of value in connection with a Federal, State, or local election from a person who is located in a room or building occupied in the discharge of official duties by an officer or employee of the United States. It shall be unlawful for an individual who is an officer or employee of the Federal Government, including the President, Vice President, and Members of Congress, to solicit or receive a donation of money or other thing of value in connection with a Federal, State, or local election, while in any room or building occupied in the discharge of official duties by an officer or employee of the United States, from any person."

152. Title VIII, Subtitle H of H.R. 1 would also necessitate a record of the use of any noncommercial, private, or chartered flight used by any senior political appointee no later than 30 days after use. The bill, however, only requires the official to submit a written statement to Congress certifying that no commercial flight was available for their travel. See also U.S. Congress, Senate, S. 1, 117th Congress, 1st sess., Title VIII, Subtitle H, www.congress.gov/bill/117th-congress/senate-bill/1/text. These provisions were removed in the 117th Congress's version of the Freedom to Vote Act. See U.S. Congress, Senate, S. 2747.

# 2

# Other Federal Conflicts of Interest and Their Enforcement

## WALTER M. SHAUB JR.

Government ethics rules have traditionally sought to ensure that public servants in all three branches of the U.S. federal government use the power that America entrusts to them solely for the people's benefit. Whether serving in the executive branch, the legislature, or the judiciary, government officials are not serving the people when they are solely focused on helping themselves, their families, or their business associates. If an official misuses government authority for personal gain, the consequences can be catastrophic.

Ethics transgressions occur in every administration.[1] But the Trump administration marked a new low. The prior chapter primarily focused on the president and the White House, with a few exceptions; this chapter will primarily concentrate on the remainder of the executive branch, again with a few exceptions.

Ethics scandals embroiled multiple Trump agency heads, sometimes leading to their resignation. Scott Pruitt, Trump's first pick for the head of the Environmental Protection Agency (EPA), resigned in July 2018 in response to pressure from watchdogs and lawmakers, including in his own party, over an array of ethically questionable conduct. Among Pruitt's most egregious behavior was keeping a secret calendar that was reportedly maintained to schedule surreptitious meetings with industry officials with whom Pruitt and the administration were allegedly intertwined.[2] His installation of a $43,000 soundproof phone booth in his EPA office, evidently to prevent people from overhearing what he was up to, didn't help either. Ryan Zinke, Trump's interior secretary, resigned in an ethics cloud not six months after Pruitt amid criticism over his dealings with industry representatives and extravagant security costs associated with personal travel taken by him and his wife.[3] Even before Pruitt and Zinke attracted intense ethics scrutiny, Health and Human Services Secretary Tom Price stepped down in September 2017 after reports emerged that he had spent more than $1 million in public funds on luxury travel, including more than twenty-six instances of his chartering a private plane for official travel when commercial routes were available.[4] The pervasive ethics issues among Trump's cabinet and subcabinet nominees resulted in experts alleging that the Trump White House was "the most corrupt presidency and administration we've ever had."[5] The remarkable clip of corruption scandals led to an ethics-related resignation count reported to be higher than any presidential administration in history by July 2019.[6] We have never seen anything like it.[7]

Government ethics programs exist to protect us all from corruption as well as from the appearance of corruption. Congress enacted criminal laws to prohibit officials from putting their own interests before the public interest.[8] In the executive branch, a variety of executive orders, regulations, and policies supplement those laws with additional requirements.[9] In Congress, the ethics committees for the two chambers also have issued rules for members and congressional staffers.[10] In the courts, district and circuit court judges are governed by judicial ethics systems.[11] But as we have just been reminded, there are gaps in this legal framework for government ethics, and the enforcement mechanisms are weak.

The biggest gap, of course, is the failure to apply conflict of interest restrictions to the president, as proven by Donald Trump and discussed in depth in the previous chapter. A president cannot, the thinking goes, recuse from anything. The people need the head of government to handle any manner of crisis. But when President Trump defied tradition and retained conflicting assets, the result was four years of ethical failure. Americans may never know the extent to which his personal financial interests influenced government policies at the expense of the public's interests. But it is clear that the bad tone from the top led to a series of ethics-related scandals that seemed to gush like water through a firehose.

The Trump administration exposed some of the problems with the government's ethics program, but it did not create them. The Trump years were a stress test for the executive branch's ethics program, and the program failed. That has important lessons for the other branches of government as well. The ethics program in Congress is even weaker than the executive branch ethics program, and the Supreme Court has no formal ethics code at all;[12] when a possible conflict or other ethics situation arises for a justice, each is left to decide what she or he thinks ethics require. A message Congress should draw from Trump's presidency is that all of the systems for ethics in government need to be strengthened. Just as the Watergate scandal prompted a wave of government reforms,[13] the ethical failure of the Trump administration should prompt significant and systemic transformation.

This chapter details a number of legislative reforms that would meaningfully strengthen the government ethics program. Most of these reforms are focused on the executive branch that Trump and his appointees so badly abused, but I also include some recommendations for Congress and the Supreme Court. They are hardly immune from Trumpery under their respective current ethics schemes; on the contrary, the weakness of those rules invites it.

The reader will note that aspects of these recommendations are necessarily in depth. That is because I hope to provide a roadmap for legislators of the sometimes highly technical fixes that are required to make sure that the corruption of the Trump era is never again repeated. That said, the basic thrust of each recommendation and its aim is easy enough to understand.

## Reducing Conflicts of Interest

When President Trump nominated Elaine Chao to be transportation secretary, she promised to sever her ties with an asphalt company that owed her a cash payment. Two years later, her financial disclosure report revealed that she had accepted shares of the company's stock instead of cash and had kept the stock.[14] The department's ethics official argued that Secretary Chao was not technically violating any rule. The relevant standard only kicked in if she was participating in any "particular matter" affecting the asphalt industry. She wasn't. But this technical legal argument did little to ease public concerns about a transportation secretary owning asphalt company stock while the administration was promising massive investments in the nation's infrastructure. Ultimately public pressure helped force Chao to divest the stock.[15]

This example of a currently allowable but troubling conflict of interest is hardly unique among officials of the Trump administration or any other. Congress should enact reforms to reduce conflicts of interest in the executive branch. If the opportunity for personal enrichment is eliminated, government officials will be more likely to put the public's interest first. The best way to achieve this risk reduction is by enacting a new law requiring top executive branch officials to get rid of (i.e., divest) financial holdings that may give rise to conflicts of interest much more broadly than is currently the case.[16]

This remedy seems obvious enough, but it would constitute a significant shift from the executive branch's current approach to ethics. No law requires a president or vice president to divest conflicting financial interests, and most of the conflict of interest laws applicable to executive branch officials do not apply to the president or vice president at all.[17] The primary conflict of interest law applicable to other executive branch officials requires only recusal, not divestiture.[18] Under that law, recusal means avoiding conflicts of interest by merely refraining from working on a matter.

But recusal can be tricky. For one thing, the primary conflict of interest law can be difficult to understand. That law does not require recusal from every matter affecting an official's financial interests. It applies only when a matter affecting an official's financial interests qualifies as a "particular matter."[19] This legal term refers to a matter that is focused on the interests of individual parties or a "discrete and identifiable class of persons," such as an industry.[20] For example, a regulation applicable to drugmakers would be a "particular matter" because it focuses on the interests of the drug manufacturing industry. But a workplace safety regulation applicable to all large employers would not be a "particular matter" because it applies to companies in a wide range of industries instead of a "discrete and identifiable class."

Making it even harder to understand the concept of a "particular matter," the government has said anything that involves a variety of topics (such as a broad-ranging speech or an international trade agreement covering a variety of sectors of the economy) does not qualify as a "particular matter"—even if any one of the topics, standing alone, would be a "particular matter." For instance, the energy secretary could legally give a speech highlighting all of the Energy Department's initiatives, including one initiative directly affecting the secretary's personal financial interests. But, after giving the speech, the secretary could not return to her or his office and work on the initiative affecting the secretary's personal financial interests because the initiative itself is a "particular matter."

With such a complicated law, relying on recusal to resolve conflicts of interest can be a risky proposition for a senior government official. That is true even when officials are operating in good faith (something that did not always seem to be the case among Trump appointees). The real world of government is not like a written law school exam that presents tidy hypothetical scenarios for thoughtful analysis. The work is hectic. Senior officials juggle a daunting volume of emails, phone calls, videoconferences, telephone conferences, and in-person meetings. Matters requiring their attention do not come with warning labels saying, "Caution: I qualify as a 'particular matter' that may implicate the complex conflict of interest law." Officials often have little understanding of the law and little time to evaluate the applicability of that law to the matters that arise. If an administration also lacks an ethical tone at the top, and an appetite to follow the rules, the situation can lend itself to even worse neglect or abuse.

Too many recusals can also limit an official's effectiveness in government. The secretary of the U.S. Department of Energy could legally keep a large portfolio of energy company stocks, but the conflict of interest law would require the secretary to recuse from a wide assortment of activities. That would not be a problem if the secretary came to Washington to sit with her or his feet on a desk reading the newspaper all day, but it is not ideal if the secretary has policy objectives. That is why many senior officials divest at least some assets when they go into government.

Deciding which assets to divest, however, is a subjective art and not a science. Divestiture is inconvenient, and it can cause an official to miss out on money-making opportunities. Having worked with thousands of senior officials, I know that most are not enthusiastic about the prospect of erring on the side of caution and divesting a wide range of assets. Their reluctance to divest can make negotiations with them over divestitures difficult. It is up to ethics officials to press high-level officials in their agencies to divest. Negotiations over divestitures can be fraught because an agency's ethics officials work under the agency's managers, the very people the ethics officials have to persuade to divest potentially conflicting assets. Even when the agency ethics officials do not work directly for a senior manager with whom they are negotiating, the senior manager wields influence with the ethics officials' bosses. It is hard for ethics officials to hold a firm line in this environment, especially when the conflict of interest law does not specifically require divestiture.

Things are slightly better in the case of presidential nominees for Senate-confirmed executive branch positions, the top layer of government outside the White House. In the case of these officials, the Office of Government Ethics (OGE) gets involved. Officials who work for OGE are independent of another agency's managers, which means OGE has greater freedom than the agency's ethics officials to demand divestitures. OGE officials can also be more objective than agency ethicists, who can sometimes be overly empathetic to the senior managers with whom they work every day. But OGE officials are limited in the pressure they can exert, because they lack the access that agency ethics officials and managers have to information about the nature of the agency's work. It is hard for OGE officials to identify conflicts of interest if they do not know what duties a nominee will perform after entering government. This dynamic does not guarantee the best results when it comes to deciding on divestitures.

Weighing against divestiture is a presidential administration's concern when recruiting candidates for political posts. White House and cabinet officials tend to worry that expansive divestiture requirements may make it harder for an administration to fill key positions. Concerns about the effect of divestiture on recruitment are legitimate, but their importance is often overstated. Underlying the argument that divestiture is bad for recruitment seems to be an assumption that the best candidates for government service are well-to-do and wealthy individuals who would turn away from public service rather than divest conflicting assets. A counterargument might be that the public's interest is best served by hiring the sort of patriots who are willing to make personal sacrifices to serve their country. After all, candidates for high-level positions are seeking authority to influence policies that affect people's lives. If those candidates are unwilling to resolve conflicts of interest through divestiture, a citizen should be skeptical of their willingness to put the public's interests before their own. While this argument may oversimplify the issue somewhat, the point is that Americans should be careful about sacrificing the public's interest in government integrity just to avoid inconveniencing government officials who want to get the best possible return on their investments.

A few examples highlight why relying on recusal (as opposed to divestiture) can undermine public confidence in government integrity, even if recusal is technically enough for an official to comply with the conflict of interest law. Proving that ethics concerns know no party, take the case of the Biden administration's energy secretary, Jennifer Granholm, who promised to divest stock options in an electric vehicle company. Deviating from the normal three-month deadline for divestiture, the government gave Secretary Granholm six months to offload her options. In the meantime, she promised that she would recuse from any "particular matter" affecting the company.[21] That is where things got complicated.

Granholm's recusal commitment meant that she needed to stay out of "particular matters" affecting her financial interest in the electric vehicle company. This generally meant recusing from matters focused on the electric vehicle industry, but not exactly. The contours of the legal term "particular matter" were such that she could arguably comply with the conflict of interest law while touting the administration's push for electric vehicle technology as long as she did so in the context of discussing energy policies affecting a variety of industries. When news reports indicated that she was, in fact, touting the administration's push for electric vehicle technology, the public had little ability to gauge whether she was complying with the conflict of interest law. What the public knew was that a government official who held stock options in an electric vehicle company was using her position to help the electric vehicle industry. Even if technically compliant, that cannot have helped public confidence in government.

Of course, the Trump administration was also rich in ethical challenges. Trump's first director of the Centers for Disease Control and Prevention (CDC), Dr. Brenda Fitzgerald, likewise found herself in hot water over her investments. She cited conflicts of interest with her financial holdings as the basis for declining an invitation to testify before Congress about her agency's activities.[22] Later, she caused a stir when she bought tobacco stock while leading the health agency. Though the conflict of interest law prescribes recusal and not divestiture as the remedy for conflicts of interest, public outrage over her actions forced her to resign.[23]

Recusal may be all the law currently requires, but it is often not the remedy for conflicts of interest that the public deserves. What the public needs is a law requiring broad divestitures by the president's top political appointees (as well as by the president and the vice president). Applying the law to all 2.1 million federal employees would be too hard to manage, so the law should focus on the officials with the most power to do harm if conflicts of interest influence their decisions.[24] Specifically, the law should apply to all presidential appointees and all full-time political appointees holding executive positions (i.e., noncareer members of the Senior Executive Service and equivalent executive systems). The divestiture law should not apply to other political appointees in nonexecutive positions or to short-term appointees (i.e., so-called "Schedule C" appointees, who are confidential advisors to more senior appointees, and special government employees, who are exempted from certain ethics rules because they are hired to serve no more than 130 days in government).[25] These individuals are generally senior advisors and support staff who lack the authority to make final decisions in significant matters. They would remain subject to the conflict of interest law, which would still necessitate recusal or divestiture when conflicts of interest arise. This carve-out for lower-level appointees would give an administration needed wiggle room to bring in experts to fulfill urgent government needs. For example, it would enable the government to avail itself of help from information technology wizards, who may hold stock options in Silicon Valley companies but may have the expertise to respond to urgent cybersecurity threats and could still come into government as nonexecutive appointees or as short-term, special government employees.

The divestiture law should include reasonable exceptions. Otherwise, covered officials would have to liquidate all of their assets and stuff their money in their mattresses. Bank accounts and Treasury bonds are unlikely to pose conflicts of interest, and should be allowed. To avoid forcing officials to sell their homes, cars, and artwork, the law would need exceptions for personal residences and belongings. An exception for personal residences could also include any individual rental property, such as a beach house. But the personal residence exception should not include other types of real estate, such as apartment buildings and strip malls, held solely for investment purposes.

The divestiture law could incorporate other regulatory exceptions that OGE has issued under the conflict of interest law. Congress has already authorized OGE to issue regulations exempting some types of financial interests from the conflict of interest law, which means ownership of these interests does not create the risk of violating that law. OGE can issue a regulatory conflict of interest exemption whenever it determines that a type of financial interest is "too remote or too inconsequential" to affect the integrity of the services that government officials provide.[26] OGE has used this authority to exempt diversified mutual funds, employer-sponsored retirement plans, and other financial interests from the conflict of interest law.[27] Because the government does not deem exempted financial interests to pose conflicts of interest, the divestiture law could allow officials to retain them—in other words, the new law would not require officials to divest any financial interests that are covered by OGE's regulatory conflict of interest exemptions.[28]

Divestiture is stronger medicine than recusal, so the divestiture law will need more exceptions than the conflict of interest law, which requires only recusal. For example, a government official may be married to a corporate executive whose compensation includes stock options or a law firm partner who has a capital account in a law firm. OGE has not exempted these financial interests from the conflict of interest law, but divestiture may not be feasible (short of divorce, which hardly seems a suitable ethics remedy). For that reason, the divestiture law should include an exception for a spouse's financial interest in a business or an employer, and the government official should be allowed to recuse from matters affecting the spouse's financial interest.

The divestiture law may also need an exception for certain family trusts. Some government officials may be beneficiaries of trusts their parents, grandparents, or great grandparents established as a way of passing on assets to heirs.[29] The trustees may be unwilling or unable to let these officials "cash out" their interests in these trusts. In such cases, officials may have no way to divest their conflicting interests without forfeiting their entire inheritances. In these cases, the divestiture law should carve out an exception. To avoid abuse, however, the exception should not apply if the government official, the official's spouse, or the official's child created the trust or contributed any money or property to the trust. Carefully drawn exceptions could apply to certain other types of trusts (e.g., a qualified blind trust or an irrevocable trust for the official's own children).

As with the conflict of interest law, Congress should give the Office of Government Ethics authority to issue additional exceptions to the divestiture law. These exceptions could take two different forms.[30] First, OGE could issue universally applicable exceptions by regulation. Second, OGE could issue individual waivers based on a person's unique circumstances when necessary to avoid undue hardship. Congress would have to create some safeguards to prevent the executive branch from gutting the divestiture law through exceptions. The law should require OGE to publish all individual waivers on its official website. Because the president can hire and fire OGE's director, the president and vice president should be ineligible for individual waivers. In addition, presidents and vice presidents should be permitted to rely on OGE's universally applicable regulatory exemptions only if those exemptions were issued in a prior administration (though an exception may be necessary for the president in office when the law is first enacted).

## Review of Agency Head Financial Disclosure Reports

Another thing lacking from government ethics laws is any requirement that the Office of Government Ethics review the financial disclosure reports filed by agency heads who are not confirmed by the Senate.[31] Take the case of major Trump and GOP donor Postmaster General Louis DeJoy, whose 2020 appointment did not require Senate advice and consent.[32] The law required OGE to review his financial disclosure report only after ethics officials at the U.S. Postal Service had completed their review.[33] As a result, when he entered government, his report was initially subject to review only by ethics officials who served under him. He entered government on June 15, 2020, and his agency's ethics officials did not complete their review of this financial disclosure report until August 6, 2020.[34] Media reports recounted the controversy after it was discovered that DeJoy had retained tens of millions of dollars' worth of stock in his former employer, XPO Logistics, Inc., a postal service contractor.[35] After postal officials sent his financial disclosure report to OGE, however, OGE determined that it was reasonably necessary for DeJoy to divest this stock to comply with a conflict of interest law.[36] Congress should also require them to obtain OGE's approval of any ethics agreements to prevent conflicts of interest from arising.[37]

The flaw in the existing requirements should be obvious. OGE has more independence than agency ethics officials, who will have to report to a new agency head. Moreover, agency heads not requiring Senate confirmation have thirty days to file a financial disclosure report and can receive two forty-five-day extensions.[38] As a result, nearly four months could pass before anyone begins reviewing their assets for potential conflicts of interest.

The problem with this arrangement became apparent during the Trump administration. As mentioned earlier, in early 2018 CDC Director Brenda Fitzgerald resigned after having served only about a half a year in the job—reportedly for reasons connected to her difficulty in divesting certain assets and her purchase of other assets.[39] One senator had expressed concern that Dr. Fitzgerald's conflicting financial interests appeared to necessitate her recusal from particular matters related to cancer and opioids.[40] Because the CDC position was not subject to Senate confirmation, however, there was no requirement for OGE to review her financial disclosure report and create an ethics agreement before she began her ill-fated appointment.[41]

To prevent a repeat of these types of situations, Congress should amend the Ethics in Government Act to require OGE to review the financial disclosure reports of all agency heads before they enter government service.[42] Congress can amend that law, 5 U.S.C. App. § 103(a), so that it requires prospective appointees for agency head positions not requiring Senate confirmation to submit their reports simultaneously to both their agency ethics officials and OGE at least thirty days before assuming the duties of the position.

## Reducing Outside Influence on Officials

The Trump administration was a cornucopia of alleged outside influence on its appointees. For example, one media outlet reported that after David Bernhardt "joined the [Interior] department in 2017, it has made at least 15 policy changes, decisions or proposals that would directly benefit Bernhardt's former clients. . . . In some cases, the former clients wrote letters addressed to Bernhardt about those issues or lobbied his colleagues before those colleagues met with Bernhardt on those matters."[43] Gaps in existing laws and regulations leave the executive branch vulnerable to the appearance or reality of outside influences in numerous ways. Congress should strengthen applicable laws to close these gaps in three areas: golden parachute payments, former employers and clients, and post-government employment.

### Golden Parachute Payments

Current law fails to prevent outside employers from making extraordinary payments to any of their employees who leave to accept executive branch positions. The issue often arises in the context of unvested interests, such as unvested stock options and restricted stock, which employers often require departing employees to forfeit when they resign. But if an employer accelerates the vesting of an unvested interest when an employee resigns to enter government, the employee can legally receive a windfall from the employer immediately before assuming a position of influence. For example, the Department of Energy authorized Trump's energy secretary, Rick Perry, to request that two energy companies, Sunoco Logistics Partners L.P. and Energy Transfer Partners, accelerate the vesting of his restricted stock in those companies.[44] He later reported that the companies paid him a total of $345,597 for these interests.[45]

A simpler way to accomplish the same concerning arrangement is to give the departing employee a cash payment. That's what happened when William Long, Trump's Federal Emergency Management Agency director, left an emergency management consulting firm to oversee the government's emergency management and the company gave him a bonus.[46] The Commerce Department similarly authorized one of its assistant secretaries,

Nazakhtar Nikakhtar, to receive a discretionary bonus.[47] Whatever concerns the public may have about these payments influencing government officials, they were legal under existing laws.

However, these types of permissible but concerning arrangements were not unique to the Trump administration. A defense contractor, Enersys, accelerated the vesting of unvested restricted stock held by Obama's secretary of the Navy, Ray Mabus, when he quit the company to enter government service.[48] And the Defense Department authorized Biden's Air Force secretary, Frank Kendall, to have the vesting of his unvested stock options and restricted stock accelerated by another defense contractor, Leidos.[49]

The current law is inadequate to prevent payments that appear designed to influence the recipient's actions once in government.[50] In his ethics executive order, President Biden took a step toward addressing these payments. It is a good improvement, but it does not go quite far enough, so citizens need federal legislation to do more. The executive order requires Biden's appointees to make the following pledge:

> I have not accepted and will not accept, including after entering Government, any salary or other cash payment from my former employer the eligibility for and payment of which is limited to individuals accepting a position in the United States Government. I also have not accepted and will not accept any noncash benefit from my former employer that is provided in lieu of such a prohibited cash payment.

This pledge seeks to thwart anyone from offering a future presidential appointee a payment conditioned on entering federal government service, possibly in the hope of the appointee later exerting governmental influence to return the favor, but the pledge has some holes. It applies only if eligibility for the payment is "limited to individuals accepting a position in the United States government." In all my years in government ethics, working with thousands of presidential nominees and appointees, I have only once seen a payment conditioned on someone accepting a position in the *federal* government.[51] The more typical arrangement has been company public service programs that allow departing employees to retain certain benefits if they accept a position in the "government" generally, which could include state and local governments as opposed to specifically a position in the federal government. That, of course, is also problematic; however, it would not be covered by the Biden ethics executive order, making a legislative fix desirable.[52]

The other gap in the executive order is that it would not apply to noncash items.[53] Its terms specify that it applies only if a cash payment is offered or something else is offered specifically as a substitute for a cash payment, and that is a good feature of the executive order. But it fails to cover other noncash offers. For instance, over the years, I have often seen officials with unvested stock options leave employers to enter government service. Typically, most of those employers required forfeiture of unvested stock options upon resignation, because that is the point of a vesting requirement. Sometimes, however, an employer offered to accelerate the vesting schedule so that the departing employee could retain the now-vested options upon resigning to accept a government position. This type of arrangement can be even more valuable than a cash severance payment. Unfortunately, the Biden ethics pledge does not address this sort of golden parachute payment.[54]

These examples show why Congress should enact a new law prohibiting golden parachute payments of all types. The prohibition should cover cash payments as well as things like the acceleration of vesting schedules for stock options and other employee benefits. The new law should apply to any benefit or payment an incoming official receives unless the official can demonstrate that the employer would have offered the benefit or payment even if the official had not accepted a government position. And the term *government* should not be limited to the *federal* government.[55]

## Former Clients and Employers

Former clients and employers of officials always pose ethical concerns due to fears that the officials will remain loyal to their former associates instead of being loyal to the public. One 2019 report catalogued 24 Trump cabinet nominees who had 188 past clients or employers who had business before the cabinet agency overseen by the nominee.[56] Of those 188, 47 actively lobbied the respective departments of the nominees on matters too numerous to count. Interior's Bernhardt alone had 20 former clients or employers who lobbied the department. An OGE regulation requires officials to recuse from certain matters involving former clients and employers. But the requirement should be codified in a statute so that a future administration cannot rescind it, and Congress should broaden the existing recusal requirement to bolster public confidence in the face of issues like those faced by Bernhardt and many other Trump officials.

The existing OGE regulation requires recusal for only one year after an official served a former client or employer, but President Biden's ethics executive order goes further—expanding that requirement to two years. The two-year period runs from the date the official enters government service, rather than the date when the official last served the client or employer, and it applies to any client or employer the employee served in the two-year period before entering government. That difference is significant. In effect, an official covered by Biden's executive order could have to recuse from matters involving a former client or employer for up to four years after the last service to that client or employer, which is much longer than the twelve-month recusal under the existing regulation.

The problem with an executive order is that a future president could rescind it. But a law would endure beyond the current administration. That is why Congress should enact a law containing the recusal requirement established in the Biden executive order. Congress should specifically adopt the Biden version of this requirement instead of the OGE version. The OGE regulation requires recusal only when "the employee determines that the circumstances would cause a reasonable person with knowledge of the relevant facts to question his impartiality in the matter."[57] That makes the rule largely unenforceable because officials can always claim they determined the public would not be concerned about their actions. But the Biden executive order strips officials of that excuse by omitting this language. In drafting the law, Congress should track the Biden executive order by omitting this language. It should also adopt the longer recusal period required under the Biden executive order.[58]

### Post-Employment Restrictions

A conflict of interest law imposes post-employment restrictions on high-level government officials. The restrictions bar these officials, after they leave government, from communicating with (or appearing before) certain other government officials on behalf of someone else with the intent to influence the government. They are needed to hold back those such as the thirty-three ex-Trump officials who, as of 2019, had reportedly become "registered federal lobbyists [or went to] work in jobs that closely resemble lobbying."[59] These restrictions are helpful to make sure that ex-officials do their lobbying away from their former colleagues over whom they still may have undue sway, but a mere one-year ban is too short to curtail that influence. Congress should increase the duration to at least two years.

Specifically, the conflict of interest law requires a *one*-year cooling-off period for "senior employees," a group of noncareer officials (i.e., political appointees) and career officials that includes deputy assistants to the president, as well as noncareer and career members of the Senior Executive Service.[60] The law imposes a longer, *two*-year cooling off period on "very senior employees," a separate, smaller group of even higher-ranking noncareer officials (i.e., political appointees) that includes assistants to the president and only the very top cabinet officials. The length of these restrictions is adequate for career officials who qualify as "senior employees" but is too short for noncareer officials (i.e., political appointees) who qualify as either "senior employees" or "very senior employees." I recommend lengthening the restriction for all of these political appointees to at least two years, a period of time in which relationships with former colleagues are more likely to cool.

There is a precedent for making this change. In 2009, President Obama issued an executive order extending the one-year restriction for former *noncareer* (i.e., politically appointed) "senior employees" to two years.[61] As a result, both "senior" and "very senior" employees were subject to a two-year restriction. (The breadth of the restriction, in terms of which government officials they could not contact after leaving government, remained broader for "very senior employees" than for "senior employees," but the length of the recusals for both groups was the same under the Obama executive order.) Unfortunately, President Trump rescinded that extension shortly after his inauguration in 2017.[62] Now, President Biden has reinstated the Obama-era two-year restriction for noncareer "senior employees."[63] Consistent with the Obama and Biden approach to political appointees, Congress should extend the restriction to two years for former noncareer "senior employees."

In the case of "very senior employees," the stakes are even higher. This category includes the highest-level officials in the federal government, such as the secretary of state and the secretary of defense. There is no reason, for example, that a former defense secretary should be permitted to represent clients before the Defense Department during the administration of the president who appointed her or him. The level of influence such a former official can wield is extreme. For this reason, the post-employment restriction for these "very senior employees" should last until the government has been turned over to a new president and not less than two years if the administration ends sooner. Thus, instead of limiting the restriction on "very senior employees" to two years, the restriction should apply for two years or until the end of the administration, whichever is longer.

In addition, President Biden's ethics executive order has expanded the scope of the restriction with respect to the type of activities it prohibits. The existing post-employment conflict of interest law restricts communications with (and appearances before) the government by former "senior" and "very senior" employees.[64] But the Biden ethics executive order goes further by also restricting these former officials from working behind the scenes to help lobbyists prepare for any contacts with the government that the former officials would be prohibited from making themselves.[65] Congress should capture this added restriction in the law so that a future president cannot simply eliminate it by rescinding the Biden ethics executive order.

## Restricting the Outside Activities of Executive Branch Officials

Federal law prohibits some outside activities for high-level political appointees, but the restrictions do not go far enough to eliminate potential conflicts of interest. For example, an oversight agency did not act when presidential advisor Jared Kushner appeared to be running the Trump campaign out of the White House.[66] At the time, the *New York Times* reported that "Mr. Kushner is positioning himself now as the person officially overseeing the entire campaign from his office in the West Wing, organizing campaign meetings and making decisions about staffing and spending."[67] Congress should impose additional restrictions on officials engaging in certain other outside activities while serving in government.

There are, in fact, several existing restrictions. The Ethics in Government Act bars high-level political appointees from earning outside income in excess of 15 percent of their federal salary. OGE's regulation goes further, barring presidential appointees from earning any outside income at all;[68] however, a future administration could rescind this regulation. The ethics statute also bars officials from serving for compensation on a corporate board or otherwise affiliating with a corporation or association; and the act also bars officials from letting certain businesses, such as law firms, use their names.[69]

To reduce the risk of conflicts of interest associated with outside positions, Congress should also prohibit the most senior political appointees (noncareer "senior" and "very senior" employees) from serving as a director, officer, employee, trustee, or general partner of any outside organization, partnership, or trust, even without compensation. The problem with serving as a director, officer, employee, trustee, or partner for any entity for free is that this outside service splits the official's loyalty between the government and the outside entity. The American people deserve leaders whose sole professional focus is the public interest, and they cannot have total confidence in the loyalty of a leader who serves two masters.

There is also a legal problem for the executive branch official who holds an outside position. The conflict of interest law imputes to the employee all of the financial interests of any outside organization, partnership, or trust that the employee serves as director, officer, employee, trustee, or partner.[70] In other words, any financial interest held by the outside organization, partnership, or trust is treated as though it is the employee's own financial interest. The possibilities for conflicts abound.

The other issue involving outside activities that needs to be addressed by Congress is the political activities of White House officials. As discussed in the preceding chapter, the Hatch Act prohibits executive branch employees from engaging in political activity while they are on duty, in government buildings, wearing uniforms or official insignia, or using a government vehicle.[71] Absent an exception, the prohibition against political activity while on duty or on government property imposes a disproportionate restriction on presidentially appointed, Senate-confirmed (PAS) appointees and White House staffers, because they are deemed to be continuously on duty twenty-four hours a day, seven days a week.[72] For this reason, Congress created an exception that excuses certain PAS appointees and White House staffers from compliance with the prohibition on political activity, provided that the government incurs no additional costs beyond their salaries.[73]

The U.S. Office of Special Counsel (OSC), the small federal agency that

enforces the Hatch Act, has publicly expressed the view that this exemption
is intended to enable only incidental activity while on duty or on government property:

> Congress expected that on-the-job political activity by [exempt] employ-
> ees would be kept to a minimum. The legislative history indicates that
> the exemption was meant to afford certain high-level officials the same
> opportunities to engage in political activity that the Hatch Act Reform
> Amendments allowed non-exempt employees, that is, to engage in po-
> litical activity off-the-job. Because they are presumed to be continuously
> on duty, the exemption was necessary to put them on equal footing with
> the rest of the federal workforce. Further, the House Report accompany-
> ing the Hatch Act Reform Amendments noted that "despite the excep-
> tion, the committee expects that most of the political activity that these
> officials engage in will be conducted off Government property and not
> during regular duty hours." Accordingly, although the plain language
> of the Hatch Act and its regulations place no limitations on the extent
> to which [exempt] employees can engage in political activity on duty
> and in the federal workplace as long as the costs are reimbursed, OSC
> maintains that imposing no restraints at all goes beyond what Congress
> intended.[74]

Whether or not OSC feels it can act on its view of the congressional
intent underlying this exception, its assessment of the aim of the law seems
correct. Unfortunately, the plain language of the statute does not state that
there is a limitation on the amount of time that individuals subject to the
exception can spend engaging in political activity while on duty or in the
federal workplace. As a result, there is significant potential for abuse of this
exception. For example, the aforementioned case of Jared Kushner apparently running the Trump campaign out of the White House stimulated a
watchdog group complaint to OSC.[75] But no action ensued. Congress can
address this potential for abuse by tightening the restriction to prohibit
anything more than incidental political activity by covered officials during
normal business hours or while in the federal workplace.[76]

## Addressing Conflicts of Interest Associated with a Spouse's Employment

The spouse of a high-level executive branch official can wield inappropriate influence over the subordinates or peers of that official. For example, a State Department Office of the Inspector General (OIG) report found that Susan Pompeo, the wife of Secretary of State Mike Pompeo, requested that "employees in the Office of the Secretary undertake work of a personal nature, such as picking up personal items, planning events unrelated to the Department's mission, and conducting such personal business as pet care and mailing personal Christmas cards. OIG found that such requests were inconsistent with Department ethics rules and the Standards of Ethical Conduct for Employees of the Executive Branch."[77] Worse still, given that level of spousal influence, existing laws actually permit the spouse of a high-level employee to represent paying clients before the employee's agency, creating a risk of the appearance of profiting inappropriately from public service. Congress should do more to prevent the spouses of top officials from representing clients before their agencies.

Though government ethics laws do not apply to the spouses of officials, they do apply to the officials themselves. Congress should deter the spouses of high-level political appointees (noncareer senior and very senior executive branch employees) from representing clients before the political appointees' agencies by imposing burdensome recusal obligations on the appointees.[78] Congress should prohibit these political appointees, for the duration of their appointments, from participating in any "particular matters" affecting the known financial interests of any clients the appointees' spouses represent before the agency at a time when the employees serve in political positions in their agencies.[79] This very broad recusal would go beyond current law to likely deter a high-level appointee's spouse from representing clients before the appointee's agency.

That is needed because less senior executive branch employees may be reluctant to adhere to ordinary procedures and apply strict legal standards in any matters in which their politically appointed supervisors' spouses are representing clients. At a minimum, these employees are likely to be faster to return calls from the spouses or agree to meet with them. A private sector client wanting speedy government service and the hope of preferential treatment would therefore have an incentive to seek out a top official's spouse when looking for representation before the government. Even when this is not the reason for a client's decision to hire the spouse as a representative, the arrangement creates a potential for an appearance of misusing public office for private gain, which can undermine public confidence in government.

Restricting the business activities of a political appointee's spouse is not simple. The spouse is a private citizen who did not make a choice to go into government. For this reason, the focus of the new restriction should be the activities of the political appointee who has undertaken the responsibilities of public service. Imposing a "particular matter" recusal on this employee for the duration of government service stands a reasonable chance of success because a "particular matter" is any matter focused on the interests of specific parties or a discrete and identifiable class of persons.[80] It is the second part of this definition that makes a "particular matter" recusal burdensome. An industry is an example of a discrete and identifiable class of persons. Thus, for instance, if the spouse of a top political appointee at the Food and Drug Administration represents a drug company before that agency with respect to a new drug application, the political appointee would be disqualified from any matter focused on the interests of the drug manufacturing industry for the rest of her or his appointment. Because that would make it difficult for the official to do her or his job, the reasonable alternative is spousal avoidance of the agency.

## Providing the Government with Stronger Tools to Enforce Ethics Rules

Executive branch ethics restrictions are of little value if violations are not addressed. The repeated flouting of ethics and related rules in the Trump administration, often without consequences or recourse, at times made a mockery of the system. The tone of impunity was set in the first weeks of the new administration when Counselor to the President Kellyanne Conway endorsed the clothing line of the president's daughter, Ivanka Trump, during a television appearance from the White House briefing room: "Go buy Ivanka's stuff is what I would tell you. . . . this is just a wonderful line. I own some of it. I fully—I'm gonna just give a free commercial here. Go buy it today everybody. You can find it online."[81] Conway's endorsement was a clear violation of the government ethics rules pertaining to federal employees. Despite a recommendation from OGE, however, Conway faced no disciplinary action for her endorsement.[82] The decision to discipline Conway was the president's and he (unsurprisingly) did nothing. Others followed Conway's lead. For example, Ivanka Trump would issue a similar endorsement of Goya products in July 2020 while her father was running for reelection, despite her status as an advisor to the president subjecting her to the same ethics rules governing Conway's conduct.[83] But Conway remained the administration's most enthusiastic transgressor of ethics and related rules (after the president himself), with one watchdog group ultimately counting sixty alleged violations.[84] The government needs more effective mechanisms for enforcing conflict of interest laws and other government ethics regulations.

As a supplement to the existing legal framework for conflict of interest and ethics restrictions, Congress should create a noncriminal law prohibiting a broader range of conduct than the criminal conflict of interest law prohibits. Congress should also establish an effective administrative mechanism for investigating suspected violations and imposing fines on violators. For minor ethics violations, Congress should authorize the Office of Government Ethics to assess a $200 fee without having to overcome significant procedural hurdles, though the employee should have a right to appeal the assessment to the Merit Systems Protection Board (MSPB). For more serious noncriminal violations, OGE should be authorized to file a complaint with the MSPB requesting significant civil penalties. The employee should have the right to seek review of a final MSPB decision by the U.S. Court of Appeals for the Federal Circuit.

In most instances, the only realistic deterrent to violations of conflict of interest laws and government ethics regulations today is the threat of disciplinary action. That system is effective with regard to career-level officials, but it only works with regard to political appointees if the president is willing to fire or otherwise meaningfully sanction those who violate the conflict of interest law. (Trump was not.) The disparity is even greater when it comes to enforcing OGE's standards of conduct regulations.

The criminal nature of the conflict of interest law seems to make the Department of Justice (DOJ) reluctant to enforce it.[85] A prosecutor will normally only pursue cases in which a violation is severe enough to merit criminal prosecution and the government can meet the very high burden of proving beyond a reasonable doubt that a crime was committed. Even then, there may be little likelihood of prosecution in an administration like Trump's, where questions arose as to whether Attorney General Bill Barr was interfering in cases to protect the president's associates.[86]

The law affords the Justice Department the option of pursuing a noncriminal civil action to seek civil monetary penalties against an employee who violates the law.[87] The standard of proof for a civil action is lower than in criminal cases, with the government only having to prove that it is more likely than not that the employee violated the law.[88] But the court must interpret the various elements of the law narrowly because any interpretation will apply to criminal defendants in other cases. Supreme Court Justice Antonin Scalia, writing for the plurality in one decision, restated this principle concisely: "We interpret ambiguous criminal statutes in favor of defendants, not prosecutors."[89]

What is needed is a new mechanism, separate from DOJ's enforcement of the conflict of interest law, that encourages enforcement by carrying lighter consequences and a broader definition of conflicts of interest. Although reducing penalties may seem counterintuitive when the goal is strengthening ethics enforcement, a noncriminal conflict of interest law would have more teeth than a criminal one if the government were more likely to enforce it against violators. I do not advocate rescinding the existing criminal law. I advocate supplementing it with a noncriminal law with a broader reach, lighter penalties, and an effective administrative mechanism for enforcement. This law would cover only noncareer employees (i.e., political appointees) because existing disciplinary remedies are generally sufficient to address concerns as to career employees.

Under this new law, the goal would be to resolve conflicts of interest rather than to criminally punish violators, who would remain subject to the separate criminal conflict of interest law and could face more serious consequences for any violation of it.[90] For this reason, OGE and the MSPB should have the authority to impose fines, but the law should also provide an off-ramp that incentivizes bad actors to resign from government. To that end, any fine should be suspended if the noncareer employee resigns within thirty days of a final decision imposing the fine and be automatically rescinded if the employee does not return to government before the end of the presidential administration in which the employee was appointed.

Returning to the example of Kellyanne Conway, President Trump's own appointee to lead the Office of Special Counsel, Henry Kerner, ultimately recommended that the president fire Conway for what Kerner determined to be repeated violations of the Hatch Act, the law prohibiting misuse of position to influence a partisan election. But, as described in the preceding chapter, President Trump refused to take action against Conway, and she remained in her position for more than a year after the recommendation that she be fired. After resigning, she reportedly signed a multimillion-dollar book deal to talk about her time in government. It would be an improvement if, in the future, a new enforcement mechanism succeeded in motivating someone like Conway to leave government, by offering a choice between paying significant civil penalties and resigning.

The administrative imposition of fines is already part of the government ethics program. OGE and agency ethics offices can—and do—impose a $200 fine when an employee misses the deadline for filing a public financial disclosure report.[91] In 2017, for example, Assistant to the President Jared Kushner was fined at least twice for failing to meet the disclosure deadline.[92] In addition, the MSPB can impose fines if the Office of Special Counsel files a complaint alleging that either a career employee or a non-Senate confirmed political appointee violates the Hatch Act.[93] In 2020, the authorized fine per Hatch Act violation was $1,112.[94]

Consistent with this existing framework, OGE should be permitted to impose a $200 fine directly whenever it finds that an employee has violated the proposed noncriminal conflict of interest law or a provision of OGE's standards of conduct regulations. For larger fines, OGE should be required to file a complaint against the employee before the MSPB, which should be authorized to levy fines ranging from $1,000 per violation up to the full value of a conflicting financial interest or payment. For violations of ethics regulations not involving a financial interest, the penalty should range from $1,000 for a first violation, with the amount doubling for each successive violation thereafter (i.e., $2,000, $4,000, $8,000, etc.), up to the full amount of the employee's annual salary.

The coverage of this new law should be limited to noncareer senior and very senior employees, and only those who are not short-term special government employees.[95] Existing disciplinary procedures are sufficient to address violations by career employees. Lower-level political appointees have less authority to harm the interests of the government. Special government employees serve for only a short time and are less likely to have the authority to make final decisions in matters.[96]

The language of the new law should be broader than that of the criminal conflict of interest law. Recall that the criminal law prohibits participation in a "particular matter" affecting an employee's financial interests. A "particular matter" is a matter that is focused narrowly on the interests of identified parties or a discrete and identifiable class of persons.[97] Instead, the noncriminal law should cover any "matter" if the effect of the matter on the employee's financial interests is direct, predictable, and substantial. There is no substantiality requirement in the criminal law, but the term *matter* is so broad—literally meaning anything at all—that the scope of the proposed noncriminal law needs to be constrained somewhat.[98]

The scope should be further circumscribed by allowing the government to treat segregable parts of a "matter" differently. In some cases, a "matter" may have discrete parts. For example, a trade agreement that covers dozens of segments of the economy affecting a wide range of industries is considered a "matter" and not a "particular matter" for purposes of the conflict of interest law because it does not focus on a discrete and identifiable class of persons. Under the criminal conflict of interest law, therefore, an employee with significant stock holdings in a social media company could be assigned to work on provisions of a multisector trade agreement directly addressing social media companies. This is a gap that would be closed by the proposed noncriminal conflict of interest law covering "matters" as opposed to "particular matters." But there is no reason the employee with the social media company stock should be barred from working on provisions of the trade agreement that address agricultural products. For this reason, the noncriminal law should provide an exception for discrete parts of a matter that can be segregated from those parts of the matter that pose conflicts of interest for an employee.[99]

The law should further authorize OGE to investigate suspected violations, and it should require agency management officials to cooperate with that investigation. OGE should have the authority to conduct investigative interviews of employees, subject to the right of an employee to invoke any applicable Fifth Amendment right if the answer could incriminate the employee under the conflict of interest law or any other criminal law.[100] OGE should also have enhanced authority to request information and documents from employees under investigation and the employees' agencies. To ensure cooperation, OGE should have authority to draw adverse factual inferences based on the refusal of an employee and the employee's agency to supply it with any requested information or document. To protect sensitive information (e.g., classified information, information related to an ongoing law enforcement investigation, etc.), an exception should prevent OGE from drawing adverse inference whenever a law or regulation prohibits the release of information or a document to OGE.[101] For the sake of fairness, another exception should prevent OGE from drawing an adverse inference against an employee under investigation if the employee's agency has refused to provide OGE with any requested information or record, provided that the employee truly lacks access to the information or document and has asked the agency to provide it to OGE.

Before imposing any penalty, OGE should be required to notify an employee in writing of its basis for suspecting a violation has occurred and should be required to provide the employee with copies of all material on which it is relying. The law should also give the employee or the employee's representative at least forty-five days to respond both orally and in writing, but the law should expressly state that, at this stage, the employee is not entitled to a hearing. After considering any response by the employee or the employee's representative and the materials provided to the employee, OGE should be authorized to issue a finding as to whether the employee violated this proposed noncriminal law.

The law should provide that if OGE finds the employee has violated or is violating the law, OGE can take several actions. OGE should be able to direct the employee to stop engaging in the violation, fine the employee $200, and direct the employee to file a corrective action plan with OGE. If the employee fails to comply within a reasonable time, OGE should be able to assess successive $200 fines every thirty days. The law should provide that the office or contractor that manages the employing agency's payroll function must comply with an order by OGE to withhold the amount fined from the employee's pay. The employee should have the right to appeal an adverse determination by OGE to the MSPB.

In the event of serious violations or continued noncompliance, OGE should have the authority to file a complaint with the MSPB seeking more significant fines. The law should require OGE to bear the burden of proving that the employee committed the violation by a preponderance of the evidence, based solely on evidence previously supplied to the employee and any reasonable adverse factual inference OGE has drawn. The MSPB should be required to adopt OGE's adverse inference unless OGE failed to advance a proper request for information; the employee either was not given adequate notice of the request or attempted in good faith to comply with the request; or the adverse inference is not one that a reasonable person would have drawn under the totality of the circumstances. In addition, the employee should be permitted to rebut any properly drawn adverse inference by submitting evidence to the MSPB, but the burden should shift to the employee to prove by a preponderance of the evidence that a properly drawn adverse inference is factually incorrect.

The case should be decided in an expedited proceeding. To ensure the process moves quickly, the law should place reasonable limits on discovery to avoid lengthy and burdensome requests. The employee should, however, be permitted to submit affidavits, witness testimony, records, and written argument, and to cross-examine witnesses. The MSPB should be authorized to request additional information from either OGE or the employee, as well as to draw adverse inferences if either party fails to supply the requested information. The employee should be entitled to appeal an adverse final decision by the MSPB to the U.S. Court of Appeals for the Federal Circuit, which should conduct the same limited review that it conducts when the MSPB has sustained the firing of a career employee.[102] Finally, the law should authorize OGE to seek a court order from a district court to enforce a final MSPB decision to impose a fine on the employee, and the law should expressly permit OGE to seek the court order directly without having to be represented in the case by DOJ.

The law should not award payment by OGE of the legal fees of an employee who prevails in an MSPB proceeding, although it should grant the employee's agency head the discretion to reimburse the employee for any legal fees if the employee prevails. This is because, as a small agency, OGE has a small budget. An unexpected expense, particularly at the end of a fiscal year, could cause OGE to incur costs in excess of its appropriated funds. A wealthy political appointee could exploit this vulnerability by running up excessive legal fees, knowing that OGE would have to drop its request that the MSPB impose a fine to avoid violating the Antideficiency Act.[103] The risk of this happening could prevent OGE from vigorously pursuing violations. Therefore, OGE should be insulated from having to pay the employee's legal fees. But fairness dictates that the employee's agency have the option to reimburse the employee for any legal fees.

To discourage a president from firing OGE's director in retaliation for the use of these new enforcement powers and replacing the director with a loyalist, the law should provide that, if the director is fired, the highest-ranking career employee with the most seniority in OGE will automatically become the acting director until the Senate confirms a replacement. The law should also give that career employee the right to file a civil action challenging any effort to block her or him from serving as OGE's acting director, as well as the right to accept related free legal services from any United States–based lawyer or law firm in connection with the case, provided that the lawyer or law firm is not reimbursed by any foreign government or foreign individual. This requirement would help to prevent a president from removing OGE's director and installing a loyalist as a way to shut down an OGE investigation of a political appointee.

Finally, to prevent abuse, the law should require OGE to suspend any investigation or enforcement action in the twelve-month period prior to a presidential election. Although this blackout period could let some bad actors off the hook for violating this law, they will remain subject to the criminal conflict of interest law. Given the continued availability of the criminal law to remedy serious conflict of interest violations, the need to protect U.S. elections outweighs the need to enforce this new noncriminal law during the year before the election.

## Ensuring Inspector General Independence

President Trump's assault on the inspector general (IG) community was remarkable, not only for its brazenness in undermining the independence of inspectors general but also for the way it was enabled by members of Congress, including some who had long crafted public images as defenders of IGs.[104] In just six weeks in the spring of 2020, Trump removed four of these watchdogs from the helms of their respective agencies' offices of inspector general.[105] The purge began with unabashed retaliation against the intelligence community inspector general who notified Congress of the whistleblower complaint relating to Trump's dealings with Ukraine that precipitated his first impeachment and trial. The president made no effort to hide his animus, stating that the IG "took a fake report and he brought it to Congress." Removals followed of acting or permanent IGs at the Departments of Defense, State, and Transportation.[106] He announced his intent to nominate a replacement for a fifth IG, an acting official at the Health and Human Services Department, but the nominee later withdrew from consideration.[107] It is clear that inspectors general lack the protection they need to do their jobs.

Congress should require the president to provide a detailed justification to Congress no less than thirty days before the effective date of any removal of an inspector general. It should prohibit placing an IG on administrative leave in the absence of reasonable suspicion that a crime has been committed. Congress should provide that an IG can be fired only for wrongdoing or a gross waste of appropriated funds, and it should give IGs the right to file a civil action challenging any firing. This may be subject to challenge after the Supreme Court greatly expanded presidential power to fire appointees in decisions regarding the head of the Consumer Financial Protection Bureau under President Trump and the Federal Housing Finance Authority under President Biden, but Congress should continue to explore creative legislative options for subjecting personnel actions against IGs to judicial review to protect the American people against abuses of executive power.

A 2008 law requires a president to give Congress thirty days' notice before firing an inspector general.[108] The idea was to increase the independence of IGs by giving Congress time to investigate the firing and pressure the president to back off any retaliatory or politically motivated firing.[109] But Congress proved unwilling to use its leverage to stop President Trump's retaliatory firings of inspectors general.[110]

Congress should strengthen the law by providing that the thirty-day waiting period does not begin until the president has provided Congress with all information and records forming the basis of an IG's termination. The current law does not compel the president to provide a detailed justification for the firing in the thirty-day notice, nor does the law prohibit the president from placing the inspector general on administrative leave during that thirty-day period.[111] Congress should amend the law to require the president to explain the firing fully. It should bar placing the IG on administrative leave, absent reasonable suspicion that the inspector general has committed a crime.

Congress should also make this law enforceable by authorizing inspectors general to file suit to challenge a termination.[112] The law should place the burden of proof on the administration to establish that the termination was for one of several prescribed causes and that it followed applicable procedures. In meeting this burden, the administration should be limited to only the information and records it provides to Congress at least thirty days before the termination becomes effective. This limitation will put pressure on the administration to be forthcoming with Congress as to the president's reasons for firing an IG.

In connection with giving inspectors general the right to challenge firings, Congress should also address the grounds on which the president may fire IGs. When Congress originally passed the Inspector General Act of 1978, the Department of Justice objected on constitutional grounds to requiring the president to articulate a reason for firing an IG.[113] Although the final version of the law did not impose substantive limitations on the president's authority to fire an inspector general, both the House of Representatives and the Senate rejected DOJ's view.[114] In 2020, the House went further and passed the Heroes Act, which included language providing that IGs could be removed only for specified causes, including permanent incapacity; inefficiency; neglect of duty; malfeasance; felony conviction; conduct involving moral turpitude; knowing violation of a law, rule, or regulation; gross mismanagement; gross waste of funds; or abuse of authority.[115] This language is so broad that it would effectively impose no real limitation on the president's authority to remove an inspector general. But a revised version could have the desired effect if coupled with a right on the part of inspectors general to challenge firings in court.

To discourage the president from taking a retaliatory personnel action against an inspector general, the law should provide that, if the IG is fired, the highest-ranking career employee with the most seniority in the inspector general's office will automatically become the acting IG until the Senate confirms a replacement. The law should also give that career employee the right to file a civil action challenging any effort to block her or him from serving as acting inspector general, as well as the right to accept related free legal services from any United States–based lawyer or law firm in connection with the case, provided that the lawyer or law firm is not reimbursed by any foreign government or foreign individual. This requirement would help to prevent a president from removing an IG and installing a loyalist to shut down an investigation of a political appointee.[116]

## Strengthening Whistleblower Protections

Congress needs to do more to protect whistleblowers, who proved to be a bane of Trump's existence and, among other things, triggered his first impeachment. He viciously and repeatedly attacked the individual whose report triggered the impeachment, at one point going so far as to say the person was "close to a spy" and should be handled as "in the old days"—reported by the media as "a veiled reference to execution."[117] And when impeachment concluded, Trump went on a rampage of revenge against those in his administration who cooperated with Congress (or whom he otherwise blamed, as reported in the *New York Times*):

> After the Senate trial ended, Mr. Trump began removing officials seen as enemies. The target list was long and varied, including Lt. Col. Alexander S. Vindman, a national security aide who testified before the House under subpoena, and his twin brother, Lt. Col. Yevgeny Vindman, who had nothing to do with impeachment other than being family. Ambassador Gordon D. Sondland, another witness, was removed. Ambassador William B. Taylor Jr., the acting chief diplomat in Ukraine who also testified, was brought home early. John C. Rood, the under secretary of defense, was ousted. Joseph Maguire, the acting director of national intelligence, was pushed out early. Elaine McCusker, a Defense Department official who questioned the aid freeze, had her nomination to be Pentagon comptroller withdrawn.[118]

Congress should take action to strengthen whistleblower protections by doing the following:

- Granting a right of anonymity to federal employees who blow the whistle;

- Making it a criminal offense for high-level legislative and executive branch officials to name any individual in public statements that will foreseeably create widespread suspicion of the individual being a whistleblower;

- Letting whistleblowers file civil actions without having to go first to the MSPB;

- Eliminating the requirement that military personnel challenging adverse personnel actions must bear the burden of proving such actions would not have been taken absent whistleblower retaliation; and

- Creating a three-judge panel to consider claims of whistleblower retaliation filed by executive branch personnel involving classified information, and granting that panel broad authority to take corrective action.

For inspectors general to function effectively, they must have access to the information that whistleblowers possess. The Trump presidency made it clear that additional protections are needed for whistleblowers who expose wrongdoing. To ensure government integrity, the American people must be able to rely on federal employees to expose fraud, waste, and abuse, as the executive branch ethics regulations require them to do.[119] In late 2019, dozens of IGs warned the Trump administration that protecting whistleblowers is crucial to their work:

> For over 40 years, since enactment of the Inspector General Act in 1978, the IG community has relied on whistleblowers, and the information they provide, to conduct non-partisan, independent oversight of the federal government. Because the effectiveness of our oversight work depends on the willingness of government employees, contractors, and grantees to come forward to us with their concerns about waste, fraud, abuse, and misconduct within government, those individuals must be protected from reprisal.[120]

During President Trump's first impeachment trial, Senator Rand Paul (R-KY) made a public statement about an individual whom conservative media had accused—correctly or incorrectly—of being the whistleblower who triggered the impeachment.[121] Although Senator Paul did not directly claim the individual was a whistleblower and denied even having independent knowledge of the whistleblower's identity, the statement created risk for the individual and may well have chilled other whistleblowing activity by federal officials.[122]

In the wake of this deeply disturbing conduct, Congress should take action to protect whistleblowers and those suspected, rightly or wrongly, of whistleblowing from being named under circumstances that could lead to harm or threats of harm. Congress should make it a criminal offense for any member of Congress, congressional staffer, or noncareer senior or very senior employee of the executive branch to make a public statement intended to create widespread suspicion that an individual is a whistleblower, unless the individual has publicly acknowledged such status.[123] The law should prohibit such statements without regard to whether the individual is actually a whistleblower. In addition, Congress should establish a special compensation fund to which federal employees and federal contractors can apply for compensatory damages in the event that harassment or other harm befalls them, a member of their household, or a relative after such a statement has been made. If the application is denied by the fund administrator, the employee or contractor should have the right to initiate a civil action for compensatory damages, naming the fund as the defendant.

Congress should also adopt two recommendations by the Project on Government Oversight.[124] First, whistleblowers should be able to bypass the MSPB and take retaliation complaints directly to court. Second, Congress should eliminate a requirement that military personnel who allege that whistleblower retaliation motivated an adverse personnel action must prove the action would not have been taken in the absence of whistleblower retaliation. No such requirement exists for civilian federal employees, and military personnel deserve the same protections as their civilian counterparts.

In the case of whistleblowing that involves classified information, Congress should create a special three-judge panel. The panel should have authority to issue an interim stay of any personnel action against a covered whistleblower upon finding probable cause to believe the action was taken partly in retaliation for lawful whistleblowing. Thereafter, the panel should be empowered to adjudicate the claim of whistleblower retaliation and take specified steps to protect whistleblowers against retaliation. The special panel could also serve as a backstop to review any claim that the executive branch has failed to provide Congress with the statutorily mandated notice of an "urgent concern" that the intelligence community IG has found to be credible.[125] In this case, the panel should have authority to compel notification of Congress.

In the event that the executive branch retaliates against an employee by rescinding the individual's security clearance, the panel should also be able to take remedial action. However, the remedy would not include restoration of the individual's security clearance. Instead, a different remedy would apply if the panel determines that the rescission of the security clearance was motivated partly by whistleblower retaliation. In that event, upon request by the employee, the panel should have the authority to order the Office of Personnel Management to reassign the employee to any comparable position in the executive branch within the same commuting area that does not require a security clearance, entails the same level of pay, and requires knowledge, skills, and abilities that the employee possesses. If no such position exists, the executive branch should be required to carry the employee in a status of paid administrative leave for up to two years while the employee seeks a new job. At its election, the executive branch could rebut the employee's presumptive entitlement to these benefits by bearing the burden of proving to the three-judge panel that the employee's security clearance would have been rescinded even in the absence of any whistleblower retaliation.[126]

## Ensuring Civil Service Protections

Although rarely thought of as ethics laws, civil service protections are among the most important components of the framework for ethics and rule of law in the federal executive branch. We were reminded of the need for civil service laws during the Trump presidency.[127] Trump frequently smeared career professionals in the government as actors in a "deep state" conspiracy arrayed from the start against him and his administration.[128] He commonly blamed these public servants for his troubles, alleging that legitimate attempts to uphold their duty to the Constitution and laws were merely their retributive machinations.[129] To restore morale and protect these essential professionals from political attacks, Congress should strengthen civil service laws to protect the public from corruption and abuses of authority. It should expand the number of employees who have the right to appeal adverse personnel actions to the Merit Systems Protection Board. And Congress should limit the president's authority to eliminate MSPB appeal and collective bargaining rights.

Some of the most important anticorruption laws are often overlooked or even maligned: namely, laws protecting civil servants from arbitrary personnel actions. These protections exist not primarily for the benefit of the public servants they cover, but to guard all Americans against corruption. These laws make it harder for political appointees to pressure career employees to ignore fraud, waste, and abuse.[130] In addition, career officials cannot be fired or demoted for refusing illegal orders.[131] Without these protections, the massive federal workforce could, over time, become filled with individuals too afraid to object to wrongdoing or too loyal to a politician to care about wrongdoing. That kind of federal workforce could pose a threat to democracy itself.

Most career federal employees who have completed probationary periods can be fired only for cause and can appeal a termination to the MSPB. Near the end of his term, however, President Trump issued an executive order laying the groundwork to eliminate appeal rights for a potentially wide swath of the federal workforce.[132] In doing so, he exploited a loophole that allows presidents to exempt positions from the law granting employees the right to appeal firings to the MSPB.[133] Although President Biden rescinded this executive order,[134] Congress should act to prevent a future president from picking up where President Trump left off. It should enact a law barring the president from exempting more than 1,500 positions and prohibiting current government employees from being swept into exempt positions.[135]

Congress should take additional steps to shore up civil service protections. It should grant MSPB appeal rights to most non-probationary employees who lack them. These include executives serving in the Department of Veterans Affairs,[136] certain employees of the Federal Aviation Administration[137] and of the Transportation Security Administration,[138] members of the Foreign Service,[139] and employees of the Federal Bureau of Investigation,[140] among others. Finally, Congress should reduce the president's authority to restrict union activity in the executive branch.[141]

Balanced against these increased due process rights, Congress should lengthen the probationary periods for executive branch employees. Often, federal managers are reluctant to give up on an employee during the first or second year of employment. Congress should lengthen all one-year probationary periods to three years, and it should lengthen all two-year probationary periods to five years. This change would create a system that rewards tenure only after executive branch supervisors have thoroughly evaluated the performance of new hires. To reduce the risk of abuse, the Office of Special Counsel should receive a line-item appropriation that can only be used for investigating claims that probationary employees have been terminated in violation of the prohibited personnel practices law.[142]

## Prohibiting Congressional Conflicts of Interest

Trump's flouting of laws and norms was a reminder of just how dangerous weak government ethics systems can be. That lesson has implications for the other two branches of the federal government, and in the last two sections of this chapter I turn to them. Congress has exempted itself from the criminal conflict of interest law that applies to executive branch employees.[143] In place of that law, Congress has imposed no meaningful conflict of interest prohibitions. The federal legislative branch has consistently held itself to a lower standard than that to which the laws it has enacted hold the executive branch. The executive branch has Congress to watch over it, but who watches over the watchers? There are few rules and even less enforcement. And in the current polarized environment, it would be naïve to think that the public would reliably vote out members of Congress based on their financial holdings. It is long past time for Congress to do the honorable thing and begin holding itself to a high ethical standard.

The congressional prohibitions on its members' conflicts of interest are hardly rigorous. The *Ethics Manual* for the House of Representatives vaguely instructs: "It is fundamental that a Member, officer, or employee of the House may not use his or her official position for personal gain."[144] In practice, this admonition has proven virtually meaningless with respect to financial interests, for members of Congress can take actions directly focused on the specific industries in which they hold company stock.[145]

The Senate conflict of interest rule is no better. Thanks to the wiggle room afforded by repeated use of the word *only* and the inclusion of the phrases *principal purpose* and *limited class*, senators are no more restricted than representatives are from advancing their financial interests in specific industries:

> No Member, officer, or employee shall knowingly use his official position to introduce or aid the progress or passage of legislation, a principal purpose of which is to further only his pecuniary interest, only the pecuniary interest of his immediate family, or only the pecuniary interest of a limited class of persons or enterprises, when he, or his immediate family, or enterprises controlled by them, are members of the affected class.[146]

Congress should subject itself to a conflict of interest restriction that prohibits any member of Congress and the member's spouse or minor child from holding a financial interest in any business enterprise.[147] Limited exceptions should permit the following:

- A member, spouse, or minor child can hold interests in diversified mutual funds.

- A member, spouse, or minor child can hold interests in other diversified investment funds through any employer-sponsored retirement plan.

- A member, spouse, or minor child can be a beneficiary of trusts, provided that none of the trust property was contributed by the member or spouse, and neither of them serves as trustee of the trust or otherwise controls its investments.

- A minor child can be a beneficiary of any irrevocable trust that cannot distribute any holdings or income to the child until the child is no longer a minor.

- The spouse can hold interests in an employer.

In addition, individual congressional staff members who are required to file public financial disclosure reports should be subject to the same criminal conflict of interest law that applies to executive branch employees, 18 U.S.C. § 208.[148]

If Congress is unwilling to take these responsible steps to institute a high ethical standard for the nation's legislature, it should at least strictly prohibit members and their spouses from buying or selling any interest in a business enterprise other than a spouse's employer. In all likelihood, members of Congress lack any interest in living up to even this much lower standard. Therefore, a third option should be considered: members of Congress and their spouses should be required to give ninety-days' notice to the Senate or House ethics committee before buying or selling any interest in a business entity. The notice should remain confidential until after the purchase or sale, and then should be posted online with other financial disclosures. This advance notice requirement would go far to prevent members of Congress from trading on their access to nonpublic information. It would go even further to eliminate the appearance of impropriety that can arise when members of Congress or their spouses make suspiciously well-timed purchases, as allegedly and notoriously happened shortly before the public became fully aware of the likely impact of the COVID-19 pandemic.[149]

## Establishing a Code of Supreme Court Ethics

Finally, I turn to the third branch of government and the institution that sits atop it: the Supreme Court. It is arguably the most powerful body in the land, since its unelected members often have the final word in determining if actions of the other two branches (not to mention state and local governments, and private organizations and individuals) have complied with the Constitution and laws. Yet, the Supreme Court has no ethics code of its own. All other federal judges and many state court judges are covered by ethics standards.[150] Chief Justice John Roberts has sought to reassure the public that "every Justice seeks to follow high ethical standards," but he has resisted adopting standards for the high court. In 2021, the House of Representatives tried to force his hand by passing the For the People Act, H.R. 1,[151] which requires the court to adopt a code of ethics. But that bill has since stalled in the Senate, and its successor, the Freedom to Vote Act, does not contain the Supreme Court ethics provisions of its predecessor. Whether through that legislation or some other bill, Congress should require the Supreme Court to adopt meaningful ethical standards.

The absence of high court ethical standards is inexcusable. Obviously, enforcement would be difficult or impossible because the Supreme Court sits atop the judicial branch and is independent. But difficulty enforcing them is no excuse for not striving to live up to a set of rigorous, uniform, transparent standards. Even without an enforcement mechanism, the standards would give the public a means to gauge the appropriateness of the conduct of justices. It would also afford justices guidance on what the body collectively believes to be the correct approach to ethics, rather than leaving them to rely on their own subjective consciences.

As things stand, the justices have been engaging in conduct that could cause the public to question their judgment or impartiality. They have earned outside income,[152] accepted offers to speak before various interest groups,[153] socialized with parties to cases,[154] ruled on cases affecting companies whose stock they owned,[155] and published books.[156] Justice Brett Kavanaugh even appeared to threaten to retaliate against those he blamed for making his confirmation difficult, with the statement that "what goes around comes around."[157]

The justices also lack any clear standards for recusal,[158] and they are not required to offer written explanations for their decisions to recuse or not recuse. Watchdog groups like Fix the Court have tracked instances where justices chose not to recuse despite reasonable public concerns.[159] In 2021, for instance, Justice Amy Coney Barrett chose to participate in a case involving a party that spent over a million dollars supporting her confirmation less than a year earlier.[160] Establishing clear standards for recusal would go far in resolving public concerns. Requiring justices to provide written explanations when they decide to recuse would also provide an evolving body of examples of how justices have handled various situations. While justices could ignore these prior examples in the future, inasmuch as the examples would not be legally binding precedents, the justices might feel pressure to recuse when they encounter circumstances similar to those in which other justices previously recused.

There may be concern that a justice's recusal could shift the balance of the court in a case because, as things currently stand, a recusing justice could not be replaced. But there is a possible fix for this problem. The Project on Government Oversight convened a panel of judicial experts to serve on its Task Force on Federal Judicial Selection, and the group's report addresses this very problem.[161] Among its many other recommendations, the group argues that Congress has authority under the Constitution to establish a mechanism by which federal appellate judges serve temporarily on rotating panels, functioning as the Supreme Court in lieu of the nine permanent justices. This mechanism would afford the court opportunities to replace recusing justices, and it would go a long way in reducing the politicization of the court.[162]

## Conclusion

The federal ethics rules strive to ensure that those whom the American people entrust with pursuing the public interest do not stray into self-service, abuse, and corruption. Even before Trump, those rules were fraught with problems. His and his administration's four years in office further damaged the ethics system and outright broke it in places. Even after Trump's assault on executive branch ethics, what remains still looks good compared to the ethics systems of Congress and the Supreme Court. It is time—past time—to do something about all of that.

## Notes

1. The author has been a frequent critic of the Biden administration. See Walter M. Shaub Jr., "Biden Condemned Trump's Nepotism. So Why Are His Aides' Relatives Getting Jobs?" *Washington Post*, June 25, 2021, www.washingtonpost.com/outlook/biden-nepotism-pledge-ethics/2021/06/25/9f70d070-d50f-11eb-9f29-e9e6c9e843c6_story.html; Lachlan Markay, "Trump Ethics Antagonist Walter Shaub Becomes Top Biden Critic," Axios, July 14, 2021, www.axios.com/bidens-trump-ethics-antagonist-walter-shaub-27d012b7-0c02-440c-9f3e-32774ab9d2ab.html.

2. Jeremy Diamond, Eli Watkins, and Juana Summers, "EPA Chief Scott Pruitt Resigns amid Scandals, Citing 'Unrelenting Attacks,'" CNN, July 5, 2018, www.cnn.com/2018/07/05/politics/scott-pruitt-epa-resigns/index.html.

3. Ellen Knickmeyer, Matthew Brown, and Jonathan Lemire, "Zinke Resigns as Interior Secretary Amid Numerous Probes," AP News, December 16, 2018, https://apnews.com/article/north-america-donald-trump-ap-top-news-cabinets-montana-842c84a03e5f405fae83277a97905841.

4. Sam Baker, "Tom Price Resigns," Axios, September 29, 2017, www.axios.com/tom-price-resigns-1513305859-22fb4062-2a3a-4c96-9862-24dbb49f5a1c.html.

5. Zephyr Teachout, *Corruption in America: From Benjamin Franklin's Snuff Box to Citizens United* (Harvard University Press, 2016).

6. Jason Easley, "Trump Has Lost More Members of His Cabinet to Ethics Violations than Any President in History," PoliticusUSA, July 15, 2019, www.politicususa.com/2019/07/15/trump-ethics-violations-record.html.

7. "Trump-proofing the Presidency," Citizens for Responsibility and Ethics in Washington (CREW), October 2, 2018, www.citizensforethics.org/reports-investigations/crew-reports/trump-proofing-the-presidency/; see also "Trump Team's Conflicts and Scandals: An Interactive Guide," Bloomberg, March 14, 2019, www.bloomberg.com/graphics/trump-administration-conflicts/; see also Donald K. Sherman and Meredith Lerner, "At Least 15 More Hatch Act Violations by Trump Officials during the Conventions," CREW, September 3, 2020, www.citizensforethics.org/reports-investigations/crew-investigations/at-least-15-more-hatch-act-violations-by-trump-officials-during-the-conventions/.

8. See, e.g., 18 U.S.C. §§ 201–209.

9. See, e.g., Exec. Order No. 12,731, 5 C.F.R. 2634; Exec. Order No. 13,989, 72 Fed. Reg. 7029.

10. See, e.g., Senate Rules "Rule XXXIV: Financial Disclosure," "Rule XXXV: Gifts," "Rule XXXVI: Outside Earned Income," "Rule XXXVII: Conflict of Interest," and "Rule XXXVIII: Prohibition of Unofficial Office Accounts," included in "Standing Rules of the Senate" (117th Congress), www.rules.senate.gov/rules-of-the-senate; "Rule XXIII: Code of Official Conduct," "Rule XXIV: Limitations on Use of Official Funds," "Rule XXV: Limitations on Outside Earned Income and Acceptance of Gifts," "Rule XXVI: Financial Disclosure," and "Rule XXVII: Disclosure by Members and Staff of Employment Negotiations," included in "Rules of the U.S. House of Representatives" (117th Congress), www.rules.house.gov/sites/democrats.rules.house.gov/files/117-House-Rules-Clerk.pdf.

11. See, e.g., Committee on Codes of Conduct, *Guide to Judiciary Policy,* vol. 2A, ch. 2, 2014, www.uscourts.gov/sites/default/files/code_of_conduct_for_united_states_judges_effective_march_12_2019.pdf (last updated, March 12, 2019).

12. Steven Lubet, "Why Won't John Roberts Accept an Ethics Code for Supreme Court Justices?" *Slate,* January 16, 2021, https://slate.com/news-and-politics/2019/01/supreme-court-ethics-code-judges-john-roberts.html.

13. Sam Berger and Alex Tausanovitch, "Lessons from Watergate," Center for American Progress, July 30, 2018, www.americanprogress.org/issues/democracy/reports/2018/07/30/454058/lessons-from-watergate/.

14. Eric Lipton, "Transportation Secretary Failed to Sever Financial Ties to Construction Company," *New York Times,* May 28, 2019, www.nytimes.com/2019/05/28/us/politics/elaine-chao-stock-divest.html.

15. Ibid.

16. Section 8012 in Title VIII, Subtitle B of H.R. 1, addresses this issue for the offices of the president and vice president. It requires that they divest financial interests that pose a conflict of interest within thirty days of assuming office, place these assets in OGE-certified blind trusts, or comply with enhanced disclosure requirements pertain-

ing to the assets. U.S. Congress, House of Representatives, H.R. 1, 117th Congress, 1st Sess., Title II, Subtitle B, www.congress.gov/bill/117th-congress/house-bill/1/text?r=30-#toc-HB3C0AD44CA8F41C0B6227788118F7DD2. These provisions in H.R. 1 are no longer in the Freedom to Vote Act. See U.S. Congress, Senate, S. 2747, 117th Congress, 1st Sess. (2021–2022), www.congress.gov/bill/117th-congress/senate-bill/2747/text.

17. 18 U.S.C. § 202(c).

18. 18 U.S.C. § 208.

19. 5 C.F.R. § 2635.402.

20. 5 C.F.R. § 2640.103.

21. "Barrasso Requests Inspector General Review of Secretary Granholm's Investments in Electric Bus Company," U.S. Senate Committee on Energy and Natural Resources, April 27, 2021, www.energy.senate.gov/2021/4/barrasso-requests-inspector-general-review-of-secretary-granholm-s-investments-in-electric-bus-company.

22. Jennifer Haberkorn and Brianna Ehley, "CDC Director's Conflicts Keep Her from Testifying," Politico, January 18, 2018, www.politico.com/story/2018/01/18/cdc-director-avoids-congressional-testimony-297284.

23. Adam Cancryn and Jennifer Haberkorn, "Why the CDC Director Had to Resign," Politico, January 31, 2018, www.politico.com/story/2018/01/31/cdc-director-resigns-fitzgerald-azar-380680.

24. Sections 8007 and 8012 of H.R. 1 take a similar approach. Section 8007 establishes requirements applicable only to presidential appointees, and section 8012 establishes requirements specific to the president and vice president. These sections do not prescribe this reform for all federal employees. See also U.S. Congress, House of Representatives, H.R. 1, 117th Congress, 1st sess., Title VIII, § 8012, www.congress.gov/bill/117th-congress/house-bill/1/text?r=30#toc-H358658EEF05E40908B5FFCBD1A31EA4E. The provisions made in Title VIII of H.R. 1 to restrict executive branch conflicts of interest are no longer in the 117th Congress's version of the Freedom to Vote Act. See U.S. Congress, Senate, S. 2747.

25. Section 8012 of H.R. 1 would require that presidents or vice presidents either divest conflicting interests or comply with enhanced disclosure requirements for retained assets. U.S. Congress, House of Representatives, H.R. 1, 117th Congress, 1st sess., Title VIII, § 8012, www.congress.gov/bill/117th-congress/house-bill/1/text?r=30#toc-H358658EEF05E40908B5FFCBD1A31EA4E. Title VIII, Subtitle G of H.R. 1 does not discuss divestiture laws by senior political appointees, but it does outline a "revolving door ban," prohibiting senior executive branch employees from participating in matters relating to former employment and contracts for two years from the date of appointment. See also U.S. Congress, Senate, S. 1, 117th Congress, 1st sess., Title VIII, Subtitle G, www.congress.gov/bill/117th-congress/house-bill/1/text?r=30#toc-H358658EEF05E40908B5FFCBD1A31EA4E. These ethics regulations made in H.R. 1 and S. 1 have been removed in the 117th Congress's version of the Freedom to Vote Act. See U.S. Congress, Senate, S. 2747.

26. 18 U.S.C. § 208(b)(2).

27. U.S. Office of Government Ethics, *Guidance for Reviewers of the OGE Form 450, Part I* (2008), www.ethics.usda.gov/science/financial-disclosure/450guide.pdf.

28. Section 8012 of H.R. 1, which would create a new section 701 in the Ethics in Government Act, effectively allows for this exemption for divestitures made by the president and vice president at OGE's discretion because it authorizes OGE to approve the retention of financial interests it deems "so remote or inconsequential as not to pose a conflict." The bill further allows the conversion of divested assets into cash. U.S. Congress, House of Representatives, H.R. 1, 117th Congress, 1st sess., Title VIII, § 8012, www.congress.gov/bill/117th-congress/house-bill/1/text?r=30#toc-H3586 58EEF05E40908B5FFCBD1A31EA4E. Similar to the other ethics provisions made in H.R. 1 and S. 1, these are also no longer in the 117th Congress's version of the Freedom to Vote Act. See U.S. Congress, Senate, S. 2747.

29. Section 8012 of H.R. 1 also provides reforms to divestiture law, but does not discuss family trust exceptions. It does, however, give OGE the power to review alternative assets, such as family trusts, and allows investments to remain in such trusts if the conflict of interest risk is low. U.S. Congress, House of Representatives, H.R. 1, 117th Congress, 1st sess., Title VIII, § 8012, www.congress.gov/bill/117th-congress/house-bill/1/text?r=30#toc-HB3C0AD44CA8F41C0B6227788118F7DD2. Reforms to divestiture law are no longer in the Freedom to Vote Act. See U.S. Congress, Senate, S. 2747.

30. Title VIII, Subtitle B, § 8012 of H.R. 1 makes a similar recommendation, allowing divested assets of the president and vice president to be transferred to a separate investment that would meet criteria established by OGE. U.S. Congress, House of Representatives, H.R. 1, 117th Congress, 1st sess., Title VIII, Subtitle B, § 8012, www.congress.gov/bill/117th-congress/house-bill/1/text?r=30#toc-HB3C0AD44CA8F41C0 B6227788118F7DD2. This recommendation is dropped in the Freedom to Vote Act (2021–2022). See U.S. Congress, Senate, S. 2747.

31. See 5 U.S.C. App. § 103(c).

32. The postmaster general is not a Senate-confirmed presidential appointee; rather, the postmaster general is appointed by the Postal Board of Governors. "About the Board of Governors," U.S. Postal Service, https://about.usps.com/who/leadership/board-governors/.

33. 5 U.S.C. App. 103(c) (requiring review of the report of the already appointed postmaster general).

34. Louis DeJoy, "OGE Form 278e, U.S. Office of Government Ethics," June 15, 2020, https://s3.amazonaws.com/storage.citizensforethics.org/wp-content/uploads/2020/08/20200937/DeJoy-Louis-2020-New-Entrant-278e-Agency-Certified-1.pdf.

35. Alison Durkee, "Postmaster General Louis DeJoy Should Resign over 'Obvious Financial Conflicts of Interest,' Experts Testify," *Forbes*, September 14, 2020, www.forbes.com/sites/alisondurkee/2020/09/14/postmaster-general-louis-dejoy-should-resign-over-obvious-financial-conflicts-of-interest-experts-testify/?sh=4bdda58a1

47c; Luke Broadwater and Catie Edmondson, "Postal Service Has Paid DeJoy's Former Company $286 Million Since 2013," *New York Times*, September 2, 2020, https://nyti.ms/37pW59F; Olivia Rubin and Soo Rin Kim, "Amid Political Controversy, Postmaster General's Stock Holdings Come Under Renewed Scrutiny," *ABC News*, August 14, 2020, https://abcn.ws/387NN5C.

36. U.S. Office of Government Ethics, "Certificate of Divestiture for Louis DeJoy" (OGE-2020-075), October 9, 2020, www.citizensforethics.org/wp-content/uploads/2020/10/DeJoy-Louis-OGE-2020-075-1.pdf.

37. Reflecting an expectation that Senate-confirmed appointees will be subject to ethics agreements, the Ethics in Government Act addresses the documentation of compliance with ethics agreements. 5 U.S.C. App. § 110.

38. 5 C.F.R. § 2634.201.

39. Cancryn and Haberkorn, "Why the CDC Director Had to Resign."

40. Debra Goldschmidt and Ben Tinker, "CDC Director Brenda Fitzgerald Resigns," CNN, January 31, 2018, www.cnn.com/2018/01/31/health/cdc-director-fitzgerald-resigns-bn/index.html; Lena H. Sun and Alice Crites, "New CDC Head Faces Questions about Financial Conflicts of Interest," *Washington Post*, December 11, 2017, www.washingtonpost.com/news/to-your-health/wp/2017/12/11/new-cdc-head-faces-questions-about-financial-conflicts-of-interest/.

41. As indicated in the "Plum Book," the position of CDC director is not a Senate-confirmed position. See Committee on Oversight and Reform, U.S. House of Representatives, 116th Congress, 2nd sess., *United States Government Policy and Supporting Positions* (Plum Book), December 2020, p. 66, www.govinfo.gov/content/pkg/GPO-PLUMBOOK-2020/pdf/GPO-PLUMBOOK-2020.pdf.

42. Title VIII, Subtitle D, § 8035, H.R. 1, makes a similar recommendation for agency ethics officials, not agency heads, to provide the director of OGE with divestitures and public financial disclosures in a searchable and downloadable format for public use. U.S. Congress, House of Representatives, H.R. 1, 117th Congress, 1st sess., Title VIII, Subtitle D, § 8035, www.congress.gov/bill/117th-congress/house-bill/1/text?r=30#toc-HB3C0AD44CA8F41C0B6227788118F7DD2.

43. Scott Bronstein, Curt Devine, Drew Griffin, and Audrey Ash, "15 Times Former Clients of the Acting Interior Secretary Got Favorable Decisions," CNN, March 5, 2019, www.cnn.com/2019/03/05/politics/david-bernhardt-interior-oil-and-gas/index.html. Bernhardt denied all allegations of misconduct. Following several complaints from eight Democratic senators and several watchdog groups, Bernhardt's spokeswoman argued that he remained "in complete compliance with his ethics agreement and all applicable laws, rules, and regulations." Coral Davenport, "Interior Dept. Opens Ethics Investigation of Its New Chief, David Bernhardt," *New York Times*, April 15, 2019, www.nytimes.com/2019/04/15/climate/bernhardt-interior-department-ethics-investigation.html.

44. "Letter from Rick Perry to Susan Beard, Designated Agency Ethics Office, U.S.

Department of Energy," January 9, 2017, https://extapps2.oge.gov/201/Presiden.nsf/PAS+Index/BFCC9856F8C16299852580C1002C7A68/$FILE/Perry,%20James%20Richard%20%20finalAMENDEDEA.pdf.

45. "Executive Branch Personnel Public Financial Disclosure Report" (OGE Form 278e) of Rick Perry, at 3, May 15, 2018 (part 2, lines 4 and 5), https://extapps2.oge.gov/201/Presiden.nsf/PAS+Index/999A37BFAC9D83F5852582AB0027D93D/$FILE/James-R-Perry-2018-278.pdf.

46. "Certification of Ethics Agreement Compliance by William Long," September 15, 2017, https://extapps2.oge.gov/201/Presiden.nsf/PAS+Index/498DA6893EC0BF4F8 52581A0002C20ED/$FILE/Long%20EA%20Certification%201%20of%201.pdf; "Letter from William Long to Joseph Maher, Designated Agency Ethics Official, Department of Homeland Security," April 24, 2017, https://extapps2.oge.gov/201/Presiden .nsf/PAS+Index/070FF466992002108525812A0026FA43/$FILE/Long,%20William% 20B.%20%20finalEA.pdf.

47. "Letter from Nazakhtar Nikakhtar to David Maggi, Designated Ethics Official, U.S. Department of Commerce," October 3, 2017, https://extapps2.oge.gov/201/ Presiden.nsf/CB914570911BF755852581B6002BF7FF/$FILE/Nikakhtar,%20Nazakhtar %20%20finalEA.pdf.

48. "Letter from Ray Mabus to Frank Jimenez, Designated Agency Ethics Official, Department of the Navy," April 21, 2009, https://extapps2.oge.gov/201/Presiden.nsf/PAS+Index/99499B3E52C9F07585257FC20010E39F/$FILE/01319-Raymond-Mabus -2010EA.pdf.

49. "Letter from Frank Kendall to Scott Thompson, Alternate Designated Agency Ethics Official, Department of Defense," May 21, 2021, https://extapps2.oge.gov/201/ Presiden.nsf/PAS+Index/DDBB84D66E69C551852586DD002E613E/$FILE/Kendall,% 20Frank%20%20finalEA.pdf.

50. President Biden's Executive Order on Ethics, issued on January 20, 2021, addresses the issue of golden parachute payments by requiring incoming officials to affirm that they have not and will not accept such payments in the form of cash bonuses, salary increases, or other noncash gifts. Executive Order 13989 of January 20, 2021, "Ethics Commitments by Executive Branch Personnel," *Federal Register*, sec. 1, par.3,title3(2021),www.oge.gov/Web/oge.nsf/Legal%20Docs/16D49D01588276F985258 668004F1094/$FILE/Exec.%20Order%2013989.pdf?open.

51. Matthew Boesler, "Citi Offered Jack Lew a Big Bonus to Secure a 'High-Level' Government Position," *Business Insider India*, February 25, 2013, www.businessinsider .in/Citi-Offered-Jack-Lew-A-Big-Bonus-To-Secure-A-High-Level-Government-Posi tion/articleshow/21321536.cms.

52. Ibid.

53. Ibid.

54. Ibid.

55. Title VIII, Subtitle A, § 8002 and § 8003, H.R. 1, also establish enhanced restrictions on private sector payments for government service, including accelerated

bonuses and other incentive payments, as this recommendation proposes. In addition, the bill lays out criminal penalties for violating conflict of interest standards, including any participation in matters relating to the employee's former contracts or employers. U.S. Congress, House of Representatives, H.R. 1, 117th Congress, 1st sess., Title VIII, Subtitle A, § 8002 and § 8003, www.congress.gov/bill/117th-congress/house-bill/1/text?r=30#toc-HEC152BFCE52249209547733ED9AC1A09. However, these proposed amendments to the United States Code are no longer in the Freedom to Vote Act (2021–2022). See U.S. Congress, Senate, S. 2747.

56. Marc Rehmann, "David Bernhardt Is President Trump's Most Conflicted Cabinet Nominee," Center for American Progress, March 15, 2019, www.americanprogress.org/issues/green/news/2019/03/15/467373/david-bernhardt-president-trumps-conflicted-cabinet-nominee/.

57. 5 C.F.R. § 2635.502.

58. Executive Order 13989 of January 20, 2021, "Ethics Commitments by Executive Branch Personnel," *Federal Register*, sec. 1, par. 2, title 3 (2021), www.oge.gov/Web/oge.nsf/Legal%20Docs/16D49D01588276F985258668004F1094/$FILE/Exec.%20Order%2013989.pdf?open.

59. Derek Kravitz, "Former Trump Officials Are Supposed to Avoid Lobbying. Except 33 Haven't," ProPublica, February 14, 2019, www.propublica.org/article/the-lobbying-swamp-is-flourishing-in-trumps-washington.

60. 18 U.S.C. § 207(c); 5 C.F.R. § 2641.104.

61. Exec. Order No. 13490 § 4.

62. Exec. Order No. 13770 § 2.

63. Exec. Order No. 13989, "Ethics Commitments by Executive Branch Personnel."

64. 18 U.S. Code § 207(c), (d).

65. Exec. Order No. 13989, "Ethics Commitments by Executive Branch Personnel."

66. Letter from Noah Bookbinder, CREW, to Special Counsel Henry J. Kerner, April 2, 2020, www.citizensforethics.org/wp-content/uploads/legacy/2020/04/2020-4-2-Jared-Kushner-7324b-ineligibility.pdf.

67. Annie Karni and Maggie Haberman, "Kushner's Global Role Shrinks as He Tackles Another: The 2020 Election," *New York Times*, January 9, 2020, www.nytimes.com/2020/01/09/us/politics/jared-kushner-trump-campaign.html.

68. 5 C.F.R. § 2635.804.

69. 5 U.S.C. App. § 502.

70. 18 U.S.C. § 208(a).

71. 5 U.S.C. § 7324.

72. "Permissibility of the Administration and Use of the Federal Payroll Allocation System by Executive Branch Employees for Contributions to Political Action Committees," 19 Op. O.L.C. 47, 79 n.56 (1995), www.justice.gov/file/20246/download.

73. 5 U.S.C. § 7324(b); 5 C.F.R. § 734.503. The exception applies to PAS appointees serving inside the United States who determine "policies to be pursued by the United States in relations with foreign powers or in the nationwide administration of Federal

laws." 5 U.S.C. § 7324(b)(2)(B)(ii). The exception applies to White House staffers whose responsibilities "continue outside normal duty hours and while away from the normal duty post" and who are "paid from an appropriation for the Executive Office of the President." 5 U.S.C. § 7324(b)(2)(B)(i).

74. U.S. Office of Special Counsel, *Investigation of Political Activities by White House and Federal Agency Officials During the 2006 Midterm Elections* 74 (January 2011), citing H.R. Rep. 103-16 at 22-23 (1993), https://s3.amazonaws.com/storage.citizensforethics .org/wp-content/uploads/2019/06/24214702/OSC-REPORT.pdf.

75. "Letter from Noah Bookbinder, CREW, to Special Counsel Henry J. Kerner," April 2, 2020.

76. Title VIII, Subtitle G, H.R. 1, echoes many of the recommendations in this section, including an ethics pledge for every appointee in every executive agency that prohibits them from participating in matters relating to their former employers and contracts for two years after the beginning of their appointment. Enhanced requirements for conflict of interest standards also criminalize involvement of agency heads with former employers that have a financial interest in their government position. U.S. Congress, House of Representatives, H.R. 1, 117th Congress, 1st sess., Title VIII, Subtitle G, www.congress.gov/bill/117th-congress/house-bill/1/text?r=30#toc-HEC152BF CE52249209547733ED9AC1A09. An ethics pledge requirement for appointees in every executive agency has been dropped in the Freedom to Vote Act (2021–2022). See U.S. Congress, Senate, S. 2747.

77. The report found that the secretary also engaged in these practices. Office of Inspector General, "Review of Allegations of Misuse of Department of State Resources," Office of Evaluations and Special Projects (ESP), 21-01, April 2021, p. 1, www .stateoig.gov/system/files/esp_21-02_-_review_of_allegations_of_misuse_of_depart ment_of_state_resources.pdf. Another alleged case of an executive official's spouse wielding undue influence is Candy Carson, wife of former Housing and Urban Development Secretary Ben Carson. In 2018, Helen Foster, a senior career official at HUD, claimed that she was "taken out of [her] position as Chief Administrative Officer" after refusing to exceed the congressionally appropriated budget for office redecoration. According to Foster, she was repeatedly asked to find additional funds "in the context of Mrs. Carson wants to do this. We have to find the money." Rene Marsh, "'$5,000 Will Not Even Buy a Decent Chair': HUD Staffer Files Complaint over Ben Carson Office Redecoration," CNN, updated February 27, 2018, www.cnn.com/2018/ 02/27/politics/ben-carson-office-furniture-whistleblower/index.html.

78. The terms *senior employee* and *very senior employee* are defined in OGE's regulations, and the term *noncareer* is used here to mean political appointees. 5 C.F.R. § 2641.104.

79. The term *particular matter* is defined in 5 C.F.R. § 2640.103(a) and is discussed in more detail below in this section.

80. 5 C.F.R. § 2640.103(a)(1).

81. Arden Farhi, "Office of Government Ethics: Discipline Kellyanne Conway," CBS News, February 14, 2017, www.cbsnews.com/news/office-of-govt-ethics-says -kellyanne-conway-should-be-disciplined-over-ivanka-product-plug/.

82. Ibid.

83. Betsy Klein, "Ivanka Trump Backs Goya: By Endorsing Black Beans She Possibly Violates Ethics Rule," CNN, July 15, 2020, www.cnn.com/2020/07/15/politics/ ivanka-trump-goya-beans-ethics/index.html.

84. "CREW Sues OSC to Hold Kellyanne Conway Accountable to the Hatch Act," CREW, December 17, 2019, www.citizensforethics.org/legal-action/lawsuits/hatch-act -kellyanne-conway-osc/.

85. A review of OGE's prosecution surveys shows that the Justice Department has occasionally prosecuted some career-level employees within the vast federal civilian workforce of about 2.1 million people, but this does not change the author's perception with regard to noncareer employees. "Conflict of Interest Prosecution Surveys," U.S. Office of Government Ethics, www.oge.gov/Web/OGE.nsf/Enforcement/D4D37D87F EAFD9FA852585B6005A0509?opendocument.

86. Randall D. Eliason, "William Barr Has Gone Rogue," *Washington Post*, September 17, 2020, https://wapo.st/356ghMb; Nicholas Fandos, Charlie Savage, and Katie Benner, "Roger Stone Sentencing Was Politicized, Prosecutor Plans to Testify," *New York Times*, June 23, 2020, https://nyti.ms/3882XJi; Katie Benner and Charlie Savage, "Dropping of Flynn Case Heightens Fears of Justice Dept. Politicization," *New York Times*, May 8, 2020, https://nyti.ms/3hDxim2.

87. 18 U.S.C. §§ 208(a), 216(b).

88. 18 U.S.C. § 216(b) (imposing a preponderance of the evidence standard).

89. *United States v. Santos*, 553 U.S. 507 (2008).

90. 18 U.S.C. §§ 208, 216.

91. 5 U.S.C. App. § 104(d); 5 C.F.R. § 2634.704. This episode is also covered at length in chapter 1.

92. Anita Kumar and Ben Wieder, "Jared Kushner Fined Again for Late Ethics Form, Ivanka Trump Fined Too," McClatchy DC Bureau, October 3, 2017, www. mcclatchydc.com/news/politics-government/white-house/article176849096.html.

93. 5 U.S.C. § 1215(a)(3)(A)(ii).

94. 5 C.F.R. § 1201.126(a) (2020).

95. The term *special government employee* is defined at 18 U.S.C. § 202(a).

96. H.R. 1 and S. 1 also define conflict of interest penalties for agency heads and covered employees. They go one step further than the fines outlined in this recommendation to include imprisonment for criminal penalties. However, S. 2747 does not define these conflict of interest penalties nor outline recommendations for its criminalization.

97. 5 C.F.R. § 2640.103.

98. See Office of Government Ethics, "'Particular Matter Involving Specific Par-

ties,' 'Particular Matter,' and 'Matter,'" Legal Advsiory DO-06-029, October 4, 2006, https://oge.gov/Web/OGE.nsf/0/84B69E98832F055E852585BA005BED07/$FILE/do-06-02_9.pdf.

99. At the risk of getting technical, it may be useful to supply an example of how this could work. I offer the following language as a suggestion, but this formulation in my own words is just one of many formulations that could achieve these goals:

(a) Except as provided in subsection (b), a noncareer senior or very senior employee of the executive branch of the United States Government, other than a special Government employee, shall not knowingly participate personally and substantially in any matter that will have a direct, predictable, and substantial effect on the financial interests of an organization with which the employee has a covered relationship.

(b) This restriction shall not prohibit the employee from participating personally and substantially in a discrete aspect of a matter that is segregable from aspects of the matter affecting the organization.

(c) Except as provided in subsection (d), an employee has a covered relationship with any for-profit business enterprise in which the employee knows that the employee, the employee's spouse, or the employee's minor child—

(1) holds stock or any other ownership interest,

(2) has a right to a share of profits or revenue,

(3) holds vested or unvested stock options or any other derivative or notional interests tied to the business enterprise,

(4) holds a financial interest in any investment fund or other pooled investment vehicle that holds any of the interests described in paragraphs (1) through (3), or

(5) is a vested beneficiary of a trust that holds any of the interests described in paragraphs (1) through (3).

(d) An employee shall not have a covered relationship with a business enterprise if the financial interest of the employee, the employee's spouse, or the employee's minor child is—

(1) covered by a regulatory exemption issued by the Office of Government Ethics pursuant to 18 U.S.C. § 208(b)(2),

(2) the subject of a waiver issued pursuant to 18 U.S.C. § 208(b)(1) or 18 U.S.C. § 208(b)(3), or

(3) is worth less than $15,000.

(e) Whether or not a meeting will have a direct, predictable, and substantial effect on the financial interests of the organization, an employee shall not, in an official capacity as a government employee, meet with an organization with which the employee has a covered relationship, unless—

(1) the meeting is open to the public,

(2) a recording of the entire meeting, containing video and audio, is available to the public, or

(3) at least five parties representing a diversity of interests participate in the meeting.

(f) To be diverse, interests need not be adversarial but must include individuals or organizations who do not represent for-profit business enterprises or the United States government.

(g) Subsections (a) and (e) shall not apply to the extent that the head of the agency has publicly released a written determination that—

(1) a reasonable person with knowledge of the relevant facts would not question the employee's impartiality in the matter, or

(2) the interests of the Government in the employee's participation in a matter or in a meeting outweighs the concern that a reasonable person may question the integrity of the agency's programs and operations.

(h) The director of the Office of Government Ethics may exempt certain covered relationships or financial interests from the coverage of this section if, by regulation applicable to all or a portion of all employees covered by this section published in the Federal Register, the Director finds that a reasonable person with knowledge of the facts would be unlikely to question an employee's participation in a matter affecting the financial interest of an organization with which the employee has a covered relationship.

100. H.R. 1 and S. 1 suggest expansion of OGE's powers in a comparable manner. They expand the powers of the director of OGE to review and approve any recusals, exemptions, or waivers from the conflicts of interest and ethics regulations and allow OGE to require and subpoena information from any agency pertinent to an investigation being carried out by OGE. S. 2747, however, does not include any suggestions to expand OGE's power.

101. H.R. 1 and S. 1 would allow the director of OGE to secure any information from any agency, including through subpoenas, that is necessary for the performance of OGE's functions. Refusal to comply with OGE's requests would be enforceable by order of district courts, per the bills. These enhanced enforcement powers of the director of OGE over agencies are dropped in the 117th Congress's version of the Freedom to Vote Act.

102. 5 U.S.C. § 7703(c) establishes the following standard of review: "(c) In any case filed in the United States Court of Appeals for the Federal Circuit, the court shall

review the record and hold unlawful and set aside any agency action, findings, or conclusions found to be (1) arbitrary, capricious, an abuse of discretion, or otherwise not in accordance with law; (2) obtained without procedures required by law, rule, or regulation having been followed; or (3) unsupported by substantial evidence; except that in the case of discrimination brought under any section referred to in subsection (b)(2) of this section, the employee or applicant shall have the right to have the facts subject to trial de novo by the reviewing court."

103. 31 U.S.C. § 1341(a)(1)(A).

104. Walter M. Shaub, "Ransacking the Republic," *New York Review of Books*, July 2, 2020, www.nybooks.com/articles/2020/07/02/trump-corruption-ransacking-republic/.

105. Melissa Quinn, "The Internal Watchdogs Trump Has Fired or Replaced," CBS News, updated May 19, 2020, www.cbsnews.com/news/trump-inspectors-general -internal-watchdogs-fired-list/.

106. Ibid.

107. Justine Coleman, "Biden Nominates HHS Official Targeted by Trump," *The Hill*, June 18, 2021, https://thehill.com/policy/healthcare/559180-biden-nominates-hhs -official-targeted-by-trump.

108. Inspector General Reform Act of 2008, Pub. L. No. 110–409, 122 Stat. 4302.

109. Todd Garvey, "Presidential Removal of IGs Under the Inspector General Act," Congressional Research Service, LSB10476, May 22, 2020, https://crsreports. congress.gov/product/pdf/LSB/LSB10476.

110. See Jen Kirby, "Trump's Purge of Inspectors General, Explained," Vox, May 28, 2020, www.vox.com/2020/5/28/21265799/inspectors-general-trump-linick -atkinson.

111. See 5 U.S.C. App. 2 § 3(b).

112. Sen. Elizabeth Warren and others have proposed similar legislation. See Coronavirus Oversight and Recovery Ethics Act of 2020, S. 3855, 116th Cong. § 2 (2020), www.congress.gov/bill/116th-congress/senate-bill/3855.

113. "Inspector General Legislation," 1 Op. O.L.C. 16 (1977), www.justice.gov/olc/ file/626791/download.

114. Garvey, "Presidential Removal of IGs."

115. Heroes Act, H.R. 6800, 116th Cong., § 70104 (2020), www.congress.gov/116/ bills/hr6800/BILLS-116hr6800pcs.pdf.

116. The author's recommendations track with the Protecting Our Democracy Act (PODA) in a number of respects. Both the author and PODA set a window of no less than thirty days before the effective removal date of an inspector general for the president to provide Congress with a notification justifying the removal. Both the author and the bill would also bar the president or relevant agency head from removing or putting an inspector general on leave without specific cause. For an additional discussion of PODA, see chapter 8.

117. Shannon Pettypiece, "Trump Says Those Who Gave Info to the Whistle-

blower Are Like Spies, Reports Say," NBC News, September 26, 2019, www.nbcnews
.com/politics/white-house/trump-says-our-country-stake-whistleblower-account
-made-public-n1059011.

118. Peter Baker, "Trump Proceeds with Post-Impeachment Purge Amid Pandemic," *New York Times*, May 19, 2020, www.nytimes.com/2020/04/04/us/politics/
trump-coronavirus-post-impeachment-purge.html?referringSource=articleShare.

119. 5 C.F.R. § 2635.101(b)(11).

120. Letter from Michael Horowitz, Chair, Council of the Inspectors General on
Integrity and Efficiency, and others to Steven Engel, Assistant Attorney General,
Office of Legal Counsel, U.S. Department of Justice, October 22, 2019, https://ignet.
gov/sites/default/files/files/CIGIE_Letter_to_OLC_Whistleblower_Disclosure.pdf.

121. Kyle Cheney and Burgess Everett, "Rand Paul Reads Alleged Whistleblower's
Name and Republicans 'Fine' with It," Politico, February 4, 2020, https://politi.co/
2UcyIJt; Michael D. Shear and Sheryl Gay Stolberg, "Chief Justice Denies Senator's Bid
to Name Person Thought to be Whistle-Blower," *New York Times*, January 30, 2020,
www.nytimes.com/2020/01/30/us/politics/rand-paul-whistle-blower-name.html.

122. Li Zhou, "Why Chief Justice Roberts Refused to Read a Question from Rand
Paul at Trump's Trial," Vox, January 30, 2020, www.vox.com/2020/1/30/21115562/john
-robert-rand-paul-impeachment-trial.

123. The terms *senior employee* and *very senior employee* are defined in OGE's regulations. 5 C.F.R. § 2641.104.

124. Liz Hempowicz, "The State of Whistleblower Protections and Ideas for
Reform," Project on Government Oversight (POGO), January 8, 2019, www.pogo.org/
testimony/2020/01/the-state-of-whistleblower-protections-and-ideas-for-reform/.
The author is affiliated with POGO.

125. The concept of an "urgent concern" is defined at 50 U.S.C. § 3033(k)(5)(G).

126. On the topic of whistleblowers, the author takes a more granular approach
than PODA does. While both generally recommend greater protections for whistleblowers, the author goes further in the recommended scope of such protections, including establishing a special compensatory fund for whistleblowers who suffer
harassment or retaliation as a result of their disclosures, and making it easier for military personnel to prove that adverse personnel decisions were taken in retaliation for
whistleblowing.

127. Walter M. Shaub Jr., "Civil Servants Are the Last Defense Against a Lawless
President. It's No Wonder Trump Didn't Trust Them," *Washington Post*, October 11,
2021, www.washingtonpost.com/politics/2021/10/11/civil-servants-are-last-defense-
against-lawless-president-its-no-wonder-trump-didnt-trust-them/.

128. Jonathan Allen, "Trump Weaponizes 'Deep State' to Investigate His Investigators," NBC News, May 23, 2018, www.nbcnews.com/politics/white-house/trump
-weaponizes-deep-state-investigate-his-investigators-n876551; see also Hope Yen and
Calvin Woodward, "AP FACT CHECK: Trump's Baseless Claim of 'Deep State' at

FDA," AP News, August 24, 2020, https://apnews.com/article/election-2020-politics-religion-virus-outbreak-iran-nuclear-d976ab2b204ac14b220d5bf6dc565b2d.

129. Peter Baker and others, "Trump's War on the 'Deep State' Turns against Him," *New York Times*, October 23, 2019, www.nytimes.com/2019/10/23/us/politics/trump-deep-state-impeachment.html.

130. See Nick Schwellenbach, "Gutting Civil Service Laws Would Reduce Senior Official Accountability," Project on Government Oversight (POGO), February 7, 2018, www.pogo.org/investigation/2018/02/gutting-civil-service-laws-would-reduce-senior-official-accountability/. The author is affiliated with POGO.

131. 5 U.S.C. § 2302(b)(9)(D).

132. Exec. Order No. 13957, 85 Fed. Reg. 67631 (Oct. 21, 2020), www.govinfo.gov/content/pkg/FR-2020-10-26/pdf/2020-23780.pdf.

133. 5 U.S.C. § 7511(b)(2)(A).

134. Exec. Order No. 14003, 86 Fed. Reg. 7231 (Jan. 27, 2021), www.govinfo.gov/content/pkg/FR-2021-01-27/pdf/2021-01924.pdf.

135. In December 2015, there were 1,501 positions exempted under Schedule C. Memorandum from Beth Cobert, Acting Director, Office of Personnel Management, to Heads of Departments and Agencies, January 9, 2017, www.chcoc.gov/content/temporary-transition-schedule-c-authority-and-temporary-transition-senior-executive-service.

136. See Department of Veterans Affairs Accountability and Whistleblower Protection Act of 2017, Pub. L. No. 11541, § 201 (2017) (codified at 38 U.S.C. § 713); 5 U.S.C. §§ 2303–2304.

137. 49 U.S.C. § 40122(g).

138. 49 U.S.C. § 114(n).          ·

139. 5 U.S.C. § 7511(b)(6).

140. 5 U.S.C. § 7511(b)(8).

141. See 5 U.S.C. § 7103(b). See also Delegation of Certain Authority under the Federal Service Labor-Management Relations Statute, 85 Fed. Reg. 10033 (Feb. 21, 2020); Jessie Bur, "Trump Moves to Cut Union Bargaining for DoD Feds," *Federal Times*, February 21, 2020, www.federaltimes.com/management/2020/02/21/trump-moves-to-cut-union-bargaining-for-dod-feds/.

142. A law applicable to probationary employees prohibits personnel actions based on political affiliation. 5 U.S.C. § 2302(b)(E); 5 C.F.R. § 315.806(b).

143. 18 U.S.C. § 208.

144. H. Comm. on Standards of Official Conduct, 110th Cong., *House Ethics Manual* 186 (2008), https://ethics.house.gov/sites/ethics.house.gov/files/documents/2008_House_Ethics_Manual.pdf.

145. Griffin Connolly, "House Conflict of Interest Rules Still Not Up to Snuff, Ethics Experts Lament," *Roll Call*, January 14, 2019, www.rollcall.com/2019/01/14/house-conflict-of-interest-rules-still-not-up-to-snuff-ethics-experts-lament/.

146. S. Select Comm. on Ethics, 114th Cong., *The Senate Code of Official Conduct* (2015), Rule XXXVII, www.ethics.senate.gov/public/_cache/files/3507e6ae-2525-40ac -9ec8-7c6dbfe35933/2015---red-book---the-senate-code-of-official-conduct.pdf.

147. H.R. 1 and S. 1 define such restrictions for family members of the president and vice president, including public disclosures and divestments. The restrictions were subsequently dropped in the Freedom to Vote Act. See U.S. Congress, Senate, S. 2747. The bills do not mention such restrictions for members of Congress but do discuss the prohibition of members of Congress from knowingly using their position to pass legislation whose principal purpose is to further the pecuniary interest of their family members.

148. H.R. 1 and S. 1 outline a similar restriction for employees of a member of Congress from knowingly using their position to pass legislation whose principal purpose is to further the pecuniary interest of their family members. They do not discuss criminal penalties. Expanded restrictions for employees of members of Congress have been removed from S. 2747. See U.S. Congress, Senate, S. 2747.

149. Stephanie Saul, Kate Kelly, and Michael LaForgia, "2,596 Trades in One Term: Inside Senator Perdue's Stock Portfolio," *New York Times*, December 2, 2020, https:// nyti.ms/3rUVULB.

150. This section is adapted from an issue of *The Bridge*, a newsletter circulated through the Project on Government Oversight (POGO), that the author wrote. This issue was released via email on July 8, 2021, and is not available online. See https:// secure.everyaction.com/12rmHB32-Eyz8IRfVgxZTw2.

151. Mike DeBonis, "House Democrats Pass Sweeping Elections Bill as GOP Legislatures Push to Restrict Voting," *Washington Post*, March 3, 2021, www.washington post.com/politics/house-elections-voting-pelosi-/2021/03/03/e434df58-7c22-11eb -a976-c028a4215c78_story.html.

152. "Newly Released Financial Disclosures Show Every Justice Supplemented His or Her Income in 2020," *Fix the Court*, June 11, 2021, https://fixthecourt.com/2021/06/ newly-released-financial-disclosures-show-every-justice-supplemented-income-2020/.

153. Adam Liptak, "Justices Get Out More, But Calendars Aren't Open to Just Anyone," *New York Times*, June 1, 2015, www.nytimes.com/2015/06/02/us/politics/ justices-get-out-more-but-calendars-arent-open-to-just-anyone.html?emci=b84e74b6 -5ddf-eb11-a7ad-501ac57b8fa7&emdi=3f94df8f-05e0-eb11-a7ad-501ac57b8fa7&ceid= 65700.

154. Sarah Turberville, "Closing the Gap in Judicial Ethics," Project On Government Oversight (POGO), January 29, 2019, www.pogo.org/testimony/2019/01/closing -the-gap-in-judicial-ethics/. The author is affiliated with POGO.

155. Andrew Ross Sorkin, "When a Brief May Find a Real Friend on the Court," *New York Times*, July 20, 2015, www.nytimes.com/2015/07/21/business/dealbook/when -a-brief-may-find-a-real-friend-on-the-court.html?_r=0; Lee Fang, "Exclusive: Supreme Court Justice Sam Alito Dismisses His Profligate Right-Wing Fundraising as

'Not Important,'" ThinkProgress, November 10, 2010, https://thinkprogress.org/exclu
sive-supreme-court-justice-sam-alito-dismisses-his-profligate-right-wing-fundrais
ing-as-not-2bc755721a5b/.

156. Ronald Collins, "353 Books by Supreme Court Justices," *SCOTUSblog,* March
12, 2012, www.scotusblog.com/2012/03/351-books-by-supreme-court-justices/.

157. "Watch: Judge Brett Kavanaugh's Opening Statement," *New York Times,* September 27, 2018 (video), 4:07, www.youtube.com/watch?v=M_NSe2oG4Xo.

158. Turberville, "Closing the Gap in Judicial Ethics."

159. "Recent Times in Which a Justice Failed to Recuse Despite a Conflict of Interests," *Fix the Court,* updated October 8, 2021, https://fixthecourt.com/2021/10/recent
-times-justice-failed-recuse-despite-clear-conflict-interest/.

160. Gabe Roth, "AFP Spent Loads of Money to Get a Justice Confirmed. Now AFP
Is a Litigant. No One's Recusing. That's a Problem," *Daily Journal,* April 20, 2021, www
.dailyjournal.com/articles/362335-afp-spent-loads-of-money-to-get-a-justice-confirm
ed-now-afp-is-a-litigant-no-one-s-recusing-that-s-a-problem?emci=b84e74b6-5ddf
-eb11-a7ad-501ac57b8fa7&emdi=3f94df8f-05e0-eb11-a7ad-501ac57b8fa7&ceid=65700.

161. Task Force on Federal Judicial Selection, "Above the Fray: Changing the
Stakes of Supreme Court Selection and Enhancing Legitimacy," Project on Government Oversight (POGO), July 8, 2021, www.pogo.org/report/2021/07/above-the-fray
-changing-the-stakes-of-supreme-court-selection-and-enhancing-legitimacy/. The
author is affiliated with POGO.

162. Ibid.

**Part II**

# Rule of Law Reforms

# 3

# Restoring the Rule of Law through Department of Justice Reform

**CLAIRE O. FINKELSTEIN | RICHARD W. PAINTER**

As the nation's principal law enforcement agency, the Department of Justice (DOJ) plays a unique role in protecting rule of law and, therefore, U.S. democracy. Despite the fact that the attorney general is appointed by the president and serves at the president's pleasure, a recognition of the comparable independence of the DOJ from the political priorities of the rest of the executive branch has been critical for maintaining the department's integrity and credibility over the course of its roughly 150-year history. To assure the American public that the actions of the DOJ are based on legitimate prosecutorial discretion rather than on political favoritism or electoral politics, prosecutions must be politically neutral and motivated only by the goal of evenhanded enforcement of the law, without prejudice produced by presidential political aims. The DOJ articulates its mission as to "enforce the law and defend the interests of the United States according to the law,"[1]

---

This chapter is partially adapted from the authors' 2020 CERL/CREW report on the Department of Justice. All material drawn from the report is properly attributed.

an aim that, when fulfilled, allows the department to serve as the guardian of the rule of law for the country as a whole. When the DOJ faithfully conforms to both law and ethics, it powerfully reinforces the foundations of democratic governance.

But the flip side is also true: the DOJ is particularly well situated to corrupt the rule of law.[2] When the department treats legal compliance as a creative exercise in public relations and political manipulation, it leads to the disintegration of rule of law values, not just in the DOJ but also in government as a whole. In that case, it threatens the very foundations of democratic governance. In short, any attempt to justify distortions of law by claiming the authority of law does disproportionate damage, given that such distortions strike at the very concept of legality itself.

With these principles in mind, in the summer of 2020, the authors of this chapter were reporters for a bipartisan working group hosted by the Center for Ethics and the Rule of Law (CERL) at the University of Pennsylvania, in conjunction with Citizens for Responsibility and Ethics in Washington (CREW), to examine the conduct of the Department of Justice during the tenure of former Attorney General William Barr.[3] The working group and consultants to the project consisted of legal and intelligence experts, including former high-ranking Justice Department officials in Republican administrations, assisted by students from CERL's 2020 summer internship program. The working group presented a number of serious concerns relating to the functioning of the DOJ in 2019–2020, which it presented in a report on October 12, 2020.[4] The CERL/CREW report examined questions about the conduct of Attorney General Barr during the roughly twenty months of his tenure at the DOJ and found serious misconduct.[5] A core theme that arose across the many different areas of the DOJ's functions was the extreme politicization of the department.[6]

One of the most concerning aspects of this politicization during the last administration was the DOJ's systematic use of its powers of investigation against critics of Donald Trump or individuals who had a role in initiating the FBI investigation into the Trump campaign's contact with Russia—an investigation known as Crossfire Hurricane.[7] The politicized investigations into the origins of the Russia probe fostered an atmosphere of suspicion and intimidation relating to the FBI and the intelligence community more generally. The politicization of the department regarding the intelligence community weakened U.S. national security by creating doubt about the motivations of intelligence investigations and federal law enforcement in general, damage that will only be repaired with great effort. In addition, the attacks on the intelligence community were amplified in Congress, where three Senate committees placed more than fifty former Obama-era officials on a subpoena list based on their role in initiating or recommending the Crossfire Hurricane probe,[8] contributing to an atmosphere of public suspicion of intelligence operations.[9] Such public relations campaigns across the branches of the government are dangerous to U.S. democracy and weaken the separation of powers.

After October 2020, when the CERL/CREW report was issued, matters got rapidly worse. Trump's politicization of the DOJ came to a head in the 2020 presidential campaign, when Attorney General Barr lent his pre-election support to the discredited view that mail-in voting would produce a fraudulent result, helping to pave the way for President Trump's post-election assault on the integrity of the election.[10] Barr, however, was not willing to stay the course with Donald Trump's assault on the election, a matter that Trump greatly resented. On December 1, 2020, Barr gave a widely circulated interview in which he rejected Trump's claim that there had been fraud in the election.[11] Two weeks later, Barr resigned, but not without furnishing the public with a sycophantic resignation letter that praised Trump's presidency to the hilt.[12] Trump complained about Barr's change of heart in a rally in July 2021, saying that Barr "became a different man when the Democrats viciously stated that they wanted to impeach him." According to the *Washington Examiner*, Trump's complaint about Democrats wanting to impeach Trump referred to the CERL/CREW report, which recommended that Congress open an impeachment investigation on Barr.[13]

Barr's successor, Acting Attorney General Jeffrey A. Rosen, also came under extraordinary pressure from President Trump to declare that there was "fraud" in the November 2020 election, and Jeffrey Clark, also a political appointee in DOJ, prepared a draft letter to state legislators in Georgia declaring that there was fraud in the election, which Rosen refused to sign.[14] Had DOJ issued this statement, Trump might have used it to invalidate the election, whether by declaring martial law and forcing a new election or otherwise. DOJ thus came perilously close to providing legal cover for an attempted coup.

Shortly before he would step down, Barr also revealed in a letter he sent to members of Congress that in October 2020 he had secretly sought to entrench the department's scrutiny of the origins of the Russia probe by elevating the then U.S. attorney for Connecticut, John Durham, to the post of special counsel.[15] As U.S. attorney, Durham had been conducting a counter-investigation into Crossfire Hurricane and the FBI's investigation into the Trump campaign and its ties to Russia.[16] Many were highly critical of this move. Former Acting Solicitor General Neal Katyal, for example, who wrote the special counsel rules as a Department of Justice staff member in 1999, characterized this appointment as violating both the special counsel rules and "fundamental democratic principles."[17] He argued it was a "devious move" by Barr, "designed to entrench a politically appointed prosecutor in a new administration and make it hard for President Biden to appoint a replacement."[18]

Ultimately, however, Durham did not play the role in the 2020 election for which Trump had hoped. In October, Barr stated that Durham would not have a report ready prior to the election, an announcement to which Trump reacted with great anger and disappointment.[19] Although the Durham investigation has now run longer than Special Counsel Mueller's investigation itself, Attorney General Merrick Garland wisely chose to allow the investigation to continue in the Biden administration, though Durham is no longer a U.S. attorney.[20] As of this writing, Durham has charged several individuals but still has not released his report or given a timeline for wrapping up his investigation. Whether it will be a balanced, evenhanded assessment of the origins of the Russia probe or the politicized instrument for which Trump had hoped remains to be seen, but the decision not to issue a report prior to November 3, 2020, may have avoided the worst politicization of the department by minimizing its impact on the election. It may also have helped to constrain Trump from even more egregious attempts to use the department post-election to further the attack on Biden's clear victory.

Nevertheless, disturbing revelations about Barr and the DOJ he led continue to emerge, and it remains the case that Barr allowed the department to be hijacked for partisan political purposes. In March 2021, federal judge Amy Berman Jackson wrote that Barr and the Justice Department were "disingenuous" in attempting to hold back internal DOJ documents relating to the Mueller report. She found that their claims "are so inconsistent with evidence in the record, they are not worthy of credence."[21] Judge Jackson was the second federal judge to make such a finding. In 2020, Judge Reggie Walton stated that Barr provided a "distorted" and "misleading" account of the Mueller report to the American people, which led the judge to question Barr's "credibility" and, with it, the department's representation of the report to the court.[22] As we discuss below, the public also learned of secret DOJ subpoenas seeking communications records of reporters in 2017 during the Trump administration.[23] Those startling disclosures were followed by the news that in 2017 and 2018, the DOJ subpoenaed Apple for data from the accounts of Democrats on the House Intelligence Committee, their aides, and their family members, in an attempt to identify who was behind leaks of classified information early on in the Trump years.[24]

This chapter seeks to identify some key areas where repair is badly needed following a period in which the department's core values were severely compromised. The chapter also presents some specific measures to hasten the process of repair and put the DOJ on the path toward regaining its credibility and its trusted role as defender of the rule of law.

## Politicization of the Department of Justice

Although the damage to the rule of law in the DOJ and the obstacles to repair are arguably even more formidable now than they were following President Nixon's resignation, it is worth heeding the example of Attorney General Edward Levi, a Republican, who was appointed by President Ford in the aftermath of the Watergate scandal.[25] Levi's reforms were inspired by what his then aide, now federal judge, Mark Wolf recalls as his philosophy of the executive branch "acting judicially."[26] The reforms included guidelines for FBI surveillance and other activities, reinforcing the ideals of professionalism and adherence to separation of powers and the rule of law, as well as new DOJ rules and structures to assure the integrity of DOJ actions.[27] According to Levi, "Nothing can more weaken the quality of life or more imperil the realization of the goals we all hold dear than our failure to make clear by words and deed that our law is not an instrument of partisan purpose, and is not to be used in ways which are careless to the higher values which are within all of us."[28] Levi's words were powerful, but his reforms were vulnerable. Embodied as they were in DOJ policies and practices, these reforms could be easily changed by a subsequent attorney general.

During the Carter administration, Attorney General Griffin Bell chose to maintain the measures Levi put in place.[29] Bell also imposed strict limits on FBI investigations and protocols for communication between the White House and the DOJ to enhance the department's independence,[30] reforms that are (in updated form) still in place to this day.[31] These protocols, for example, require White House staff to communicate with the DOJ about particular investigations and prosecutions strictly through the White House Counsel's office, rather than by contacting individual employees of the DOJ.[32]

Decades earlier, Edward Levi and Griffin Bell understood that politicization on the part of government lawyers is particularly damaging.[33] A series of irresponsible and misleading memos emanated from the Office of Legal Counsel (OLC) in 2002 and 2003—memos that sought to justify the CIA-led abusive interrogation of detainees using methods amounting to torture.[34] Some of these memos were subsequently withdrawn,[35] but not before the credibility of both the CIA and the DOJ had been badly damaged.

Other examples of politicization have unfortunately damaged the department over the years and compromised its commitment to the rule of law. In 2006, for example, several U.S. attorneys were fired, at least one upon the urging of a senator.[36] The apparent reason for the firings was that the DOJ had refused to conduct criminal investigations having to do with alleged voter fraud.[37] Attorney General Alberto Gonzales in 2007 resigned after giving testimony about the U.S. attorney firings—testimony that some members of Congress found to be misleading.[38] Years earlier in March 1993, President Clinton fired all of the U.S. attorneys from the George H. W. Bush administration, a move that was also perceived as highly political.[39] In the Obama administration, results-oriented reasoning was once again on display in the DOJ in the form of a controversial memo issued by OLC on the authorization to use military force in Libya.[40] Similarly, in the domain of war powers, the 2010 Obama-era OLC memo authorizing the targeted killing in Yemen of Anwar al-Awlaki, an American citizen, has been regarded as highly problematic as well, given that Yemen is a sovereign nation with which the United States was not at war and given the memo's somewhat distorted treatment of the concept of "imminence" under International Humanitarian Law (IHL).[41]

These earlier instances of politicization at the DOJ under presidents of both parties, and the failure to correct these excesses, set the stage for what was to come. During the Trump administration, politicized use of the department's powers was more the norm than the exception in cases where President Trump's interests were affected. Under Barr's leadership, for example, there was a striking use of the department's prosecutorial function apparently to punish political enemies and to buy the cooperation of potential friends. There was political interference in DOJ criminal investigations and prosecutions, such as that on display in the Roger Stone and Michael Flynn cases.[42] There was also evident vindictiveness against those who spoke out against the administration or Donald Trump, like that unleashed on the president's former lawyer, Michael Cohen, who was reimprisoned before the publication of his book about Donald Trump, following his release from prison on a medical furlough. A judge promptly and properly ordered the government to re-release him.[43]

The public also now knows that during the Trump years, the department secretly obtained phone records of journalists, seeking to find the source of leaks to the press about the Russia investigation.[44] Except under the most extraordinary circumstances, DOJ surveillance of journalists is a violation of the First Amendment freedom of the press and should not be countenanced. In this case, President Trump's loudly proclaimed concerns about leaks in the Russia investigation were politically motivated, and there was no national security justification for targeting journalists. Trump's attacks on journalists, which began on day one of his presidency and continued throughout his time in office, were aimed at blunting criticism of his own conduct by calling any unflattering portraits he received in the media "fake news." His public attacks, as well as the DOJ's clandestine investigations of legitimate journalistic activities, were offensive and damaging to democratic values.

The department similarly targeted Democratic members of Congress as well as their aides and members of their families, including at least one minor. DOJ accomplished this by secretly obtaining the family members' phone records and other metadata by subpoena from Apple. Among those targeted in this way were members of the House Intelligence Committee that was investigating the 2016 Trump campaign's ties to Russia, including

Representative Adam Schiff (D-CA), then the committee's ranking member, and Representative Eric Swalwell (D-CA). The subpoenas also involved a gag order that made it impossible for Apple to speak out against these incursions.[45] In 2018 the DOJ also sent a subpoena to Apple to seize the phone records of former White House Counsel Don McGahn while he was still in office.[46] The foregoing privacy violations were an abuse of legitimate law enforcement investigatory powers as well as a direct affront to the separation of powers contemplated by the Constitution. Members of Congress have the constitutional right and duty to conduct oversight of executive branch functions without themselves being surveilled by that very branch. Such conduct by the nation's chief law enforcement agency is antithetical to the principles of representative democracy.

Other politicized actions in DOJ included unjustified criminal investigations,[47] allegedly politically motivated targeting of companies in antitrust enforcement,[48] using federal offices to influence elections in violation of the Hatch Act,[49] and allegedly unauthorized use of force against protestors and others exercising their First Amendment rights.[50] Many of these actions appeared to violate DOJ policy or federal law. Under Attorney General Barr, for example, the DOJ sought to justify the president's attempts to solicit the assistance of foreign countries with his bid for reelection, such as the infamous call to the president of Ukraine in 2019, for which Trump was impeached, though not removed.[51] This kind of interference compromised U.S. relationships with key allies abroad and placed a personal, domestic political agenda ahead of U.S. national security.

Decades earlier, Edward Levi and Griffin Bell understood the damage that politicization on the part of government lawyers would particularly inflict on OLC in the undermining of democratic values. When the OLC uses the law as a political tool to achieve partisan aims, particularly if it distorts the law for this purpose, its conduct profoundly undermines the rule of law. This is because using the trappings and language of law to justify violating the law damages the very concept of legality itself.[52] In particular, the willingness of OLC in the Bush years to distort the law to justify the use of torture contributed to the distrust of OLC's opinions and has conveyed the sense that OLC is primarily oriented toward providing legal cover for White House policies. Results-oriented reasoning masquerading as genuine legal advice resurfaced in Donald Trump's DOJ under the leadership of William

Barr. Barr too often seemed to regard himself as the president's personal lawyer rather than the head of a federal agency committed to enforcing the law.

Damage to the rule of law can be accomplished in an instant, but repair takes time. It will take much work and focused attention to repair the damage from the politicization of the DOJ's central functions—work that must be undertaken function by function within the DOJ. Politicization of the DOJ strikes not only at the foundations of democratic governance at home, but also damages U.S. national security interests in the domain of foreign relations. The CERL/CREW working group found that, in several different areas, "the actions of the DOJ under Mr. Barr compromised U.S. national security and increased risks to U.S. national interests relative to foreign and domestic enemies."[53] OLC memos like the one defending the 2020 strike on Iranian state actor Qassim Suleimani damage the rule of law by casting doubt on fundamental principles relating domestic law to the Law of Armed Conflict (LOAC).[54] Such distortions of law impact national security for the worse. The working group found the risk to national security from the department's actions to be particularly concerning under Barr's leadership, and found that Barr was "more interested in supporting the president's reelection bid" than in protecting U.S. security priorities or upholding the law.[55] The risk he posed to national security went well beyond the politicization of OLC memos relating to the law of war, given the role Barr may have played in the aforementioned Ukraine matter. The risk of collusion between a runaway president or attorney general and a malign foreign power is significant, and in retrospect it may seem surprising that it has not occurred more frequently. Particular attention must be paid to ensure that the attorney general does not damage U.S. national security interests under pressure from a corrupt president, and to guard against the possibility of collusion between executive branch officials and foreign powers.

Restoring commitment to the rule of law will not be an easy task, particularly in light of the erosion of the norms and practices that have served as informal guardrails for U.S. democracy. In an ideal world, legal constraints provide the outlines of what democracy requires, while a shared commitment to democratic values allows citizens to trust that those outlines will be filled in with integrity. In the absence of shared values, the survival of democracy will depend on the country's ability to replace informal norms with formal rules and laws, such as those we detail in this chapter. While it would be a mistake to think the United States can restore and secure those traditions by legislating them back into existence, the country must nevertheless attempt the task of codifying as many of the guardrails of democracy as will lend themselves to such an exercise.

New rules alone, however, cannot repair the many different forms of damage to the rule of law from acts of the past. Indeed, in many instances there were optimal rules in place, but those rules were violated with impunity. In the next section, we discuss another important aspect of restoring integrity and repairing damage to the rule of law, namely the role of accountability and the need to address legal violations, particularly those that occur within the DOJ.

## Violations and Accountability in Prior Administrations

Preserving and restoring the rule of law in a democracy requires accountability for past misdeeds, particular for those of government actors. Accountability requires the country to confront and address illegal and immoral conduct on the part of various U.S. institutions that has occurred in the past.[56] Without transparency about the past and accountability of government for its actions, future administrations are likely to repeat former mistakes.

Setting the scene for the excesses of the Trump era, formal legal condemnation of senior officials in prior administrations in the United States has been rare, and most criminal activity by government officials remains unaddressed. Exceptions have included several Watergate defendants[57] (though President Nixon himself evaded accountability by receiving a pardon from President Ford), as well as several senior officials from the Reagan administration who were involved in the Iran-Contra scandal, most of whom were pardoned by President George H.W. Bush in 1992. Federal prosecutors are concerned about appearing to be political and often do not like to prosecute officials from a previous administration. With respect to allegations of international wrongdoing, the disdain of the United States for international mechanisms of accountability has undermined its ability to serve as a standard-bearer for the rule of law across the globe. For example, the refusal of the United States to ratify the Rome Statute establishing the jurisdiction of the International Criminal Court (ICC) weakens the ability of the international community to hold senior officials, including U.S. officials, accountable for serious crimes.[58] In general, the United States has not looked favorably on attempts to hold U.S. officials accountable, even in instances of clearly illegal conduct.[59]

Following this pattern, the Obama administration made the decision in 2009 not to investigate or prosecute officials from the George W. Bush administration who had been involved with the use of torture in the war on terror.[60] Upon assuming office in 2009, President Obama said that "we need to look forward as opposed to looking backwards."[61] Subsequently, detailed findings were released by the Senate Select Committee on Intelligence (SSCI) documenting a high-level, CIA-driven program to engage in the torture and mistreatment of numerous detainees captured in Iraq and Afghanistan, which also attracted the support of other sectors of government, including the DOJ.[62] Contemporaneous with the release of the SSCI report, Attorney General Eric Holder announced that the department would not prosecute anyone following the mistaken and distorted OLC memos justifying the use of torture.[63] As a result, there have been no prosecutions of any of the architects or high-level participants in the Rendition, Detention, and Interrogation (RDI) program, and very few prosecutions of anyone who actually carried out the torture either. That is despite powerful evidence that the use of waterboarding and other harsh interrogation methods constituted torture, in violation of both U.S. federal law and U.S. treaty obligations under the Geneva Conventions and the UN Convention against Torture, as well as the Uniform Code of Military Justice (UCMJ).[64] Other countries have been at least superficially more willing to self-examine around this issue. The U.K., for example, authorized an investigation into crimes that were carried out by British forces in Iraq and Afghanistan,[65] but ultimately the vast majority of the charges were dropped due to lack of evidence.[66]

While the SSCI report laid the greatest responsibility for the use of illegal methods of interrogation at the doorstep of the CIA, it is hard to overstate the role played by DOJ lawyers at the Office of Legal Counsel who knowingly provided the CIA and the Department of Defense (DOD) with the incorrect legal advice that so-called enhanced interrogation was legal and could be used on detainees in the war on terror.[67] Given that the Holder

Justice Department argued for immunity on the part of those who inflicted the torture because they were relying on the OLC memos,[68] one might have thought that would serve as a basis for finding those who falsely designed that justification responsible. Yet, Holder offered no explanation for why the authors of the memos were never investigated by the DOJ for their role in creating false legal advice that hundreds in the White House, the CIA, and the armed services would rely on to ensure the legality of their actions.

Moreover, the idea that those who relied on the OLC memos had a clear basis for exoneration was incorrect. The truth is considerably more complicated. The "just following the OLC memos" defense should not, in theory, be any more effective for deflecting responsibility than the "just following orders" defense was at Nuremberg.[69] No such defense can be claimed where the individual making the claim knew that the action was illegal, or where an actor knew that the proposed illegal act would be unable to meet its military or civilian objective. The rule against torture under international law is *jus cogens,* meaning that everyone is expected to know the law.[70] In the United States, public servants, including the military and members of the CIA, take an oath to defend and uphold the Constitution. That oath imposes a duty to refuse to follow a patently illegal order and to report illegality up the chain of command. Those who followed the memos could try to argue an "advice of counsel" defense, comparable to the "just following orders" defense. Yet, once again, neither defense should immunize someone who authorizes or engages in torture where the conduct in question is patently illegal and the individual knows, or has reason to know, that this is so.

Why, then, did President Obama so willingly embrace the no-accountability approach, when it flew in the face of both the Nuremberg tradition and the clear approach to illegal orders demanded by U.S. constitutional jurisprudence? There have been many rationalizations offered for the decision not to prosecute those involved in the RDI program, but they fall flat when one considers the conspiracy of silence that has surrounded even less formal means for sanctioning those who designed and implemented that program. Almost without exception, those who were most supportive of the use of torture were promoted and found further positions in government, academia, or think tanks. Jay Bybee, the former head of OLC, became a federal judge in 2003.[71] John Yoo returned to legal academia as a chaired professor at the University of California at Berkeley School of Law,[72] and his history at OLC did not prevent the Heritage Foundation,[73] the National Constitution Center,[74] the American Enterprise Institute,[75] and the Federalist Society from embracing him as a fellow or for regular talks and engagements.

Gina Haspel, who served as director of the CIA under Trump, not only allegedly assisted in implementing the use of torture at a CIA so-called "black site" in Thailand during the Bush administration. As chief of staff to Jose Rodriguez, head of the CIA's clandestine service, she also issued the order in November 2005 for the destruction of videotapes of torture sessions, some of which took place under her watch.[76] The White House counsel in 2005 had been informed of the destruction of the tapes, supposedly after the fact, and expressed grave concern, but no investigation ensued.[77] In an eight-page memo, then CIA deputy director Mike Morell exonerated Haspel for her role in destroying these tapes during the Bush administration,[78] but there appears to be no other comprehensive report on this matter.[79] For her commitment to the program and her willingness to protect other members of the CIA, Haspel was held in high regard by members of the intelligence community, support that helped her bid to secure Donald Trump's nomination and Senate confirmation as director of the CIA.[80] Despite the controversy, Haspel was confirmed 54-45, with several key Democrats joining Republicans to support her.[81]

Moreover, while there have been significant investigations into the Rendition, Detention, and Investigation program, some of the resulting reports, such as U.S. Attorney John Durham's 2012 report for DOJ on torture and the Senate Select Committee on Intelligence (SSCI) report, have not been fully declassified.[82] Only 500 or so pages of the executive summary, out of more than 6,700 pages of the SSCI report, have been released, despite repeated requests by Senator Dianne Feinstein (D-CA), who chaired the committee, for greater public disclosure.[83] The failure to produce the full, unredacted text of the SSCI report stands in stark contrast with the treatment of an earlier Senate Armed Services Committee report, which was released in 2009.[84] The secrecy surrounding the CIA's role, along with information that continues to dribble out in connection with the military commissions, means that the country cannot fully put its past use of torture to rest.[85] President Biden should declassify the remaining documents relating to the RDI program so Congress and the public can have full transparency and ensure that it never happens again. He should also put an end to the continued abuse and miscarriage of justice of the remaining detainees at Guantanamo Bay by closing the prison and either trying the remaining detainees in federal court or repatriating them to their home countries, as would be required for those with prisoner of war (POW) status by the Geneva Conventions.[86]

Most importantly for present purposes, any reform of the DOJ will require a thorough examination of its Office of Legal Counsel, for which an investigation of the role its lawyers played in greenlighting the use of torture will be essential. While the Senate examined the role of the armed services and that of the CIA in the use of torture and did hold one hearing regarding the role of the DOJ in approving and coordinating the use of torture,[87] there is no report from either the House or the Senate Judiciary Committees on the OLC torture memos. That unwritten chapter in U.S. history continues to damage faith in the DOJ, particularly in its OLC, and creates continuing doubt about the legality and legitimacy of OLC legal advice.

From the standpoint of the rule of law, this failure of accountability is profoundly corrosive. The decision to "look forward, not back" on torture, and the legal precedent that was therefore never fully excised and rejected by the U.S. legal system, damaged the country's ability to hold government officials to the constraints of law. It also had a damaging effect on U.S. respect for the LOAC and on the very concept of the rule of law itself.[88] As such, lack of accountability badly discredited the OLC and weakened the normative authority of its legal opinions.[89] It also created deep mistrust of the intelligence community, particularly the CIA. Damage from both sources arguably made itself felt in the Trump administration, which might have been held more in check had abuses of executive authority been reined in by the DOJ at an earlier point in time.[90]

The failure to hold prior administrations accountable recurred in the transition from the Trump to the Biden administration. The Biden DOJ, for example, has thus far failed to announce any investigation into the potential crimes of Donald Trump or his administration, including in connection with the former president's role in inciting the attack on the Capitol on January 6, 2021. However, the House of Representatives has engaged in a robust investigation of this incident, which has included issuing subpoenas to former members of President Trump's inner circle, and the DOJ has announced that it will not honor Trump's assertion of executive privilege to block the enforcement of such subpoenas.[91]

In other matters, however, Attorney General Merrick Garland has filed a flurry of motions and other papers siding with former President Trump in important cases implicating his interests. The DOJ has appealed a federal judge's order that a secret 2019 DOJ memo discussing possible indictment of President Trump be released under the Freedom of Information Act.[92] It has also asserted executive privilege over the congressional testimony of former White House Counsel Don McGahn[93] in response to a House subpoena, although it ultimately settled the matter and allowed a deposition to proceed, albeit with significant constraints.[94] The Biden DOJ has also sided with Trump in urging dismissal of a suit by Black Lives Matter and other plaintiffs over the violent clearing of peaceful protestors from Lafayette Park in 2020 to facilitate a Trump campaign photo op.[95] And the department has filed briefs with the Second Circuit Court of Appeals siding with Trump in his appeal of a federal district court decision refusing to dismiss E. Jean Carroll's federal defamation suit against him.[96] The DOJ continues to take the position that Trump's statements about Carroll—who had accused Trump of a rape that took place in New York City twenty years ago—were issued in his "official" capacity. The current DOJ is maintaining that stance even though Trump called her a liar about events that had nothing to do with his presidency (and then for good measure added that Carroll was "not my type").[97]

Fortunately, DOJ did not apply this same logic to a lawsuit against a member of Congress, Representative Mo Brooks (R-AL), who was sued by Representative Eric Swalwell (D-CA) over Brooks's incendiary speech near the White House shortly before the January 6 insurrection on the Capitol. Brooks repeated unfounded allegations of election fraud and urged supporters to "start taking down names and kicking ass." Brooks claimed that his statements were, like Trump's against Carroll, made in his official capacity and that the DOJ was obligated, under the Westfall Act, to defend him as well. The DOJ rejected this argument, determining that Brooks's statements were personal capacity "campaign activity" and declined to defend him.[98] It remains to be seen whether the DOJ would take the same stance in a civil lawsuit over the events of January 6 against former President Trump.

Which way will the DOJ ultimately go on Trump and his administration? The attorney general has the discretion to determine DOJ policy. However, the DOJ's stance in some of these cases also shows an alarming degree of deference to presidential power, an orientation that has been fairly consistently maintained by different attorneys general for a number of years. What is particularly concerning about the deference shown to presidential power in these various contexts is that the broad scope of executive authority becomes a tool on the part of the president and other executive branch officials for avoiding accountability, and even for obstructing justice by interfering with legitimate investigations. Efforts to investigate and, ultimately, to hold executive branch officials accountable must be protected against manipulation. Even the appointment of a special counsel by the attorney general cannot adequately protect against presidential interference with attempts to establish responsibility and transparency, as shown, for instance, by the outcome of the Mueller investigation. That is particularly the case in the absence of the appointment of a special counsel to investigate the potential crimes of past administrations and the unwillingness at times on the part of the Garland DOJ to hold prior executive branch officials accountable for illegal acts of the past.

If crimes were committed by the government, even by the president himself, the architects of those crimes should be investigated and, if the evidence warrants, prosecuted. The decision whether to prosecute former government officials is a complex one, but it is best depoliticized by having the determination made by an independent counsel whose mandate allows him or her to operate substantially independently of the DOJ's current leadership. Had the Obama administration chosen to provide the American people with a full accounting of the illegalities of the previous administration, and had Obama chosen to prosecute the most significant architects of the RDI program, it would have traveled some distance toward reversing and repairing the distortion of law the administration inherited from the war on terror. Undoing legal distortions and clearly identifying and repudiating the mistakes of the past might have helped to prevent the politicization of the DOJ during the Trump administration.

Whether there is any cause and effect between the prior failures of accountability and the subsequent more wholesale dismantlement of integrity at the DOJ is a matter of speculation. But in an atmosphere in which the department has become increasingly politicized, the way was paved for further and deepening abuse of the powers of the DOJ to satisfy the political ambitions of the current occupant of the Oval Office. Clarifying the role of the DOJ, along with enhanced transparency, accountability, and apologies for the mistakes of the past, would go some way toward reestablishing the faith once placed in the department by the American people.

## Presidential Obstruction of Justice

In numerous instances, Donald Trump attempted to interfere with independent investigations of the 2016 Trump campaign, along with other potential matters of criminal interest. For example, it emerged in the course of the Mueller investigation that Trump had indeed asked White House Counsel Don McGahn to have Robert Mueller fired, and that McGahn had refused to comply.[99] Instead, Trump ultimately fired his attorney general, Jeff Sessions, and installed William Barr in his place to supervise Mueller and the rollout of the special counsel's report.

The special counsel's report describes the holes in the evidence his team gathered from witnesses who lied or withheld information, and President Trump refused to be interviewed in person by the Mueller team.[100] Once Mueller submitted his final report to Barr, the attorney general purported to characterize the special counsel's principal findings in a March 24, 2019, letter to the chairs and ranking members of the Senate and House Judiciary Committees.[101] But the inaccuracy of this letter led Mueller to respond with his own letter to Barr about the "public confusion about critical aspects of the results" that the attorney general's letter had generated.[102] Two federal judges have since sharply criticized Barr's "lack of candor" in his handling of the Mueller report. Judge Reggie Walton stated that Barr provided a "distorted" and "misleading" account of the report to the American people, which led the judge to question Barr's "credibility" and, with it, the department's representation of the report to the judge.[103] One year later, Judge Amy Berman Jackson echoed Judge Walton's opinion, writing that Barr and the Justice Department were "disingenuous" and that DOJ's descriptions of an OLC memorandum drafted to lend an air of legitimacy to Barr's preformed views on obstruction of justice "are so inconsistent with evidence in the record, they are not worthy of credence."[104]

In volume II of his report, Mueller indicated he could not indict President

Trump because the DOJ has a policy against indicting a sitting president.[105] What transpired next—including Barr's noted misrepresentation of the Mueller report's findings to Congress—is a clear indication that the DOJ's current special counsel regulations and related policies fail to protect the independence and transparency of an investigation involving the president. As we explain more fully in a forthcoming article,[106] the DOJ policy against indicting a sitting president is not mandated by the Constitution. That point became even more obvious when the Supreme Court ruled in *Trump* v. *Vance* that a sitting president is subject to criminal process, including a state grand jury subpoena.[107] Mueller nonetheless had no choice; his boss, Attorney General William Barr, was not going to authorize indictment of the president. After President Trump left office, however, indictment became a realistic option.[108] Indeed, the Mueller report contemplates just that post-presidency possibility when discussing the importance of preserving the evidence and documenting what President Trump and others did. The importance of preserving and documenting the evidence was one of the justifications in the report for the detail in volume II on obstruction of justice.

This chapter does not fully explore the merits of Mueller's obstruction of justice case against President Trump, as this is already the subject of considerable analysis.[109] Much of the argument for finding Trump responsible for obstructing justice is built around specific actions he took in connection with the Russia investigation—such as firing FBI Director James Comey and attempting to fire Mueller himself—all actions intended to impede the investigation and violate the obstruction of justice statutes.[110] As a private sector lawyer in 2018 before his second term as attorney general, William Barr had laid out a detailed argument in a letter to President Trump explaining his belief that Mueller's "obstruction theory" was wrong and why the supposed acts of obstruction were actually within the president's powers under Article II of the Constitution.[111] This self-serving memorandum apparently helped induce Trump to nominate Barr as attorney general. However, we believe that Mueller was right on the question of obstruction and that Barr was clearly wrong: Article II does not empower the president to obstruct justice, a point later underscored in 2020 by the Supreme Court's clear message in *Trump* v. *Vance* that nothing in Article II of the Constitution exempts the president from criminal process.

A second category of rule of law violation in past administrations involves conduct where the executive branch has exceeded its authority, but where the action is not necessarily criminal. Alternatively, this could be categorized as conduct that is illegal but that for various reasons has become unprosecutable, such as because the statute of limitations has run out or there is a general grant of immunity against prosecution.[112] True accountability would address this conduct in addition to conduct that is identifiably illegal and prosecutable. The unavailability of prosecution should not be taken to mean there are no resources to remedy the past. In such instances, the DOJ or other executive branch agencies must seek to establish accountability, coupled with transparency, along alternative lines.

The emphasis here is more on institutional accountability than on individual accountability, yet both are important. Governments can only act through individuals who serve as their agents, and thus any focus on crimes of government must also hold individuals responsible. Yet there is a great difference between accepting institutional responsibility for past failings and blaming institutional wrongdoing on individual agents, which sometimes only serves to deflect from true public accountability. The use of torture under the Bush administration, the excessive and possibly illegal use of drone strikes under the Obama administration, and the inhumane treatment of immigrants in detention facilities during the Trump administration all raised serious questions about expanding presidential war powers and executive authority more generally, as well as the ability of the other branches of the federal government to ensure that the executive branch adheres to the rule of law.[113]

## Alternate Forms of Accountability

Criminal investigation and prosecution of current or former senior governmental leaders who violate the law is one of the most important means of establishing responsibility and repairing damage to the rule of law. Often the opposite occurs: low-level government employees who carry out the policies of their leaders are prosecuted while the architects walk free. Accountability requires particularly that we identify the crimes of senior government leaders, as it helps to establish the systematic nature of the wrongdoing and the fact that it was part of a concerted plan on the part of the state to violate the law. However, when individual prosecution of senior leaders is legally or politically infeasible, we may still be able to hold government accountable, as well as to make significant progress toward repairing damage to the rule of law.

There are a number of ways for a government to acknowledge responsibility without conducting criminal prosecutions. For example, Japanese Americans who had been incarcerated in internment camps during World War II under a 1942 presidential executive order were partially and belatedly compensated for lost property beginning in the Truman administration, pursuant to the Japanese American Evacuation Claims Act of 1948.[114] This statute merely compensated for seized and lost property, refusing to acknowledge that the United States government had done anything wrong, a point already made by the Supreme Court in 1944 in *Korematsu* v. *United States*, when it upheld the constitutionality of the executive order.[115] A Supreme Court majority did not revisit the erroneous decision upholding the executive order until seventy-four years later, in dicta rejecting the reasoning of *Korematsu*, but in an opinion where the court nonetheless refused to strike down another executive order of dubious constitutionality, this one by President Trump banning entry to the United States of people from a group of principally Muslim countries.[116] Hopefully in future cases, it will take less than seventy-four years to complete the process of acknowledging that the United States government was legally as well as morally wrong, a process that in this instance was only completed in 2018 when the Supreme Court may very well have blindly given its approval to yet another wrong.

Most victims of torture after 9/11 thus far have not received compensation,[117] and some of them remain in Guantanamo indefinitely without charge or awaiting a trial that may never come. Under the UN Convention against Torture, victims of torture are entitled to "redress and . . . an enforceable right to fair and adequate compensation."[118] The DOJ should work accordingly with the legal advisor to the State Department to (1) determine the extent of the U.S. obligation under the circumstances of the war on terror to pay reparations and (2) make a good-faith effort to address its own liability in advance of potential litigation in international courts.[119] This would be a particularly important move to make in light of President Biden's decision to end the war in Afghanistan by withdrawing all U.S. troops, coupled with his insistence that American involvement in hostilities in the region has ceased.[120]

Some victims of rule of law breaches by the Trump administration—including children who were illegally separated from their parents and were held in deeply inhumane conditions—also should receive compensation for their suffering. First, there is the importance of wholly or at least partially compensating the victim of illegal federal government conduct for violation of rights as one would compensate the victim of any tort, particularly an intentional tort. Of equal importance is the message to the public and to future administrations that certain actions by the federal government are illegal, and that if injury results therefrom, these actions are tortious and must be compensated. Once required to publicly acknowledge fault and to pay compensation for illegal actions, the government is less likely to perform these or similar actions again.

In addition to compensation, there is often enhanced accountability in mere transparency itself. Even many years after the injury occurred, a full and unequivocal acknowledgement of the wrongs that were inflicted can help to heal some of the wounds for the victims and also contribute to enhanced accountability on the part of government actors, even if no penalty is paid other than in the court of public opinion. Commissions established for truth and reconciliation in South Africa following apartheid, for example, were designed with precisely this function in view, though their success has been debated.[121] Japan agreed to apologize as well as to pay $8.3 million in compensation to Korean women who had been forced into sexual slavery during the Second World War,[122] though the final resolution of the matter between the two nations has remained elusive.[123] And in 2013, an association of Chilean judges issued an apology for the court system's role in the human rights abuses committed during the regime of dictator Augusto Pinochet.[124]

While apologies or compensation offered many years after the initial fact may seem pointless, especially if paid to a succeeding generation from that which was originally wronged, there is a forward-looking purpose to symbolic acts of this sort. Apologies or even relatively modest monetary awards serve an expressive function: they acknowledge that a wrong was committed and identify a need not to repeat the conduct again. This is as important for clarifying the culpability of the government as it is for helping victims move past the injury. It constitutes a clear commitment to a different path in the future and to different values from the ones manifested in the wrongful act. That this has failed to occur in the case of the illegal methods of interrogation that occurred at Guantanamo and Abu Ghraib prisons, among other U.S.-run bases and black sites, may explain the lack of reprobation and the continued personal success of Bush administration officials who had a role in furthering the torture program.

## The Advisory Function of the DOJ

Revisiting illegal conduct of previous administrations requires introspection and accountability within the DOJ itself. Much of the conduct that appeared to be contrary to law during the Trump administration occurred inside the DOJ or was approved by the department. This conduct included the DOJ's role in approving and then defending in the courts some of the executive orders and other administrative actions discussed above. DOJ lawyers, mostly political appointees of the president, and their subordinates were intimately involved in many of these activities. Among other forms of accountability, the DOJ's inspector general and Office of Professional Responsibility (OPR) should investigate this conduct and report on whether policy or legal violations occurred. Persons found to have violated the law or engaged in other serious misconduct in most instances should be barred from federal employment in the future rather than rewarded for being stalwart in defending their former colleagues in the face of political pressure to come clean.[125] Referrals should also be made to state bar disciplinary committees.

In addition to investigations of culpable individuals, the DOJ should conduct a review of legally questionable actions in previous administrations to guide the present and future administrations. A written evaluation of the legality of questionable government conduct is needed even if such conduct is not presently under consideration. If prior conduct is illegal, the DOJ should be on record indicating as much. Only in this way can the DOJ learn from the mistakes of the past and improve the legal consistency of the department over time.

## Recommendations for Restoring the Rule of Law at DOJ

The CERL/CREW report, released in October 2020, included specific recommendations as to how to restore the independence of the DOJ from partisan politics and assure the department's commitment to the rule of law.[126] As coauthors of the CERL/CREW report, we incorporate those recommendations here, in some cases expanding upon the discussion in the original CERL/CREW document.

Reform efforts involving the DOJ are most likely to be implemented in one of three ways: a change in DOJ policy; an executive order (EO) by the president; or congressional action, specifically legislation. Many of the post-Watergate reforms to the DOJ were implemented by changes to DOJ policies and procedures under Attorney General Edward Levi and his successor, Griffin Bell. As noted above, such reforms are vulnerable because they can be easily reversed by subsequent attorneys general.

An EO, on the other hand, needs to be rescinded by a president, forcing future presidents to accept political accountability for the change. An EO can also give agencies outside the DOJ, such as the Office of Government Ethics (OGE) or the Office of Special Counsel (OSC), a role in monitoring and reporting to the president and to Congress about what is happening within the DOJ. From the standpoint of strengthening the ethical and legal core of the DOJ's conduct, this arrangement is preferable to one in which the attorney general has exclusive control over the department's compliance with its own rules.

Finally, the most permanent changes to DOJ policies and procedures can be accomplished by statute, which can only be reversed by an act of Congress. Because of concerns about abuse of presidential power,[127] legislative reforms are preferable whenever possible. Although ethics reform by statute can be politically fraught, this may be the right moment. The White House is currently controlled by a political party that has complained about abuses at the DOJ under the previous administration.[128] The other party, having lost the White House, may have a renewed interest in restraining the power of the executive branch, including the DOJ. However, passing legislation takes time, and therefore an executive order from the president may be the most effective means to implement these recommendations in a sufficiently timely manner until statutory reform becomes possible. Meanwhile, and despite some policy differences we have with the current attorney general, we have full confidence that Merrick Garland will informally do everything in his power to reduce the overall atmosphere of politicization of the department while more lasting reforms are being established.

Recommendations for further structural changes are set out in the discussion that follows.

### Strengthen the Independence of the Special Counsel

Currently, special counsels must be appointed by the attorney general or the acting attorney general, and authorization for such an appointment lies solely within the executive branch. This was not always the case, however. After Watergate, Congress passed legislation authorizing the appointment of an independent counsel, but Congress allowed the law to lapse in 1999.[129] To protect the independence of this critical role, Congress should renew the special prosecutor legislation, with particular attention to the need to ensure the independence of that office. In particular, in the absence of congressional action to establish an independent prosecutor, those investigating the president or other high-level officials will be continuously vulnerable to dismissal, which will allow the president to exercise considerable control over any investigation into her or his own potential wrongdoing or wrongdoing of persons close to the president. Independent prosecutors must be protected against arbitrary dismissal. No federal prosecutor or investigator—whether an independent counsel, an inspector general, or a U.S. attorney[130]—should be fired by a superior if the motivation for the firing is to stop or obstruct an investigation of alleged criminal activity. The power to hire and fire in the federal government should not include the power to obstruct justice.

There are two main arguments against the passage of an independent counsel law: (1) that it is unconstitutional and (2) that its prior iterations led to gross prosecutorial overreach. Both fail on close examination.

First, there are those who believe that restricting the power of the president to remove an independent prosecutor would be unconstitutional. In 1988, the Supreme Court in *Morrison* v. *Olson*[131] upheld the independent counsel statute against arguments that it unconstitutionally infringed on the power of the executive. In the face of objections that the independent counsel statute infringed on the power of the president, the Court said:

This case does not involve an attempt by Congress itself to gain a role in the removal of executive officials other than its established powers of impeachment and conviction. The Act instead puts the removal power squarely in the hands of the Executive Branch; an independent counsel may be removed from office "only by the personal action of the Attorney General, and only for good cause."[132]

One justice, Antonin Scalia, issued a famous dissent in which he complained that the majority opinion violated the framers' intent with regard to the separation of powers and also unduly weakened the executive branch:

This is what this suit is about. Power. The allocation of power among Congress, the President, and the courts in such fashion as to preserve the equilibrium the Constitution sought to establish—so that "a gradual concentration of the several powers in the same department," can effectively be resisted. Frequently an issue of this sort will come before the Court clad, so to speak, in sheep's clothing: the potential of the asserted principle to effect important change in the equilibrium of power is not immediately evident, and must be discerned by a careful and perceptive analysis. But this wolf comes as a wolf.[133]

Scalia and other critics of that decision point to *Myers* v. *United States* (1926), which established the president's right to remove members of the executive branch as a broader removal power than *Morrison* would suggest.[134] Indeed, the *Myers* case defends a theory of presidential power known as the "unitary executive theory," which interprets the president's power to remove executive branch officials under Article II as nearly absolute, and thus if the president wants to fire a member of the executive branch, no ordinary legislation can stop him or her. Adherents of the unitary executive theory maintain that Trump had the right to fire Robert Mueller, even if he had done so explicitly to put an end to the investigation into himself and his 2016 campaign. The same could be said under this theory of Trump's firing of FBI Director Jim Comey, despite the fact that Trump explicitly admitted after he fired Comey that he "faced great pressure" because of the Russia inquiry.[135]

We reject this expansive view of presidential removal power and do not believe that *Myers* can be understood as extending presidential removal in cases involving obstruction of justice. Indeed, *Myers* held that Congress could not restrict the president's power to remove a postmaster, but this is quite a far cry from removing a prosecutor in the middle of an ongoing investigation of the president or of persons close to the president. Contrary to what Scalia may have thought, *Myers* should not be read as suggesting that the president's removal power is in fact unlimited, especially when that case is read in conjunction with *Morrison*. Although *Myers* does recognize "a legislative declaration that the power to remove officers appointed by the President and the Senate vested in the President alone,"[136] the court in that case was addressing the narrower question of whether the fact that the Senate must approve appointments gave it the implied power of being able to exercise a veto over removals. *Myers* laid to rest the idea that the Senate might exercise such a veto, but it failed to address whether Article II constrains Congress's ability to limit the president's removal powers.

A further development in this line of cases was the court's decision in *Humphry's Executor* v. *United States*,[137] in which the court refined *Myers* to suggest that congressional control over executive appointments might differ depending on the agency involved. Thus the court found that *Myers* did not apply to Congress's ability to limit the president's power to remove a member of the Federal Trade Commission,[138] similar to its ruling in *Morrison*. In another case, however, the court distinguished the two cases and struck down statutory restrictions on the president's power to remove officers from the Public Company Accounting Oversight Board (PCAOB) in *Free Enterprise Fund* v. *PCAOB*,[139] as well as the Consumer Financial Protection Bureau (CFPB) in *Seila Law LLC* v. *CFPB*.[140] While this area of law is somewhat in flux, *Morrison* is still good law, and there is no current legal impediment to reenacting the special counsel law in some form. In particular, the existence of an independent counsel who is subject to dismissal only for cause is fully consistent with broad presidential authority under Article II,[141] and the same might be said for an independent counsel appointed by the attorney general in the absence of special counsel legislation.

Second, bringing back the independent counsel law is controversial among some who otherwise are strong supporters of presidential accountability because of concern about an overzealous independent counsel free of supervision by the attorney general. For example, Bob Bauer and Jack Goldsmith in their 2020 book rejected the idea of bringing back an independent counsel statute and advocated that the DOJ should retain a check on the special prosecutor.[142] A 1999 joint report of the American Enterprise

Institute (AEI) and the Brookings Institution also concluded that the attorney general's responsibilities for appointing a special counsel should be fully restored.[143] As the 1999 AEI-Brookings report observed:

> Like many, we believe the Act's reach has been too broad and too arbitrary. Instead of promoting public confidence, the Act has failed to produce public consensus that outside counsel are being appointed when, but only when, it is in the public interest that a matter be removed from the Department of Justice's jurisdiction.[144]

The report recommended an arrangement similar to what the United States has had for the past twenty years—namely, that the attorney general once again have the power to make decisions concerning the scope of the independent counsel's jurisdiction, the budget of the special counsel, measures to make sure that the independent counsel is both independent and conforms to Justice Department policies and procedures, and whether to remove the independent counsel for cause.

This concern about runaway independent prosecutors was fueled in particular by two lengthy investigations by special counsels: the Iran-Contra investigation by independent counsel Lawrence Walsh, and Ken Starr's investigation of President Clinton. Following these inquiries, worry about the unchecked power of independent counsel was paramount, and removing the federal judiciary from its role in appointing and supervising the independent counsel and restoring the authority of the attorney general were thought to be the route to achieving a balance between independence and accountability for independent counsels. The result, however, is that today, as in 1973, the special counsel can be dismissed by the DOJ. There is thus little protection against a recurrence of what happened to Archibald Cox on President Nixon's orders in the "Saturday Night Massacre," and indeed, President Trump very nearly did fire Robert Mueller.

In 2017, Congress considered legislation that would have protected Mueller from being fired except for good cause,[145] but the bill, despite being sponsored by Trump ally Senator Lindsey Graham (R-SC), never passed. During consideration of that bill, constitutional law experts like Akhil Amar, who derided *Morrison*, were called to testify about the "unconstitutionality" of Congress constraining presidential removal power and Trump's "right" to fire Mueller.[146] As we have explained, we strongly disagree with Amar.

Whatever the case may have been in 2017, given the abuses of the Trump DOJ since, there should be skepticism about delegating so much responsibility over the special counsel to the attorney general. By contrast, during the Trump administration, federal judges—even Trump-appointed ones—were sometimes more courageous, both in standing up to the administration and in their willingness to criticize the DOJ.[147] Restoring to the federal judiciary a role in supervising an independent counsel, as provided for in the Ethics in Government Act of 1978, might therefore be an attractive option. The federal judiciary would likely provide a better constraint on presidential abuse of power than the attorney general, underscoring the wisdom of the arrangement in the 1978 independent counsel statute.

Even recognizing the risks of runaway independent counsels, the importance of accountability in preserving the rule of law still speaks in favor of restoring the independent counsel law, albeit with careful reflection on checks that can be put in place for the special counsel. A compromise position, however, might be a statute that leaves DOJ special counsel regulations in place but requires the DOJ to appoint a special counsel in certain specified circumstances, such as a criminal investigation involving the president, a former president, or persons close to the president. The statute might or might not require a judicial finding of "cause" for the attorney general to remove the special counsel—the most contentious point of any independent counsel law. If removal of the special counsel by the DOJ were permitted, the statute should require the attorney general to notify Congress in writing of the reasons for removing the special counsel,[148] and to appear and testify before both houses of Congress to answer questions about the circumstances of the special counsel's removal and plans for appointment of a new one.

## Protect Special Counsel Investigations
## Through Revised Obstruction Laws

Despite the change in control of the Justice Department in January 2021, there is ample evidence that DOJ political appointees' decisions concerning a president, including even a former president of the opposite political party, are highly deferential to the president.

In theory, there is protection beyond the mere powers of a special counsel in federal law. Federal obstruction of justice law already criminalizes the removal of any prosecutor, whether by the president or anyone else, for the purpose of interfering with an ongoing investigation.[149] Special Counsel Robert Mueller expressed a similar view in volume II of his 2019 report.[150] In addition to reviving the special counsel legislation, Congress should also consider amending federal obstruction of justice law to make clear that if any prosecutor is fired for the purpose of obstructing an ongoing investigation, the firing would violate federal obstruction of justice law.[151]

It is also important to protect against efforts to obstruct investigations through the destruction of documents or through denying the special counsel's access to information needed to encourage a thorough and fully informed investigation. Following the precedent established in *United States* v. *Nixon*, there must be compliance with special counsel subpoenas of the executive branch, including those issued to the White House.[152] If a new independent counsel law is enacted, it should include a provision for expedited judicial review of special counsel subpoenas that are challenged. Accordingly, the destruction of government documents and other records from previous administrations, or from the current administration, should not be tolerated.[153] Any destruction of government records should trigger a DOJ investigation, not just an investigation inside the agency where the destruction of the document occurred. As discussed in the preceding section, the RDI program should have been the subject of a special counsel investigation during the Obama administration, if not the Bush administration, and destruction of relevant documents would have undermined that investigation if it had occurred.[154] The DOJ needs to make clear that destruction of government records in any executive branch agency will be investigated as a possible criminal offense and may be prosecuted as such.

## Protect Federal Prosecutors

Appointment of U.S. attorneys for fixed terms would avoid some of the problems that occur when U.S. attorneys are removed for political reasons, including reasons that may amount to obstruction of justice.[155] U.S. attorneys could be protected from removal by a statute that provides for fixed terms in office—for example, ten years. Initial terms could be staggered to assure that each presidential term has an equal number of vacancies to fill. Such a statute could prevent the president from removing a U.S. attorney for any-thing else but cause. While such an arrangement would have required the Biden DOJ to retain some U.S. attorneys appointed by Trump, the Trump DOJ also would have been required to retain some U.S. attorneys appointed by Obama. All of these U.S. attorneys would still work under the supervision of the attorney general, but such an arrangement very likely would provide more checks and balances in the DOJ than there are today, when a president can fire and replace all of the U.S. attorneys at once. Of course, any such reform would need to account for the myriad contingencies of professional life, such as a U.S. attorney who resigns or dies. In these instances, the sitting president should be allowed to nominate a replacement for the remainder of the unfinished term.

Like the independent counsel statute, a restriction on the power of the president to remove United States attorneys would be subject to constitutional challenge on the grounds that it was inconsistent with the president's Article II powers.[156] While it is beyond the scope of this chapter to fully address how insulating a U.S. attorney from presidential removal can nevertheless coexist with the extensive removal powers the court has recognized in *Myers*, *CFPB*, and *PCAOB*, it is clear from cases like *Morrison* that the two are indeed reconcilable.[157] Indeed, in 2020 the Supreme Court held in *Trump v. Vance* that the president is subject to criminal process, including the subpoena power of a prosecutor.[158] Given the unique functions of prosecutors, who are responsible for enforcing existing laws—not making policies or promulgating regulations[159]—providing job protections for U.S. attorneys is within Congress's mandate.

Other parts of the DOJ also should be insulated from partisan politics, even when the president's removal powers are recognized as fully applicable. The DOJ should accordingly enhance the role of its career attorneys in policy decisions as well as decisions in individual investigations, civil cases, and criminal prosecutions. One way to do that is to reduce the number of political appointees in the DOJ. This could be the number of presidentially appointed and Senate-confirmed (PAS) appointees or the number of middle-ranked Schedule C positions filled with political appointees chosen by the PAS appointees.[160] Another approach is to require the DOJ to document, in writing, material disagreements between career DOJ attorneys and political appointees unless the political appointees defer to the career attorneys. Such documentation should in most instances be shared with congressional oversight committees upon request. Yet another priority should be enforcing existing civil service laws that prohibit politicization of the hiring process for career civil servants, and that provide job protections to career civil servants in the DOJ and other federal agencies.[161] Political appointees should not be allowed to intrude into the hiring, evaluation, promotion, and firing process for career civil servants. If existing statutes and regulations are not sufficient, they should be tightened by amendment. The Office of Special Counsel, which is charged with enforcing the civil service laws and the Hatch Act, should strengthen its enforcement activities and keep a close watch on the DOJ.

Finally, ethics statutes and regulations do not change from administration to administration and should not be interpreted based upon political ideology.[162] Most DOJ ethics officials are career DOJ attorneys rather than political appointees and, with civil service job protections, are well suited to give ethics advice that may not be popular with senior DOJ officials.[163] Congress should require, preferably by statute, the DOJ to disclose to Congress instances in which a presidentially appointed DOJ official intentionally disregards the direct advice of DOJ ethics lawyers.[164]

### Add Legal Protections and Heighten Responsibilities for Inspectors General

Some instances of criminal conduct in the executive branch are never referred to the DOJ because the conduct is not reported and investigated in the agency where it occurred.[165] This is usually the job of agency inspectors general (IGs), who need independence and cooperation from other executive branch officials to do their job.[166] Inspectors general are part of the executive branch, but they also have a critically important independent role in investigating abuse in their agencies as part of their mission to "promote integrity, efficiency, and accountability."[167] Inspectors general are frequently the bearers of bad news and negative information, as the officers tasked with verifying compliance with laws, regulations, and policies within their respective governmental agencies. It is important to protect IGs from reprisals, lest the agency and the government writ large lose the primary benefit of the IG position.

As evident during the Trump administration, inspectors general who failed to toe the party line were fired or forced to resign by the president.[168] In at least one case, namely, the firing of Michael Atkinson, the inspector general of the intelligence community, the dismissal took place with the endorsement of the attorney general.[169] For IGs to be sufficiently independent that they feel free to report wrongdoing in the agency to which they are assigned, the ability of the president to fire them must be limited, compatible with prevailing Supreme Court guidance regarding limitations on the scope of the president's removal power.

One approach is to have fixed terms for IGs as suggested above for U.S. attorneys. Appointment of inspectors general for fixed terms would avoid some of the problems that occur when IGs are removed in the middle of investigations. Inspectors general, like prosecutors, do not have a policymaking role in the executive branch, making the case for unrestrained presidential removal power under Article II of the Constitution a weak one. Although there is uncertainty about whether a statutory restriction on presidential removal power is constitutional, we believe it is essential to the independence of an inspector general.[170]

Other than giving inspectors general fixed terms in office and making them removable only for cause, other protections should be given to IGs to enable them to do their job free of interference. Sometimes the investigative work of IGs will displease political superiors and even the president, but it is important that this work continue undisturbed. Additional regulations, and perhaps also criminal statutes, may be needed to prohibit interference with the independence of the IGs. All persons including the president should be subject to those same regulations and statutes.

Inspectors general should also report information to Congress not only at the conclusion of investigations, but also in appropriate circumstances at the outset or during an investigation, and IGs should not be removed by the president for fulfilling this duty. OLC opinions stating that IGs do not have to report certain information to Congress before the conclusion of an investigation—including the opinion OLC rendered in 2019 in connection with the Ukraine whistleblower[171]—should be rescinded. Better yet, such reports by IGs to Congress should be specifically required by an amended statute.

Finally, inside the DOJ itself, the inspector general needs the power to proceed promptly and unimpeded with investigations of alleged wrongdoing. Unlike most other federal agencies, the DOJ has a separate Office of Professional Responsibility.[172] Investigations should not languish under the "exclusive jurisdiction" of the DOJ's OPR[173] before the IG begins to investigate. In addition, IG reports to Congress should not be delayed because there is also an OPR investigation. This goal would be assisted by the transfer of some responsibilities from the OPR to the DOJ IG. The Inspector General Access Act of 2019 (S. 685 / H.R. 202) provided for this needed change and had sponsors from both sides of the aisle.[174]

## Expand Recusal of Presidential Appointees

DOJ attorneys appointed by the president should recuse from participation in criminal cases and investigations in which the president has a personal interest. Generally applicable recusal rules for particular party matters in the executive branch,[175] if properly interpreted, would preclude political appointees from participating in some of these cases, but these rules are too subjective, and waivers are too easy to obtain. Bright-line recusal rules in the DOJ are therefore needed. A preferable approach is to embed this recusal rule in a federal statute to ensure it cannot be undone by executive order. The point is simple: in a democratic society, criminal investigation and prosecution decisions turn on the facts and an evenhanded application of the law, not on personal favoritism or politics. DOJ attorneys close to the president should not decide whether to investigate or prosecute the friends, family, or enemies of the president.

DOJ's presidential appointees should recuse from any matter involving the president in a personal capacity, the president's family, business entities owned by the president, and the president's campaign. Other items on the recusal list should include matters involving close associates of the president and people appointed by the president to positions in the United States government. Presidential appointees in the DOJ probably should also recuse from matters involving members of Congress and candidates for election to Congress, as well as matters involving presidential candidates and their families. Another category meriting recusal of presidential appointees in the DOJ involves investigations and prosecutions of people whom the president has identified as requiring investigation even before they are charged with a crime.[176]

Most of these matters can be handled by career DOJ attorneys in the main Justice Department or U.S. attorneys' offices with supervision by a senior career attorney rather than by very senior officials appointed by the president. If additional supervision of a matter is required, a senior career DOJ attorney from another part of the DOJ or a different district can assume that responsibility. For particularly complex matters, such as the 2017–2019 Russia investigation undertaken by Robert Mueller, a special counsel can be appointed.

Finally, investigations and prosecutions involving a prior president or the president's family members or appointees also should be undertaken by DOJ attorneys who are not appointees of the current president. For reasons explained above, a retrospective examination of potentially criminal conduct in previous administrations is important for preserving and restoring democratic norms. But to avoid the appearance of retaliation against a vanquished political foe by supporters of the winner, this task should not be undertaken by DOJ attorneys who are appointees of the current president.

### Enhance Protections for the Intelligence Community

Many lessons regarding the intelligence community emerged from the 2016 election. Some suggest the need for greater protection for members of the intelligence community who are faithfully trying to protect U.S. national security, but others suggest a need for greater transparency on the part of intelligence agencies as well as more careful adherence to agency protocol.[177] Following a sustained attack on the intelligence community on the part of the Trump administration, former members of the Obama-era intelligence community were repeatedly targeted by both the president and the DOJ, with public attacks as well as counter-investigations into the origins of the Russia probe.[178] In particular, as discussed above, the investigation by Special Counsel John Durham held out hope for Donald Trump of exposing a conspiracy on the part of the Obama administration to bring down the Trump campaign.[179]

The DOJ investigations occurred simultaneously with investigations by three committees in the Republican-controlled Senate, in which former members of the intelligence community or those involved in the Russia probe on the national security side were placed on a subpoena list.[180] Neither the

DOJ investigations nor the Senate investigations appear to have borne fruit. The highly awaited Durham probe, in particular, ended up a great disappointment to the former president when Durham told Barr, who in turn notified Trump, that Durham would not be able to issue a report prior to the election.[181] A December 2019 report by DOJ Inspector General Michael Horowitz meanwhile found that the Russia probe was correctly predicated and duly authorized under law, meaning that the FBI had met the legal criteria for undertaking the investigation under the circumstances.[182]

Nevertheless, these counter-investigations and the suspicion they raised of the FBI may have caused lasting damage to the United States intelligence community. At the same time, the Horowitz IG report identified significant difficulties within the FBI, ones that must be attended to going forward. In an earlier, August 2019 report, for example, Horowitz found that there were leaks in connection with Crossfire Hurricane and that then FBI Director James Comey was himself responsible for leaking sensitive information that he should have kept confidential.[183] Horowitz also identified difficulties of accountability within the FBI, and noted that Crossfire Hurricane was started by career officials who had not run their investigative plans all the way up the chain and, most notably, had not consulted with the DOJ as per agency guidelines.[184] He also discussed the low threshold for opening an investigation of a political campaign in the first place, which is necessarily politically sensitive,[185] as well as a lack of care and diligence in presenting information honestly to Foreign Intelligence Surveillance Act (FISA) court judges.[186] This latter point became apparent when Horowitz examined the highly controversial wiretap and other surveillance that was ordered on Carter Page, a member of the Trump campaign. While there were good grounds to be concerned about Page's contact with the Russians, Horowitz found FBI agents failed to reveal that Page had previously provided information to another U.S. intelligence agency and therefore the level of suspicion of his activities might have been exaggerated.[187] Nevertheless, Horowitz concluded that "we did not find documentary or testimonial evidence that political bias or improper motivation influenced the FBI's decision to seek FISA authority on Carter Page,"[188] which was at the heart of the objections to Crossfire Hurricane raised by Donald Trump and his advisors.[189] The report therefore suggested that the probe of Page was warranted and no laws were broken. But the report also pointed to the need for greater care in adhering to agency protocol, as well as much greater attention to agency guidelines for ensuring the confidentiality of intelligence within the department.[190]

Although the December 2019 Horowitz report largely vindicated the FBI and Crossfire Hurricane, some important lessons emerged from it for the department and the intelligence community. Carelessly handled DOJ investigations in the intelligence community could compromise sources and methods of obtaining intelligence, and the Horowitz report pointed to the need to handle that risk with greater care.[191] In addition, there must be better coordination with the DOJ surrounding sensitive political probes, especially those with a significant criminal dimension. While the CERL/CREW report identified concerns with DOJ restrictions on FBI intelligence protocol,[192] it is also the case that the DOJ must have an opportunity to weigh in on criminal investigations from the outset. This suggests that the DOJ should engage in better coordination with the Office of the Director of National Intelligence (ODNI), and that the ODNI inspector general's office should have enhanced opportunities to guide DOJ investigations within ODNI. The DOJ should be required to coordinate with the ODNI IG's office to make sure investigations do not compromise the quality of U.S. intelligence or unfairly intimidate intelligence employees.[193]

### Restrict Exercise of Prosecutorial Discretion to Domestic Considerations

With the exception of cases like those involving extradition, which necessarily involve negotiations with foreign governments, the DOJ's prosecutorial decisions should not be affected by U.S. interests relating to foreign countries. As shown by Bill Barr's overtures to a wide array of other nations in support of Trump's illegitimate attacks on the Mueller investigation, the potential for abuse is great. It can take the form of American politicians seeking to involve foreign nations in politicized DOJ activity, or of foreign governments seeking to involve the United States' criminal justice system in political disputes abroad. DOJ requests from a foreign nation for legal assistance, as well as DOJ willingness to provide legal assistance to a foreign nation, should be justified on law enforcement grounds. And given the possibility of mixed purposes in a case involving the prosecution of a foreign national, Congress should act to prohibit the exercise of federal prosecutorial discretion with regard to domestic considerations and thus forbid trade-offs based on foreign relations. Although there are some restrictions built into the system by the Foreign Agents Registration Act (FARA), which requires individuals or organizations who engage in political activities on behalf of a foreign principal to register with the DOJ,[194] there are few constraints that would limit the DOJ from using its prosecutorial authority to secure the assistance or cooperation of a foreign nation.[195] While such decisions may on occasion occur in even a healthy democracy, the potential for abuse makes such trade-offs too risky and ultimately untenable in an agency that strives to adhere to rule of law values.

Examples of prosecutorial abuses during the tenure of Bill Barr include the aforementioned attempts by President Trump to persuade Australia, Ukraine, Italy, and the United Kingdom to assist Attorney General Barr in a counter-investigation of the origins of the Russia investigation.[196] Trump administration discussions with Australia[197] in particular may have matured into cooperation that reportedly also involved the United States in Australia's negotiation for the release of hostages in a third country, Iran.[198] Sometimes, foreign governments seek to influence criminal investigations inside the United States, as the Turkish government allegedly did in asking the Trump administration to scale back a criminal investigation of Halkbank, a politically influential Turkish bank, by the U.S. attorney in the Southern District of New York.[199]

Cooperation and coordination with other nations in criminal investigations is sometimes appropriate. The United States has entered into mutual legal assistance treaties (MLATs) with other nations, and these arrangements are helpful in combatting crimes that cross international boundaries, such as narcotics trafficking, sex trafficking, money laundering, and terrorism.[200] Prosecutors are urged to consult the DOJ's Office of International Affairs (OIA) to determine whether the United States has an MLAT with a country from which evidence or other cooperation is sought. This procedure is a shortcut for the DOJ because it is considered faster and more reliable than letters rogatory—that is, a formal request from a U.S. court addressed to a foreign court and asking for assistance in a particular matter.[201]

The United States should of course abide by its treaty obligations and, when appropriate under these treaties or when letters rogatory are obtained from a court, should call upon foreign nations for reciprocal legal assistance.

Such requests should also be reviewed by career DOJ lawyers, not just political appointees, and the requests must never be politically motivated. In addition, they should fall squarely within the treaty obligations or treaty rights of the United States. Most importantly, any such agreement between U.S. law enforcement and a foreign nation should be as transparent as possible; secret deals in this domain are almost always highly suspect. Congressional oversight committees—the judiciary and intelligence committees of the House and Senate—should be informed of instances in which foreign legal assistance is requested or given, and the reasons therefor.

### Enhance Privacy Protections for Journalists and Private Citizens

Finally, we return to the abuses that occurred with regard to journalists, members of Congress, and private citizens. These are difficult to correct, and there is a long and complex history regarding the reach of DOJ's investigatory powers. The surveillance of journalists and members of Congress and their families discussed above is particularly concerning, all the more so given that these investigations were judicially authorized. As a result, there is now a House review of the surveillance of lawmakers and journalists, an internal Justice Department review of the surveillance, and a review by the inspector general for the DOJ.[202] The critical question is what Congress will eventually do with the information it receives. Will it stand up to executive branch overreach or will it once more defer to the executive branch, even when the security and privacy of its own members are concerned?

The surveillance of journalists and members of Congress suggests the need for congressional reform of the DOJ's investigatory powers as well as constraints on the willingness of federal judges to acquiesce to executive branch demands. Surveillance that targets domestic subjects, let alone government officials, is justified under the Constitution only under the most extraordinary of circumstances, notably where the target is being directly investigated for the commission of a crime and the methods of surveillance fully satisfy the subject's Fourth Amendment rights. Federal courts should be particularly parsimonious with authorizing surveillance of journalists, as such surveillance can easily infringe upon their First Amendment rights. Surveillance and other forms of interference with a free press will over time prove particularly damaging to democratic governance.

## Conclusion

The CERL/CREW working group concluded that Donald Trump's Department of Justice "compromised the interests of the United States and jeopardized our national security by failing to enforce the law evenhandedly."[203] At a minimum, the department undermined public confidence by creating the perception that the law was being used as a political tool to support the reelection of the president. In some cases, the working group concluded, Attorney General Barr went so far as to violate rules of professional conduct and government ethics rules. The working group also expressed great concern about lack of congressional oversight of the DOJ and refusal of the attorney general to cooperate with Congress.[204]

Barr's leadership of the DOJ provided a test case for the ability of the department to withstand political pressure from the White House, allowing for an evaluation of whether adequate protections are in place to guard against the politicization of the department's core functions. The Trump DOJ failed that test miserably, thus exposing weaknesses in the current legal framework by which the department functions. In the case of Barr, who substantially shared the president's autocratic view of presidential power, the constraints that the DOJ observed were too often based on political consequences rather than a sense of duty or fidelity to the law.[205] This suggests that the current guardrails that are in place to ensure that DOJ conforms to the rule of law are inadequate to protect against the destructive force of an attorney general who views his or her own extensive authority as flowing from a nearly unbounded view of presidential power.

Congress needs to be more assertive in exercising its authority under Article I to oversee the conduct of the DOJ and other executive branch agencies and departments.[206] Although Article II puts these agencies and departments under the authority of the president, Congress sets their budget.[207] Congress should use the power of the purse to assure greater accountability from the DOJ. This includes requiring regular testimony from the attorney general before Congress and compliance with congressional subpoenas.[208] At a minimum, the elected representatives who decide disbursement of public funds are entitled to information on how that money is being spent by executive branch agencies, including the DOJ, and as part of the budgetary process, Congress should make sure that information is provided.

During the Trump administration, the DOJ transitioned from a department that regarded itself as bound by the rule of law to a department that treated law as a tool for achieving political ends and that treated adherence to law as optional. Using law as a weapon against political enemies poses a lasting threat, both to the integrity of the DOJ and to the United States' ability to protect democracy against erosion due to weakening moral and legal standards.[209] The American people can no longer afford to rely on the softer constraints of conscience or political opprobrium to constrain an attorney general intent on abusing her or his authority. It is time for a second major reform effort, in the spirit of the Levi-Bell reforms, to return the Department of Justice to being a champion of the rule of law, and to restore confidence in the impartiality of its operations and comparable independence from White House political pressures.

## Notes

1. "About DOJ," U.S. Department of Justice, www.justice.gov/about.

2. Jonathan Greenberg, "Twelve Signs Trump Would Try to Run a Fascist Dictatorship in a Second Term," *Washington Post*, July 10, 2020, www.washingtonpost.com /outlook/fascist-dictatorship-trump-second-term/2020/07/10/63fdd938-c166-11ea -b4f6-cb39cd8940fb_story.html.

3. The editor of this volume is the cofounder and former board chair of Citizens for Responsibility and Ethics in Washington (CREW), and one of the coauthors of this chapter also previously served on its board. Neither is currently associated with the organization.

4. CERL and CREW, *Report on the Department of Justice and the Rule of Law Under the Tenure of Attorney General William Barr,* University of Pennsylvania Center for Ethics and the Rule of Law, October 12, 2020, www.law.upenn.edu/live/files/10900 -report-on-the-doj-and-the-rule-of-law.

5. Ibid.

6. Ibid., p. 14.

7. See, e.g., George Croner, "What Durham Is Investigating and Why It Poses a Danger to U.S. Intelligence Analysis," Just Security, July 25, 2020, www.justsecurity. org/71647/what-durham-is-investigating-and-why-it-poses-a-danger-to-us-intelli gence-analysis. Croner was a member of the CERL/CREW working group and also authored a substantial portion of the discussion of this same topic in the CERL/CREW report above. See note 6.

8. The relevant committees are the Senate Judiciary Committee, the Senate Homeland Security Committee, and the Senate Finance Committee. See Karoun Demirjian, "Senate Republicans Accelerate Public Scrutiny of Trump-Russia Investi-

gation as Election Looms," *Washington Post,* September 29, 2020, www.washington
post.com/national-security/lindsey-graham-comey-fbi-russia/2020/09/29/0e6196a8
-0276-11eb-b7ed-141dd88560ea_story.html.

9. Jordain Carney, "GOP Votes to Give Chairman Authority to Subpoena Obama
Officials," *The Hill,* June 4, 2020, https://thehill.com/homenews/senate/501106-senate
-homeland-security-panel-approves-subpoenas-of-obama-officials; see also Tim
Ryan, "Senate Targets Obama with Subpoena Vote, Putting Virus & Protests in Back
Seat," Courthouse News Service, June 4, 2020, www.courthousenews.com/senate
-targets-obama-with-in-subpoena-vote-putting-virus-protests-in-back-seat/.

10. See, e.g., Bob Christie, "U.S. Attorney General Barr Attacks Voting by Mail
While in Arizona," *PBS News Hour,* September 10, 2020, www.pbs.org/newshour/
nation/u-s-attorney-general-barr-attacks-voting-by-mail-while-in-arizona. Barr did
state after the election that there was no widespread election fraud.

11. Jonathan D. Karl, "How Barr Finally Turned on Trump," *Atlantic,* June 27, 2021,
www.theatlantic.com/politics/archive/2021/06/william-barrs-trump-administration
-attorney-general/619298/.

12. Norman Eisen and Donald Ayer, "William Barr's Resignation Is One Final
Parting Shot to the Rule of Law," *Washington Post,* December 15, 2020, www.washing
tonpost.com/outlook/2020/12/15/barr-resignation-rule-law/.

13. See Kaelan Deese, "Trump: Barr Was 'Unable' to Hold Kavanaugh Accusers and
Steele Dossier Sources 'Accountable,'" *Washington Examiner,* July 11, 2021, www.wash
ingtonexaminer.com/news/barr-was-unable-to-hold-kavanaugh-accusers-steele-dos
sier-sources-accountable; Mark Hosenball, "U.S. Ethics Groups Say Barr Uses DOJ as
Political Tool, Calls for His Impeachment," Reuters, October 12, 2020, www.reuters
.com/article/us-usa-justice-barr/u-s-ethics-groups-say-barr-uses-doj-as-political-tool
-call-for-his-impeachment-idUSKBN26X2RS.

14. Josh Dawsey and Devlin Barrett, "As Trump Pushed for Probes of 2020 Election, He Called Acting AG Rosen Almost Daily," *Washington Post,* July 28, 2021, www
.washingtonpost.com/national-security/trump-rosen-election-calls/2021/07/28/4310
6ab6-efd6-11eb-bf80-e3877d9c5f06_story.html.

15. Charlie Savage, "Barr Makes Durham a Special Counsel in a Bid to Entrench
Scrutiny of the Russia Inquiry," *New York Times,* December 1, 2020, www.nytimes.com
/2020/12/01/us/politics/john-durham-special-counsel-russia-investigation.html.

16. Michael Balsamo and Eric Tucker, "Barr Appoints Special Counsel in Russia
Probe Investigation," AP News, December 1, 2020, https://apnews.com/article/election
-2020-donald-trump-robert-mueller-statutes-elections-ae0275b4eb23981c1e6fbf9fc
49c3239.

17. Neal Katyal, "I Wrote the Special Counsel Rules. Barr Has Abused Them," *New
York Times,* December 3, 2020, www.nytimes.com/2020/12/03/opinion/bill-barr-john
-durham-prosecutor.html.

18. Ibid.

19. Kevin Breuninger and Dan Mangan, "Trump Fumes When Told Durham Probe

Findings Might Not Come Out Before Election Day," CNBC, October 9, 2020, www .cnbc.com/2020/10/09/trump-fumes-when-told-durham-probe-findings-might-not -come-out-before-election-day.html.

20. Aruna Viswanatha and Sadie Gurman, "Durham Probe of What Sparked Russia Investigation Examines FBI Tipsters," *Wall Street Journal*, August 13, 2021, www.wsj.com/articles/durham-probe-of-what-sparked-russia-investigation-exam ines-fbi-tipsters-11628857851.

21. *Citizens for Responsibility and Ethics in Washington* v. *U.S. Department of Justice*, No. 19-1552, 2021 WL 1749763 (D.D.C. 2021).

22. *Electronic Privacy Information Center* v. *United States Department of Justice*, No. 19-810, at 145 (D.D.C. 2020), and *Jason Leopold and Buzzfeed, Inc.*, v. *United States Department of Justice, et al.*, 487 F. Supp. 3d 1 (D.D.C. 2020), https://int.nyt.com/data/docu menthelper/6805-judge-walton-ruling-on-barr-cr/2df9b5c6d7de0fef1e35/optimized/ full.pdf#page=1.

23. Devlin Barrett, "Trump Justice Department Secretly Obtained Post Reporters' Phone Records, " *Washington Post,* May 8, 2021, www.washingtonpost.com/national -security/trump-justice-dept-seized-post-reporters-phone-records/2021/05/07/933cd fc6-af5b-11eb-b476-c3b287e52a01_story.html.

24. Katie Benner and others, "Hunting Leaks, Trump Officials Focused on Demo-crats in Congress," *New York Times,* June 10, 2021, www.nytimes.com/2021/06/10/us/ politics/justice-department-leaks-trump-administration.html.

25. Jack Fuller, ed., *Restoring Justice: The Speeches of Attorney General Edward H. Levi* (University of Chicago Press, 2013).

26. David Frank Levi and others, "Restoring Justice: The Legacy of Edward H. Levi," American Academy of Arts and Sciences, 2014, www.amacad.org/news/restoring -justice-legacy-edward-h-levi.

27. Ibid.; David Leonhardt, "The Sense of Justice That We're Losing," *New York Times*, April 29, 2018, www.nytimes.com/2018/04/29/opinion/the-sense-of-justice -that-were-losing.html; "The Attorney General's Guidelines," Electronic Privacy In-formation Center, https://epic.org/privacy/fbi/.

28. Edward H. Levi, Attorney General of the United States, "Farewell Remarks before the Employees of the U.S. Department of Justice," January 17, 1977, www. justice.gov/sites/default/files/ag/legacy/2011/08/23/01-17-1977.pdf.

29. Griffin B. Bell and Ronald J. Ostrow, *Taking Care of the Law* (Mercer University Press, 1986).

30. CERL/CREW, *Report on the Department of Justice*, p. 20.

31. "Memorandum from Donald F. McGahn II, Counsel to the President, to all White House Staff," Politico, January 27, 2017, www.politico.com/f/?id=0000015a -dde8-d23c-a7ff-dfef4d530000. Restrictions on communication between DOJ and the White House have been reissued under the Biden administration. See Josh Gerstein, "Justice Department Issues Policy Limiting White House Contact," Politico, July 21,

2021, www.politico.com/news/2021/07/21/justice-white-house-contact-biden-trump
-500476.

32. Ibid.

33. CERL/CREW, *Report on the Department of Justice.*

34. See, e.g., Claire Finkelstein and Stephen N. Xenakis, "Repairing the Damage from Illegal Acts of State: The Costs of Failed Accountability for Torture," in *Interrogation and Torture,* edited by Steven J. Barela and others (Oxford University Press, 2020), p. 49; "A Guide to the Torture Memos," *New York Times,* https://archive.nytimes .com/www.nytimes.com/ref/international/24MEMO-GUIDE.html?. See also Richard W. Painter, *Getting the Government America Deserves: How Ethics Reform Can Make a Difference* (Oxford University Press, 2009), p. 130–32.

35. Jeffrey Rosen, "Conscience of a Conservative," *New York Times Magazine,* September 9, 2007, www.nytimes.com/2007/09/09/magazine/09rosen.html; Ariane de Vogue, "DOJ Releases Controversial 'Torture Memos,'" ABC News, April 15, 2009, https://abcnews.go.com/Politics/LawPolitics/story?id=7343497&page=1.

36. See Mike Gallagher, "Domenici Sought Iglesias Ouster," *Albuquerque Journal,* April 15, 2007, www.abqjournal.com/news/special/554986nm04-15-07.htm.

37. Office of the Inspector General and Office of Personal Responsibility, U.S. Department of Justice, *An Investigation into the Removal of Nine U.S. Attorneys in 2006* (September 2008), www.justice.gov/opr/page/file/1206601/download; Dan Eggen and Amy Goldstein, "Voter-Fraud Complaints by GOP Drove Dismissals," *Washington Post,* May 14, 2007, www.washingtonpost.com/wp-dyn/content/article/2007/05/13/AR 2007051301106.html.

38. Steven Lee Myers and Philip Shenon, "Embattled Attorney General Resigns," *New York Times,* August 27, 2007, www.nytimes.com/2007/08/27/washington/27cnd -gonzales.html.

39. David Johnston, "Attorney General Seeks Resignations from Prosecutors," *New York Times,* March 24, 1993, www.nytimes.com/1993/03/24/us/attorney-general -seeks-resignations-from-prosecutors.html.

40. Office of Legal Counsel, "Authority to Use Military Force in Libya," Memorandum Opinion for the Attorney General, April 1, 2011, https://fas.org/irp/agency/doj/olc /libya.pdf.

41. Charlie Savage, "First Justice Department Memo on Killing Anwar Al-Awlaki," *New York Times,* August 15, 2014, www.nytimes.com/interactive/2014/08/16/us/ 16firstolcawlakimemo.html. A summary of the memo was first leaked by NBC News in 2014.

42. CERL/CREW, *Report on the Department of Justice,* pp. 78–80.

43. Maggie Haberman, William K. Rashbaum, and Nicole Hong, "Michael Cohen Returned to Jail in Dispute Over Trump Book," *New York Times,* August 13, 2020, www .nytimes.com/2020/07/09/nyregion/michael-cohen-arrested.html.

44. Charlie Savage and Katie Benner, "Trump Administration Secretly Seized

Phone Records of Times Reporters," *New York Times*, June 3, 2021, www.nytimes.com /2021/06/02/us/trump-administration-phone-records-times-reporters.html; Adam Goldman, "Trump's Justice Dept. Seized CNN Reporter's Email and Phone Records," *New York Times*, May 20, 2021, www.nytimes.com/2021/05/20/us/politics/cnn-trump -barbara-starr.html.

45. Benner and others, "Trump Officials Focused on Democrats in Congress."

46. Ryan Lucas, "DOJ Subpoenaed Apple for Data on Trump White House Lawyer," NPR, June 13, 2021, www.npr.org/2021/06/13/1006082436/doj-subpoenaed-apple-for -data-on-trump-white-house-lawyer.

47. CERL/CREW, *Report on the Department of Justice*, pp. 128–130.

48. Ibid., 138–146.

49. Ibid., 146–147.

50. Ibid., 95–100.

51. "Full Document: Trump's Call with the Ukrainian President," *New York Times*, October 30, 2019, www.nytimes.com/interactive/2019/09/25/us/politics/trump -ukraine-transcript.html.

52. Finkelstein and Xenakis, "Repairing the Damage," p. 49.

53. CERL/CREW, *Report on the Department of Justice*, p. 8.

54. Office of Legal Counsel, "January 2020 Airstrike in Iraq against Qassem Soleimani," Memorandum for John A. Eisenberg, Legal Advisor to the National Security Council, March 10, 2020, https://s3.documentcloud.org/documents/21012045/redacted -olc-memo-justification-of-soleimani-strike.pdf.

55. Ibid., pp. 8–9.

56. See Claire Finkelstein, "Vindicating the Rule of Law: Prosecuting Free Riders on Human Rights," in *When Governments Break the Law: The Rule of Law and the Prosecution of the Bush Administration,* edited by Austin Sarat and Nasser Hussein (New York University Press, 2010).

57. Lesley Oelsner, "Mitchell, Haldeman, Ehrlichman Are Sentenced to 2½ to 8 Years, Mardian to 10 Months to 3 Years," *New York Times*, February 22, 1975, www.ny times.com/1975/02/22/archives/mitchell-haldeman-ehrlichman-are-sentenced-to-2 -to-8-years-mardian.html.

58. President Clinton signed the Rome treaty, but the agreement was never sent to the Senate for ratification. The Bush administration later withdrew support for the ICC, in effect nullifying President Clinton's signature to the treaty. Curtis A. Bradley, "U.S. Announces Intent Not to Ratify International Criminal Court Treaty," *American Society of International Law 7*, no. 7 (May 11, 2002), www.asil.org/insights/volume/7/ issue/7/us-announces-intent-not-ratify-international-criminal-court-treaty.

59. Maggie Jo Buchanan, Tom Jawetz, and Stephanie Wylie, "Promoting Accountability: State and Federal Officials Shouldn't Be Above the Law," Center for American Progress, December 17, 2020, www.americanprogress.org/issues/courts/reports/2020/ 12/17/493748/promoting-accountability-state-federal-officials-shouldnt-law/.

60. For an argument in favor of prosecution, see Claire Finkelstein and Michael

Lewis, "Should Bush Administration Lawyers be Prosecuted for Authorizing Torture?" *University of Pennsylvania Law Review (PENNumbra)* 158 (2010), p. 195.

61. David Johnston and Charlie Savage, "Obama Reluctant to Look into Bush Programs," *New York Times,* January 11, 2009, www.nytimes.com/2009/01/12/us/politics/12inquire.html.

62. The SSCI report was completed in 2012, yet it took two years for just the 500-plus page executive summary to be released in redacted form. Despite persistent requests by the chair of the report committee, Sen. Dianne Feinstein, the full report, totaling thousands of pages, has yet to be released. See Staff of S. Select Comm. on Intelligence, 113th Cong., *Study of the Central Intelligence Agency's Detention and Interrogation Program* (2014), www.congress.gov/congressional-report/113th-congress/senate-report/288/1.

63. Glenn Greenwald, "Obama's Justice Department Grants Final Immunity to Bush's CIA Torturers," *Guardian,* August 31, 2012, www.theguardian.com/commentisfree/2012/aug/31/obama-justice-department-immunity-bush-cia-torturer.

64. See Staff of S. Select Comm. on Intelligence, 113th Cong., *Study of the Central Intelligence Agency's Detention and Interrogation Program* (2014), www.congress.gov/congressional-report/113th-congress/senate-report/288/1; Pub. L. No. 108–375, § 1091, 118 Stat. 2068 (2004); "No More Excuses: A Roadmap to Justice for CIA Torture," Human Rights Watch, December 1, 2015, www.hrw.org/report/2015/12/01/no-more-excuses/roadmap-justice-cia-torture.

65. Jonathan Owen, "British Soldiers 'Face Prosecution' over 55 Iraq War Deaths," *Independent,* January 8, 2016, www.independent.co.uk/news/uk/home-news/british-soldiers-face-prosecution-over-55-iraq-war-deaths-a6803211.html; Owen Bowcott, "UK Military Investigating Hundreds of Alleged Abuses in Afghanistan," *Guardian,* September 22, 2016, www.theguardian.com/uk-news/2016/sep/22/uk-military-investigating-hundreds-of-alleged-abuses-in-afghanistan.

66. Mark Duell and Martin Robinson, "UK Soldiers Hit by War Crimes Claims Unlikely to Face Criminal Trials," *Daily Mail,* June 2, 2020, www.dailymail.co.uk/news/article-8379245/UK-soldiers-hit-war-crimes-claims-unlikely-face-criminal-trials.html; Luke Andrews, "No more British troops will be prosecuted over Afghanistan war crimes," *Daily Mail,* June 21, 2020, www.dailymail.co.uk/news/article-8444251/No-British-troops-prosecuted-alleged-war-crimes-Afghanistan.html.

67. Finkelstein, "Vindicating the Rule of Law."

68. Greenwald, "Bush's CIA Torturers."

69. "Nuremburg Trials," United States Holocaust Museum, last edited January 5, 2018, https://encyclopedia.ushmm.org/content/en/article/the-nuremberg-trials.

70. *Report of the International Law Commission,* UN General Assembly Official Records, 74th Sess., Supp. No. 10. U.N. Doc. A/74/10 (2019).

71. "Bybee, Jay S.," Federal Judicial Center, www.fjc.gov/history/judges/bybee-jay-s.

72. See "John Yoo," Faculty Profiles, Berkeley Law, www.law.berkeley.edu/our-faculty/faculty-profiles/john-yoo/.

73. See "Virtual Event: Is the President Trumping Constitutional Norms?" Heritage Foundation, August 3, 2020, www.heritage.org/the-constitution/event/virtual-event-the-president-trumping-constitutional-norms.

74. See Jeffrey Rosen, Kimberly Wehle, and John Yoo, "The Executive and the Rule of Law," *We the People*, podcast produced by the National Constitution Center, February 27, 2020, https://constitutioncenter.org/interactive-constitution/podcast/the-executive-and-the-rule-of-law.

75. "Visiting Scholar Profile for John Yoo," American Enterprise Institute, www.aei.org/profile/john-yoo/.

76. Glenn Kessler, "CIA Director Nominee Haspel and the Destruction of Interrogation Tapes: Contradictions and Questions," *Washington Post*, May 11, 2018, www.washingtonpost.com/news/fact-checker/wp/2018/05/11/cia-director-nominee-haspel-and-destruction-of-interrogation-tapes-contradictions-and-questions/. See also Claire Finkelstein and Steve Xenakis, "Lawyers Told Gina Haspel Torture Was Legal. But It Never Was," *New York Times*, May 9, 2018, www.nytimes.com/2018/05/09/opinion/gina-haspel-cia-torture.html.

77. See memorandum from Michael J. Morell, Deputy Director, Central Intelligence Agency, to the Director of the Central Intelligence Agency re: "Disciplinary Review Related to Destruction of Interrogation Tapes," republished in Mathew Kahn, "CIA Releases Memo on Haspel Involvement in Destruction of Tapes," *Lawfare*, April 20, 2018, www.lawfareblog.com/cia-releases-declassified-memo-haspel-involvement-destruction-tapes.

78. Ibid.

79. The issue might have been discussed by John Durham in his report on torture, but that report is still classified as of this writing.

80. Finkelstein and Xenakis, "Lawyers Told Gina Haspel Torture Was Legal."

81. Associated Press, "Gina Haspel Confirmed as CIA Director after Key Democrats Vote in Favor," *Guardian*, May 17, 2018, www.theguardian.com/us-news/2018/may/17/gina-haspel-cia-director-senate-vote.

82. Laura Pitter, "Delusion of Justice on CIA Torture," *The Hill*, December 14, 2015, thehill.com/blogs/congress-blog/262947-delusion-of-justice-on-cia-torture.

83. President Obama made the decision before the end of his term not to make the report public, but he did preserve it by including it in his presidential records. Josh Gerstein, "Obama Won't Declassify Senate 'Torture Report' Now, But Will Preserve It," Politico, December 12, 2016, www.politico.com/blogs/under-the-radar/2016/12/barack-obama-torture-report-declassify-preserve-232519.

84. Staff of S. Comm. on Armed Services, 110th Cong. Rep., *Inquiry into the Treatment of Detainees in U.S. Custody* (2008), https://media.npr.org/documents/2009/apr/senatereport.pdf.

85. Sheri Fink, James Risen, and Charlie Savage, "C.I.A. Torture Detailed in Newly Disclosed Documents," *New York Times*, January 19, 2017, www.nytimes.com/2017/01/19/us/politics/cia-torture.html.

86. See Geneva Conventions Relative to the Treatment of Prisoners of War art. 118-119, Aug. 12, 1949, 5 U.S.T. 3316, 75 U.N.T.S. 135.

87. There was a hearing in 2009. See *What Went Wrong: Hearing on Torture and the Office of Legal Counsel in the Bush Administration Before the S. Subcomm. on Administrative Oversight and the Courts of the S. Comm. of the Judiciary*, 111th Cong. (2009), https://fas.org/irp/congress/2009_hr/wrong.html.

88. See "Shortchanging Justice Carries High Price," Human Rights Watch, July 7, 2009, www.hrw.org/report/2009/07/07/selling-justice-short/why-accountability-matters-peace.

89. See Shalev Rolsman, "The Real Decline of OLC," Just Security, October 8, 2019, www.justsecurity.org/66495/the-real-decline-of-olc/. "After all, the more OLC unfailingly says 'Yes' to proposed executive action, the more the White House Counsel will be tempted to ask its view. Increased involvement might thus sometimes (but not always) be the result of reliably saying 'Yes'—conduct that is likely to decrease OLC's legitimacy."

90. Ibid. "In recent months, OLC has been on the frontlines defending some of the Trump Administration's most politically fraught policies. It approved President Trump's proclamation reallocating funds to pay for his long sought-after border wall. It was the legal face of the Secretary of Treasury's refusal to turn over President Trump's personal tax returns to Congress. It has provided the legal justification for some of the Trump White House's most extreme claims relating to executive privilege. And, most recently, it provided the public legal justification for the Trump Administration's initial refusal to turn over the Ukraine whistleblower complaint to Congress." See also Chris Smith, "'There Has Never Been Accountability': Ali Soufan on How the 9/11 Disinformation Campaign Paved the Way for Political Armageddon," *Vanity Fair*, September 8, 2020, www.vanityfair.com/news/2020/09/how-the-911 -disinformation-campaign-paved-the-way-for-political-armageddon.

91. Nicholas Wu, Kyle Cheney, Betsy Woodruff Swan, and Meridith Mcgraw, "Biden White House Waives Executive Privilege for Initial Set of Trump-Era Documents Sought by Jan. 6 Panel," Politico, October 8, 2021, www.politico.com/news/2021 /10/08/bannon-jan-6-subpoena-515681.

92. See *Citizens for Responsibility and Ethics in Washington v. U.S. Department of Justice*, Civ. No. 19-1522 (D.D.C. 2020), www.citizensforethics.org/wp-content/uploads /2021/05/show_public_doc.pdf; Claire O. Finkelstein and Richard W. Painter, "Biden Is Defending Trump's Sweeping View of Executive Power," *Washington Post*, May 29, 2021 (criticizing the DOJ's decision to appeal this order), www.washingtonpost.com/ politics/2021/06/03/daily-202-biden-is-guarding-some-trumps-big-secrets/.

93. See Claire O. Finkelstein and Richard W. Painter, "Why Is Merrick Garland's DOJ Covering for Trump?" *Slate*, June 3, 2021 (criticizing DOJ's continued assertion of executive privilege over Don McGahn's Congressional testimony), https://slate. com/news-and-politics/2021/06/don-mcgahn-testimony-trump-doj-interference. html.

94. See *U.S. House Judiciary Comm.* v. *McGahn*, 968 F.3d. 755 (D.C. Cir., 2020). The D.C. Circuit upheld the enforceability of the House subpoena and explicitly left open the question of whether portions of McGahn's potential testimony would be privileged.

95. *Black Lives Matter D.C., et al.* v. *Joseph R. Biden, Jr., President of the United States of America, et al.* (D.D.C., No. 20-1469, 2021), https://storage.courtlistener.com/recap/gov.uscourts.dcd.218706/gov.uscourts.dcd.218706.158.0.pdf. See also Celine Castronuovo, "DOJ Asks Judge to Dismiss Cases Against Trump, Barr for Lafayette Square Clearing," *The Hill*, May 29, 2021, https://thehill.com/regulation/court-battles/556077-doj-asks-judge-to-dismiss-cases-against-trump-barr-for-lafayette.

96. See Reply Brief of Appellant United States of America, filed June 7, 2021, in *Carroll* v. *Trump*, No. 20-3977 and 20-3978 (2nd Cir., 2021), http://cdn.cnn.com/cnn/2021/images/06/07/jean.carroll.pdf.

97. Ibid.

98. Joe Walsh, "DOJ Says It Won't Defend Mo Brooks in Jan. 6 Lawsuit from Eric Swalwell," *Forbes*, July 27, 2021, www.forbes.com/sites/joewalsh/2021/07/27/doj-says-it-wont-defend-mo-brooks-in-jan-6-lawsuit-from-eric-swalwell/?sh=425837a62b3a; Paul Figley, "Expert Backgrounder: The Westfall Act and Representative Brooks's Speech," Just Security, July 23, 2021, www.justsecurity.org/77561/expert-backgrounder-the-westfall-act-and-representative-brookss-speech/. Other encouraging signs of DOJ's attention to accountability include the investigation of and raid on Trump's former lawyer Rudy Giuliani, the prosecution of Trump friend and inaugural committee chair Tom Barrack, the decision to allow Trump administration officials to testify before Congress regarding the January 6 insurrection and Trump's conduct leading up to it, and of course the prosecution of over 600 of the insurrectionists as of this writing; see also Norman Eisen and Donald Ayer, "Merrick Garland Is Doing More to Hold Trump Accountable than It Appears," *Washington Post*, July 28, 2021, www.washingtonpost.com/outlook/2021/07/28/garland-brooks-jan-6-immunity/.

99. See Robert S. Mueller III, U.S. Department of Justice, *Report on the Investigation into Russian Interference in the 2016 Presidential Election*, vol II, at p. 211, March 2019, www.justice.gov/storage/report_volume2.pdf.

100. Ibid.

101. "Letter from William P. Barr, Attorney General, U.S. Department of Justice, to Sen. Lindsey Graham, Sen. Dianne Feinstein, Sen. Jerrold Nadler, and Sen. Doug Collins," March 24, 2019, https://assets.documentcloud.org/documents/5779688/AG-March-24-2019-Letter-to-House-and-Senate.pdf.

102. "Letter from Robert S. Mueller III, Special Counsel, to William P. Barr, U.S. Attorney General," March 27, 2019, https://assets.documentcloud.org/documents/5984410/Mueller-letter-to-Barr.pdf.

103. *EPIC*, No. 19-810, at 145, and *Leopold*, at 487 F. Supp. 3d 1.

104. *Citizens for Responsibility and Ethics in Washington*, No. 19-1552.

105. Robert S. Mueller III, U.S. Department of Justice, *Report on the Investigation*

*into Russian Interference in the 2016 Presidential Election,* vol. II, p. 1 (March 2019), www .justice.gov/storage/report_volume2.pdf.

106. Claire O. Finkelstein and Richard W. Painter, "Presidential Accountability and the Rule of Law: Can the President Claim Immunity If He Shoots Someone on Fifth Avenue?" *University of Pennsylvania Journal of Constitutional Law* 24, no. 1 (2021), https://ssrn.com/abstract=3879702.

107. *Trump* v. *Vance,* 591 U.S. __ (2020).

108. "Recognizing an immunity from prosecution for a sitting President would not preclude such prosecution once the President's term is over or he is otherwise removed from office by resignation or impeachment." *A Sitting President's Amenability to Indictment and Criminal Prosecution,* 24 Op. O.L.C. 222, 255 (2000), www.justice.gov/ sites/default/files/olc/opinions/2000/10/31/op-olc-v024-p0222_0.pdf.

109. Barry H. Berke, Noah Bookbinder, and Norman Eisen, "Presidential Obstruction of Justice: The Case of Donald J. Trump," Brookings Institution, August 22, 2018, www.brookings.edu/research/presidential-obstruction-of-justice-the-case-of-donald -j-trump-2nd-edition/; Quinta Jurecic, "Obstruction of Justice in the Mueller Report: A Heat Map," *Lawfare,* April 21, 2019, www.lawfareblog.com/obstruction-justice -mueller-report-heat-map.

110. 18 U.S.C. § 1512(c)(2). See Robert S. Mueller III, "Executive Summary to Volume II," pp. 3–7 (2019), www.snopes.com/uploads/2019/05/Mueller-Summary-Vol ume-II.pdf.

111. Mikhaila Fogel and Benjamin Wittes, "Bill Barr's Very Strange Memo on Obstruction of Justice," *Lawfare,* December 20, 2018, www.lawfareblog.com/bill-barrs -very-strange-memo-obstruction-justice.

112. See Shalev Roisman, "The Real Decline of OLC," Just Security, October 8, 2019, www.justsecurity.org/66495/the-real-decline-of-olc, discussing OLC's involvement with Trump reallocating funds to pay for a border wall, the Treasury secretary's refusal to turn over President Trump's personal tax returns to Congress, expansive claims by the White House to executive privilege, and the refusal to turn over the Ukraine whistleblower complaint to Congress.

113. Louis Charbonneau, "U.S. Drone Strikes Violate Pakistan's Sovereignty: U.N.," Reuters, March 15, 2013, www.reuters.com/article/us-un-drones/u-s-drone -strikes-violate-pakistans-sovereignty-u-n-idUSBRE92E0Y320130315; ACLU, Human Rights Watch, National Immigrant Justice Center, *Justice-Free Zones: U.S. Immigration Detention Under the Trump Administration,* April 2020, www.hrw.org/sites/default/files /supporting_resources/justice_free_zones_immigrant_detention.pdf.

114. Exec. Order No. 9066, 7 Fed. Reg. 1407 (Feb. 19, 1942), www.archives.gov/ historical-docs/todays-doc/?dod-date=219; Japanese-American Evacuation Claims Act of 1948, Pub. L. No. 80–886, 62 Stat. 1231.

115. *Korematsu* v. *United States,* 323 U.S. 214 (1944). A formal apology for the internment and partial reparations for interned Japanese Americans did not begin until President Reagan signed the Civil Liberties Act of 1988, Pub. L. No. 100–383, 102 Stat. 904.

116. Chief Justice Roberts wrote, "The dissent's reference to *Korematsu*, however, affords this Court the opportunity to make express what is already obvious: *Korematsu* was gravely wrong the day it was decided, has been overruled in the court of history, and—to be clear—'has no place in law under the Constitution.'" *Trump* v. *Hawaii*, 585 U.S. ___ (2018) (Jackson, J., dissenting) (quoting *Korematsu*, 323 U.S. at 248). The majority opinion in *Hawaii* nonetheless refused to enter an injunction against Presidential Proclamation No. 9645, 82 Fed. Reg. 45, 161 (Sept. 24, 2017) which had banned entry immigration from seven predominantly Muslim countries.

117. See Dorothy Samuels, "At Last, Some Justice for Torture Victims," Brennan Center for Justice, October 2, 2017, www.brennancenter.org/our-work/analysis -opinion/last-some-justice-torture-victims.

118. United Nations Convention against Torture and Other Cruel, Inhuman or Degrading Treatment or Punishment, art. 14 (Dec. 10, 1984), 1465 U.N.T.S. 113.

119. See Fionnuala Ní Aoláin, "What Is the Remedy for American Torture?" Just Security, November 25, 2014, www.justsecurity.org/17720/remedy-american-torture/. "A starting point to addressing why the United States has an obligation of reparations is to recall why remedies exist for human rights violations under international treaty law. Reparations exist because they provide a concrete means to show a desire for non-repetition, to give redress to persons who have been harmed and to individually confirm meaningful condemnation in the aftermath of grievous harm to a human being."

120. Terri Moon Cronk, "Biden Announces Full U.S. Troop Withdrawal from Afghanistan by Sept. 11," U.S. Department of Defense News, April 14, 2021, www.defense .gov/Explore/News/Article/Article/2573268/biden-announces-full-us-troop-withdrawal -from-afghanistan-by-sept-11/; Ellen Knickmeyer, "Biden Ending US Support for Saudi-Led Offensive in Yemen," AP News, February 4, 2021, https://apnews.com/article/biden -end-support-saudi-offenseive-yemen-b68f58493dbfc530b9fcfdb80a13098f.

121. Truth and Reconciliation Commission, www.justice.gov.za/trc/index.html.

122. Choe Sang-Hun, "Japan and South Korea Settle Dispute Over Wartime 'Comfort Women,'" *New York Times*, December 28, 2015, www.nytimes.com/2015/12/29/ world/asia/comfort-women-south-korea-japan.html.

123. Motoko Rich, "Japan Balks at Call for New Apology to South Korea Over 'Comfort Women,'" *New York Times*, January 12, 2018, www.nytimes.com/2018/01/12/ world/asia/japan-south-korea-comfort-women.html. A Korean judge has also entered an order that Japan pay reparations to the victims. See Choe Sang-Hun, "South Korean Court Orders Japan to Pay Reparations for Wartime Sexual Slavery," *New York Times*, January 7, 2021, www.nytimes.com/2021/01/07/world/asia/south-korea-comfort -women-japan.html.

124. Alexander Besant, "Chile Judges Apologize for Role in Pinochet Regime Abuses," *The World*, PRI, September 5, 2013, www.pri.org/stories/2013-09-05/chile -judges-apologize-role-pinochet-regime-abuses.

125. This was surely the case with Gina Haspel, who allegedly destroyed video-tapes of torture sessions, in violation of federal law, to protect the CIA. While the de-

struction of evidence was an issue at her confirmation hearing, she was likely so strongly supported by the intelligence circles in which she was influential because she was understood to be a "team player." See Finkelstein and Xenakis, "Lawyers Told Gina Haspel Torture Was Legal"; Nicholas Fandos, "Senate Confirms Gina Haspel to Lead C.I.A. Despite Torture Concerns," *New York Times*, May 17, 2018, www.nytimes. com/2018/05/17/us/politics/haspel-confirmed.html?searchResultPosition=17.

126. CERL/CREW, *Report on the Department of Justice*, pp. 175–79.

127. In the past fifty years, two presidents have been impeached by the House (one of them impeached twice) and one president has resigned under threat of impeachment. Tara Law, "What to Know about the U.S. Presidents Who've Been Impeached," *Time*, January 13, 2021, https://time.com/5552679/impeached-presidents.

128. H. Comm. on Oversight and Reform, "House Democrats Introduce Landmark Reforms Package, the Protecting Our Democracy Act," press release, September 23, 2020, https://oversight.house.gov/news/press-releases/house-democrats-introduce -landmark-reforms-package-the-protecting-our-democracy.

129. Ethics in Government Act of 1978, Pub. L. No. 95–521, 92 Stat. 1824. Title VI amended Title 28 of the United States Code to provide for the independent counsel. Title VI expired in June 1999.

130. See, e.g., Claire O. Finkelstein and Richard W. Painter, "The 'Friday Night Massacre' Spells the Downfall of William Barr," *Newsweek*, June 23, 2020, www. newsweek.com/friday-night-massacre-spells-downfall-william-barr-opinion-1512935, discussing the sudden firing of Geoffrey Berman, the U.S. Attorney for the Southern District of New York, in the middle of several investigations that were politically and personally sensitive to President Trump.

131. *Morrison* v. *Olson*, 487 U.S. 654 (1988).

132. Ibid., at 686.

133. Ibid., at 699, citing Federalist No. 51, p. 321 (J. Madison).

134. *Myers* v. *United States*, 272 U.S. 52 (1926).

135. Linda Qiu, "Did Trump Fire Comey Over the Russia Inquiry or Not?" *New York Times*, May 31, 2018, www.nytimes.com/2018/05/31/us/politics/fact-check-trump -fire-comey-russia.html.

136. *Myers*, 272 U.S., at 117.

137. *Humphrey's Executor* v. *United States*, 295 U.S. 602 (1935).

138. Ibid., at 626-628.

139. *Free Enterprise Fund* v. *Public Company Accounting Oversight Board*, 561 U.S. 477 (2010).

140. *Seila Law LLC* v. *Consumer Financial Protection Bureau*, 591 U.S. ___ (2020).

141. This view runs into some difficulty because of a recent case, *Seila Law* v. *CFPB*, which held that the Constitution does not permit Congress to create nonremovable positions in other areas of the executive branch, as that would infringe on the president's Article II powers and violate the necessary separation between Congress and the executive branch. We believe *Seila Law* is distinguishable, however. The policy-

making role of the CFPB director is very different from the narrow, case-specific focus of the investigatory and prosecutorial functions of an independent counsel.

142. Bob Bauer and Jack Goldsmith, *After Trump: Reconstructing the Presidency,* (Lawfare Institute 2020), proposing changes to internal DOJ regulations but not statutory controls on prosecutorial functions similar to the 1978 independent counsel statute. For a critique of Bauer and Goldsmith's approach, see William G. Howell and Terry M. Moe, "Reforming the Presidency: How Far is Far Enough," *Judicature* 104, no. 3 (Fall/Winter 2020–2021), https://judicature.duke.edu/articles/reforming-the-presi dency-how-far-is-far-enough/. Bauer and Goldsmith "see serious downsides to having executive officials and agencies that are securely insulated from presidential control— worrying that they will go rogue (as, for example, many think independent counsel Kenneth Starr did)—and they put great stock in the political accountability allegedly gained when presidents and their appointees have almost total control over the executive branch, its officials, and its operations."

143. "Project on the Independent Counsel Statute, Report and Recommendations," American Enterprise Institute and Brookings Institution, May 1999, www. brookings.edu/wp-content/uploads/2016/06/icreport.pdf.

144. Ibid., p. 10.

145. See S. 1735 (Graham-Booker) and S. 1741 (Tillis-Coons) on providing job protections for the special counsel. See also "Booker, Graham, Coons, Tillis Introduce Merged Legislation, The Special Counsel Independence and Integrity Act," press release from the office of Sen. Cory Booker, April 11, 2018, www.booker.senate.gov/news /press/booker-graham-coons-tillis-introduce-merged-legislation-the-special-counsel -independence-and-integrity-act.

146. See testimony of Akhil Reed Amar before the United States Senate Committee on the Judiciary, September 26, 2017, www.judiciary.senate.gov/imo/media/doc/09 -26-17%20Amar%20Testimony.pdf, stating, among other things, that a proposed bill protecting Mueller from being fired by Trump would be unconstitutional and that *Morrison* v. *Olson* had been wrongly decided.

147. See *EPIC,* No. 19-810; and *Leopold,* 19-957, Memorandum and Opinion, at 19. "The inconsistencies between Attorney General Barr's statements, made at a time when the public did not have access to the redacted version of the Mueller Report to assess the veracity of his statements, and portions of the redacted version of the Mueller Report that conflict with those statements cause the Court to seriously question whether Attorney General Barr made a calculated attempt to influence public discourse about the Mueller Report in favor of President Trump despite certain findings in the redacted version of the Mueller Report to the contrary."

148. The AEI-Brookings report (above) at p. 18, also recommended that the attorney general be required to report to Congress to explain removal of a special counsel.

149. See, e.g., Claire Finkelstein and Richard Painter, "Bloomberg Insights, Trump's Unitary Executive Theory Meets Cyrus Vance on Fifth Avenue," Bloomberg,

July 17, 2020, https://news.bloomberglaw.com/us-law-week/insight-trumps-unitary-executive-theory-meets-cyrus-vance-on-fifth-avenue.

150. Mueller, *2016 Presidential Election*, vol. II, p. 169.

151. This is the topic discussed in volume II of the Mueller report and a topic that we also address in a separate law review article. Even if the firing of a prosecutor is within the purported powers of the president under Article II of the Constitution or the powers delegated by the president to another officer of the executive branch, that power cannot lawfully be used to obstruct justice in an ongoing investigation.

152. Todd Garvey, *Congressional Subpoenas: Enforcing Executive Branch Compliance*, Congressional Research Service, R45653 (2019), https://crsreports.congress.gov/product/pdf/R/R45653.

153. See Kessler, "CIA Destruction of Interrogation Tapes."

154. Criminal statutes implicated by destruction of government records include 18 USC § 641 (public money, property, or records), 18 USC § 1361 (government property or contracts), 18 USC § 2071 (concealment, removal, or mutilation generally), 18 USC § 793 (gathering, transmitting, or losing defense information), and 18 USC § 1512 (tampering with a witness, a victim, or an informant). See Richard W. Painter, "Destroying Federal Documents During a Presidential Transition Is a Federal Crime," Just Security, November 5, 2020, www.justsecurity.org/73265/destroying-federal-documents-during-a-presidential-transition-is-a-federal-crime/.

155. See "Fired U.S. Attorneys: A Who's Who," NPR, April 15, 2007, www.npr.org/templates/story/story.php?storyId=7777925; Tierney Sneed and Manu Raju, "Former U.S. Attorney Tells Investigators He Quit Because He Heard Trump Was Considering Firing Him," CNN, August 11, 2021, www.cnn.com/2021/08/11/politics/pak-trump-georgia-election-testimony/index.html.

156. Saikrishna Prakash, "Removal and Tenure in Office," *Virginia Law Review* 92, no. 8 (2006), pp. 1779–1852, https://papers.ssrn.com/sol3/papers.cfm?abstract_id=889378. See also discussion of the Supreme Court's holding in *Myers* and *CFPB* above.

157. See Pratin Vallabhaneni, "U.S. Supreme Court Rules CFPB's Leadership Structure is Unconstitutional But Leaves CFPB Intact," White & Case, July 8, 2020, www.whitecase.com/publications/alert/us-supreme-court-rules-cfpbs-leadership-structure-unconstitutional-leaves-cfpb.

158. *Vance*, 591 U.S. ___.

159. See "9-27.000—Principles of Federal Prosecution," U.S. Department of Justice, www.justice.gov/jm/jm-9-27000-principles-federal-prosecution.

160. See H. Comm. on Oversight and Reform, 116th Cong., *Policy and Supporting Positions* (2020), www.govinfo.gov/content/pkg/GPO-PLUMBOOK-2020/pdf/GPO-PLUMBOOK-2020.pdf; "3-4.000—Personnel Management," U.S. Department of Justice, www.justice.gov/jm/jm-3-4000-personnel-management.

161. See Troy Cribb, "Politicizing the Civil Service: How a New Executive Order Destabilizes the U.S. Government," Just Security, November 2, 2020, www.justsecurity

.org/73213/politicizing-the-civil-service-how-a-new-executive-order-destabilizes-the
-u-s-government/.

162. Presidents Obama, Trump, and Biden issued executive orders imposing additional ethics restrictions on presidential appointees in their administrations, but these restrictions are in addition to, and do not preempt, the federal statutes and Office of Government Ethics regulations that govern executive branch ethics from administration to administration.

163. H. Comm. on Oversight and Reform, 116th Cong., *Policy and Supporting Positions* (2020), www.govinfo.gov/content/pkg/GPO-PLUMBOOK-2020/pdf/GPO-PLUM BOOK-2020.pdf. Among the Trump executive orders that need to be rescinded by President Biden is one diminishing civil service job protections for career federal employees. See Cribb, "Politicizing the Civil Service."

164. Title VI, Section 603 of PODA remains unchanged in the version introduced in the 117th Congress. Title VI would mandate that the attorney general keep a log of specified communications between the White House and the DOJ. The communications would include correspondence relating to any investigation or litigation underway by the Department of Justice in any civil or criminal matter. The statute would require the attorney general to furnish the communications log to the DOJ inspector general every six months. The IG would be mandated by the statute to review the log and share with Congress any communications reflecting improper political interference or other inappropriate conduct. See H.R. 5314, 117th Congress (2021–2022), Title VI, § 603, www.congress.gov/bill/117th-congress/house-bill/5314.

165. A discussion about insulating inspectors general from political retribution is also included in chapter 2, this volume.

166. Robert Longley, "About the U.S. Inspectors General: The U.S. Government's Built-In Watchdogs," ThoughtCo., December 5, 2020, www.thoughtco.com/about-the -office-of-inspector-general-3322191#:~:text=A%20U.S.%20federal%20inspector% 20general,government%20procedures%20occurring%20within%20the.

167. "About the Office," Office of the Inspector General, U.S. Department of Justice, https://oig.justice.gov/about.

168. Melissa Quinn, "The Internal Watchdogs Trump Has Fired or Replaced," CBS News, May 19, 2020, www.cbsnews.com/news/trump-inspectors-general-internal -watchdogs-fired-list.

169. Charlie Savage, "Endorsing Trump's Firing of Inspector General, Barr Paints Distorted Picture," *New York Times*, April 10, 2020, www.nytimes.com/2020/04/10/us/ politics/barr-inspector-general-firing.html.

170. "About the Office," Office of the Inspector General.

171. *"Urgent Concern" Determination by the Inspector General of the Intelligence Community,* 43 Op. O.L.C. __ (2019), www.justice.gov/olc/opinion/file/1205711/download.

172. "Office of Professional Responsibility," U.S. Department of Justice, www. justice.gov/opr.

173. See "Jurisdiction and Relationship to the Office of Inspector General," Office

of Professional Responsibility, U.S. Department of Justice, June 5, 2019, www.justice
.gov/opr/jurisdiction-and-relationship-office-inspector-general, stating that the OPR
has exclusive jurisdiction over investigations of allegations of impropriety against
DOJ attorneys relating to exercise of their power to investigate, litigate, and provide
legal advice, and that the DOJ inspector general should refer such investigations to
OPR.

174. Inspector General Access Act of 2019, S. 685, 116th Cong. § 2.

175. 5 C.F.R. § 2635.502 (2020). This Office of Government Ethics rule is known as
the "impartiality regulation," but outside of very specific situations, mostly involving
former employers or family members of government officials, the rule depends upon
subjective assessment by government officials of their own bias. The rule also requires
similarly subjective determinations by their superiors, themselves also political appointees, who may grant "authorizations"—i.e. waivers.

176. This recommendation is also made in H.R. 1 and S. 1, which would amend the
U.S. Code to require any presidential appointee to recuse himself or herself from any
matter in which the president has a personal interest. Sen. Joe Manchin has indicated
support for this recommendation from the bill as well.

177. See Carrie Cordero, "Intelligence Transparency and Foreign Threats to Elections: Responsibilities, Risks, and Recommendations," Center for a New American
Security, July 23, 2020, www.cnas.org/publications/reports/intelligence-transparency
-and-foreign-threats-to-elections.

178. CERL/CREW, *Report on the Department of Justice*, pp. 37–45.

179. Ibid., pp. 14, 37. See also Jen Kirby, "'Obamagate': Trump's Latest Conspiracy
Theory, Explained," Vox, May 15, 2020, www.vox.com/2020/5/15/21257299/obamagate
-trump-flynn-unmasking-conspiracy.

180. Jeremy Herb, "GOP-Led Senate Panel Authorizes Subpoenas of Top Obama
Officials," CNN, June 11, 2020, www.cnn.com/2020/06/11/politics/subpoenas-obama
-officials-lindsey-graham/index.html.

181. Murray Waas, "How Trump and Barr's October Surprise Went Bust," *New
York Magazine*, November 2, 2020, https://nymag.com/intelligencer/2020/11/durham
-investigation-how-trumps-october-surprise-went-bust.html.

182. Office of the Inspector General, U.S. Department of Justice, *Review of Four
FISA Applications and Other Aspects of the FBI's Crossfire Hurricane Investigation* (2019),
p. iv, www.justice.gov/storage/120919-examination.pdf.

183. Office of the Inspector General, U.S. Department of Justice, *Report of Investigation of Former Federal Bureau of Investigation Director James Comey's Disclosure*
(2019), https://oig.justice.gov/reports/2019/o1902.pdf. See also Bauer and Goldsmith,
*After Trump*, p. 210.

184. Bauer and Goldsmith, *After Trump*, p. 209; U.S. Department of Justice, *Review
of Four FISA Applications*, pp. 410–11.

185. U.S. Department of Justice, *Review of Four FISA Applications*, p. iii.

186. Ibid., p. v.

187. Ibid., pp. viii–ix.

188. Ibid., p. vi.

189. "Trump says he is the victim of a politicized F.B.I. He says senior agents tried to rig the election by declining to prosecute Mrs. Clinton, then drummed up the Russia investigation to undermine his presidency. He has declared that a deeply rooted cabal—including his own appointees—is working against him." Matt Apuzzo, Adam Goldman, and Nicholas Fandos, "Code Name Crossfire Hurricane: The Secret Origins of the Trump Investigation," New York Times, May 16, 2018, www.nytimes.com/2018/05/16/us/politics/crossfire-hurricane-trump-russia-fbi-mueller-investigation.html.

190. U.S. Department of Justice, Review of Four FISA Applications, p. xix.

191. Ibid., pp. 410–14.

192. CERL/CREW, Report on the Department of Justice, pp. 57–58.

193. H.R. 1 and S. 1 also propose mechanisms to increase coordination between DOJ and ODNI, specifically requiring that the DNI and heads of offices of the federal government, including the AG, submit a joint report on foreign threats no later than 180 days before the date of the next federal election. Further, the bills require the president, DNI, AG, and other agency heads to issue a national strategy to protect the country's democratic institutions from threats. Finally, they establish a unit in the DOJ dedicated to FARA investigations, recommending that the AG consult with the DNI in investigations relating to foreign threats. The requirement of a joint report on foreign threats and the establishment of a unit within the DOJ dedicated to enforcing FARA is no longer found in the 117th Congress's version of the Freedom to Vote Act (2021–2022). S. 2747 does keep the proposed amendments to the FEC requiring disclosure of "reportable foreign contact," establishing a foreign contact reporting compliance system, and establishing criminal penalties for violation. See S. 2747, 117th Congress (2021–2022), 1st Sess., Division B, Title III, Subtitle I, §§ 3802–3806, www.congress.gov/bill/117th-congress/senate-bill/2747/text.

194. 22 U.S.C. § 611 et seq., discussed in detail in chapter 4 of this volume.

195. See 22 U.S.C. §§ 612–613.

196. Zachary B. Wolf and Sean O'Key, "The Trump-Ukraine Impeachment Inquiry Report, Annotated," CNN, December 3, 2019, www.cnn.com/interactive/2019/12/politics/trump-ukraine-impeachment-inquiry-report-annotated/; Andy Sullivan, "Barr Gives Top Priority to Investigating the Investigators of Russian Meddling," Reuters, October 1, 2019, www.reuters.com/article/us-usa-trump-whistleblower-barr-explaine/explainer-barr-gives-top-priority-to-investigating-the-investigators-of-russian-meddling-idUSKBN1WG4QZ.

197. See Mark Mazzetti and Katie Benner, "Trump Pressed Australian Leader to Help Barr Investigate Mueller Inquiry's Origins," New York Times, September 30, 2019, www.nytimes.com/2019/09/30/us/politics/trump-australia-barr-mueller.html.

198. Quoting Claire Finkelstein: "This story suggests that the president is continuing to use the authority of his office to pressure foreign leaders into assisting him

in covering up Russia's assistance with his 2016 victory. This is the same conduct for which Trump was impeached, and the reporting suggests that he is undeterred." See Erin Banco, "Barr Pressed Australia for Help on Mueller Review as DOJ Worked to Free its Hostages," *Daily Beast*, June 16, 2020, www.thedailybeast.com/bill-barr -pressed-australia-for-help-on-mueller-review-as-doj-worked-to-free-its-hostages.

199. Eric Lipton and Benjamin Weiser, "Turkish Bank Case Shows Erdogan's Influence with Trump," *New York Times*, October 29, 2020, www.nytimes.com/2020/10/29/ us/politics/trump-erdogan-halkbank.html.

200. See Bureau of International Narcotics and Law Enforcement Affairs, U.S. Department of State, *International Narcotics Control Strategy Report: Money Laundering* (March 2020), www.state.gov/wp-content/uploads/2020/03/Tab-2-INCSR-Vol-2 -508.pdf.

201. "Criminal Resource Manual," U.S. Department of Justice, January 22, 2020, www.justice.gov/archives/jm/criminal-resource-manual-276-treaty-requests.

202. Benjamin Swasey, "A House Panel Will Investigate Trump DOJ Surveillance of Lawmakers and Journalists," NPR, June 14, 2021, www.npr.org/2021/06/14/1006417 513/a-house-panel-will-investigate-trump-era-surveillance-by-the-department-of -justi; Matt Zapotosky, Felicia Sonmez, and Karoun Demirjian, "Justice Dept. Watchdog to Probe Trump-Era Leak Investigations, Including Secret Subpoenas for Data from Congress, Journalists," *Washington Post*, June 11, 2021, www.washingtonpost. com/powerpost/trump-justice-department-democrats-congress/2021/06/11/7c2b1aa8 -cace-11eb-a11b-6c6191ccd599_story.html.

203. CERL/CREW, *Report on the Department of Justice*, p. 168.

204. Ibid., pp. 168–69.

205. Ibid.

206. See Christopher M. Davis, Todd Garvey, and Ben Wilhelm, Cong. Rsch. Serv., RL30240, *Congressional Oversight Manual* (2020), https://fas.org/sgp/crs/misc/RL30 240.pdf.

207. U.S. Const. art. II; "Budget of the U.S. Government," USA.gov, October 26, 2021, www.usa.gov/budget#:~:text=Each%20year%2C%20Congress%20works%20on ,includes%20a%20detailed%20spending%20plan.

208. "FY 2021 Congressional Budget Submission," U.S. Department of Justice, www.justice.gov/doj/fy-2021-congressional-budget-submission.

209. CERL/CREW, *Report on the Department of Justice*, p. 8.

# 4

# Protecting Democracy Against Foreign Interference

## CLAIRE O. FINKELSTEIN

The era of Donald Trump was a dangerous one from the standpoint of foreign interference with U.S. politics. Russian attempts to influence U.S. democracy were highly impactful in the run up to the 2016 presidential election, when Russian social media propaganda, as well as Russian hacking into sensitive Democratic Party sites, played a major role in Trump's victory. Indeed, Trump signaled his dependence on the Kremlin in July 2016, when he famously remarked, "Russia, if you're listening—I hope you are able to find the 30,000 emails that are missing."[1] Though the Kremlin's efforts to repeat their victory failed in the 2020 presidential election, Russia has continued its attack on democracy, both in the United States and elsewhere around the globe.[2]

The danger of foreign interference in democratic governance seems to increase as other countries learn from Russia's example. China, North Korea, Saudi Arabia, and Iran[3] have mounted sophisticated cyber campaigns in recent years that display an evolving understanding of the power of social media and that prey on the weakness of U.S. cyber defenses. In the long run, advanced democracies will need to examine their own practices relating to free expression and the internet and weigh the benefits of having unfettered open expression on social media platforms against the vulnerabilities such platforms create. With their robust tradition of free speech, democratic nations are particularly subject to attack in cyberspace.[4] If democratic nations do not find a way to protect themselves against the dangers posed by social media, the very openness to differing viewpoints that makes democracies strong could ultimately prove to be their undoing.[5] In a world connected by social media and internet functionality, it may no longer be possible to remain internally open yet adequately guarded with respect to malign foreign actors.

This chapter reviews an important tool for combatting foreign interference within the United States: the Foreign Agents Registration Act (FARA). FARA addresses one aspect of foreign interference in U.S. democracy, namely the use of American citizens by foreign entities to lobby on their behalf with U.S. lawmakers and the American public. While the statute does not forbid such lobbying, it requires that any American engaging in political, legislative, or public relations activities on behalf of the foreign power do so openly, namely by registering with the Department of Justice (DOJ). A unit within the National Security Division (NSD) of the DOJ is tasked with enforcing this registration requirement.

Unfortunately, FARA enforcement has been less effective than it might have been, though recent efforts on the part of the DOJ, as well as Special Counsel Robert Mueller's office, have seen enhanced investigations and prosecutions under FARA and related provisions. A number of cases emerged from the foreign contacts of individuals in the Trump orbit. For example, the DOJ is currently investigating Trump's former counsel Rudy Giuliani for possible activity as an unregistered foreign agent of Ukraine. Trump friend Tom Barrack, who served as chair of Trump's 2017 inaugural committee, has been charged with conspiracy to act as an unregistered agent of the United Arab Emirates, an offense that is closely related to FARA. Trump's first National Security Advisor Michael Flynn was revealed to have accepted hundreds of thousands of dollars from the government of Turkey, yet he failed to register under FARA despite being warned that such registration was required. Ultimately Flynn was not charged with FARA violations, but the threat to charge him under FARA helped to secure his initial guilty plea of lying to investigators.[6] Other highly visible cases during the Trump era under FARA or related provisions include that of Elliot Broidy, a former top fundraiser for Trump who pled guilty to conspiring to violate foreign lobbying laws on behalf of Chinese and Malaysian interests. Similarly, Paul Manafort, Trump's former campaign manager, pled guilty to conspiring to defraud the United States in connection with failure to register under FARA as an agent of the government of Ukraine. And Manafort's one-time office-mate, W. Samuel Patten, pled guilty to violating FARA, once again based on Ukraine-related activity in the United States. Broidy, Flynn, and Manafort were all pardoned by Trump.[7]

This handful of high-profile prosecutions no doubt barely scratches the surface of the number of Americans lobbying on behalf of foreign governments, especially during the Trump years, yet it serves the purpose of drawing attention to FARA and its registration requirement. Challenges to bringing such prosecutions, however, have also drawn attention to the many problems with the current statute and have created momentum for bids to enact reform.[8] Experts rightly perceive that until the act is replaced or at least supplemented with more effective weapons in the battle against foreign influence, reform efforts must concentrate on making the existing statute more effective as a tool for fighting foreign interference. This chapter offers some suggestions for how that might be accomplished.

## Understanding the Foreign Agents Registration Act

Prior to the 2016 U.S. elections, few Americans had heard of FARA,[9] a disclosure statute originally passed in 1938 pursuant to the recommendations of a congressional committee investigating anti-American activities in the United States.[10] The statute was sparked by concerns about Nazi and Communist propaganda, particularly as introduced into circulation by Americans under the control of or acting in conjunction with foreign powers.[11] FARA was not designed to curb lobbying efforts on the part of foreign powers directly, but to ensure that the American people and U.S. policymakers know when political, legislative, and public relations are being carried out in furtherance of the interests of a foreign principal.[12] Transparency, as opposed to regulation, was the method chosen, as this would avoid the need to evaluate the motivations, aims, and content of foreign influence campaigns.[13] Americans who were found to be "foreign agents" as defined by the statute would need to register with the DOJ, and in this way their status as foreign agents would be publicly displayed for all to see.[14] FARA was passed in particular to forestall the use of American citizens to influence domestic public opinion while concealing the true source of the sponsoring entity.[15]

Recent cases, however, have shown just how ineffectual FARA is at combatting the use of propaganda in foreign covert operations in the United States and the weakness of the DOJ's tools for combatting foreign influence and cyber intrusions more generally.[16] Despite an increase in the enforcement efforts of DOJ's National Security Division,[17] there have been very few prosecutions brought on the basis of FARA violations and even fewer convictions. For example, a DOJ 2016 inspector general's report found that there were only seven prosecutions brought under FARA between 1966 and 2015.[18] The rare FARA violation that does come to the attention of DOJ enforcement generally results either in compliance on the part of the subjects or in an agreement that the subject does not need to register under the statute.[19] Where prosecutions take place, they are usually on the basis of false statements made to DOJ investigators in the course of a FARA investigation.[20] It should be noted that some enforcement of the registration statute takes place under a closely related statute, 18 U.S.C. § 951, which makes it a crime to act "as an agent of a foreign government without prior notification to the Attorney General," as required by DOJ regulations.[21]

Broadly speaking, there have been at least four impediments to making FARA an effective tool in fighting foreign interference. As discussed above, the first is the small number of prosecutions that DOJ has brought to enforce FARA over the years, which is at least in part a function of the statute's poor design. FARA requires voluntary disclosure of foreign lobbying efforts, and it contains no provision for civil investigation prior to filing litigation. This makes it all the more difficult to detect violators.[22] Unsurprisingly, the statute fails to motivate compliance and generates only minimal penalties for violators.

Second, there is the difficulty of bringing effective enforcement under the statute once an action has been initiated.[23] FARA enforcement actions have typically resulted in very few convictions, since a DOJ determination that someone is a foreign agent can usually be addressed through voluntary compliance, which blunts the deterrent effect of FARA-related prosecutions. Between 1938 and 1965, one source indicates that there were only nine reported completed cases and thirty-one indictments.[24]

Third, in addition to the foregoing problems with prosecution, several of the exemptions from the reporting requirements significantly limit the reach of the statute as well as undermine compliance. The Lobbying Disclosure Act (LDA) exemption, for example, allows agents of foreign principals to avoid registration under FARA if they are registered under the LDA. But the latter registration process is significantly more streamlined and involves less direct supervision than FARA does, and thus the LDA exemption weakens FARA enforcement.[25] Two additional exemptions that have weakened FARA's effectiveness are § 613(d)(1), which exempts anyone engaged in "private and nonpolitical activities," and § 613(e), which exempts persons engaged in "religious, scholastic, academic, or scientific pursuits or . . . the fine arts." Given the vagueness of these categories, and the paucity of cases interpreting the provisions, the weakness in enforcement has allowed foreign agents seeking to hide their activities a ready means to do so.[26] Almost by design, such loosely worded exemptions coupled with a voluntary compliance scheme are prone to exploitation.

Fourth, there are significant problems enforcing FARA due to lack of clarity regarding the scope of the act.[27] Indeed, the statute is so vaguely worded that there is a question of whether it violates a fundamental principle of due process and creates a constitutional problem of notice. As Judge Amy Berman Jackson noted in her dismissal of the second of the two charges against Skadden attorney Greg Craig, who was prosecuted by Robert Mueller because of work he allegedly did for the Ukrainian government without registering under FARA, the "rule of lenity" requires that vagueness in Congress's intent about who should fall within the scope of the statute gives the benefit of the doubt to the defendant.[28] (Craig was ultimately acquitted at trial.)

## How Effective Can FARA Be at Combating Foreign Influence?

Even with perfect legislative and prosecutorial efforts, however, FARA will always be a somewhat blunt instrument for fighting foreign influence, given the narrow focus of its aims. Foreign propaganda and lobbying by foreign entities have been persistent and seemingly intractable problems, but some of that does not depend on the assistance of U.S. persons in any respect. More significantly, foreign propaganda and lobbying are far from the only or even the most concerning forms of foreign influence the United States and other advanced democracies confront. Funding of right-wing candidates has also played a significant role in recent elections, as well as Russian funding of right-wing charitable organizations that wield significant power in issue-related politics. Thus, for example, Russian funding of far-right candidates was a significant factor in the 2018 French elections.[29] The far-right party of the "Front Nationale" in France received over $12 million in financing from a Russian bank starting in 2014—loans that eventually resulted in a lawsuit for repayment.[30] And the candidacies of both Jill Stein and Bernie Sanders in 2016 received a boost with Russian-funded social media campaigns on Facebook.[31] The National Rifle Association (NRA) reportedly has had close ties to Moscow, with entanglement involving the case of Maria Butina coming to light in a minority-led report by the Senate Finance Committee.[32] Nothing in FARA, even in the event of perfect compliance, would address the impact of foreign money in U.S. politics.[33]

Moreover, even if the focus is restricted to efforts to influence and manipulate public opinion and government officials, the role of propaganda from foreign governments in swaying U.S. elections and other political events is not entirely clear. As some scholars have concluded, the hack-and-dump strategies on the part of the Russians in the run-up to the 2016 election were at least as influential, if not more influential, in influencing the result of the election and controlling the public narrative as use of social media to convey disinformation.[34] And as the 2020 cyberattack on U.S. government websites through SolarWinds software makes clear, the greatest national security vulnerabilities come from covert operations involving cyber hacking, not propaganda.[35]

In some sense, this is as it should be, in that the topics of foreign propaganda through social media and foreign hacking into vulnerable governmental websites are entirely distinguishable. FARA was never meant as a tool for addressing overall cybersecurity, nor even to address general information security. FARA was always only a statute with the narrow target of exposing Americans whose public messaging reflects the will of a foreign country. Without other measures in place for fighting foreign propaganda, the United States has been left vulnerable both to direct foreign propaganda efforts and to invasive cyberattacks and release of confidential information, such as occurred in the 2016 hack of the Democratic National Committee (DNC) and posting of information on WikiLeaks.

Moreover, FARA leaves a lot to be desired where social media is concerned. Even with perfect enforcement and compliance with FARA's basic terms, it is not clear that a mere registration requirement can provide sufficient deterrent value to dissuade Americans from engaging with foreign powers around political matters. More importantly, there is some reason to think that U.S. elected officials are not particularly deterred by a lobbyist's status as a FARA registrant when they conduct meetings with special interest groups or individual lobbyists. An examination of the public calendars of members of Congress reveals a significant number of meetings with foreign lobbyists, even those who are registered under FARA.[36] Not only are members of Congress willing to be lobbied by foreign governments, but lawmakers may in fact intentionally seek connection with Americans acting on behalf of wealthy foreign governments, given that connecting with a U.S. person who is willing to serve as an intermediary may facilitate a profitable arrangement.[37]

For this reason, even if perfectly enforced, FARA may do little to deter foreign influence. It may not even do much to reduce foreign influence exerted through the intermediary of American citizens disseminating online or other media propaganda, the core case for FARA enforcement. Moreover, as discussed below, FARA has the potential to deter the protected First Amendment activities of media organizations, as well as to chill the scholarly pursuits of think tanks, many of which receive foreign funds in the form of grants. I turn to the problem of overdeterrence, specifically of media organizations and think tanks, in the next section, and reforms to address both under- and overdeterrence in the section after that.

## The Risk of Overdeterrence: FARA as a Threat to Media and Research Organizations

As lawmakers consider badly needed reforms of FARA, especially focused on ways to enhance enforcement of the statute, they should bear in mind that enforcement comes with risks of overdeterrence as well. One of the greatest concerns has to do with the possibility that enhanced enforcement provisions would have a chilling effect on media outlets or think tanks that do not fall squarely under the exemption for such organizations. There is a similar concern that FARA may have a negative impact on universities and research organizations—many of whom receive foreign grant assistance and other forms of financial support from foreign governments—and that the scholarly exemptions may not be clearly enough articulated to forestall such effects. A solution to this risk of overdeterrence must be found before FARA can be adequately strengthened to serve its purpose. However, this chapter will argue, there is a reasonably clear solution to the First Amendment concerns with the statute, one that can be easily implemented.[38]

Although press organizations are generally exempt from registration requirements under 22 U.S.C. § 611(d), the exemption does not apply when the organization is largely under the control of a foreign governmental or private entity.[39] In such cases, the press or media organization is considered to be acting in the political or publicity interests of the foreign entity.[40]

Worries relating to foreign-controlled media outlets that have been required to register as agents of foreign principals under FARA have sparked concern among First Amendment advocates along with those focused on academic freedom and respect for academic research.[41] The critical question is whether FARA can be made more effective in its essential purpose without infringing on the rights of the press under the First Amendment, as well as the general commitment in a free and open society to protect the independence of media organizations. Protection of national security is one of the rare and cautious exceptions to these principles. FARA seeks to strike an effective balance between protecting media organizations and protecting the right of citizens to guard against foreign interference in the foundations of U.S. democracy, by identifying rather than censuring press organizations whose primary purpose is to advocate for the interests of a foreign principal. The need to register as a foreign agent is not a direct imposition on First Amendment rights of the press.[42] However, registration under FARA does entail loss of congressional press credentials as well as a certain amount of social stigma that may serve to discredit the work of any organization so situated.[43]

The vagueness of the statute in its present form has had a particularly damaging impact on press organizations, an ironic result in light of the fact that the statute contains an explicit exemption for media organizations.[44] The ambiguity creates uncertainty and, arguably, a serious risk of lack of adequate notice to prospective registrants under the statute, which raises constitutional concerns. Whenever the potential targets of an enforcement action involving speech are identified with insufficient clarity, there is a risk of unduly chilling speech and overdeterring or abusing the legislative scheme for political purposes.[45]

The exemption contained in § 611(d) makes clear that the term "agent of a foreign principal," a prerequisite for requiring registration under the statute, does not apply to media organizations. Under § 612(a), FARA does not include "any news or press service or association organized under the laws of the United States," provided that the organization is (1) at least 80 percent owned by a U.S. person or U.S. persons, and (2) such a news organization "is not owned, directed, supervised, controlled, subsidized, or financed, and none of its policies are determined by any foreign principal defined in subsection (b) of this section, or by any agent of a foreign principal required to register under this subchapter." One of the principal difficulties is the need to interpret the concept of "control by a foreign principal." What exactly constitutes control? When is a U.S. person or organization engaged in "political activities" on behalf of a foreign principal? When is a U.S. person or organization acting as a "publicity agent" of a foreign principal?

The difficulties of the statutory scheme were made clear in two recent cases in which the Department of Justice sent letters to media outlets informing them they must register under FARA. The first concerned a court judgment secured by the DOJ in 2019 that Florida-based RM Broadcasting must register as a foreign agent, a decision affirmed by a federal court two years later.[46] That case, the first FARA civil enforcement action since 1991, found that the broadcaster violated FARA because it broadcast Russia's "Sputnik" radio programs on AM radio without editing or alteration.[47] In the wake of that decision, concern began to arise that the increased enforcement activity by FARA would end up implicating legitimate media outlets.[48]

More recently, a determination letter was released stating that the U.S. branch office of Turkish national public broadcaster TRT was acting as an agent of foreign principals.[49] Despite TRT's insistence that it "is funded by public fees and advertising and is financially and editorially independent of the Turkish government," the DOJ determined that TRT was a foreign principal and that the U.S. branch acted at the direction and control of TRT and the ruling Turkish regime. The determination letter found that the U.S. branch engaged in three categories of activities in the United States on behalf of these foreign principals, each of which triggered its obligation to register pursuant to FARA: (1) it engaged in political activities; (2) it acted as a publicity agent; and (3) it acted as an information service employee.[50]

Some First Amendment advocacy organizations, such as the Knight Foundation, have expressed concerns about requiring media and press organizations to register under FARA under any circumstances.[51] The price paid for increased control over foreign propaganda, they believe, is not worth the risk that such press organizations will have their activities chilled by the concern of being perceived as under the control of a foreign principal, or that think tanks will be concerned about accepting foreign funds because of potential allegations of falling under the auspices of FARA, thus potentially chilling or impairing legitimate research.[52]

The logic is the same as the debate that takes place in First Amendment litigation regarding who should count as "press" for constitutional purposes. This question has similarly divided national security and First Amendment advocates, arising, for example, in the debate over whether Julian Assange and WikiLeaks should count as "press" as a publisher and provider of online content.[53] National security experts have questioned whether Assange and WikiLeaks should be understood as forfeiting their status as protected press at the point where it can be demonstrated that they were acting in the interests of the Russian government or acting as a "publicity agent" of the Kremlin. First Amendment advocacy groups, by contrast, are against picking and choosing among publishers of online content, believing that weakening the protection for some in turn weakens the protection for all.[54]

Another example of this tension can be found in the long-running battle, pressed by the United Arab Emirates (UAE), to force Al Jazeera to register under FARA.[55] Al Jazeera is funded substantially by the government of Qatar, not dissimilar to the way in which the British government funds the BBC.[56] Over the course of many years, with the assistance of U.S. lawyers the UAE has spent substantial sums attempting to induce the DOJ to take enforcement action against Al Jazeera under FARA.[57] This had the effect of discrediting a prominent media outlet within the Middle East and globally, but also of discrediting the Qatari government. Whatever the merits of the arguments in favor of forcing Al Jazeera to register, U.S. law and U.S. taxpayer dollars should not be the vehicle for Middle East countries to settle their political scores against one another. Ironically, FARA's enforcer—the DOJ—has been subject to the very same foreign influence that FARA is designed to help regulate.

Moreover, there are many reasons to believe that Al Jazeera, and even more so the BBC, should not be considered on a par with RM Broadcasting and TRT. Both of the former have independent standards of journalism, and neither appears to be a mere mouthpiece for the respective governments that help to fund them. In the case of the BBC in particular, the government is arguably bypassed, since there is an independent tax that creates the public funding for the parent company and that is paid directly to support public broadcasting.[58] There is grave concern among First Amendment activists and watchdog groups that any FARA enforcement actions against foreign-funded media will have a chilling effect on all foreign media broadcasting in the United States. This suggests that Section 611(d) of FARA, which provides some limited exclusions for press organizations, should be broadened to include any media outlet. This would, however, have rendered impossible the registration of TRT as well as of RM Broadcasting, enforcement decisions on DOJ's part that seem appropriate.

## Critical Reforms of FARA

Reflecting the current imperfect nature of FARA as an enforcement tool, numerous bills have been introduced in both the House and the Senate in recent years in an attempt to reform FARA. Lawmakers have sought to strengthen its enforcement, tighten its exemptions, or otherwise amend FARA to better face the challenges posed by foreign influence in today's global media environment.[59] The large number of pending FARA bills proposed by members of Congress come from both sides of the aisle. The bills' sponsors hope that by addressing the loose exemptions and other holes in FARA legislation, they may mitigate the "widespread abuses" of current FARA requirements.[60] The most recent of these attempts is contained in the For the People Act, H.R. 1, an anti-corruption effort introduced by the Democrats and passed in the House in March 2021.[61] H.R. 1 was subsequently introduced in the Senate as

S. 1, but eventually tabled and replaced in that same legislative term by S. 2747. The FARA provisions from S. 1 did not carry over to S. 2747.[62] All that remains of the original FARA-related measures in H.R. 1 are several provisions placing restrictions on financial donations from foreign entities, as well as a reporting requirement relating to certain classes of financial donations. It is a shame that the FARA provisions were not included in S. 2747, as several of the suggestions were proposed and supported by Democrats and Republicans alike. The original FARA provision in H.R. 1 would have "created a special enforcement unit within the Justice Department with the power to take appropriate legal action, establish civil fines to allow recourse in cases that do not rise to the level of prosecution, and otherwise extend FARA."[63] This provision and others took inspiration from legislation originally proposed by Senator Charles Grassley (R-IA), among others.[64]

This section addresses several of the more important FARA-related reform proposals, and in addition will present several proposals for minimizing the risk of First Amendment infringements due to overdeterrence. The focus is to make FARA a more effective law enforcement tool while ensuring that greater FARA enforcement will not chill media engagement or stifle research efforts on the part of academics and think tanks. These two goals must be kept constantly in equipoise. The more vigorous the enforcement efforts, the more overdeterrence there is likely to be. If the United States enhances enforcement, it is even more critical to assure relevant stakeholders that the First Amendment and other protected activities will not be illegitimately targeted by an overzealous or politically motivated DOJ.

### Improve FARA's Key Definitional Sections

Several key terms in FARA have created great uncertainty about how the statute is to be applied in particular cases due to lack of adequate definition. Perhaps the worst offender in this regard is the phrase "agent of a foreign principal," as contained within 22 U.S.C. § 611(c). Although the statute contains a detailed definition of who should count as an agent of a foreign principal, the definition itself contains several circular and ambiguous phrases. In (c)(1), for example, the phrase "agent of a foreign principal" is defined as "any person who acts as an agent, representative, employee, or servant, or any person who acts in any other capacity at the order, request or under the direction or control, of a foreign principal." Apart from the obvious circularity stemming from the fact that the word "agent" is found in the definition of the phrase "agent of a foreign principal," there is a more serious problem that stems from the ambiguity of the phrase "who acts . . . under the direction or control . . . of a foreign principal." Much debate and some litigation has taken place grappling with the question of what being "under the direction or control" means. This question arises with particular urgency in cases involving foreign media outlets, as with Al Jazeera. The media exemption in 22 U.S.C. 611(d) attempts to clarify matters, but the highly technical definition in that subsection does not fully resolve the issue, since terms like "owned, directed, supervised, and controlled" also appear within the exemption.

Accordingly, the exemption for media under 22 U.S.C. § 611(d) should be reformed to maximize First Amendment protection and avoid overdeterrence based on ambiguity regarding who satisfies the conditions of the exemption. As discussed above, clarity regarding the press exemption from the FARA provisions is urgently needed. There are several possible reforms that may be worth considering in the immediate future. One is to amend 22 U.S.C. § 611(d) to require registration only for news organizations that are subject to the direction and control of content by a foreign government or foreign political party. The current approach of the provision is conjunctive: a media organization is exempt if it is owned 80 percent or more by U.S. persons and "none of its policies are determined by any foreign principal defined in subsection (b) of this section, or by any agent of a foreign principal required to register under this subchapter."[65] However, a media organization more than 80 percent owned by U.S. persons would have to register under FARA if, under the final subsection of § 611(d), the organization was found to have its policies "determined" by a foreign principal.[66] Under my suggestion, the only question would be whether the organization is "subject to the direction and control of content" by a foreign government or foreign political party.[67]

In short, 22 U.S.C. § 611(d) requires clarification regarding the phrase "owned, directed, supervised, controlled, subsidized, or financed," as well as the phrase "determined by any foreign principal."[68] The relevant amendment should provide a substantive test for identifying media organizations whose policies are "determined" by a foreign principal, as formal factors alone do not reliably establish individuals or organizations that should be thought of as agents of a foreign principal.

Insofar as future legislation seeks to enhance protections against foreign interference, it is important to ensure that the legislation includes corresponding protections against overenforcement that might unduly burden protected speech or media activity.

### Establish Civil Investigative Demand Authority

Congress should provide the Department of Justice with civil investigative demand (CID) authority to enable effective investigation of possible FARA violations. This would result in far greater compliance versus leaving the department with the choice of dropping the investigation of a potential FARA violation or engaging in a criminal investigation.[69] Civil investigatory power would allow the DOJ to conduct more frequent investigations, but it would also expand DOJ's power to conduct preliminary investigations and gather information prior to opening a criminal case. This would enable DOJ to have the additional ability to force those who fall under the statute to register without having to turn to criminal prosecution for noncompliance. Similar to the Securities and Exchange Commission (SEC), the DOJ will have more flexible and effective enforcement powers if it has a broader range of tools available.

The expansion to CID authority is consistent with H.R. 1, sections 7101 and 7102, which provide for the establishment of an enforcement unit within the National Security Division empowered to impose civil fines.[70] The proposed act as it currently stands, however, is not entirely clear. Two suggested revisions recommend themselves. First, the bill should clarify that the relevant authority indeed is "civil investigative demand authority," which would give the relevant unit the power to impose and enforce subpoenas and other binding investigatory tools. Second, the relevant CID authority should be established within the Counterintelligence and Export Control Section (CES) in the NSD, rather than in the "counterespionage section" of the DOJ, as currently provided. FARA enforcement was moved into the NSD and out of the DOJ criminal division in 2006, though in order to bring a FARA prosecution, the FARA unit must receive approval from both CES and NSD.[71] Keeping FARA enforcement authority within the NSD locates the emphasis in the right place, namely on compliance rather than on criminal prosecution. This is consistent with the suggestion to add CID authority to the range of tools DOJ investigators have at their disposal to enhance compliance with FARA's registration requirement.

For FARA to effectively deter propagandistic relationships with foreign powers on the part of Americans, the contours of the statute must be intuitive and the stigma of having a promotional relationship with a foreign government must be obvious. Avoiding overly technical definitions and multiple terms for the same concept would improve FARA's clarity but it might also strengthen the stigma associated with noncompliance. The more technical the statute, the more its requirements appear to be formal requirements with no obvious connection to U.S. national security. The public needs to understand the purpose served by the registration and to have concerns about the influence agents for foreign principals exert on our political system.

### Reform the Relationship of FARA to the Lobbying Disclosure Act

Congress should amend 22 U.S.C. 613(h) and its relationship to the Lobbying Disclosure Act of 1995, 2 U.S.C.A. 1601 et seq. Because FARA and the LDA serve different purposes, duplicative registration would not be excessive. I strongly suggest that Congress should amend FARA to eliminate the exemption for prior registration under the LDA.[72] While this would result in duplicate registrations in some cases, the redundant registrations would be a welcome check on activities relating to foreign lobbying. Repealing the LDA exemption should increase FARA registrations and thereby better represent the body of foreign agents at work. To expand the authorization of the DOJ in handling FARA cases, the United States may begin to enable better enforcement mechanisms for FARA.

*Improve Public Notice and Transparency*
*under FARA Disclosure Rules*

Congress should also amend FARA to include additional notice requirements that would help identify agents of foreign principals under the statute and enhance public awareness of their status. Improved notification
requirements could include the following:

- Require the DOJ to send a separate notification to all members of Congress containing copies of all new determination letters, as well as notify
  members of Congress of any new registrations under FARA or pending
  court cases involving registration.

- Require that all determination letters, as well as all filings, be published
  on the DOJ website in a FARA enforcement database. This change would
  be consistent with H.R. 1's 7104 (a) and (b), though this specific requirement should be explicitly added to the language of H.R. 1.

- Require the FARA registration unit to submit periodic reports to Congress regarding all civil or criminal investigations under the statute, as
  well as the number of cases referred to the DOJ for investigation where
  further action was declined.

- Require members of Congress to file periodic reports with the DOJ disclosing the time, place, and purpose of all meetings with agents of foreign principals registered under FARA.

- Amend FARA to include a provision requiring new registrants under the
  act to disclose any knowledge of any gift or other thing of financial value
  paid by the foreign principal of which that registrant is an agent to any
  federal or state officeholder. This provision is set out in H.R. 1 and would
  require a supplemental filing by any registrant under FARA.

Several of these provisions, as well as others not mentioned here, are
contained within the now defunct Foreign Agent Lobbying Transparency
Enforcement Act, or S. 1679, sponsored in 2017 by Senators Tammy Duck-
worth (D-IL), Richard Blumenthal (D-CT), Dick Durbin (D-IL), and Mazie

Hirono (D-HI). It would appear, however, that as currently written, H.R. 1 only scratches the surface of the reforms to FARA that would be needed to address the concerns detailed above, and to make the statute a basis for effective enforcement. The question remains, with the number of bills drawing attention to FARA's shortcomings, of why only one has received a markup and why none have advanced from their assigned committees.[73] In the face of significant bipartisan efforts to improve FARA's impact and usefulness, and a great need to strengthen the country's defenses against foreign interference, FARA reform is both achievable and urgent. The For the People Act has been mired in controversy, principally because of its voting rights provisions, but there is no reason that FARA reform efforts must be coupled with voting rights reform, critical though the latter is. Given the large number of bills from both sides of the aisle over the past several years attempting to reform FARA, it would make a great deal of sense to craft a bill that accomplishes the aims of both Republicans and Democrats in strengthening the country's defenses against foreign propaganda and foreign influence. To that end, a more detailed discussion of FARA reform can be found in the 2021 report put out by a committee of the American Bar Association (ABA), of which the current author was a contributing member.[74]

## Is FARA Enough? Is It Too Much?

Reform efforts are badly needed to revise and update FARA to make enforcement under the act more effective. But at the same time, the more capacious the DOJ's enforcement capabilities, the greater the risk of overbreadth and the more concerned the American people should be about the possibility of chilling constitutionally protected activities such as freedom of the press and scholarly activities funded by foreign governments. As discussed above, FARA requires significant revision on the enforcement side, principally the addition of civil investigative demand authority and the possibility for civil fines, and hence enhanced investigatory powers. However, these new enforcement powers must be complemented by enhanced precision with regard to media and scholarly exemptions, as well as improvement in basic definitional concepts whose nebulous character can import too much unpredictability on the part of DOJ in its enforcement of the act and a risk of constitutionally insufficient notice. Indeed, such reforms are urgent, because the risk that FARA may ultimately be found constitutionally defective in its current form increases with every determination letter.

It is also critical that such reform efforts are not undertaken piecemeal. A number of other areas of legislation are inextricably related to or affected by foreign agent registration rules, such as the Lobbying Disclosure Act, campaign finance restrictions, and weak personal ethics rules for executive branch employees that may pose a greater risk of encouraging the development of foreign agent-principal relationships. FARA, then, is only one piece of a larger puzzle, the totality of which must be viewed when considering ways to minimize foreign interference with democratic institutions across the board. In addition, measures designed to minimize the injection of foreign propaganda into the American consciousness must also be considered as part of an overall strategic approach to cybersecurity, as foreign political discourse and disinformation are ultimately only a small portion of the national security risks that the United States faces from foreign governments.[75]

Two big picture questions ultimately arise with regard to FARA reform. First, is there a risk that with greater enforcement, and hence expanded compliance, the stigma of foreign agency will start to diminish, as indeed may already have occurred as FARA enforcement activities have expanded? Might there not, in effect, be an inverse relationship between the number of agents of foreign principals that can be made to comply with registration requirements and the disfavor with which interacting with such agents is regarded among U.S. lawmakers and members of the public? The more routine it becomes for individuals and organizations to be registered agents of foreign governments, the less concern U.S. lawmakers will have about interacting with FARA registrants. If this turns out to be the case, then ultimately the experiment of handling foreign propaganda disseminated by Americans through the mechanism of transparency rather than through a system of prohibitions will have failed.

Second, even if enhanced FARA enforcement should prove successful in both producing and ultimately deterring the transmission of foreign propaganda by Americans, will a reduction in foreign propaganda as conveyed by U.S. intermediaries in fact reduce the effectiveness of foreign influence? Or will foreign adversaries simply dispense with a U.S. intermediary and find they can be equally effective in achieving their political aims by targeting an American audience through direct transmission or propaganda on the internet, or by turning to noninformation-based methods of impacting U.S. patterns of behavior?

While the answers to these questions are presently unknown, it is clear that protecting U.S. democracy against foreign influence and foreign interference will require a broad array of sophisticated tools that evolve with the nature of the threats. For too long, FARA has been one of the few resources available to combat the induction of Americans into the efforts of foreign governments to undermine democratic governance through propaganda. While even a perfect FARA statute will not do everything that is needed to protect against the insidious effect of foreign efforts to influence the course of democratic governance, FARA reform is a potentially effective place to begin.

## Notes

1. Ashley Parker and David E. Sanger, "Donald Trump Calls on Russia to Find Hillary Clinton's Missing Emails," *New York Times*, July 27, 2016, www.nytimes.com/2016/07/28/us/politics/donald-trump-russia-clinton-emails.html.

2. Jane Mayer, "How Russia Helped Swing the Election for Trump," *New Yorker*, September 24, 2018, www.newyorker.com/magazine/2018/10/01/how-russia-helped-to-swing-the-election-for-trump; Ellen Nakashima, "Fewer Opportunities and a Changed Political Environment in the U.S. May Have Curbed Moscow's Election Interference This Year, Analysts Say," *Washington Post*, November 17, 2020, www.washingtonpost.com/national-security/russia-failed-to-mount-major-election-interference-operations-in-2020-analysts-say/2020/11/16/72c62b0c-1880-11eb-82db-60b15c874105_story.html.

3. Eric Tucker and Frank Bajak, "U.S. Officials Link Iran to Emails Meant to Intimidate Voters," AP News, October 21, 2020, https://apnews.com/article/donald-trump-florida-elections-voting-2020-voting-2124f257f89649630e123952df34b186; Kevin Collier, "Russia, China and Iran Launched Cyberattacks on Presidential Campaigns, Microsoft Says," NBC News, September 10, 2020, www.nbcnews.com/tech/security/russian-china-iran-launched-cyberattacks-presidential-campaigns-microsoft-says-n1239803; Stephanie Kirchgaessner, "Revealed: Saudis Suspected of Phone Spying Campaign in U.S.," *Guardian*, March 29, 2020, www.theguardian.com/world/2020/mar/29/revealed-saudis-suspected-of-phone-spying-campaign-in-us.

4. Claire O. Finkelstein, "How Democracy in the Kremlin's Crosshairs Can Fight

Back," *Zocalo Public Square*, May 11, 2017, www.zocalopublicsquare.org/2017/05/11/dem
ocracy-kremlins-crosshairs-can-fight-back/ideas/nexus/.

5. Janna Anderson and Lee Rainie, "Concerns about Democracy in the Digital
Age," Pew Research Center, February 21, 2020, www.pewresearch.org/internet/2020/
02/21/concerns-about-democracy-in-the-digital-age/.

6. Norman Eisen, Claire Finkelstein, and Richard Painter, "Arrest of a Trump
Friend Sends Key Message," CNN Opinion, July 23, 2021, www.cnn.com/2021/07/22/
opinions/tom-barrack-foreign-agent-charges-eisen-finkelstein-painter/index.html;
Murray Waas, "Michael Flynn Ignored Official Warnings about Receiving Foreign
Payments," *Guardian*, April 8, 2021, www.theguardian.com/us-news/2021/apr/08/mi
chael-flynn-ignored-official-warnings-receiving-foreign-payments.

7. Kenneth P. Vogel, "Elliott Broidy Pleads Guilty in Foreign Lobbying Case," *New
York Times*, October 20, 2020, www.nytimes.com/2020/10/20/us/politics/elliott-broidy
-foreign-lobbying.html; David Laufman, "Paul Manafort Guilty Plea Highlights Increased Enforcement of Foreign Agents Registration Act," *Lawfare*, September 14,
2018, www.lawfareblog.com/paul-manafort-guilty-plea-highlights-increased-enforce
ment-foreign-agents-registration-act; Katelyn Polantz, "Sam Patten Sentenced to 3
Years Probation, No Jail Time after Cooperating with Mueller," CNN, April 12, 2019,
www.cnn.com/2019/04/12/politics/sam-patten-sentencing/index.html; "Recent FARA
Cases," U.S. Department of Justice, www.justice.gov/nsd-fara/recent-cases; Lachlan
Markay, "Trump Pardons Former GOP Fundraiser Elliot Broidy," Axios, January 20,
2021, www.axios.com/trump-elliott-broidy-pardon-474b53d4-81b1-48ae-9ead-1b6e
bcb17733.html; "President Trump as Acting Pardon Attorney, Executive Grant of
Clemency to Adjmi, Banki, Bannon, Bernadett, and others," U.S. Department of Justice (January 19, 2021), www.justice.gov/pardon/page/file/1358801/download; "President Trump as Acting Pardon Attorney, Executive Grant of Clemency for Paul J.
Manafort, Jr.," U.S. Department of Justice (December 23, 2020), www.justice.gov/par
don/page/file/1358801/download.

8. The author served on a committee of the American Bar Association for FARA
Reform. See Caitlin Oprysko with Daniel Lippman, "How to fix FARA, According to
FARA Lawyers," Politico,  September 29, 2021, www.politico.com/newsletters/politico
-influence/2021/09/29/how-to-fix-fara-according-to-fara-lawyers-797929. The recommendations contained in this chapter do not perfectly align with the ABA report's
suggestions, as the latter reflect the views of the entire committee, which differ in
some instances from the author's own stance. Nevertheless, the ABA report provides
a set of workable and potentially effective reforms to enhance FARA's efficacy.

9. 22 U.S.C. § 611 et seq.

10. U.S. Department of Justice, Office of the Inspector General, Audit Division
16-24, *Audit of the National Security Division's Enforcement and Administration of the
Foreign Agents Registration Act* (September 2016), hereinafter *FARA Audit*, www
.oversight.gov/sites/default/files/oig-reports/a1624.pdf.

11. Cynthia Brown, *The Foreign Agents Registration Act (FARA): A Legal Overview*,

Congressional Research Service, R45037, December 4, 2017, p. 2, https://fas.org/sgp/crs/misc/R45037.pdf.

12. Ibid.

13. Ibid.

14. 22 U.S.C. § 614 (a)–(f).

15. Brown, *FARA: A Legal Overview*.

16. Consider, for example, the failed attempt to prosecute Greg Craig, from the law firm of Skadden, Arps, for his dealings with Ukraine. See Sharon LaFraniere, "Gregory Craig Acquitted on Charge of Lying to Justice Department," *New York Times*, September 4, 2019, www.nytimes.com/2019/09/04/us/politics/gregory-craig-acquitted.html.

17. "FARA Enforcement," U.S. Department of Justice, www.justice.gov/nsd-fara/fara-enforcement.

18. See U.S. Department of Justice, *FARA Audit*, Office of the Inspector General, 2016, p. 8.

19. U.S. Department of Justice, *FARA Audit*.

20. See, e.g., the prosecutions of Greg Craig, W. Samuel Patten, Richard Gates, and Michael Flynn. See "Recent FARA Cases," U.S. Department of Justice, last updated December 3, 2021, www.justice.gov/nsd-fara/recent-cases.

21. For example, Trump associate Thomas Barrack was prosecuted under this provision. See Eisen, Finkelstein, and Painter, "Arrest of a Trump Friend Sends Key Message."

22. Ibid., p. 9.

23. U.S. Department of Justice, *FARA Audit*, pp. 9–13.

24. Francis R. O'Hara, "The Foreign Agents Registration Act—The Spotlight of Pitiless Publicity," *Villanova Law Review* 10, no. 3 (1965), p. 441, https://digitalcommons.law.villanova.edu/cgi/viewcontent.cgi?article=1663&context=vlr.

25. 22 U.S.C. § 613 (as amended by Pub. L. 104–65, § 9(3)).

26. 22 U.S.C. § 613.

27. Ibid.; U.S. Department of Justice, *FARA Audit*, pp. 8–12.

28. *United States* v. *Craig*, 401 F. Supp. 3d 49 (D.D.C. 2019).

29. Alan Crosby, "Putin May End Up the Winner in French Presidential Vote," RadioFreeEurope/RadioLiberty, April 22, 2017, www.rferl.org/a/france-election-macron-le-pen-fillon-melenchon-putin-russia/28445679.html.

30. Paul Sonne, "A Russian Bank Gave Marine Le Pen's Party a Loan. Then Weird Things Began Happening," *Washington Post*, December 27, 2018, www.washingtonpost.com/world/national-security/a-russian-bank-gave-marine-le-pens-party-a-loan-then-weird-things-began-happening/2018/12/27/960c7906-d320-11e8-a275-81c671a50422_story.html. See also Reuters Staff, "Russian Firm Suing France's Far-Right Party over Loan Debt—Court Document," Reuters, February 18, 2020, www.reuters.com/article/russia-france/russian-firm-suing-frances-far-right-party-over-loan-debt-court-document-idUKL8N2AI57L.

31. Josh Dawsey, "Russian-Funded Facebook Ads Backed Stein, Sanders and

Trump," Politico, September 26, 2017, www.politico.com/story/2017/09/26/facebook
-russia-trump-sanders-stein-243172.

32. U.S. Senate Committee on Finance Minority Staff Report, *The NRA and Russia: How a Tax-Exempt Organization Became a Foreign Asset*, September 2019, https://assets .documentcloud.org/documents/6432520/The-NRA-Russia-How-a-Tax-Exempt -Organization.pdf.

33. On this theme, see Richard Painter's chapter on campaign finance reform (chapter 6, this volume).

34. See Kathleen Hall Jamieson, *Cyberwar*, 2nd ed. (Oxford University Press, 2020).

35. David E. Sanger, Nicole Perlroth, and Eric Schmitt, "Scope of Russian Hacking Becomes Clear: Multiple U.S. Agencies Were Hit," *New York Times*, December 14, 2020, www.nytimes.com/2020/12/14/us/politics/russia-hack-nsa-homeland-security -pentagon.html.

36. Ben Freeman and Lydia Dennet, "Loopholes, Filing Failures, and Lax Enforcement: How the Foreign Agents Registration Act Falls Short," Project on Government Oversight (POGO), December 16, 2014, https://docs.pogo.org/report/2014/pogo-fara -report-20141216.pdf?mtime=20180803144208&focal=none&_ga=2.101501768.894585 58.1635456144-357539079.1635456144.

37. Ben Freeman and Ryan Summer, "Governments Abroad Are Shaping Our Foreign Policy in Broad Daylight," *The Nation*, November 13, 2019, www.thenation.com/ article/archive/trump-saudi-arabia-lobbying/.

38. Nick Robinson, "'Foreign Agents' in an Interconnected World: FARA and the Weaponization of Transparency," *Duke Law Journal* 69 (2020), pp. 1075–1147, https:// scholarship.law.duke.edu/dlj/vol69/iss5/2; Doug Rutzen and Nick Robinson, "The Unintended 'Foreign Agents,'" Just Security, March 16, 2018, www.justsecurity.org/53967 /unintended-foreign-agents/.

39. 22 U.S.C. § 611(d).

40. Ibid.

41. See, e.g., Robinson, "'Foreign Agents' in an Interconnected World," pp. 1113–15; Alexandra Ellerbeck and Avi Asher-Schapiro, "Everything to Know about FARA, and Why It Shouldn't Be Used against the Press," *Columbia Journalism Review*, June 11, 2018, www.cjr.org/analysis/fara-press.php.

42. Brown, *FARA: A Legal Overview*, p. 1.

43. "Accreditation Criteria," House Radio Television Correspondents' Gallery, https://radiotv.house.gov/membership/accreditation-criteria; Rutzen and Robinson, "The Unintended 'Foreign Agents.'"

44. Ellerbeck and Asher-Schapiro, "Everything to Know about FARA."

45. See Robinson, "'Foreign Agents' in an Interconnected World," pp. 1113–16.

46. Office of Public Affairs, "Court Finds RM Broadcasting Must Register as a Foreign Agent," U.S. Department of State, May 14, 2019, www.justice.gov/opa/pr/court -finds-rm-broadcasting-must-register-foreign-agent.

47. Ibid.

48. Ellerbeck and Asher-Schapiro, "Everything to Know about FARA."

49. Letter from Brandon Van Grack, Chief, FARA Unit, U.S. Department of Justice, "Obligation of Turkish Radio & Television Corporation to Register under the Foreign Agents Registration Act," August 1, 2019, www.al-monitor.com/sites/default/files/documents/2020/trt_world_justice_department_fara_determination_letter.pdf.

50. Ibid.

51. See, e.g., Joel Simon, "Propaganda or Not, Forcing RT to Register Sets a Bad Precedent," *Columbia Journalism Review*, December 1, 2017, www.cjr.org/analysis/fara-press.php,%20https://www.cjr.org/opinion/rt-propaganda-foreign-agent.php.

52. See event, "Protecting Democracy: Modernizing the Foreign Agents Registration Act," American Enterprise Institute, April 17, 2019, www.aei.org/events/protecting-democracy-modernizing-the-foreign-agents-registration-act/; Rutzen, Robinson, "The Unintended 'Foreign Agents.'"

53. Emily Stewart, "The Debate over What Julian Assange's Arrest Means for Freedom of the Press, Explained," *Vox*, April 12, 2019, www.vox.com/policy-and-politics/2019/4/12/18308186/assange-arrest-freedom-of-press.

54. See generally "Are WikiLeaks' Actions Protected by the First Amendment?" First Amendment Watch, https://firstamendmentwatch.org/deep-dive/are-wikileaks-actions-protected-by-the-first-amendment/#tab-analysis-opinion.

55. Marc Tracy and Lara Jakes, "U.S. Orders Al Jazeera Affiliate to Register as Foreign Agent," *New York Times*, September 15, 2020, www.nytimes.com/2020/09/15/business/media/aj-al-jazeera-fara.html.

56. Kevin Ponniah, "Qatar Crisis: Can Al Jazeera Survive?" BBC News, June 8, 2017, www.bbc.com/news/world-middle-east-40187414.

57. Dan Friedman, "The Trump Administration Orders an Al Jazeera Affiliate to Register as a Foreign Agent," *Mother Jones*, September 15, 2020, www.motherjones.com/politics/2020/09/trump-doj-al-jazeera-fara-uae-qatar/.

58. Jill Lawless, "U.K. Government, at Odds with Media, Eyes BBC Funding Change," AP News, February 5, 2020, https://apnews.com/article/20fd0363b96823e55b1e56d0591e268e.

59. Lydia Dennett, "Comparing Current Foreign Influence Reform Legislation," POGO, August 9, 2018, www.pogo.org/analysis/2018/08/comparing-current-foreign-influence-reform-legislation/.

60. Brown, *FARA: A Legal Overview.*

61. H.R. 1, or the For the People Act of 2019, was sponsored by John Sarbanes and Cheri Bustos in 2020. The bill was intended to expand access to the ballot box, reduce the influence of money in politics, and strengthen ethics rules for public servants.

62. See S. 2747, 117th Congress (2021–2022), 1st session, www.congress.gov/bill/117th-congress/senate-bill/2747/text.

63. Eisen, Finkelstein, and Painter, "Arrest of a Trump Friend Sends a Key Message."

64. Chuck Grassley, "Grassley Leads Relaunch Of Foreign Lobbying Disclosure Reforms," news release, May 20, 2021, www.grassley.senate.gov/news/news-releases/grassley-leads-relaunch-of-foreign-lobbying-disclosure-reforms; Disclosing Foreign Influence Act, S. 2039, 115th Cong., 1st sess., introduced October 31, 2017, www.congress.gov/bill/115th-congress/senate-bill/2039/actions.

65. 22 U.S.C. § 611(d).

66. Ibid.

67. Ibid.

68. Ibid.

69. H.R. 1 addresses this issue by establishing a unit within the counterespionage section of the DOJ responsible for the enforcement of FARA. Like this recommendation, the bill would authorize the new FARA unit to take appropriate legal action against suspects in violation of FARA and coordinate legal action with the U.S. attorney. Sen. Joe Manchin has also noted this recommendation as a provision of the bill that he would support. The 117th Congress's version of the Freedom to Vote Act (2021–2022) does not address the issue of FARA enforcement by establishing a counterespionage section in the DOJ. See S. 2747, 117th Congress (2021–2022), 1st session, www.congress.gov/bill/117th-congress/senate-bill/2747/text.

70. The For the People Act of 2019, H.R. 1, 116th Cong., was passed by the House in 2019 but blocked from reaching the floor of the Senate by Senate Majority Leader Mitch McConnell. See Wendy Weiser, Daniel I. Weiner, and Dominique Erney, "The Case for H.R. 1," Brennan Center for Justice, April 10, 2020, www.brennancenter.org/sites/default/files/2020-04/2020_04_Case%20for%20HR1_Final.pdf.

71. Matthew T. Sanderson and Olivia N. Marshall, "United States: A History of the FARA Unit," Mondaq, May 28, 2020, www.mondaq.com/unitedstates/terrorism-homeland-security-defence/941882/a-history-of-the-fara-unit.

72. Jacob R. Straus, Cong. Rsch. Serv., R46435, *Foreign Agents Registration Act (FARA): Background Issues for Congress* (2020), pp. 20–21, https://fas.org/sgp/crs/misc/R46435.pdf.

73. Disclosing Foreign Influence Act, H.R. 4170, 115th Cong. (2017), www.congress.gov/bill/115th-congress/house-bill/4170.

74. The current chapter does not reflect the official views of the ABA FARA Reform Committee or the views of any of its members except the author's own.

75. Such a measure is also laid out in H.R. 1, authorizing several senior officials, including the president, attorney general, and chairman of the FEC, to issue a national strategy to protect against disinformation campaigns and cyberattacks. The DISCLOSE Act, a companion bill to the For the People Act, would additionally require the FEC to submit to Congress an analysis of the extent to which illicit foreign money was used to carry out disinformation and propaganda campaigns. Also, the Protecting Our Democracy Act (PODA), introduced in the 117th Congress as H. R. 5314, would add limits to foreign interference in elections. See H. R. 5314, 117th Congress (2021–2022), Division C, Titles XIII and XIV, www.congress.gov/bill/117th-congress/house-bill/5314.

**Part III**

# Democracy Reforms

## Elections, Voting, and Campaign Finance

# 5

# Countering Voter Suppression and Election Subversion

## VICTORIA BASSETTI

Most of the chapters in this volume focus on the harm President Trump did while in office and how it can be addressed. But toward the end of his term, and persisting since he left the White House, Trump has helped to stimulate a new and worrying set of threats. He continues to make and inspire persis-

---

This chapter is based in part on and adapts from *A Democracy Crisis in the Making* (April 2021 report and June 2021 report update) and *The Impact of H.R. 1 & S. 1 on Voting: An Analysis of Key States*. Thanks go to the States United Democracy Center and the coauthors of the first two, Protect Democracy and Law Forward, for permitting this author to adapt the material. See States United Democracy Center, Protect Democracy, and Law Forward, "Democracy Crisis Report Update: New Data and Trends Show the Warning Signs Have Intensified in the Last Two Months," memorandum, June 10, 2021, https://statesuniteddemocracy.org/wp-content/uploads/2021/06/Democracy-Crisis -Part-II_June-10_Final_v7.pdf; States United Democracy Center, Protect Democracy, and Law Forward, *Democracy Crisis in the Making*, report, April 22, 2021, https: //statesuniteddemocracy.org/wp-content/uploads/2021/04/FINAL-Democracy-Crisis -Report-April-21.pdf; States United Democracy Center, *The Impact of H.R. 1 & S. 1 on Voting: An Analysis of Key States*, report, May 6, 2021, https://statesuniteddemocracy.org/ wp-content/uploads/2021/05/HR1Report_UPDATED_5.06.21_800PM.pdf.

tent, widespread, and virulent attacks on the integrity of the American election system. One could call these threats electoral Trumpery—and these threats are no less in need of redress.

The 2020 election set a modern record for voter participation rates and was rightly hailed as the most secure and accurate contest in U.S. history.[1] Hundreds of thousands of election administrators and workers gave their utmost to count every vote and to protect the election, all in the midst of a global pandemic. Yet, in the days and months up to and following November 3, 2020, Trump initiated a wholesale assault on the election results. Before the election, he stated that if he did not win, it could only be because it was rigged.[2] After, he or his allies filed or backed more than sixty often frivolous legal challenges to the election results.[3] He launched a sustained propaganda campaign to persuade millions of Americans to break from reality and believe the lie that the election was stolen.[4] And in the days leading up to Congress's meeting to certify the Electoral College vote, he laid the foundation for and then incited an illegal, armed, and fatal attack on the Capitol.[5]

When Trump finally left office on January 20, 2021, there was some basis for hope that the worst of his assaults on the election system would stop. But 2021 has shown that the poison of Trumpery has spread far and wide. Throughout the country, state legislators and other elected officials have joined Trump in his attacks on the U.S. election system and have also accelerated voter suppression efforts.

One organization, the Voting Rights Lab, has identified more than 2,000 bills that were introduced in state legislatures in 2021 that deal in one way or another with how elections are administered.[6] Many of these proposals have been pro-voter or neutral in effect. But a frightening proportion are hostile to voters and the electoral system. These can be viewed as an aggressive expansion of the long-standing trends in voter suppression that have afflicted America for its entire history. However, some of this legislation is part of a newer and more shocking phenomenon: hundreds of these proposals seek to alter basic principles about how elections should be run, aspiring to reverse almost a century of concerted work to ensure that elections are fairly and professionally administered and that the worst partisan impulses are controlled.

Ten years ago, most voting rights observers were focused on two major threats: strict and disenfranchising voter identification requirements, and racial and partisan gerrymandering. But today, the problem has morphed and diverged. The voter suppression movement has grown far more sophisticated and insidious. Rather than one single anti-voting measure, states are passing comprehensive bills that weave a web of suppression. The cumulative effect of such packages in any given state is substantial. These efforts to inhibit individual voters—as well as the ongoing threat of redistricting, which I deal with briefly in this chapter—are now coupled with broader and brazen attempts to undermine the objective and professional administration of elections. All of this has taken place in the context of the Supreme Court's persistent undermining of voting rights, including through insulating partisan gerrymandering from federal review and issuing a series of decisions that guts provisions of the Voting Rights Act (the most recent of which, *Brnovich* v. *Democratic National Committee*, was decided in July 2021).[7]

This chapter first outlines the evolving present threats to voting via Trump-stimulated or inspired voter suppression and election subversion. Voter suppression consists of efforts to discourage individuals from voting by, for example, making it harder to register, restricting the ability to vote by mail, and limiting where and when voters can cast their ballots. Election subversion consists of the new wave of efforts to undermine competent and fair election administration by, for example, conducting sham audits of the 2020 election or criminalizing minor administrative errors related to elections. I also include a discussion of upcoming efforts in the states to draw new election district boundaries, as is standard practice every decade after the decennial census is completed. These upcoming redistricting efforts pose an increased risk of extreme gerrymandering, which threatens to strip voters of a meaningful voice in elections.

The chapter then details available responses. What the states can take away, Congress can guarantee or restore to federal elections. It can do so by using its broad constitutional authority to pass legislation that would set minimum requirements in key areas under state assault. That includes automatic voter registration, voting by mail, and early voting. These measures could be coupled with legislation to end partisan gerrymandering, renew the Voting Rights Act to counteract Supreme Court decisions that undermine that statute, and to reform the Electoral Count Act. Indeed, legislation to do all those things is pending or expected before Congress. The chapter analyzes various legislative approaches pending as of this writing and how they might operate to address the challenges. Consistent with Brookings policy, I neither endorse nor oppose active legislation. Instead, the chapter is confined to describing how various proposed congressional remedies would work in practice and offers some alternative ideas that have not yet been introduced. I explain why the only available comprehensive solution is through congressional action; executive orders, regulation, and other options will not suffice, given the scale and scope of the issues nationally.

## Voter Suppression

Before 2013, the preclearance system established in 1965 by the Voting Rights Act stymied many efforts to depress voter participation. The act's preclearance requirement barred states and jurisdictions with a history of discrimination from making changes to their voting procedures without first clearing it through the U.S. Department of Justice (DOJ).[8] Preclearance was viewed as "the most powerful weapon in the civil rights arsenal."[9] But in 2013 the Supreme Court invalidated the preclearance process in *Shelby County* v. *Holder*, 570 U.S. 529 (2013). With that, the door was opened to a new era of voter suppression.[10]

The year 2021 may prove to be a pivotal moment in that new era, a point when the small-scale production of anti-voter laws enabled by *Shelby* turned into a high-volume factory—driven by the relentless efforts of Trump and his supporters to attack the democracy that they believe drove them from power. By February 2021, state legislators had introduced four times as many anti-voting laws as they had by the same point in 2020.[11] By July, the number of bills introduced had grown again, and the number that had been enacted had surged. According to the Brennan Center for Justice, between January 1 and July 14, 2021, at least eighteen states enacted thirty new laws that restrict access to the vote, setting up 2021 to be one of the most suppressive years in the post-civil rights era, before the year was even half over.[12] In July, the Supreme Court also decided a parallel case to *Shelby*: *Brnovich* v. *Democratic National Committee*, 141 S.Ct. 1263 (2021). That case severely limited the ability of individual litigants to use the Voting Rights Act to challenge many of the state laws that they believe restrict the right to vote on account of race.

State legislators are also tightening the screws on every step a voter has to take to cast a ballot. Registering to vote is more difficult. Staying registered is harder, as states redouble efforts to purge voter rolls. Voting hours are shrinking. Already strict voter identification requirements are tightening. Regulations of polling places that have the effect of making lines to vote longer are being imposed. Obtaining an absentee or mail-in ballot is becoming harder. The paperwork to cast a mail-in ballot is growing more onerous, and mistakes made in that paperwork are now fatal. Delivering an absentee or mail-in ballot is becoming harder as drop boxes are limited. Partisan and untrained challengers are being empowered to stand at the polls or at vote-counting centers to question voters' eligibility. Getting third-party help anywhere in the process is being restricted—which is a direct assault on mobilization and organization as a counterweight to the suppression techniques. Finally, voter errors are drawing criminal penalties. In Texas, for example, a Houston man, Hervis Earl Rogers, was arrested and held on $100,000 bail in July 2021 for voting illegally. Rogers, who is on parole and did not realize he was ineligible to cast a ballot, stood in line for six hours to vote in the 2020 primary. He now faces four decades in prison.[13]

Although many tools are being deployed to make voting harder, four forms of suppression efforts illustrate my point.[14]

### Restricting the Ability to Get Vote-by-Mail Ballots

Many states are tightening requirements for what information and materials people need to provide on their vote-by-mail applications. For example, as the result of recently enacted laws, people will now have to provide their driver's license number or identification card number on their absentee ballot applications in Georgia, Florida, and Texas.[15] These provisions will have an outsized impact on Black voters. In Georgia, according to one report, more than 270,000 registered voters—or 3.5 percent of electors in the state—do not have the requisite identification. And more than half of them are Black. In a state that Joe Biden won by slightly fewer than 13,000 votes, or a margin of 0.25 percent, the new provision could change the arc of an election.[16]

In addition, once-permanent absentee ballot lists—where voters sign up for an absentee ballot and receive it every election—are being cut back. Arizona, which had used a permanent early voting list since 2007, effectively eliminated it in 2021. Now if a voter fails to vote via an early ballot in all elec tions for two consecutive election cycles, that voter will be removed from the permanent list. As with Georgia, imposing small hurdles to small numbers of ballots may alter election outcomes. Biden won Arizona's Electoral College votes in 2020, but by fewer than 12,000 votes.[17]

### Limiting Delivery of Mail-in Ballots

Once voters run an obstacle course to obtain ballots, they now face increasing challenges delivering them. In the last decade, many states have innovated new ways for voters to return their ballots, and one of the most effective has been drop boxes, which are secure mailbox-style containers designed exclusively for elections. In the 2016 election, nearly one in six voters nationwide made use of drop boxes, and in some states the number of voters using them was even higher.[18] During the 2020 election, their use surged further. Drop boxes were largely uncontroversial, with many voters preferring them to the vagaries of the U.S. Postal Service's unpredictable service levels.[19]

But in the wake of the 2020 election and Trump's assault on the system, some partisan legislatures fixated on hobbling safe and secure drop boxes. In Georgia, the state's election overhaul law dramatically cut the number of drop boxes that cities and counties can use. In Fulton County, home to Atlanta, where half of all absentee ballots were returned at a drop box in the 2020 general election, the number of drop boxes will fall from thirty-eight to eight as a result of the new law. In Florida, rather than restricting the number of drop boxes outright, the legislature achieved virtually the same goal by imposing a requirement that all drop boxes be continuously staffed and fining election supervisors $25,000 if they violate the rule.[20] Texas also curtailed the use of drop boxes in legislation passed in September 2021.[21]

### Tightening Identification Requirements and
### Limiting Hours for In-Person Voting

For Americans who still vote in person, the difficulties are set to increase in several states. In Georgia, Iowa, and Montana, legislatures passed laws that limit voting hours or restrict polling places.[22] And Arkansas, New Hampshire, Montana, and Wyoming imposed stricter requirements on the sort of identification a voter has to show at the polls.[23]

### Kicking Voters Off the Registration Rolls

Another cluster of laws has expanded efforts to kick registered voters off the rolls or has created a risk that flawed procedures—like those that use close rather than precise name matches to deregister people—will be used to check the rolls. While it is perfectly normal and desirable for election officials to make sure the lists of registered voters are correct and up to date, there is a long, unfortunate history of overzealous and biased efforts to do so—ones that end up disproportionately and incorrectly disenfranchising people of color, students, or the elderly.[24] A recent effort in Ohio to purge voters had an error rate of 20 percent—in other words 20 percent of the people, or 40,000 voters who were poised to be stricken from the rolls, had been wrongly singled out.

In the wake of the 2020 election, however, a number of states passed or are considering laws that increase the chance of erroneously kicking potential voters out of the system. Arizona, Iowa, Florida, Kentucky, Louisiana, Texas, and Utah all passed laws to set in motion new, potentially faulty purge efforts.[25]

### Election Subversion

In 2020, one of the more brazen and lawless efforts to overturn the election consisted of threats by legislators to appoint the losing candidate's electors despite the voting results. That was then followed up by attempts by multiple state Republican parties to craft faux Electoral College slates and submit phony certificates to Congress.[26] Today, some legislatures are finding new, creative ways to politicize and interfere with election administration or, potentially, to usurp the power to call winners and losers in elections.

Throughout most of American history, elections have been administered by local governments, which are attuned to their communities and the way their voters live their lives. In the twentieth century, local administrators were driven to increase their levels of professionalism and to limit the effects of partisanship, while state officials, usually the secretaries of state, created a base level of uniformity and coherence on a statewide basis.[27] At the federal level, a variety of laws, from the Voting Rights Act of 1965 to the National Voter Registration Act and the Help America Vote Act, have assured a minimum level of national uniformity. Altogether, this system of robust, interwoven federal, state, and local procedures and decentralized administration has created a stable election system.[28] It is imperfect, to be sure, but Americans have been confident for decades that their vote would be counted, in large part because of this system.[29]

In 2020, these long-standing arrangements, embraced by both parties, produced an election that was free and fair, and with some of the highest turnout numbers in recent decades. But 2021 threatens to introduce a new volatility into the system as the balance of power in administering elections has come under multiple attacks.

In 2021, state legislatures across the country—through at least 216 proposed laws in forty-one states—have moved to muscle their way into election administration, as they attempt to dislodge or unsettle the executive branch and/or local election officials who, traditionally, have run voting systems.[30] Some of these attempts to consolidate power would give state legislatures the ability to disrupt election administration and the reporting of results beyond any authority they had in 2020 or, indeed, throughout much of the last century. Had these bills been in place in 2020, they would have significantly added to the turmoil that surrounded the election, and they could have raised the alarming prospect that the outcome of the presidential election could have been decided contrary to how the people voted. If enacted, many of the proposals could make elections unworkable, render results far more difficult to finalize, and in the worst-case scenario, allow state legislatures to substitute their preferred candidates for those chosen by the voters.

Thus far (as of fall 2021), twenty-four bills that undermine America's traditional election administration system have been enacted.[31] These new laws and related efforts (like the sham audits discussed below) force public officials who are attempting to administer elections into an untenable position. These officials must constantly look over their shoulder, comply with Byzantine rules, seek permission for standard operating practices, work without being able to accept special funding in a crisis, and live in fear that a mistake will land them in the middle of a criminal investigation. They will know that even after they have professionally counted and certified the votes, their decisions may be subject to relentless and baseless attacks.

Many efforts are being made to undermine election administration, and I detail three of them to illustrate my point.

## Sham Audits

Several state legislatures have launched so-called audits of the 2020 election results, unleashing a wave of distrust of election administrators.[32] The Arizona legislature has led the way in these legislature-driven, post-election partisan ballot inspections and the confusion they sow.[33] The purported state senate review of the Maricopa County presidential election results grabbed headlines when it began in April and illustrated the danger of partisan state legislators becoming enmeshed in complex aspects of election administration best left to experienced professionals. The state senate's chosen vendor, Cyber Ninjas—whose CEO, Doug Logan, supported the "Stop the Steal" movement—conducted the ballot inspection with disregard for election best practices, including a rushed count, inadequate verification measures, and inconsistent procedures.[34] At the same time, the "auditors" have chased wild conspiracy theories, including looking for bamboo fibers in ballots because of a false story that thousands of fake ballots were flown in from Asia. Nevertheless, the "audit" continued for months, and when its results were finally announced, revealed that the Maricopa vote count was accurate. The audit also tried to cast doubt on the eligibility of many voters who cast ballots in 2020.[35]

Commentators have warned that the Arizona debacle is a "disinformation blueprint."[36] Still, it appears that other state legislatures are working from that new blueprint for election subversion, as activities akin to the Arizona post-election ballot inspection scheme have moved to other states. In August 2021, the head of Pennsylvania's state senate announced that it would commence an Arizona-style audit, although by the fall the effort had mutated into an inspection of registration rolls.[37] In Wisconsin, the state's assembly leader announced that he was hiring three former police officers and an attorney to conduct a three-month investigation into unsubstantiated claims of 2020 "election fraud."[38] Separately, Wisconsin's Joint Legislative Audit Committee voted earlier in 2021 to conduct an audit of the election results.[39] In Texas, an effort to undertake an audit of the 2020 election results gained momentum in August and as of this writing is poised to be addressed in an upcoming special legislative session.[40] On a county level in Michigan, while a lawsuit to force an audit of 2020 results in Antrim County was dismissed by a state court judge in mid-May 2021, the push for it continues.[41] Meanwhile, in Cheboygan County, local officials have indicated they want to proceed with an "audit" of the 2020 results, although the Michigan state elections director has warned that it is not allowed under state law.[42]

### Penalizing Minor Election Administration Errors

Bills that would create additional criminal and civil penalties for election administrators (and in some cases, voters) mark another recent legislative trend. Given that neither voter fraud nor deliberate maladministration of elections occurs with much frequency, it is tempting to dismiss these bills as solutions in search of a problem and to assume, therefore, they are unlikely to cause much harm. That would be a mistake. Many of these bills change legal standards, rewrite existing investigative processes, or shift legal burdens in ways that will increase the incidence of litigation over election processes and outcomes in the states.

These bills seek to impose penalties on local and state actors who administer elections. Given that such administrators typically are individual community members, often working to administer elections on a volunteer or part-time basis, these bills could very well paralyze election administration in communities across the country. By creating a well-founded fear of criminal or civil penalties (not to mention the expense of legal defense fees),[43] these bills likely will dissuade people from stepping up and helping to make elections work. Even with respect to full-time government employees and officials who administer elections in larger communities, there will be negative consequences. When officials believe they cannot perform even the most basic ministerial functions without opening themselves up to harsh legal penalties, the election system will become ossified and unable to react to changing circumstances. Officials who fear that any attempt to solve a practical problem facing a voter or poll worker could lead to personal liability will be unable to function effectively.

In Texas, legislators have taken the trend to unprecedented levels. In September 2021, Texas passed a sweeping elections law during a special legislative session after a number of other, smaller measures had also passed. The omnibus law contained the most extensive (and often vague) set of civil and criminal penalties for election administrators and workers pursued by any state since Trump was sworn into office in 2016. All told, election administrators face criminal penalties in sixteen new scenarios. Activities involving counting ballots and dealing with mail-in ballot applications, provisional ballots, ballot duplication, and poll watchers now have criminal penalties attached if the law is not strictly followed. In addition, the bill creates another cluster of actions that, if taken, would expose election administrators to civil penalties and lawsuits.[44]

The most sweeping provision in the bill makes it a civil offense for a public official to "create, alter, modify, waive, or suspend any election standard, practice, or procedure mandated by law or rule in a manner not expressly authorized by this code." This provision is so expansive and unclear that it could effectively freeze every local election official and worker in their tracks when faced with any need to adapt their practices to local circumstances or to emergency situations, which is not uncommon in a state that has faced both natural and other disasters regularly in the last decade. The provision would suppress reasonable and customary efforts to approach the myriad problems that inevitably arise in complex voting systems. That requirement is coupled with a new provision that penalizes an election official who violates any part of the election code with the loss of his or her job and employment benefits.[45]

Texas has been far from alone in its efforts to criminalize aspects of election administration.[46] Arizona has passed a law that makes it a felony for an official to modify an election-related date or deadline unless ordered by a court to do so.[47] Iowa makes it a felony for a local election official to fail to follow guidance issued by the state's election commissioner. An Iowa election official who fails to perform list maintenance duties could face up to two years in jail.[48] North Dakota's newly enacted prohibition of the acceptance of private funds for election administration comes with a misdemeanor penalty.[49] And other states continue to consider legislation of this ilk.

## Partisan Gerrymandering

Every decade, most state legislatures redraw the boundaries for electoral districts using newly collected data from the decennial census. New congressional, state senate, and state house lines are drawn, as are city council and school board lines, and indeed those for any political district. In an ideal world, political boundaries would be drawn to ensure equal political representation as required by the one-person, one-vote principle established by the Supreme Court in *Reynolds* v. *Sims,* 377 U.S. 533 (1964). They also would be drawn in a way that complies with the Voting Rights Act and that gathers communities of interest together to ensure that their representatives reflect and respond to their voice. At base level, then, the way lines are drawn is a critical part of the way American democracy creates a positive feedback loop between the people who live in a community and their representatives.

Sadly, a more invidious set of practices has infected the process of drawing jurisdictional boundaries, with lines drawn in ways that benefit incumbents or political parties or that discriminate against minorities and dilute the power of their votes. These gerrymandered lines are drawn to benefit individuals or political parties rather than to enable the realization of fundamental democratic principles. As a top Republican redistricting consultant put it, "redistricting [is] the only legalized form of vote-stealing left in the United States today."[50] To be sure, these sorts of practices have plagued America virtually since its founding. The term "gerrymandering" was coined in 1812 after all.[51] But these practices have been steadily growing worse in recent decades. In the redistricting cycle that followed the 2010 decennial census, gerrymandering played a key role. In seven states—Michigan, Florida, North Carolina, Ohio, Pennsylvania, Texas, and Virginia—the level of partisan gerrymandering was so high that for a time it determined the composition of the House of Representatives and could again after 2021. The partisan bias in the maps in those states appears to have generated so many House of Representative districts that Republicans dominate that the control of that chamber is unfairly tilted toward the GOP, one analysis found. "[T]here is clear evidence that aggressive gerrymandering is distorting the nation's congressional maps, resulting in both large and remarkably durable levels of partisan bias," the report concluded.[52]

2021 is poised to usher in some of the most extreme gerrymandering in American history with the road paved by the loss of the Voting Rights Act's protections and the Supreme Court's 2019 decision in *Rucho* v. *Common Cause*.[53] In that case, the Supreme Court evaluated a challenge to the 2010 gerrymander accomplished by the North Carolina legislature. That state's district lines were drawn with such partisan vigor that in 2012, Republican congressional candidates won nine out of thirteen seats in the U.S. House of Representatives even though they garnered less than half—49 percent—of the statewide vote. When the case challenging the gerrymander reached the Supreme Court, it declined to review the matter. Instead, the court concluded that federal courts have no role in reviewing the constitutionality of partisan gerrymanders; the issues were nonjusticiable.[54]

Because of the delay in the release of census data in 2021, most states have as of this writing only just begun the redistricting process.[55] Nevertheless, observers are concerned that the combination of the *Rucho* decision with a less-than-ideal census process and substantial demographic shifts portends danger.[56] One report has warned that more than 188 million people living in thirty-five states are at risk of gerrymandering based on a number of factors about their state's redistricting process, which may be controlled by incumbent politicians who can craft districts in secret and then face little to no legal scrutiny.[57] When biased legislators can draw lines to insulate themselves from accountability and to effectively keep the majority of voters from proper representation, then the future of our democratic system is in peril.

## Solutions to Address Voter Suppression and Election Subversion

American democracy is at a crossroads. A determined group of officials and advocates are unwilling to stop their assaults on voting rights, despite the dangerous consequences—including the January 6 insurrection. However, an equally committed group of federal, state, and local officials have emerged from the unprecedented and unjustified attacks on the 2020 election determined to build on the historic voter participation witnessed in 2020 and to improve the way Americans vote.

Inasmuch as current suppression efforts attack every part of the elections system, the solutions must defend it just as comprehensively. Several important congressional proposals, taken together, strive to do just that.[58] The Freedom to Vote Act, S. 2747, would establish a series of minimum requirements that would counteract the voter suppression wave. The bills also contain federal remedies to end partisan redistricting. Another companion bill, H.R. 4, constitutes a renewal of the Voting Rights Act, and that approach has attracted bipartisan voices, with Senators Joe Manchin (D-WV) and Lisa Murkowski (R-AK) speaking out in support (at least in principle).[59] And Congress has begun consideration of bills to combat election subversion as well, such as H.R. 4064 and S. 2626, which would create a series of federal remedies for election officials who are undermined or attacked.[60] Below, I address each in turn, as well as other options and the feasibility of any bills becoming law. Consistent with Brookings policy, I do not endorse or oppose any of these specific bills, but instead analyze how they would or would not work.

## The For the People and Freedom to Vote Acts

H.R. 1, which passed the U.S. House on March 4, 2021, and its Senate companion, S. 1, which remains under consideration in the Senate as of this writing (after votes to advance, it failed along party lines in June and August 2021), contain sweeping ideas about how America's federal elections should be run. In the fall, a new version of those bills, S. 2747, or the Freedom to Vote Act, was introduced in the Senate, though it also failed to proceed (once again along party lines) in October 2021. The proposals in these bills represent an effort by Congress to establish nationwide rules using some of the pro-voter practices deployed in various states over the last decade. Together, the For the People Act and Freedom to Vote Act aim to help protect the unimpeded right to vote and block attempts to build barriers to voting.

First, the bills would establish a clear and open gateway to elections for all American citizens. Automatic voter registration would have to be implemented for federal elections; so, too, would same-day, in-person registration on election day. Accurate techniques for maintaining automatic registration rolls—ones that are based on an application for a new driver's license and that involve the voter him- or herself—would be required. Inaccurate voter purging practices, such as those adopted in Arizona, Iowa, Florida, Kentucky, and Utah, would be barred, as would a discredited practice known as caging, whereby voters are taken off registration lists because a piece of mail sent to them was returned as undeliverable. States would not be able to drop people from the rolls based on unreliable list matching. For example, striking a person from a voter list because his name is the same as one on a list of people who have recently died would be barred unless there was reliable information such as a signature or photograph that the match was correct.

Further along in the voting process, no-excuse absentee voting would be allowed for all voters in federal elections. States would not be allowed to impose unnecessary and discriminatory identification requirements to get a mail-in ballot. Drop boxes for absentee votes would have to be deployed through the counties based on voter population.

In-person voters, likewise, would have their freedom to vote better protected. All states would have to offer a minimum number of early voting hours. Voters would be allowed to provide written statements, sworn under penalty of perjury, attesting to their identity so they can vote in federal elections.

The legislation contains a wealth of other provisions, ranging from improving the ability of overseas and military voters to cast ballots, to requiring that states modernize and strengthen their voting systems against attacks by mandating threat assessments, security requirements for voting machines, and audits. Paper ballots that voters can verify are accurate are required. And previously convicted people must have their voting rights restored for federal elections.

Other portions of the legislation provide that partisan gerrymandering would be barred. Voting rights advocates have long called for congressional action on this front in light of the Supreme Court's jurisprudence closing off avenues for federal judicial relief. In addition to making partisan gerrymandering illegal and therefore reviewable by the courts, H.R. 1 also adopts a trend in some states: if enacted, federal congressional districts would be drawn by independent commissions in every state. This would take power from partisan legislators and deliver it to disinterested line drawers who are more likely to respect communities of interest and voters rather than politicians, though S. 2747 does not contain this requirement. (In addition, as discussed in chapter 6, campaign finance laws would be substantially modified to limit the effects of big money on the U.S. system of government. H.R. 1 also addresses ethics issues at length, as discussed in chapters 1 and 2, while S. 2747 does not.)

## *The John Lewis Voting Rights Advancement Act (H.R. 4)*

Undoing the impact of *Shelby* is critical for dealing with current and future waves of anti-voting legislation. In 2019 and again in 2021, the House of Representatives passed the John Lewis Voting Rights Advancement Act, which would have restored the preclearance system set in place by the Voting Rights Act of 1965. The proposal is named after the recently deceased civil rights and congressional icon John Lewis, whose beating in 1965 by law enforcement as he marched for voting rights helped inspire passage of the Voting Rights Act.

If enacted, the measure could significantly slow the spread of many of the most pernicious suppression efforts. Before a state subject to the act's provisions could implement new voting qualifications or prerequisites (or voting standards, practices, or procedures), the state would have to submit them to the Department of Justice.[61] If the DOJ determined that the new proposal has the purpose or effect of diminishing the voting power of citizens on account of race, color, or membership in a language minority group, then the department could stop the new proposal in its tracks.[62] States that wanted to change polling sites, alter identification requirements, or rework their list maintenance practices would be required to do the work to show that the changes are justified and that they do not have a discriminatory impact.

In addition, the act contains provisions that address the *Brnovich* decision by clearly articulating what suffices for proving in a court that a voter of color has had his or her vote denied or diluted by a state practice. This portion of H.R. 4 would not only enable people to go to court to challenge some of the more noxious voter suppression practices currently underway, but would also apply to many gerrymandering efforts.

## *Constraining Election Subversion*

The recent surge in efforts to undermine election administration has inspired a number of proposals to counter the trend. Far from being impossible to address, these recent election subversion ploys can indeed be dealt with. While states have significant discretion over how to administer their own elections, including those for federal offices, this flexibility is not limitless. State election policies are bound by a state's own constitution and laws, and by the federal Constitution and laws.

New proposals for federal legislation could also check this emerging trend. For example, under one proposal introduced in 2021 as H.R. 4064, state election officials who are improperly removed could seek redress in federal court.[63] In addition, intimidation and harassment of election officials under federal law would be directly outlawed by the bill. Likewise, interfering with or attempting to coerce officials as they tabulate, canvass, or certify vote results could be barred, as is set forth in a 2021 Senate proposal introduced as S. 2626. Other possible ways to immunize against the new forms of election subversion include creating a federal statutory right to have one's "ballot counted and included in the appropriate totals of votes cast," enforceable in federal court. Congress could require courts to apply heightened scrutiny to government actions that diminish or impair the right to have one's vote counted. This would ensure judicial review of how votes are counted in federal elections. If, for example, partisan state election officials were to refuse to count certain ballots without sufficient justification, voters could seek relief in court to ensure their votes were counted—with a clear framework for the courts to apply in reviewing the decision. All of these proposals are also contained in the Freedom to Vote Act.

## Other Options and Feasibility

Of course, some will be dubious about the prospects for congressional action on these or other similar measures, such as badly needed Electoral Count Act reform. Yet, the House has shown a willingness to act. And as intractable as the situation seems to be in the Senate as of this writing, there are solutions for improving the functioning of that body. As explained in chapter 9, the hopes for reforming the filibuster are less dim than many believe.

If America is to meet the Trump-inspired renewal of threats of voter suppression and election sabotage, there is little other choice. Options such as litigation will not address those threats comprehensively. Cases under the existing constitutional and statutory scheme, such as the Department of Justice's lawsuit against Georgia for its voter suppression bill,[64] should still be brought. They may succeed in the more outrageous instances, given the brazen nature of some states' actions. But the Supreme Court has made it difficult to challenge much of the assault on voting through its recent decisions curtailing the Voting Rights Act. The hurdles are high and the threats too far-flung and comprehensive for litigation to meet the challenge. In the absence of comprehensive legislation, executive action—such as the Biden administration's commendable executive order to promote access to voting[65]—has too narrow an available range to meet the scope of the threats. And while "get out the vote" campaigns by stakeholders of all parties are an important part of the American electoral experiment, they will now face tornado-level headwinds unless Congress acts.

## Conclusion

The course of voting rights in America has never run smoothly. Almost every step forward has been met with concerted efforts to push back. Today, in the wake of the January 6 insurrection and the relentless suppression efforts by Trump and his allies, the situation may feel grim. The need for strong voting rights and for a renewed dedication to U.S. democracy is as strong as ever. American democracy deserves and requires better, and less politically motivated, approaches. Above all, it deserves a consensus that respects voters and their choices regardless of who ultimately prevails. In the wake of the Civil War, America had a second founding. In the wake of the civil rights movement, America could feel proud in the new strength of its democracy. In the wake of the Trump presidency, the country now has another opportunity to revitalize the U.S. election system, to prove American resilience, and to decisively reject Trumpery in the electoral system.

### Notes

1. "Joint Statement from Elections Infrastructure Government Coordinating Council and the Election Infrastructure Sector Coordinating Executive Committees," Cybersecurity & Infrastructure Security Agency, November 12, 2020, www.Cisa.Gov/News/2020/11/12/Joint-statement-elections-infrastructure-government-coordinating-council-election; Kevin Schaul, Kate Rabinowitz, and Ted Mellnik, "2020 Turnout Is the Highest in Over a Century," *Washington Post*, last updated December 28, 2020, www.washingtonpost.com/graphics/2020/elections/voter-turnout/.

2. Morgan Chalfant, "Trump: 'The Only Way We're Going to Lose This Election Is

if the Election Is Rigged," *The Hill*, August 17, 2020, https://thehill.com/homenews/administration/512424-trump-the-only-way-we-are-going-to-lose-this-election-is-if-the.

3. William Cummings, Joey Garrison, and Jim Sergent, "By the Numbers: President Donald Trump's Failed Efforts to Overturn the Election," *USA Today*, January 6, 2021, www.usatoday.com/in-depth/news/politics/elections/2021/01/06/trumps-failed-efforts-overturn-election-numbers/4130307001/.

4. Ibid.

5. Norman Eisen and Katherine Reisner, "Whatever Legal or Constitutional Test You Apply, Trump Incited the Violent Capitol Attack," *USA Today*, last updated February 4, 2021, www.usatoday.com/story/opinion/2021/02/03/donald-trump-incited-capitol-attack-by-any-legal-test-column/4370622001/.

6. See "Issue Areas," Voting Rights Lab, https://tracker.votingrightslab.org/issue-areas (searchable database of voting legislation introduced this year).

7. In 2013, the Supreme Court significantly cut back the Voting Rights Act in *Shelby County* v. *Holder*, 570 U.S. 529 (2013). Six years later, in *Rucho* v. *Common Cause*, 588 U.S. ___ (2019), the Supreme Court concluded that partisan gerrymandering claims were nonjusticiable, in other words that federal courts could not decide those sorts of claims. Finally, in *Brnovich* v. *Democratic National Committee*, 594 U.S. ___ (2021), the Supreme Court restricted the ability of individual plaintiffs to bring certain claims under the Voting Rights Act.

8. "Shelby County v. Holder," Brennan Center for Justice, August 4, 2018, www.brennancenter.org/our-work/court-cases/shelby-county-v-holder.

9. Heather K. Gerken, "A Third Way for the Voting Rights Act: Section 5 and the Opt-In Approach," *Columbia Law Review* 106, no. 708 (2006), p. 709.

10. Kevin Morris and others, "Purges: A Growing Threat to the Right to Vote," Brennan Center for Justice, July 20, 2018, www.brennancenter.org/our-work/research-reports/purges-growing-threat-right-vote; Wendy R. Weiser and Max Feldman, "The State of Voting 2018," Brennan Center for Justice, June 5, 2018, www.brennancenter.org/our-work/research-reports/state-voting-2018.

11. "Voting Laws Roundup: February 2021," Brennan Center for Justice, February 8, 2021, www.brennancenter.org/our-work/research-reports/voting-laws-roundup-february-2021.

12. "Voting Laws Roundup: July 2021," Brennan Center for Justice, July 22, 2021, www.brennancenter.org/our-work/research-reports/voting-laws-roundup-july-2021.

13. Isabella Grullón Paz, "Texas Man Who Waited Hours to Vote Is Arrested on Charges of Illegal Voting," *New York Times*, July 10, 2021, www.nytimes.com/2021/07/10/us/texas-primary-voter-arrested.html.

14. The following analysis is drawn from the sources set forth in notes 10–12, this chapter, and citations for the data provided may be found in those sources.

15. S.B. Res. 202, Sess. of 2021 (Ga. 2021), https://legiscan.com/GA/text/SB202/id/2348602/Georgia-2021-SB202-Enrolled.pdf; S.B. Res. 90, Sess. of 2021 (Fl. 2021), www

.flsenate.gov/Session/Bill/2021/90/BillText/er/PDF. Florida also allows the last four digits of an applicant's social security number to be used as identification on a voter registration application; a Pennsylvania bill passed by the state legislature contained similar provisions but was vetoed by the state's governor. H.B. Res. 1300, Sess. of 2021–2022 (Pa. 2021), www.legis.state.pa.us/cfdocs/billInfo/billInfo.cfm?sYear=2021&sInd=0&body=H&type=B&bn=1300.

16. Kate Brumback, "Georgia Again Certified Election Results Showing Biden Won," AP News, December, 7, 2020, https://apnews.com/article/election-2020-joe-biden-donald-trump-georgia-elections-4eeea3b24f10de886bcdeab6c26b680a.

17. Rob O'Dell, "'Seismic Shift': As Election Day Arrives, Republicans Hold a Slight Edge over Democrats in Early Arizona Ballots," *AZCentral*, November 3, 2020, www.azcentral.com/story/news/politics/elections/2020/11/03/arizona-early-voting-results-republicans-hold-light-edge-over-democrats/6077972002/.

18. Axel Hufford, "The Rise of Ballot Drop Boxes Due to the Coronavirus," *Lawfare*, August 27, 2020, www.lawfareblog.com/rise-ballot-drop-boxes-due-coronavirus.

19. Amy Sherman, "Ballot Drop Boxes Have Long Been Used Without Controversy. Then Trump Got Involved," *Politfact*, October 16, 2020, www.politifact.com/article/2020/oct/16/ballot-drop-boxes-have-long-been-used-without-cont/.

20. State of Florida, Senate, SB 90, 2021 regular sess., introduced February 3, 2021, and signed into effect by Gov. Ron DeSantis on May 6, 2021, www.flsenate.gov/Session/Bill/2021/90. Iowa and Indiana have also restricted the use of drop boxes. See State of Iowa, Senate, SF413, 89th Gen. Assembly, 2021 regular sess., introduced in Senate February 18, 2021, and signed into effect by Gov. Kim Reynolds on March 8, 2021, www.legis.iowa.gov/docs/publications/LGE/89/SF413.pdf.; State of Indiana, Senate, SB398, 122nd Gen. Assembly., 1st sess., introduced in Senate January 14, 2021, and signed into effect by Gov. Eric Holcomb on April 23, 2021, http://in-proxy.openstates.org/2021/bills/SB0398/versions/SB0398.06.ENRH.

21. S.B. 1, special sess. 2 of 2021 (Tex. 2021), https://capitol.texas.gov/tlodocs/872/billtext/pdf/SB00001F.pdf#navpanes=0.

22. State of Georgia, Senate, SB 202, 2021 regular sess., https://legiscan.com/GA/text/SB202/id/2348602; State of Iowa, Senate, SF413, 89th Gen. Assembly, 2021 regular sess., introduced in Senate February 18, 2021, and signed into effect by Gov. Kim Reynolds on March 8, 2021, www.legis.iowa.gov/docs/publications/LGE/89/SF413.pdf.; State of Montana, Senate, SB196, 2021 regular sess., https://legiscan.com/MT/bill/SB196/2021.

23. State of Arkansas, House, HB1112, 93rd Gen. Assembly, 2021 regular sess., introduced in House January 11, 2021, www.arkleg.state.ar.us/Bills/FTPDocument?path=%2FBills%2F2021R%2FPublic%2FHB1112.pdf; State of Arkansas, House, HB1244, 93rd Gen. Assembly, 2021 regular sess., introduced in House January 25, 2021, www.arkleg.state.ar.us/Bills/FTPDocument?path=%2FBills%2F2021R%2FPublic%2FHB1244.pdf; State of New Hampshire, House, H.B. 523, 2021 regular sess., http://gencourt.state.nh.us/bill_status/billText.aspx?sy=2021&id=747&txtFormat=html; State

of Montana, Senate, SB196, 2021 regular sess., https://legiscan.com/MT/bill/SB196/
2021; State of Wyoming, House, HB0075, 66th Leg., 2021 general sess., https://legiscan
.com/WY/text/HB0075/2021.

24. See Alan Judd, "Georgia's Strict Laws Lead to Large Purge of Voters," *Atlanta Journal-Constitution*, October 27, 2018, www.ajc.com/news/state--regional-govt--poli
tics/voter-purge-begs-question-what-the-matter-with-georgia/YAFvuk3Bu95kJIM
aDiDFqJ/.

25. State of Arizona, Senate, SB1819, 55th Leg., 1st reg. sess., introduced in Senate
May 25, 2021, https://legiscan.com/AZ/bill/SB1819/2021; State of Iowa, Senate, SF413,
89th Gen. Assembly, 2021 regular sess., introduced in Senate February 18, 2021, www
.legis.iowa.gov/docs/publications/LGE/89/SF413.pdf; State of Florida, Senate, SB 90,
2021 regular sess., introduced February 3, 2021, www.flsenate.gov/Session/Bill/2021/
90; State of Kentucky, House, HB574, 2021 reg. sess., https://legiscan.com/KY/bill/
HB574/2021; State of Louisiana, House, HB167, 2021 reg. sess., https://legiscan.com/LA
/text/HB167/2020; State of Texas, Senate, SB7, 2021, https://legiscan.com/TX/text/SB7
/2021; State of Utah, House, HB0012, 2021 reg. sess., https://legiscan.com/UT/bill/HB
0012/2021.

26. Paul McLeod, "Pro-Trump Republicans Are Holding Fake Electoral College
Votes While the Real Electoral College Meets to Formalize Biden's Win," Buzzfeed
News, December 14, 2020, www.buzzfeednews.com/article/paulmcleod/electoral-col
lege-trump-supporters.

27. See Ernest Hawkins, "Creating Professionalism in the Field," in *The Future of Election Administration*, edited by Mitchell Brown, Kathleen Hale, and Bridgett A. King
(London: Palgrave MacMillan, 2019), https://doi.org/10.1007/978-3-030-18541-1_13.

28. Polling shows that people have the utmost faith in their local leaders and election officials. See "New Poll Finds Americans Want Every Legal Vote Counted," States
United Democracy Center, November 4, 2020, https://statesuniteddemocracy.org/
2020/11/04/new-poll-finds-americans-want-every-legal-vote-counted/; Kim Hart,
"Golden Age of Local Leaders," Axios, October 2, 2019, www.axios.com/local-state
-government-trust-congress-b820f103-7952-429d-bfea-adf7fc7beaa4.html. Recent
polling shows 64 percent of voters believe local elected officials provide fair and accurate information to the public. See "Why Americans Don't Fully Trust Many Who
Hold Positions of Power and Responsibility," Pew Research Center, September 19,
2019, www.pewresearch.org/politics/2019/09/19/why-americans-dont-fully-trust
-many-who-hold-positions-of-power-and-responsibility/. Local officials are also
viewed more favorably than state elected leaders by both Democrats and Republicans,
something that has been a trend for the last decade. See Justin McCarthy, "Americans
Still More Trusting of Local Than State Government," Gallup, October 8, 2018, https:
//news.gallup.com/poll/243563/americans-trusting-local-state-government.aspx.

29. In general, while Americans are often mistrustful of overall election results,
they have tended to believe that their vote will be counted accurately. See "Voter Confidence," MIT Election Data and Science Lab, April 19, 2021, https://electionlab.mit.

edu/research/voter-confidence. "Research by scholars such as Lonna Atkeson, Mike Alvarez, Thad Hall, and Paul Gronke tells us that voters tend to be more confident when they don't wait a long time to vote, when they encounter polling place officials who seem competent, and when they vote in person rather than by mail. Some of these factors certainly can be affected by state policies, but more often, they are influenced by local administrators' decisions about how to allocate resources to polling places and how rigorously they train poll workers."

30. "Democracy Crisis Report Update: New Data and Trends Show the Warning Signs Have Intensified in the Last Two Months," States United Democracy Center, June 10, 2021, https://statesuniteddemocracy.org/wp-content/uploads/2021/06/Demo cracy-Crisis-Part-II_June-10_Final_v7.pdf.

31. Ibid.

32. For expert auditors' assessment of the Arizona activity, see Trey Grayson and Barry Burden, "Report on the Cyber Ninjas Review of the 2020 Presidential and U.S. Senatorial Elections in Maricopa County, Arizona," States United Democracy Center, June 22, 2021, https://statesuniteddemocracy.org/resources/report-on-the-cyber -ninjas-review-of-the-2020-presidential-and-u-s-senatorial-elections-in-maricopa -county-arizona/; Jen Fifield, "Is the Maricopa County Election Audit Truly an Audit? Here's What Professional Auditors Have to Say," *AZCentral*, June 1, 2021, www. azcentral.com/story/news/politics/elections/2021/06/01/professional-auditors-take-a -look-at-arizona-senate-audit-of-maricopacounty-2020-election/5212065001/; Jenni- fer Morrell, "I Watched the GOP's Arizona Election Audit. It Was Worse than You Think," *Washington Post*, May 19, 2021, www.washingtonpost.com/outlook/2021/05/19/ gop-arizona-election-audit/.

33. Ibid.

34. Ibid.

35. Laurie Roberts, "So Now It's Bamboo in the Ballots? Are There Are Any Limits to the Senate's Audit Lunacy?" *Arizona Republic*, May 7, 2021, www.azcentral.com/ story/opinion/op-ed/laurieroberts/2021/05/06/arizona-election-audit-now-searching -bamboo-our-ballots/4974025001/; Mark Phillips, Garrett Archer, and Melissa Blasius, "Hand Count Shows Biden Won Maricopa County, Republicans Now Want AG to In- vestigate," ABC15 (AZ), September 27, 2021, www.abc15.com/news/arizona-election -audit/election-audit-hand-count-shows-biden-won-maricopa-county-no-evidence -of-voter-fraud.

36. Miles Park, "Experts Call It a 'Clown Show' But Arizona 'Audit' Is a Disinfor- mation Blueprint," NPR, June 3, 2021, www.npr.org/2021/06/03/1000954549/experts -call-it-a-clown-show-but-arizona-audit-is-a-disinformation-blueprint.

37. Marc Levy, "Will an Election 'Audit' Happen in Pennsylvania?" AP News, August 28, 2021, https://apnews.com/article/elections-pennsylvania-election-2020-75 9084e8fecf29949549bc78e5dc7cf0.

38. Katie Shepard, "Despite Little Evidence of Fraud, Wisconsin Republican

Leader Hires Retired Police to Probe 2020 Election," *Washington Post*, May 27, 2021, www.washingtonpost.com/nation/2021/05/27/wisconsin-robin-vos-election-fraud/.

39. Patrick Marley, "Republican Lawmakers Order an Audit of Wisconsin's Elections," *Milwaukee Journal Sentinel*, February 11, 2021, www.jsonline.com/story/news/politics/2021/02/11/wisconsin-republicans-order-audit-2020-elections/6722833002/.

40. Reid Wilson, "Texas Republicans Plan Expanded Election Audits," *The Hill*, September 8, 2021, https://thehill.com/homenews/state-watch/571314-texas-republicans-plan-expanded-election-audits.

41. Rosalind S. Helderman, "Michigan Judge Dismisses Lawsuit Seeking New Audit of Antrim County Vote, One of the Last Remaining 2020 Legal Challenges," *Washington Post*, May 18, 2021, www.washingtonpost.com/politics/antrim-county-lawsuit/2021/05/18/e324451a-b802-11eba5fe-bb49dc89a248_story.html.

42. Craig Mauger, "Cheboygan Board Can't Require Access to Voting Machines, Michigan Elections Director Says," *Detroit News*, last modified May 26, 2021, www.detroitnews.com/story/news/politics/2021/05/25/michigan-county-board-cant-require-access-voting-machines/7436649002/.

43. Jim Small, "Senate GOP All Back Arresting Maricopa County Supervisors for Contempt," *Arizona Mirror*, February 3, 2021, www.azmirror.com/2021/02/03/senate-gop-all-back-arresting-maricopa-county-supervisors-for-contempt/; "Trump Campaign Sues to Block Mail-In Ballot Rule Changes," AP News, September 28, 2020, https://apnews.com/article/election-2020-virus-outbreak-voting-state-elections-lawsuits-7104cfbeb854710ebe7ff9528560249a; Caroline Bleakley and David Charns, "Federal Judge in Nevada Rejects Emergency Motion Claiming Voter Fraud, Signature Verification Issues," KSN, last modified November 5, 2020, www.ksn.com/news/your-localelection-hq/live-trump-campaign-to-hold-news-conference-in-las-vegas-at-830-a-m-republicans-filing-lawsuit/.

44. S.B. Res. 7, Sess. of 2021 (Tex. 2021).

45. S.B. 1, special sess. 2 (Tex. 2021). Some but not all of the new offenses created in the law likely warrant criminalization. But in a highly partisan environment, election officials in Democratic counties may fear selective prosecution. See also Allie Morris, "New Texas Elections Law Carries Costs and Threat of Litigation for All 254 Counties," *Dallas Morning News*, September 9, 2021, www.dallasnews.com/news/politics/2021/09/09/new-texas-elections-law-carries-costs-and-threat-of-litigation-for-all-254-counties/.

46. See Bob Bauer and Ben Ginsberg, "State Election Officials Are Under Attack. We Will Defend Them," *New York Times*, June 4, 2021, www.nytimes.com/2021/06/04/opinion/republican-state-laws-election-officials.html.

47. H.R. Res. 2794, Sess. of 2021 (Ariz. 2021), www.azleg.gov/legtext/55leg/1R/bills/HB2794H.pdf.

48. S.F. Res. 413, Sess. of 2021 (Iowa 2021), www.legis.iowa.gov/legislation/BillBook?ga=89&ba=sf413.

49. H.R. Res. 1253, Sess. of 2021 (N. Dak. 2021), https://legiscan.com/ND/text/1253 /id/2389045/North_Dakota-2021-1253-Enrolled.pdf.

50. Thomas Hofeller, "User Clip: Hofeller Defines Redistricting," C-SPAN (video), April 2, 1991, www.c-span.org/video/?c4801547/user-clip-hofeller-defines -redistricting.

51. Jessie Kratz, "The 'Gerry' in Gerrymandering," National Archives, June 21, 2018, https://prologue.blogs.archives.gov/2018/06/21/the-gerry-in-gerrymandering/.

52. Laura Royden and Michael Li, "Extreme Maps," Brennan Center for Justice, May 9, 2017, www.brennancenter.org/our-work/research-reports/extreme-maps.

53. *Rucho*, 588 U.S. ___.

54. Ibid.

55. Grace Panetta, "Census Delays Are Scrambling the Once-in-a-Decade Redistricting That Will Shape the 2022 Midterms," *Business Insider*, April 26, 2021, www.businessinsider.com/why-census-delays-are-upending-the-redistricting-process-explainer-2021-2.

56. Michael Li, "The Redistricting Landscape, 2021–22," Brennan Center for Justice, July 12, 2021, www.brennancenter.org/our-work/research-reports/redistricting -landscape-2021-22.

57. "Gerrymandering Threat Index," Represent.Us, May 2021, https://represent.us /wp-content/uploads/2021/05/Gerrymandering-Threat-Index-May-6.pdf.

58. This section discusses several bills introduced in the U.S. Congress. For ease of reference, readers can find citations for all of them here: H.R. 1, 117th Cong., introduced January 4, 2021, www.congress.gov/bill/117th-congress/house-bill/1; H.R. 4, 117th Cong., introduced August 17, 2021, www.https://www.congress.gov/bill/117th -congress/house-bill/4; H.R. 4064, 117th Cong., introduced June 22, 2021, www.congress.gov/bill/117th-congress/house-bill/4064/text?r=10&s=1; S. 1, 117th Cong., introduced March 17, 2021, www.congress.gov/bill/117th-congress/senate-bill/1; S. 2626, 117th Cong., introduced August 5, 2021, www.congress.gov/bill/117th-congress/senate -bill/2626; S. 2747, 117th Cong., introduced September 14, 2021, www.congress.gov/bill /117th-congress/senate-bill/2747.

59. Sahil Kapur, "Manchin, Murkowski, Call on Congress to Reauthorize Voting Rights Act," NBC News, May 17, 2021, www.nbcnews.com/politics/congress/manchin -murkowski-call-congress-reauthorize-voting-rights-act-n1267644.

60. H.R. 4064, 117th Cong., introduced June 22, 2021, www.congress.gov/bill/117th -congress/house-bill/4064/text?r=10&s=1. "To amend title 18, United States Code, and the Help America Vote Act of 2002 to provide increased protections for election workers and voters in elections for Federal office, and for other purposes."

61. The version of H.R. 4 that passed the House of Representatives in 2019 did not impact all states. Instead, the bill created a formula for determining which states (or parts of states) would be subject to its provisions. The coverage formula asks whether states have a recent history of voting rights violations, and if the number of those violations is high enough, then the state will be required to go through the preclearance

process. At the time the Supreme Court handed down the *Shelby* decision, the pre-clearance requirements of the Voting Rights Act were applied to nine ex-Confederate states and several cities or counties in California, Florida, Michigan, New York, North Carolina, and South Dakota.

62. A state could nevertheless still implement them, but only after a court has considered the matter.

63. H.R. 4064, 117th Cong., introduced June 22, 2021, www.congress.gov/bill/117th-congress/house-bill/4064/text?r=10&s=1.

64. In the wake of the Senate's latest failure to adjust filibuster rules and pass comprehensive federal voting rights legislation, bipartisan talks are as of this writing reported to be underway. See Lauren Fox, Morgan Rimmer, and Clare Foran, "Bipartisan Group of Senators Seeks Common Ground on Changing Electoral Count Act," CNN, January 20, 2022, www.cnn.com/2022/01/20/politics/electoral-count-act-reform-senate/index.html. In the House of Representatives, the Committee on House Administration has released recommendations for ECA reform as well. See U.S. House of Representatives Committee on House Administration, *The Electoral Count Act of 1887: Proposals for Reform* (2022), https://cha.house.gov/sites/democrats.cha.house.gov/files/documents/Electoral%20Count%20Act%20Staff%20Report.pdf. Electoral Count Act reform by itself is important, but is no substitute for comprehensive voting rights reform. See Fred Wertheimer and Norman Eisen, "Fixing the Electoral Count Act Is No Substitute for Real Election Reform," *Washington Post*, January 6, 2022, www.washingtonpost.com/outlook/2022/01/06/eca-reform-voting-rights/. However, there are important issues that need to be addressed with respect to the Electoral Count Act. See Joshua Matz, Norman Eisen, and Harmann Singh, "Guide to Counting Electoral College Votes and the January 6, 2021, Meeting of Congress," States United Democracy Center, January 4, 2021, https://statesuniteddemocracy.org/wp-content/uploads/2021/01/VPP-Guide-to-Counting-Electoral-Votes.pdf.

65. Executive Order 14019, "Promoting Access to Voting," *Federal Register* (2021), www.federalregister.gov/documents/2021/03/10/2021-05087/promoting-access-to-voting.

# 6

# A Three-Step Approach to Money in Politics

## RICHARD W. PAINTER

Big money in politics is a threat to American democracy.[1] Americans of all political views share a common abhorrence of the corruption inherent in the U.S. campaign finance system.[2] Although Russia contrived novel ways of interfering in the 2016 election through computer hacking and social media propaganda,[3] and foreign interference was also an issue in 2020, the United States' biggest election interference problem remains the infusion of large amounts of cash into electioneering communications.[4]

Indeed, Donald Trump ran in 2016 on the slogan "Drain the Swamp," and promised "to inoculate himself from the influence of donors."[5] The reality of his administration proved to be different. Trump campaign donors openly

---

Several recommendations put forth in this chapter, including the proposal for a tax rebate for small-dollar campaign contributions, were originally written about by the author in his 2016 book on taxation and campaign finance reform. For more, see Richard W. Painter, *Taxation Only with Representation: The Conservative Conscience and Campaign Finance Reform* (Auburn, AL: Take Back Our Republic, 2016).

wielded influence at all levels of his administration, laying the groundwork for one of the most corrupt presidencies in history.[6] Trump's properties, such as his D.C. luxury hotel and his Mar-a-Lago Club in Florida, became ground zero for the nexus of campaign cash and special interests, at times more closely resembling bazaars of influence peddling than hospitality venues (with funds flowing to both the campaign coffers of Trump and his allies as well as to Trump's own wallet).[7] Little wonder that a series of scandals involving large contributors ensued, including prosecutions linked to allegations that mega-donors Elliott Broidy and Tom Barrack utilized their ability to influence the administration on behalf of foreign governments.[8] Meanwhile, a completely dysfunctional Federal Election Commission (FEC) enabled dark money to continue its unrestrained impact on democratic processes. Instead of the swamp being drained, it was flooded with dark money on all sides, topping more than $1 billion in the 2020 cycle—a new record. Proving that special interests have no regard for party, only power, "[a]fter years of dark money overwhelmingly boosting Republicans, [2020 was] the first presidential election cycle where dark money benefited Democrats."[9]

Trump may be gone, but the crisis rages on. It was already a catastrophe—he just made it worse. The consequences of the ongoing failure to address this problem are severe. First, direct and indirect campaign contributions, including money spent on electioneering communications not paid for directly by a campaign, can be a form of bribery (whether illegal or squeezed through loopholes in the law).[10] Candidates want the money desperately, and substantial sums are provided by persons and organizations that spend the money because they want something in return.[11] The fact that some industry sectors, such as the financial services industry, spend massive amounts supporting both Democrats and Republicans, with corporate donors in particular often splitting their donations between the two parties,[12] suggests that influence could be as much a motivating factor as ideology.

Bribery is an ancient plague in government. The late professor and judge John T. Noonan Jr. traced bribery back thousands of years in his 1984 book *Bribes: The Intellectual History of a Moral Idea*.[13] Judge Noonan explained, with a multitude of examples, how bribery often manifests itself through campaign contributions in the American political system. Senator Russell

B. Long, son of Louisiana politician and power broker Huey Long, in 1971 said that "the distinction between a campaign contribution and a bribe is a hairline's difference."[14] In the past several decades, the influence of campaign expenditures has only increased, with billions of dollars now entering the U.S. campaign finance system in each election cycle.[15] Even the Supreme Court, in striking down regulation of corporate spending on electioneering communications in *Citizens United* v. *Federal Election Commission*, acknowledged that campaign contributions buy "access,"[16] although the court limited its definition of *corruption* to a demonstrable quid pro quo.[17]

Researchers have explored the appearance of quid pro quo ("this for that") in the U.S. campaign finance system using at least two methods. In one study, when mock grand jurors were presented with basic facts that are common occurrences in politics, the jurors found corruption in a large number of cases.[18] Other studies have shown substantial statistical correlation between legislators' voting patterns and campaign contributions.[19] This latter category of studies confronts the difficulty of distinguishing between situations where contributors donate to legislators already predisposed to support certain policy preferences and situations where contributions likely change a legislator's vote.[20] Even if statistical studies get mired in the chicken and egg problem (which comes first, a legislator's predisposition or a campaign contribution?), there can be little doubt that the influence of campaign money on legislative bodies is powerful and corrupting.

Yet another way of looking at this problem is the concept of "dependence corruption," explained by Lawrence Lessig in his book *Republic, Lost*.[21] Lessig uses the analogy of a magnet held close to a magnetic compass and exerting a force that, while unseen, causes the compass to point somewhere other than magnetic north. Legislators, Lessig argues, rather than being dependent only upon the people who elect them, are dependent on their funders, a dependency that is reflected in the legislators' policies.[22]

Make no mistake about the danger this poses. Even where there is no unlawful corruption, the appearance of corruption can be debilitating for a representative democracy, which depends on public trust.[23] The mere appearance can feed public enthusiasm for demagogues who promise to root out "corruption" by rooting out their political opponents. In the notorious Barmat Scandal in the Weimar Republic, leading Social Democratic politicians in 1924 and 1925 were accused of taking bribes from an influential businessman.[24] This scandal was one of many weaknesses of the Weimar regime exploited by Adolf Hitler and his fascist supporters to attack both the German political establishment and the Jewish business community.[25] The world knows what eventually happened.

The United States is not at that pass. But widespread public anger at corruption, including the enormous influence of money in politics, could feed a nasty populist turn. Candidates who say they want to "drain the swamp" in Washington can propel themselves to power through demagoguery, and through using their own sources of campaign finance and support from home and from abroad.[26] Yet, after gaining power, elected officials may do little to cure the system of corruption. "Alternative facts" and conspiracy theories about a "deep state" and "election fraud" may find fertile ground in a political climate already poisoned by corruption in politics. The United States has not yet experienced what happened in Germany in 1933, but history shows that rooting out actual corruption and the appearance of corruption in the U.S. political system will be important to protecting the future of the republic.

Reforming the U.S. campaign finance system is one of America's most pressing concerns. This chapter proposes a three-step program for minimizing, disclosing, and counterbalancing the influence that big money has on American elections.

## Minimizing Big Money in Politics

The first objective is to keep as much big money out of U.S. elections as possible. This is critically important not only to the health of democracy, but also to national security. Cash is fungible. In a global economy, corporate money of multinationals or their affiliates domiciled in the United States is often foreign money (and many United States corporations also send their money overseas).[27] Even on the domestic side, there is something fundamentally wrong with a political system that goes by the mantra of "one dollar, one vote" instead of "one person, one vote." The ensuing cynicism and polarization can easily be the undoing of a representative democracy.

The Supreme Court needs to be persuaded to revisit its decision in *Citizens United* v. *Federal Election Commission* that corporations and similar business entities are "people" entitled to a First Amendment right to inject limitless amounts of money into electioneering communications up to election day.[28] The problem is that with the conservative majority now on the Supreme Court, reversal of the court's ruling in *Citizens United* is not likely.[29] Appointment of justices who understand the difference between corporate personhood and natural persons should be a priority, but who knows how long it will take to build a consensus on the court to overturn *Citizens United*?[30]

Another approach is to pass a constitutional amendment that would reverse the rulings in *Citizens United* and similar cases.[31] There is, however, an extremely high threshold for amending the Constitution. An amendment may be proposed by a two-thirds vote of the House or Senate; or if two-thirds of the states request it, a constitutional convention can be called for the purpose of considering amendments.[32] A proposed amendment must then be ratified by three-fourths of the state legislatures or three-fourths of the ratification conventions in each state.[33]

An amendment that is politically polarizing along ideological or geographic lines, or that is perceived to favor big states or small states, almost certainly will not pass and be ratified. However, the role of money in politics is a subject about which voters across the political spectrum largely agree in their antipathy for the status quo. At least at the grassroots level, there is enough consensus to make a proposed amendment appealing, assuming voters can be persuaded to get behind the same amendment.[34] Getting an amendment passed by Congress could be more difficult, as could the process of persuading state legislatures to ratify it. The problem is that some members of Congress and state legislators may listen to corporate money rather than their own constituents. Still, there is at least enough of a chance of success that an amendment to the Constitution is worth exploring.

I will not delve here into detail on the proposed text for such an amendment. One of the simplest proposed amendments was introduced on January 4, 2019, by Representatives Ted Deutch (D-FL), Jim McGovern (D-MA), Jamie Raskin (D-MD), and John Katko (R-NY).[35] The amendment affirms the right of states and the federal government to pass laws that regulate spending in elections.[36]

Yet another approach is to enact campaign finance reform legislation that does not fly in the face of *Citizens United* and other Supreme Court case law. Dollar limits on contributions by an individual to any one candidate were upheld by the Supreme Court in *Buckley* v. *Valeo* (1976),[37] even though aggregate dollar limits on an individual's total campaign contributions were struck down in *McCutcheon* v. *Federal Election Commission* (2014).[38] Very low dollar limits on individual contributions also have been overturned by the court.[39] Nonetheless, dollar limits that have withstood constitutional challenges should be enforced, and enforcement efforts should be heightened to target illegal "straw donor" arrangements in which one person pays for a campaign contribution while another person makes the contribution.[40]

To the extent that it is constitutionally permissible, political fundraising by lobbyists who solicit their clients for contributions should be restricted. Presently, disclosure of these aggregate campaign contributions is required, but there are no dollar limits on the aggregate.[41] However, these contributions from clients solicited by a lobbyist should be attributed to the lobbyist, on the theory that the client contributions are really part of the consideration paid for the lobbyist's services. Lobbyists bundle these contributions, presumably to persuade lawmakers to give the lobbyists and their clients what they want.[42] Lobbyists should be banned entirely from fundraising for political candidates—or at a minimum, dollar limits should be imposed on the size of the contribution bundles assembled by lobbyists.[43]

Also, the courts have not struck down laws prohibiting campaign contributions by foreign nationals.[44] The federal district court in Washington, D.C., held in *Bluman* v. *FEC* that the First Amendment protections in *Citizens United* do not apply to electioneering expenditures by foreign entities.[45] This ruling, upheld in an opinion by Judge Brett Kavanaugh, was then affirmed without an opinion by the Supreme Court. This means, for now at least, that the FEC can tighten up on enforcement against electioneering expenditures by foreign nationals, and if new legislation is needed to facilitate enforcement, ask Congress to enact it.[46] Americans may disagree about which foreign nationals are trying to influence U.S. elections in favor of which candidates in a particular election, but all should be able to agree that foreign money in U.S. elections is not a good thing and should be prohibited.[47]

Devising effective regulation of all foreign-influenced electioneering expenditures inside the United States, however, could be difficult given the close and often opaque financial ties between American corporations and business entities overseas. Then Judge (now Justice) Kavanaugh in his 2011 opinion in *Bluman* ruled that American corporate money is constitutionally protected in U.S. elections but foreign money is not, a distinction that some foreign nationals may perceive as unjust and that is unusual in First Amendment jurisprudence, which generally protects foreigners' conduct within U.S. borders. The perceived unjustness and unenforceability of this distinction may inspire many to seek ways to work with American counterparts to get around the rule. Kavanaugh's ruling means that while there is a large, boisterous, and constitutionally protected money party in Washington and state capitols, it is a party to which foreign nationals are not invited.

Another area for consideration is the tax treatment of 501(c)(4) civic groups.[48] Today, 501(c)(4) civic groups are used for very different purposes than when this provision of the Internal Revenue Code was enacted, and Congress should consider whether the favorable tax treatment of such organizations remains warranted when they are extensively used as vehicles to conceal independent campaign expenditures.[49] Currently, "contributions to civic leagues and other 501(c)(4) organizations generally are not deductible as charitable contributions . . . [but] may be deductible as trade or business expenses, if ordinary and necessary in the conduct of the taxpayer's business."[50] This business expense deduction should be reconsidered; there is no reason U.S. taxpayers should subsidize efforts to conceal donors who are shaping partisan political outcomes.

### Disclosing Big Money in Politics

Political expenditures that cannot constitutionally be restricted should at least be disclosed. A more robust disclosure regime will go a long way toward helping the media and voters connect the dots between persons or entities making political expenditures and the public officials who benefit from those expenditures.[51, 52]

In the realm of political action committees (PACs), contributors to Super PACs are already disclosed, but there is insufficient information about the business entities behind these contributors.[53] The FEC needs to vigorously enforce the disclosure rules already in place, and Congress needs to enact new legislation that will make the actual sources of Super PAC funding more transparent.[54] Another problem is that in the weeks before an election, Super PACs can spend large amounts of money that is borrowed from media vendors or others, and then pay down debt with contributions or transfers from other Super PACs that are reported only after the election.[55] These loopholes in the reporting regime should be closed—for example, by requiring a Super PAC to report anticipated expenditures as soon as they become definite (such as when a television advertising contract is signed), as well as information about the Super PAC's intended sources of funding to pay for those expenditures.[56]

A 501(c)(4) organization, which can engage in a broader range of functions than a 501(c)(3), including political activity, should be required to disclose the sources of its funding. That in particular should include contributions over a certain dollar threshold. Currently, 501(c)(4)s must keep records of contributors of $5,000 or more,[57] but information identifying contributors is not publicly available.[58] This information should be made publicly available.

Although 501(c)(3) "charitable" organizations under Internal Revenue Service (IRS) rules may not support or oppose candidates in partisan elections, these organizations may engage in "issue advocacy."[59] Such advocacy, particularly immediately prior to an election, can have an impact similar to electioneering communications.[60] The federal and state tax subsidy for 501(c)(3) organizations through tax deductions should be conditioned on more transparency. Tax deductions for 501(c)(3) contributions over a certain amount should be disallowed unless the identities of the donors are publicly disclosed. Foundations that contribute to 501(c)(3) organizations should be required to reveal the contribution on their IRS Form 990 and not donate through donor-advised funds (e.g., DonorsTrust) that allow donors to conceal their identity by using the fund as a conduit.[61, 62]

On July 1, 2021, the Supreme Court announced its decision in *Americans for Prosperity Foundation* v. *Bonta*, in which a 6-3 majority struck down a California rule requiring donations over $5,000 to be disclosed by charities to the state attorney general. First Amendment–protected freedom of association, the court ruled, was offended by the rule at issue, because of the chilling effect of the disclosures under the circumstances of this case. The ruling allowed charities to keep these donations secret, at least from the state attorney general.[63]

This decision, if expanded to protect the secrecy of even larger donations to U.S. charities, could be a serious threat to U.S. independence from special interests, both foreign and domestic. For decades, leading American universities have taken large contributions from foreign interests. Harvard, for example, took large donations from the Bin Laden family before 9/11. The University of Pennsylvania was recently reported to have taken substantial and secret donations from China and Saudi Arabia.[64] These and other charitable institutions in turn have a substantial influence on the U.S. political system. The *Bonta* decision magnifies the disastrous effect of *Citizens United* and related cases, which allow political spending by nonprofit organizations. *Bonta* adds a constitutionally protected layer of secrecy to at least some of the flow of money into organizations that influence U.S. elections and many other aspects of American public policy.

*Bonta*, however, is not an absolute bar to mandated disclosure. The Supreme Court imposed an "exacting scrutiny" test to charitable contribution disclosure laws such as California's, saying that "[while] exacting scrutiny does not require that disclosure regimes be the least restrictive means of achieving their ends, it does require that they be narrowly tailored to the government's asserted interest."[65] The court went on to say that "a substantial relation to an important interest is not enough to save a disclosure regime that is insufficiently tailored."[66]

The ruling thus provides an opening for Congress to at least try to devise a disclosure regime narrowly tailored to confronting the greatest dangers of secret money entering American nonprofits. One approach would be to amend the Internal Revenue Code to condition an organization's tax-exempt status on its disclosing at least some of its donations. These disclosures would be made not only to the IRS, which already requires disclosure on Schedule B of Form 990, but also to the Department of Homeland Security and other federal agencies that safeguard national security. In the case of the largest charitable donations, public disclosure should be mandated. Congress could require that the IRS internally release to federal national security agencies the lists of donations over $5,000 on a charity's Schedule B. Congress could also provide that donations over $50,000 from foreign sources and donations over $100,000 from domestic sources must be publicly disclosed. The Supreme Court hopefully would distinguish such a narrowly tailored disclosure rule from the California rule in *Bonta*, where the line was drawn by the state at the lower sum of $5,000, and where the court believed the California attorney general had not demonstrated a true need for the information. Whether the court would recognize this distinction is uncertain, but Congress should proceed regardless.

Congress has also considered requiring Securities and Exchange Commission (SEC) rulemaking that would mandate all public companies (companies filling annual SEC Form 10-K) to disclose all expenditures on electioneering communications, whether those expenditures are direct or are payments made to 501(c)(4) organizations, Super PACs, or any other organizations that fund electioneering communications.[67, 68] Expenditures by public companies on issue advocacy—often a veiled form of electioneering communication[69]—should also be publicly disclosed.[70] Furthermore, a public company should be required to submit to its shareholders for a proxy vote any proposal from a shareholder to the effect that the company cease or restrict electioneering expenditures.

Congress took an important first step by including in the National Defense Authorization Act of 2020 a provision that requires the Treasury Department to collect beneficial ownership information on shell companies registered in the United States.[71] This provision effectively prohibits anonymously owned shell companies that can be used for, among other purposes, money laundering, transferring funds to U.S. public officials, or making electioneering communications. Such communications are not constitutionally protected under *Citizens United* if they are paid for by foreign nationals (that was the aforementioned ruling in *Bluman*), but foreign nationals can try to hide electioneering payments in shell companies unless disclosure of beneficial ownership of shell companies is required. Information obtained by the Treasury Department under this provision will hopefully be shared with the FEC and state agencies charged with enforcing campaign finance laws.

## Counterbalancing Big Money in Politics

The third step in campaign finance reform is to bring more small donors in to counterbalance the influence of big money in politics. The more candidates depend upon smaller donors, the more the candidates can free themselves from the big donors and big electioneering communications spenders who often want something in return.

One approach passed the House in March 2021 in the For the People Act, which would implement a small donor matching system to magnify the contributions of average Americans. The match would be six to one for presidential and congressional contributions. Thus a $100 contribution would be matched with $600 for a total of $700 to the candidate of choice. This would be done at no cost to the taxpayer; funding would be primarily generated by a surcharge on corporate criminal penalties and similar civil and regulatory payments. The slimmed-down Senate successor of the For the People Act now pending in the Senate as S. 2747 contains provisions for optional small dollar financing of elections for the House of Representatives and other innovations in Title VIII.

Other approaches also have been advanced. While rejecting the ruling in *Citizens United* and advocating enhanced disclosure of campaign spending, Lawrence Lessig in *Republic, Lost*[72] recognized the practical as well as constitutional limitations to both of these approaches. Lessig relied heavily on a government-funded voucher system as part of his proposed remedy. The vouchers would be good for contributions up to a certain amount ($100, $200, or whatever amount is determined by Congress) to the political candidates and parties of a voter's choice. Candidates could be required to forgo some other sources of large-dollar funding (e.g., PAC funding) to be eligible to receive the vouchers. S. 2747 contains an optional Democracy Credit Program as one of the innovations in Title VIII. It would pilot this approach with $25 vouchers that voters could contribute to House candidates.

A similar approach is to use a tax rebate. I have proposed elsewhere that every American taxpayer should get a $200 tax credit for contributions to a political candidate or candidates of the taxpayer's choice.[73] Given the substantial amount of tax revenue collected from most Americans, it seems reasonable that the first $200 should be allocated by the taxpayer to have a meaningful voice in choosing the elected officials who will decide how to spend the rest.[74] This tax credit, if offered to 143 million taxpayers and used by 100 million taxpayers, could cost the government $20 billion every two-year election cycle. However, the tax credit would probably reduce the size of the federal budget,[75] keeping in mind that the annual federal budget is around $4 trillion,[76] the defense budget alone is over $700 billion,[77] and much of this spending is influenced by campaign contributions. For instance, Defense Department and other federal expenditures are heavily influenced by the political spending of federal contractors in the defense industry.[78]

Making elected officials less dependent upon these contributions could go a long way toward cutting government waste.

Some states, including Minnesota, already have in place a modest tax credit for contributions to political candidates.[79] Enacting such a program on a national scale—preferably with direct access to the funds via the internet as an alternative to contributing and then claiming the tax credit—would facilitate many more Americans participating in this important phase of the candidate selection process in both primaries and general elections.[80] The "green primary," as Professor Lessig calls the party primary system fueled by campaign cash, would be open to all Americans by virtue of their paying taxes to the government.[81]

## Conclusion

In his famous address after the Battle of Gettysburg, President Lincoln resolved that "these dead shall not have died in vain—that this nation, under God, shall have a new birth of freedom—and that government of the people, by the people, for the people, shall not perish from the earth."[82] It is doubtful that by "the people" he meant the many industrial giants that would emerge in the aftermath of the Civil War profiting in part from the war itself.[83] It is also doubtful that the drafters of the Constitution in 1789 were thinking of any corporation as a "person" in need of constitutional protection in electioneering activity when they drafted the First Amendment, guaranteeing that Congress shall pass no law abridging "the freedom of speech, or of the press" or the "right of the people peaceably to assemble, and to petition the Government for a redress of grievances." The Supreme Court in *Citizens United* imagines a "personhood" of fictional corporate entities that is on par with the rights of natural persons. Such corporate personhood, at least in the context of elections, will be a growing threat to the republic if the rights that "personhood" bestows are not minimized by law, disclosed to the public, and counterbalanced by the influence of real people. Increasingly, corporate political spending will also be a foreign threat.[84]

The Trump years were a demonstration of just how decadent our campaign finance system has become. Protecting the American political system from internal decay and domestic and foreign special influence requires a fundamental reassessment of the role of money in the U.S. campaign finance system. The president, Congress, the Federal Election Commission, and state legislatures should work together to find ways to regulate, disclose to the public, and counterbalance the influence that big money has on elections. The courts should defer to the will of the people in making such laws. The future of America as a stable representative democracy depends upon it.

### Notes

1. During the 2016 primaries, Donald Trump was far more critical of the campaign finance system than the other Republican candidates, a message that clearly resonated with voters: "Like Sanders, Donald Trump has made money in politics one of the biggest targets of his campaign—and an emblem of his outsider status. He has called super PACs 'horrible' and insists the separation between candidates and the independent groups backing them is a charade. Trump says he supports campaign finance reform, though a specific plan is not available on his website. When he launched his campaign in June, Trump promised supporters that he would inoculate himself from the influence of donors. 'I don't need anybody's money. I'm using my own money. I'm not using the lobbyists. I'm not using donors. I don't care. I'm really rich,' Trump said." See Peter Overby, "Presidential Candidates Pledge to Undo Citizens United," NPR, February 14, 2016, www.npr.org/2016/02/14/466668949/presidential-candidates-pledge-to-undo-citizens-united-but-can-they; see Donald J. Trump, "Presidential Campaign Announcement Speech," June 16, 2015, *Time*, https://time.com/3923128/donald-trump-announcement-speech/.

2. Nicholas Confessore and Megan Thee-Brenan, "Poll Shows Americans Favor Overhaul of Campaign Financing," *New York Times*, June 2, 2015, www.nytimes.com/2015/06/03/us/politics/poll-shows-americans-favor-overhaul-of-campaign-financing.html; "Money in Politics Poll," *New York Times*, June 2, 2015, www.nytimes.com/interactive/2015/06/02/us/politics/money-in-politics-poll.html. See also Bradley Jones, "Most Americans Want to Limit Campaign Spending, Say Big Donors Have Greater Political Influence," Pew Research Center, May 8, 2018, www.pewresearch.org/fact-tank/2018/05/08/most-americans-want-to-limit-campaign-spending-say-big-donors-have-greater-political-influence/.

3. Miles Parks, "FACT CHECK: Russian Interference Went Far Beyond 'Facebook Ads' Kushner Described," NPR, April 24, 2019, www.npr.org/2019/04/24/716374421/fact-check-russian-interference-went-far-beyond-facebook-ads-kushner-described; Nathaniel Gleicher, "Removing Coordinated Inauthentic Behavior from Russia," Facebook, January 17, 2019, https://about.fb.com/news/2019/01/removing-cib-from-russia/.

4. Brian Schwartz and Lauren Hirsch, "Presidential Elections Have Turned into Money Wars—Thanks to a Supreme Court Decision in 2010," CNBC, December 20, 2019, www.cnbc.com/2019/12/19/presidential-elections-are-now-money-battlesthanks

-to-supreme-court.html; Emma Green, "The Local Consequences of *Citizens United*," *Atlantic*, July 2, 2015, www.theatlantic.com/politics/archive/2015/07/the-local-conse quences-of-citizens-united/397586/.

5. Peter Overby, "Presidential Candidates Pledge to Undo 'Citizens United.' But Can They?," NPR, February 14, 2016, www.npr.org/2016/02/14/466668949/presidential -candidates-pledge-to-undo-citizens-united-but-can-they; Peter Overby, "Trump's Efforts to 'Drain The Swamp' Lagging Behind His Campaign Rhetoric," NPR, April 26, 2017, www.npr.org/2017/04/26/525551816/trumps-efforts-to-drain-the-swamp-lagging -behind-his-campaign-rhetoric.

6. Isaac Arnsdorf, "Trump Rewards Big Donors with Jobs and Access," Politico, December 27, 2016, www.politico.com/story/2016/12/donald-trump-donors-rewards -232974.

7. These include unconstitutional foreign government emoluments. See Norman Eisen, Richard Painter, and Laurence H. Tribe, "The Emoluments Clause: Its text, Meaning, and Application to Donald J. Trump," Brookings Institution, December 16, 2016, www.brookings.edu/research/the-emoluments-clause-its-text-meaning-and -application-to-donald-j-trump/; Trump's foreign and domestic emoluments clause violations are also discussed in chapter 1, this volume; see also Fredreka Schouten, Brad Heath, and Steve Reilly, "Trump Nominates Some Club Members to Plum Gov- ernment Jobs," *USA Today*, November 2, 2017, www.usatoday.com/story/news/2017/11/ 02/trump-nominates-some-club-members-plum-government-jobs/823231001/.

8. Norman Eisen, Claire Finkelstein, and Richard Painter, "Arrest of a Trump Friend Sends Key Message," CNN, July 23, 2021, www.cnn.com/2021/07/22/opinions/ tom-barrack-foreign-agent-charges-eisen-finkelstein-painter/index.html.

9. Anna Massoglia and Karl Evers-Hillstrom, "'Dark Money' Topped $1 billion in 2020, Largely Boosting Democrats," OpenSecrets, March 17, 2021, www.opensecrets .org/news/2021/03/one-billion-dark-money-2020-electioncycle/.

10. See Brian F. Jordan, "Disclosing Bribes in Disguise: Campaign Contributions as Implicit Bribery and Enforcing Violations Impartially," *University of Pennsylvania Journal of Constitutional Law* 17, no. 5 (2015), pp. 1435–62, https://scholarship.law.upenn .edu/jcl/vol17/iss5/4/; Robert Barnes, "The High Court: When Is a Campaign Contribu- tion a Bribe?," *Washington Post*, August 12, 2012, www.washingtonpost.com/politics/ the-high-court-when-is-a-campaign-contribution-a-bribe/2012/08/12/68cdd94e-e2f9 -11e1-a25e-15067bb31849_story.html.

11. For example, according to data published by OpenSecrets.org, "The financial sector is far and away the largest source of campaign contributions to federal candi- dates and parties, with insurance companies, securities and investment firms, real estate interests and commercial banks providing the bulk of that money." The data shows a total of approximately 1.8 billion dollars in total political expenditures in 2020 from this industry sector, split roughly evenly between Democrats (53%) and Republicans (47%), with securities and investment firms, real estate interests, and commercial banks providing the bulk of that money. See Alex Glorioso, "Finance/In-

surance/Real Estate," OpenSecrets, March 2016, www.opensecrets.org/industries/indus.php?Ind=F.

12. Ibid.

13. John T. Noonan Jr., *Bribes: The Intellectual History of a Moral Idea* (University of California Press, 1984).

14. See John H. Cushman Jr., "Russell B. Long, 84, Senator Who Influenced Tax Laws," Obituaries, *New York Times,* May 11, 2003, www.nytimes.com/2003/05/11/us/russell-b-long-84-senator-who-influenced-tax-laws.html.

15. "The total cost of the races for the White House, the Senate and the House is expected to hit nearly $14 billion." See Shane Goldmacher, "The 2020 Campaign Is the Most Expensive Ever (by a Lot)," *New York Times,* October 28, 2020, www.nytimes.com/2020/10/28/us/politics/2020-race-money.html; "Cost of Elections," OpenSecrets, www.opensecrets.org/elections-overview/cost-of-election?cycle=2020&display=T&infl=N.

16. *Citizens United* v. *Federal Election Commission,* 558 U.S. 310 (2010).

17. Ibid.

18. "First . . . three [mock] grand juries deliberated on charges that a campaign spender bribed a Congressperson. Second, 1271 representative online respondents considered whether to convict, with five variables manipulated randomly. In both studies, jurors found *quid pro quo* corruption for behaviors they believed to be common." Christopher Robertson and others, "The Appearance and the Reality of *Quid Pro Quo* Corruption: An Empirical Investigation," *Journal of Legal Analysis* 8, no. 2, (2016), pp. 375–438, https://academic.oup.com/jla/article/8/2/375/2502553.

19. See Douglas D. Roscoe and Shannon Jenkins, "A Meta-Analysis of Campaign Contributions' Impact on Roll Call Voting," *Social Science Quarterly* 86, no. 1 (2005), pp. 52–68, www.jstor.org/stable/42956049?seq=1.

20. Ibid., p. 1. "Models that control for friendly giving by including a measure of legislators' ideology and that include more than one contributions variable are less likely to produce significant results. . . . After considering the impact of model choice on study results, we conclude that one-third of roll call votes exhibit the impact of campaign contributions."

21. Lawrence Lessig, *Republic, Lost: How Money Corrupts Congress—and a Plan to Stop It* (New York: Hachette Book Group, 2011).

22. Ibid.

23. See Confessore and Thee-Brenan, "Poll."

24. "BERLIN, Feb. 6.—Ex-Chancellor Gustav Bauer, prominent Socialist leader, was forced today to resign as a member of the Reichstag. His resignation was due to publication by the Lokal-Anzeiger of a letter tending to show he profited financially from association with the Barmat brothers, now under arrest pending investigation of credits obtained by them from the Prussian State Bank." T. R. Ybarran, "Ex-Chancellor Hit by Barmat Scandal," *New York Times,* February 7, 1925, www.nytimes.com/1925/02/07/archives/exchancellor-hit-by-barmat-scandal-bauer-resigns-from-reichstag

-on.html. See also Martin H. Geyer, "Contested Narratives of the Weimar Republic: The Case of the 'Kutisker-Barmat Scandal,'" in *Weimar Publics/Weimar Subjects: Rethinking the Political Culture of Germany in the 1920s*, edited by Kathleen Canning, Kerstin Barndt, and Kristin McGuire (New York: Berghahn Books, 2010), pp. 223–29, www.jstor.org/stable/j.ctt9qd2vx.

25. "Nationalist Press Makes Anti-Semitic Propaganda of Barmat Brothers Trial," from the archives of Jewish Telegraphic Agency, February 13, 1927, www.jta.org/1927/01/13/archive/nationalist-press-makes-anti-semitic-propaganda-of-barmat-brothers-trial. See also Brendan Fay, "The Nazi Conspiracy Theory: German Fantasies and Jewish Power in the Third Reich," *Library and Information History* 35, no. 2, (2019), pp. 75–97, www.tandfonline.com/doi/abs/10.1080/17583489.2019.1632574?journalCode=ylbh20.

26. See note 1 on statements made by candidate Donald Trump in the 2016 primaries. See also Ryan Balisacan, "Link between Corruption and the Global Surge of Populism," *Global Anticorruption Blog*, October 6, 2017, https://globalanticorruptionblog.com/2017/10/06/the-link-between-corruption-and-the-global-surge-of-populism/.

27. Christine Romans, "Why Big American Companies Stash Cash Overseas," CNN Business, November 3, 2017, https://money.cnn.com/2017/11/03/news/companies/romans-numeral-overseas-cash/index.html.

28. "*Citizens United* v. *FEC* (Supreme Court)," Federal Election Commission, February 1, 2010, www.fec.gov/updates/citizens-united-v-fecsupreme-court/; Ted Deutch, "Supreme Court's Citizens United Mistake Just Turned 10 Years Old. It's Time to Reverse It," NBC News, January 21, 2020, www.nbcnews.com/think/opinion/supreme-court-s-citizens-united-mistake-just-turned-ten-years-ncna1119826.

29. Joan Biskupic, "The Supreme Court Hasn't Been This Conservative Since the 1930s," CNN, September 26, 2020, www.cnn.com/2020/09/26/politics/supreme-court-conservative/index.html.

30. See David Cole, "How to Reverse *Citizens United*," *Atlantic*, April 2016, www.theatlantic.com/magazine/archive/2016/04/how-to-reverse-citizens-united/471504/.

31. See Deutch, "Citizens United Mistake."

32. U.S. Const. art. V.

33. Ibid.

34. See Jones, "Limit Campaign Spending"; Ashley Balcerzak, "Study: Most Americans Want to Kill Citizens United with Constitutional Amendment," Center for Public Integrity, May 10, 2018, www.pri.org/stories/2018-05-10/study-most-americans-want-kill-citizens-united-constitutional-amendment.

35. Democracy for All Amendment, H.R.J. Res. 2, 116th Cong. (2019).

36. Ibid. The Democracy for All Amendment includes the following:

"Section I. To advance democratic self-government and political equality, and to protect the integrity of government and the electoral process, Congress and the States may regulate and set reasonable limits on the raising and spending of money by candidates and others to influence elections.

"Section II. Congress and the States shall have power to implement and enforce this article by appropriate legislation, and may distinguish between natural persons and corporations or other artificial entities created by law, including by prohibiting such entities from spending money to influence elections.

"Section III. Nothing in this article shall be construed to grant Congress or the States the power to abridge the freedom of the press."

See also Mark Steininger, "The Importance of the Democracy for All Amendment, with American Promise Director of Political Strategy Ben Gubits," American Promise, January 7, 2019, americanpromise.net/blog/2019/01/07/director_of_political_strategy_ben_gubits_discusses_importance_of_the_democracy_for_all_amendment/.

37. *Buckley* v. *Valeo*, 424 U.S. 1 (1976).

38. *McCutcheon* v. *Federal Election Commission*, 572 U.S. 185 (2014).

39. In 2019 in *Thompson* v. *Hebdon*, 589 U.S. __ (2019), the Supreme Court vacated and remanded a decision by the Ninth Circuit that upheld Alaska's statutory $500 campaign contribution limit, suggesting that the Ninth Circuit reconsider whether its ruling was consistent with the Supreme Court's precedent striking down low dollar limits in Vermont. *Randall* v. *Sorrell*, 548 U.S. 230 (2006), ruled unconstitutional a Vermont law that limited the amount any single individual can contribute to a candidate for state office during a "two-year general election cycle" as follows: governor, lieutenant governor, and other statewide offices, $400; state senator, $300; and state representative, $200. The Court ruled that these limits were too low.

40. Brendan Parets, "Avoiding Straw Donor Issues," *Inside Political Law*, September 11, 2020, www.insidepoliticallaw.com/2020/09/11/avoiding-straw-donor-issues/.

41. As the FEC explains: "The Federal Election Campaign Act and Commission regulations require special reporting of certain contributions that are collected or 'bundled' by lobbyists/registrants, or by political action committees (PACs) that are established or controlled by lobbyists/registrants, on behalf of authorized committees of federal candidates, political party committees, and leadership PACs. Committees receiving these contributions must file Form 3L and disclose certain information about any lobbyist/registrant or lobbyist/registrant PAC that forwards, or is credited with raising, two or more bundled contributions aggregating in excess of a specific reporting threshold within a certain 'covered period' of time. These requirements apply to both in-kind and monetary contributions. The reporting threshold for calendar year 2021 is $19,300. See "Lobbyist Bundling Disclosure," Federal Election Commission, www.fec.gov/help-candidates-and-committees/lobbyist-bundling-disclosure/.

42. Ibid. See also Kate Ackley, "Lobbyists Bundle Donations to Senate Democrats, Trump Victory," *Roll Call*, July 20, 2020, www.rollcall.com/2020/07/20/lobbyists-bundle-donations-to-senate-democrats-trump-victory/.

43. "Ban Lobbyists from Fundraising for Politicians," Center for American Progress, April 25, 2018, www.americanprogress.org/issues/democracy/reports/2018/04/25/

448596/ban-lobbyists-fundraising-politicians/; "New Lobbyist Bundling Threshold and Coordinated Party Expenditure Limits," Federal Election Commission, March 2, 2020, www.fec.gov/updates/tip2020-new-lobbyist-bundling-threshold-and-coordi nated-party-expenditure-limits/.

44. "Who Can and Can't Contribute," Federal Election Commission, www.fec.gov /help-candidates-and-committees/candidate-taking-receipts/who-can-and-cant-con tribute/#:~:text=a%20federal%20election).-,Foreign%20nationals,%E2%80%94%20 federal%2C%20state%20or%20local.

45. *Bluman* v. *FEC*, 800 F. Supp. 2d 281 (D.D.C. 2011), found that foreign citizens living in the United States have no constitutional right to spend or contribute money in connection with U.S. elections. See also *"Bluman v. FEC* (Supreme Court)," Federal Election Commission, January 18, 2012, www.fec.gov/updates/bluman-v-fec-supreme -court/; and *Bluman* v. *Federal Election Commission*, No. 565 U.S. (2012).

46. Ibid. See also Michael Sozan, "Ending Foreign-Influenced Corporate Spending in U.S. Elections," Center for American Progress, November 21, 2019, www.american progress.org/issues/democracy/reports/2019/11/21/477466/ending-foreign-influenced -corporate-spending-u-s-elections/.

47. Ibid.

48. See John Francis Reilly, Carter C. Hull, and Barbara A. Braig Allen, "IRC 501(c) (4) Organizations," Internal Revenue Service, October 2002, https://pdf4pro.com/ view/irc-501-c-4-organizations-irs-gov-564e66.html. See also "Exempt Organization Types," Internal Revenue Service, last updated September 23, 2021, www.irs.gov/ charities-non-profits/exempt-organization-types.

49. Reilly, Hull, and Allen, "IRC 501(c)(4) Organizations."

50. "Donations to Section 501(c)(4) Organizations," Internal Revenue Service, last updated September 23, 2021, www.irs.gov/charities-non-profits/other-non-profits/do nations-to-section-501c4-organizations#:~:text=Contributions%20to%20civic%20 leagues%20or,conduct%20of%20the%20taxpayer's%20business.

51. Abby K. Wood, "Citizen's United Turns 10 Today. Here's What We've Learned about Dark Money," *Washington Post*, January 21, 2020, www.washingtonpost.com/pol itics/2020/01/21/citizens-united-turns-10-today-heres-what-weve-learned-about-dark -money/.

52. H.R. 1 and S. 1 aim to resolve this issue by requiring disclosure of contributions made to appointees that promote or oppose changes in federal laws or regulations to be administered by the agency to which that individual was appointed. Second, they require the director of the Office of Government Ethics (OGE) to disclose to Con gress, upon request, any ethics agreement report filed by a covered individual, includ ing gifts and contributions from certain political organizations. Sen. Joe Manchin has further communicated support for additional disclosure reforms, including creating a reporting requirement for reportable foreign contacts and barring super PACs from operating as "arms of campaigns." The contribution disclosure and OGE reporting

requirements are not present in the current Senate substitute for S. 1, the Freedom to Vote Act (FTVA), and portions of the DISCLOSE Act have been cut from the FTVA. See S. 2747, §§ 6001–6022, 117th Cong. (2021–2022), 1st Sess., www.congress.gov/bill /117th-congress/senate-bill/2747/text.

53. Ian Vandewalker, "10 Years of Super PACs Show Courts Were Wrong on Corruption Risks," Brennan Center for Justice, March 25, 2020, www.brennancenter.org/ our-work/analysis-opinion/10-years-super-pacs-show-courts-were-wrong-corruption -risks; Braden Goyette, "Cheat Sheet: How Super PACs Work, and Why They're So Controversial," *New York Daily News*, January 13, 2012, www.nydailynews.com/news/ politics/cheat-sheet-super-pacs-work-controversial-article-1.1005804; Chisun Lee and Douglas Keith, "How Semi-Secret Spending Took Over Politics," *Atlantic*, June 28, 2016, www.theatlantic.com/politics/archive/2016/06/the-rise-of-gray-money-in -politics/489002/; Trevor Potter, "Five Myths about Super PACs," *Washington Post*, April 13, 2012, www.washingtonpost.com/opinions/five-myths-about-super-pacs/2012/ 04/13/gIQAGPnEFT_story.html; "Super PACs," OpenSecrets, last updated October 29, 2021, www.opensecrets.org/political-action-committees-pacs/super-pacs/2020.

54. H.R. 1 and S. 1 make a similar recommendation, requiring the FEC to conduct an analysis of political donors, specifically to identify segregated funds of corporations. The DISCLOSE Act would also increase the reporting requirements for disbursements made to super PACs under penalty of perjury. Sen. Joe Manchin has also shown support for adding a "coordinated spender" category to campaign finance laws that would constrain super PACs from operating as extensions of campaigns. The FEC reporting requirement remains in the FTVA, as does the DISCLOSE Act, albeit with a narrower scope. See S. 2747, §§ 6001–6022, 117th Cong. (2021–2022), 1st Sess., www .congress.gov/bill/117th-congress/senate-bill/2747/text#toc-HAA77B42F73514409 AAF7B669743BED0D.

55. Maggie Severns, "'Oh, That's Cool—Do That!': Super PACs Use New Trick to Hide Donors," Politico, August 17, 2018, www.politico.com/story/2018/08/17/super -pacs-hidden-donors-disclosures-741795.

56. H.R. 1 proposes a solution to this loophole, requiring super PACs to disclose any donations over $5,000 received up to 20 days before an election. The DISCLOSE Act would also require any covered political organization to disclose campaign disbursements over $10,000 to Congress. A comparable recommendation is not included in S. 1 or the FTVA.

57. "Organizations Not Required to File Form 1023," Internal Revenue Service, last updated September 23, 2021, www.irs.gov/charities-non-profits/charitable-organi zations/organizations-not-required-to-file-form-1023.

58. "Public Disclosure and Availability of Exempt Organizations Returns and Applications: Contributors' Identities Not Subject to Disclosure," Internal Revenue Service, last updated September 7, 2021, www.irs.gov/charities-non-profits/public-disclo sure-and-availability-of-exempt-organizations-returns-and-applications-contribu tors-identities-not-subject-to-disclosure.

59. "Lobbying," Internal Revenue Service, last updated September 7, 2021, www.irs.gov/charities-non-profits/lobbying#:~:text=In%20general%2C%20no%20organiza tion%20may,loss%20of%20tax%2Dexempt%20status.

60. Craig B. Holman and Luke P. McLoughlin, *Buying Time 2000: Television Advertising in the 2000 Federal Elections*, Brennan Center for Justice, 2001, pp. 22–26, www.brennancenter.org/sites/default/files/2019-08/Report_Buying_Time_2000.pdf.

61. See Nicholas Confessore and David Gelles, "Facebook Fallout Deals Blow to Mercers' Political Clout," *New York Times*, April 10, 2018, www.nytimes.com/2018/04/10/us/politics/mercer-family-cambridge-analytica.html.

62. H.R. 1 and S. 1 also aim to increase transparency in donations of nonprofits through disclosure of donor identity. They go further to detail that any corporation, union, or nonprofit spending more than $10,000 per cycle should disclose their identity unless the funds were received in the ordinary course of business or disclosure would lead to serious threats of harassment. Additionally, they call for all campaign-related disbursements above $1,000 to be reported with certification that the spending was not coordinated with any candidate. This provision remains in the FTVA. See S. 2747, § 6011, 117th Cong. (2021–2022), 1st Sess., www.congress.gov/bill/117th-con gress/senate-bill/2747/text#toc-HAA77B42F73514409AAF7B669743BED0D.

63. *Americans for Prosperity Foundation* v. *Bonta, Attorney General of California*, 594 U.S. __ (2021), www.supremecourt.gov/opinions/20pdf/19-251_p86b.pdf.

64. Jacques Steinberg, "A Nation Challenged: Scholarships; Endowments from bin Ladens Prove Awkward," *New York Times*, October 3, 2001, www.nytimes.com/2001/10/03/us/a-nation-challenged-scholarships-endowments-from-bin-ladens-prove-awkward.html; Catherine Dunn, "Penn Got $258 Million in Foreign Money, and There May be More It Hadn't Disclosed," *Philadelphia Inquirer*, February 24, 2020, www.inquirer.com/business/university-pennsylvania-foreign-donations-china-saudi-arabia-20200224.html.

65. 594 U.S., slip op. at 3.

66. Ibid.

67. See Corporate Political Disclosure Act of 2019, H.R. 1053, § 1, 116th Cong. (2019–2020), 1st Sess., www.congress.gov/bill/116th-congress/house-bill/1053/text; Cydney Posner, "Is It Time for Corporate Political Spending Disclosure?" Harvard Law School Forum on Corporate Governance, March 17, 2019, https://corpgov.law.har vard.edu/2019/03/17/is-it-time-for-corporate-political-spending-disclosure/. See also Lucian Bebchuk and Robert Jackson, "Shining a Light on Corporate Political Spending," *Georgetown Law Journal* 101 (2013), pp. 923–67, https://papers.ssrn.com/sol3/papers.cfm?abstract_id=2142115.

68. H.R. 1 and S. 1 also propose this requirement, calling to repeal a budget rider that allows 501(c) organizations to conceal their donors. The DISCLOSE Act of 2021 makes a similar recommendation, requiring corporations and LLCs to disclose any campaign-related disbursement worth over $10,000 to Congress. Such disbursements would include public and electioneering communications. See S. 2747, § 6011(a)(a),

§ 6011(a)(d), § 6011(a)(e)(2), 117th Cong. (2021–2022), 1st Sess., www.congress.gov/bill /117th-congress/senate-bill/2747/text#toc-HAA77B42F73514409AAF7B669743 BEDoD.

69. See Holman and McLoughlin, *Buying Time 2000*, pp. 22–26.

70. The DISCLOSE Act of 2021 makes a similar recommendation, requiring corporations and LLCs to disclose any campaign-related disbursement worth over $10,000 to Congress. Such disbursements would include express advocacy payments, public communications, and electioneering communications. See S. 2747, § 6011(a)(a), § 6011(a)(d), § 6011(a)(e)(2), 117th Cong. (2021–2022), 1st Sess., www.congress.gov/bill /117th-congress/senate-bill/2747/text#toc-HAA77B42F73514409AAF7B669743 BEDoD.

71. See Morris Pearl, "Congress Just Passed the Most Important Anti-Corruption Reform in Decades, But Hardly Anyone Knows about It," *Fortune*, December 26, 2020, https://fortune.com/2020/12/26/ndaa-2021-shell-companies-corporate-transparency -act/.

72. Lessig, *Republic, Lost.*

73. Painter, *Taxation Only with Representation*, p. 13.

74. Ibid., p. 168.

75. Ibid., pp. 72–74, 172–173.

76. Kimberly Amadeo, "U.S. Federal Budget Breakdown," *The Balance*, October 29, 2020, www.thebalance.com/u-s-federal-budget-breakdown-3305789.

77. David Vergun, "2020 Budget Focuses on High-End Threats, DOD Leaders Say," U.S. Department of Defense, March 14, 2019, www.defense.gov/Explore/News/Article /Article/1785329/2020-budget-focuses-on-high-end-threats-dod-leaders-say/.

78. "Top Federal Contractors Spend Millions on Influence, Get Billions in Contracts," Project on Government Oversight (POGO), August 31, 2017, www.pogo.org/ press/release/2017/top-federal-contractors-spend-millions-on-influence-get-billions -in-contracts/.

79. "A taxpayer may claim a refund equal to the amount of the taxpayer's contributions made in the calendar year to candidates and to a political party. The maximum refund for an individual must not exceed $50 and for a married couple, filing jointly, must not exceed $100." Minn. Stat. § 290.06.23 (2020).

80. H.R. 1 and S. 1 also seek to promote a system of voluntary small donor public financing for elections and a "Freedom from Influence Fund," a public financing mechanism funded without taxpayer money. As previously noted, S. 2747 features a Democracy Credit Program and a system of small dollar matching funds, both optional and both for House elections. See S. 2747, §§ 8101–8114, 117th Cong. (2021–2022), 1st Sess., www.congress.gov/bill/117th-congress/senate-bill/2747/text#toc-HAA1809 633091423084CCC272E7FC1EC4.

81. See Lessig, *Republic, Lost.* See also Cenk Uygur and Lawrence Lessig, "Can Lawrence Lessig Win the Presidency AND Get Money Out of Politics?" TY's the Conversation, August 20, 2015 (video, 54:17), www.youtube.com/watch?v=F45J85c5vCI&

feature=emb_logo. Considering the proportionately high impact of sales taxes and other state taxes besides income taxes on low-income Americans, it is highly unlikely that any United States citizen pays directly and indirectly less than $200 in taxes a year. For this and other reasons, this political contribution tax rebate program should be available to all.

82. Abraham Lincoln, "Gettysburg Address," November 19, 1863, www.ourdocu ments.gov/doc.php?flash=true&doc=36&page=transcript.

83. See Adam Winkler, "'Corporations Are People' Is Built on an Incredible 19th-Century Lie," *Atlantic*, March 5, 2018, www.theatlantic.com/business/archive/2018/03/corporations-people-adam-winkler/554852/. Recounting how arguments by lawyers for the Southern Pacific Railroad in the 1880s transformed the understanding of personhood in the post–Civil War Fourteenth Amendment, this same conflation of corporations with natural persons is also evident a century later in *Citizens United*.

84. The FEC's startling decision to allow foreign donors to finance U.S. ballot referenda committees worsens the situation. See Federal Election Commission, "Factual and Legal Analysis," MUR:7523, www.documentcloud.org/documents/21096628 -fec-ballot-measure-ruling. The author has strongly urged that both Congress and state legislatures pass laws to prohibit such spending on ballot initiatives. See Richard W. Painter, "Opinion: FEC Is 'Dangerously Wrong' to Let Foreign Companies Spend in U.S. Elections," MSNBC, November 11, 2021, www.msnbc.com/opinion/fcc-dangerous ly-wrong-let-foreign-companies-spend-u-s-elections-n1283685.

## Part IV

# Other Democracy Reforms, Domestic and International

# 7

# The Role of Transparency in Repairing Democracy

**ANNE WEISMANN**

The actions of the Trump administration revealed the critical role that an open government plays generally in countering attacks on the foundations of democracy. Many proposals on how to restore the presidency and U.S. democracy post-Trump focus on actions that Congress and a new administration can take to right the wrongs of the past and set the country on a better course. But those proposals tend to deemphasize a key component: the ongoing oversight role of the American public. Rather than give in to the cynicism that contributed to the rise of Donald Trump and Trumpery, citizens must play a prominent part in reinstating norms, a role that does not end at the ballot box. The images of large groups of citizens peacefully and lawfully crowding the office hallways, hearing rooms, and galleries of their congressional representatives to demand action to preserve the Affordable Care Act, and a host of other policies during the Trump years, serve as a vivid example of the power of the people. But to maximize its effect, Congress must arm citizens with the necessary tools for transparency: a Freedom of Information Act (FOIA) that works, record-keeping laws that ensure the preservation of the nation's history, and access to a wealth of reliable data ranging from accurate and current ethics information on public officials to important scientific data.

Far from an abstract concept, transparency represents a structural necessity that allows the public to hold government officials accountable and enables full public participation in U.S. democracy.[1] Trump's presidency exposed the serious flaws in the systems established to provide that transparency. The Biden administration faces the daunting task of not only repairing these breaches in mechanisms designed to shed light on how the U.S. government works, but also of going further to fulfill the promise of open government in statutes like the Freedom of Information Act. Both the message and the medium comprise an essential part of any plan to restore and reinforce government accountability. As a starting point, President Biden must embrace transparency as a core value and reinforce that message with concrete actions that enhance transparency on issues ranging from how law enforcement functions to address systemic racial inequality, to how government funds are spent. The Biden administration must proactively release a wide range of high-value information, such as ethics information on government officials; must revise classification policies and procedures to counter the problem of overclassification; and must improve the quality and usability of data.[2]

At the same time, the administration has faced calls to take actions that hold the Trump administration accountable. A chorus of individuals and groups, acting on the well-founded belief that the nation cannot move forward without understanding its past, has called for some kind of truth and reconciliation process to fully examine the conduct of the Trump administration and provide a platform for accountability.[3] Others counter that the cost of a "truth tribunal" is too high, as it undermines the democratic tradition of ending an election with a winner and a loser, and moving on from there. Harvard professor and author Jill Lepore, for example, advocates instead for "the ordinary working of justice, the strengthening of democratic institutions and the writing of history over time, through the study of carefully preserved records."[4] Despite the daylight between these approaches, they both recognize that at the very least the United States must assemble and preserve the record of the Trump presidency. For that, the country need not await the appointment of a truth-seeking commission but can look to FOIA requests as the best barometer of those documents likely to be most useful in evaluating the Trump presidency.

During the Trump administration, the number of new FOIA requests soared.[5] A wide range of requesters—journalists, good government groups, historians, and everyday citizens—used the statute to determine what the Trump administration was doing and why, whether it was the White House's decision to rip children from their parents' arms at the border,[6] or its choice to send armed troops to Portland, Oregon, and other Democrat-controlled cities.[7] Some requesters were laser focused on a specific subset of documents, while others sought to vacuum up all documents on a policy or action. Whatever their approach, the information seekers understood that knowing what the Trump administration was doing and why was critical to holding that administration accountable now and in the future. FOIA litigation also spiked. The FOIA Project reported an average of between forty-three and forty-five new cases per month for 2015; by 2019, the new-case-per-month average had risen to seventy-three.[8] At the same time, government overreliance on the FOIA's exemptions continued.[9]

The Trump-era FOIA requests, particularly those in litigation, provide a roadmap for identifying the information most useful in revealing the actions of the Trump administration. The requests track that administration's most notable failings and seek to learn more about key events and to answer key questions. For example, when the Government Accountability Project wanted to learn more about the role former National Security Advisor Michael Flynn and other top Trump officials played in working with outside groups to sell nuclear technology to Saudi Arabia—bypassing the statutory guardrails in place to protect U.S. interests—the group filed FOIA requests with the six agencies involved.[10] Months later, after receiving no documents, the Government Accountability Project filed suit and continued to press for full disclosure of records that would help explain the Trump administration's continued efforts to provide Saudi Arabia with nuclear technology despite that country's anti-democratic actions.[11] The House Oversight Committee also opened an investigation into the push by the Trump White House to transfer technology to Saudi Arabia, but the committee was stymied in its efforts to obtain relevant documents from the administration.[12]

Without the missing information, the public will remain in the dark about what may be one of the more egregious scandals of the Trump administration yet to be fully revealed.[13]

Whether or not the Biden White House appoints a truth commission or takes more robust steps toward determining the roles and actions of individual Trump officials in formulating and carrying out the most heinous policies, the new administration should start with a pledge to publicly disgorge all the Trump administration documents requested through the FOIA, focusing first on those requests in active litigation. Early actions by the Biden administration, however, are cause for concern, as they suggest that the Department of Justice (DOJ) remains committed to litigating questionable positions in FOIA cases that the agency took in the prior administration. For example, the DOJ has appealed a ruling ordering it to disclose an Office of Legal Counsel (OLC) memorandum that the district court's *in camera* review revealed was prepared to help Attorney General William Barr publicly undermine Special Counsel Robert Mueller's evidence on the former president's obstruction of justice.[14] Despite the district court ruling and its conclusion that the DOJ and the attorney general had acted in bad faith, the DOJ has appealed the ruling and continues to press for keeping secret a document that would reveal how the attorney general misused the power of his office to falsely exonerate President Trump.

In disgorging Trump-era documents, the Biden administration should limit redactions to classified and personal information rather than hiding behind exemptions to prevent the truth from coming out. The individuals, journalists, and groups that made the requests can best mine the documents for useful information and place it in a larger context. This approach, as a form of crowdsourcing, would capitalize on the expertise and work already done by a large number of FOIA requesters and expand that group to the public at large. And it would save the Biden administration years of litigation over past events, freeing up its resources to focus on a new vision of America.

There is precedent for this approach, though not on such a grand scale. As attorney general, Janet Reno called on the Department of Justice to review pending FOIA litigation for compliance with her newly imposed foreseeable harm standard, which required a showing of concrete harm before an agency could invoke FOIA Exemption 5 and its incorporated discovery privileges.[15]

That review resulted in the disclosure of documents in a handful of cases.[16] But neither the Clinton administration nor any other previous administration has made such a bold and encompassing commitment to transparency as that called for here. However, none has also faced the need to reconstruct U.S. democracy by restoring and building anew the norms and rules of law that the Trump administration battered away. That reconstruction depends on understanding what happened and why; a nation that cannot remember and understand its past is, as the philosopher George Santayana noted, "condemned to repeat it."[17] Only by leveraging the tools of transparency can the nation hope to strengthen the norms that failed in the Trump era to rein in the president's most autocratic and anti-democratic impulses.

The Biden administration should take additional steps to ferret out evidence of misconduct, or worse, in the Trump administration. Biden officials should conduct an audit, or request that Congress direct the Government Accountability Office to conduct an audit, of all federal funds paid to Trump's businesses.[18] A large part of President Trump's graft and corruption stemmed from his efforts to use the power of his office for his and his family's personal enrichment, whether it was advocating for the G-7 Summit to be held at one of his golf resorts in Florida or the forty-one trademarks that China fast-tracked for companies linked to Ivanka Trump right after she joined the White House.[19] According to the *Washington Post*, the former president's businesses received at least $8.1 million dollars from U.S. taxpayers and political supporters during his term in office,[20] while Trump repeatedly accepted emoluments in the form of payments to his businesses by foreign governments, despite the constitutional prohibition against accepting such payments absent congressional approval.[21] Profits at his Washington, D.C., hotel alone exceeded $40 million in 2018, with at least part of that money paid by foreign governments, lobbyists, and state officials seeking to curry favor with the president.[22] At the same time, the Trump administration thwarted efforts by both Congress and the public to ascertain the full scope of the president's corruption.[23]

Beyond looking to the FOIA as a vehicle to shed light on the past, the Biden administration must also support major FOIA reforms and commit to a radically different level of transparency in its own actions. The last four years have revealed the full extent to which the FOIA is broken.[24] Repudiating the FOIA's guiding principle of disclosure, agencies have made compliance with their obligations under the statute the lowest of priorities.[25] Problems with the FOIA have been mounting steadily over the last decade, but the outcry for documents explaining the actions and policies of the Trump administration exposed the statute's serious shortcomings during the COVID-19 pandemic, when the public needed maximum transparency and quick access to critical information that literally was the difference between life and death.[26]

On paper the FOIA holds much promise, but it has rarely lived up to that promise. Its command for a twenty-business-day response remains elusive; many agencies rarely respond within two months, and for some the wait is years.[27] Congress provided for expedition as a means to quickly secure documents when the need is particularly acute or the public interest especially compelling and time-sensitive, but in reality, expedition offers no guarantee of a much shorter response time.[28] Agencies wrongly apply and over-rely on the FOIA's nine exemptions, especially to withhold records that would reveal the flaws in an agency's policy.[29] And during the Trump administration, at least some agencies exercised undue political influence over their FOIA processes, tainting the results and depriving the media and good government groups—their perceived "enemies"—of critical information.[30]

To restore the statute's promise of government accountability through transparency, the FOIA and the agency process for responding to FOIA requests must undergo a fundamental overhaul. The government must shift from a culture of secrecy and withholding to one of disclosure. Attorney General Merrick Garland should direct agencies not to rely on discretionary FOIA exemptions—such as Exemption 5, which protects documents subject to litigation privileges—except in the most limited of cases where the need for secrecy overwhelmingly outweighs the public interest.[31] Agencies must devote significant and sufficient resources to ensure timely processing of requests. This will require Congress to appropriate additional resources, including through a separate budget line item to ensure agencies do not divert those funds to other uses. Agencies must be accountable to Congress and should be directed to report on the specific resources, including funds and full-time employees (or their equivalents), that they dedicate to the FOIA to evaluate their sufficiency. And most fundamentally, agencies must treat the FOIA as mission critical, not a responsibility that can be readily abandoned when meeting its requirements becomes politically inconvenient. These represent policy choices that an administration can make without legislative action.

On the legislative front, Congress also must act boldly to reimagine how the United States moves past the "foot-dragging" and a "widespread reluctance . . . to honor the public's legal right to know" that have plagued the FOIA for decades.[32] To address the chronic underfunding of FOIA operations,[33] Congress must make the FOIA a line item on agency budgets and commit sufficient resources for agencies to invest in technologies that will ease their FOIA burden, such as e-discovery tools and machine learning. Congress should broaden the FOIA's reach to encompass records of private entities performing inherently governmental functions, such as private prisons. Congress should also amend the statute to make the litigation process more effective. The provision of the FOIA conferring jurisdiction on federal courts to "enjoin the agency from withholding agency records and to order the production of any agency records improperly withheld," 5 U.S.C. § 552(4)(B), gives requesters a powerful tool to counter agency intractability and worse. But FOIA lawsuits clog already crowded court dockets, leading to long waits for judicial relief. Congress should consider establishing a special FOIA court with Article III powers as a nationwide alternative to district courts to relieve the burden that FOIA litigation places on individual district court judges. Through legislative reform, Congress should also reset the FOIA's judicial review provisions to rein in the level of deference that agencies now receive. Under the present system, as judicially interpreted, agency declarations are afforded undue deference, and FOIA litigators are denied the processes typically afforded other litigators, such as discovery and the ability to exclude hearsay evidence.

President Biden need not await legislative reform to reinforce his commitment to transparency. His administration took a critical first step toward this objective by reverting to the policy, implemented by the Obama administration, that provided public access to White House visitor logs.[34] The Biden administration should now expand that access to visitor logs to other locations the president frequents or at which White House officials conduct business, as well as to virtual meetings.[35] Cloaking the White House in a veil of secrecy fundamentally conflicts with an agenda that fosters openness and recognizes the public's right to know. Every agency should adopt a robust, proactive disclosure policy that includes agency visitor logs and

other frequently requested documents, such as the use by senior agency officials of federal and private aircraft—a topic that generated significant FOIA
requests during the Trump administration.[36, 37]

The Department of Justice should publish all OLC opinions, subject to
redactions only for classified or personal information and excluding purely
legal advice it provides to the president or attorney general.[38] The D.C. Circuit has described OLC as "for decades . . . the most significant and central-
ized source of legal advice in the Executive Branch."[39] Despite its prominent
role in providing interpretations of law that bind the executive branch,
OLC keeps its opinions secret unless disclosure is politically expedient.[40]
An office not known for its political independence, OLC during the Trump
administration provided the president with justifications for some of his
most autocratic tendencies and his administration's most heinous policies.
For example, a May 2019 OLC opinion claimed White House advisors had
"absolute immunity" from testifying in the impeachment inquiry,[41] while a
June 2019 OLC opinion justified Treasury Secretary Steve Mnuchin's refusal
to turn over President Trump's tax returns to congressional committees
authorized by statute to request such returns.[42] A January 2017 OLC memorandum blessed President Trump's executive order banning immigrants
and refugees from several Muslim-majority countries.[43] This governance by
secret law undermines U.S. democracy, which functions best in the sunlight.

Efforts to assemble and digest the history of the Trump presidency
can succeed only if the administration fulfills its record-keeping obligations under the Federal Records Act (FRA) and the Presidential Records
Act (PRA). On both fronts, the Trump administration failed. From early
on, President Trump showed his disregard, if not outright contempt, for
his record-keeping obligations by ripping up his notes and insisting that no
notetakers be present for some of his most consequential meetings with foreign leaders.[44] Because the courts have interpreted the PRA as giving presidents almost unreviewable discretion in how they implement the statute,[45]
there is a very real risk that President Trump not only failed to create, but
also destroyed significant numbers of his documents, fearing they would
reveal his "potential malfeasance and crimes."[46]

Congress must amend the statute to guard against this risk and protect
records that belong to the American public. Among needed reforms, Congress should impose on the White House a periodic reporting requirement

to Congress and the archivist of the United States concerning White House compliance with record-keeping statutes, as a way to guard against systemic noncompliance. Congress should also authorize the archivist to monitor and review the president's compliance with the PRA and to make known any actions that undermine the ability of the public to access a president's records after leaving office. President Trump's actions revealed the danger in trusting presidents to "honor their statutory obligations to keep a complete record of their administrations," as Congress did when it enacted the PRA.[47] With evidence that trust has been abused, Congress should tie federal funds and contributions for a presidential library to the president's compliance with the PRA while in office, thereby creating an incentive for compliance. Even without legislation, the Biden administration should commit to being transparent about its presidential record-keeping practices and promise to err on the side of preservation, not destruction.

Agencies during the Trump administration were equally cavalier about fulfilling their responsibilities under the FRA. Most notably, EPA Administrator Scott Pruitt imposed a culture of secrecy on the agency, installing a $43,000 soundproof telephone booth to prevent anyone from hearing his phone calls, and directing staff not to take notes at meetings with him.[48] Congress must amend the FRA to provide expressly for a private right of action that more readily gives members of the public the ability to act when their government's records are destroyed or not created in the first place to cloak agency actions in secrecy. Congress must also provide greater penalties, both civil and criminal, for willful noncompliance with the FRA.

Overclassification presents another threat to transparency—a threat illustrated during the Trump administration by the transcript of a telephone call between the president and Ukraine's president Volodymyr Zelensky, which came to light only after a whistleblower filed a complaint with the chairs of the Senate and House Select Committees on Intelligence concerning the contents of the conversation that were captured in a classified summary of the call.[49] Publication of the summary revealed that President Trump had threatened to withhold nearly $400 million in military aid unless Zelensky investigated allegations concerning the work of Hunter Biden, son of then presidential candidate Joe Biden, in Ukraine.[50] Classifying the summary was not an uncommon practice, but the White House went a step further and reportedly placed the document on a highly classified computer system, an unorthodox move that seemed designed to prevent embarrassing information about the president from ever becoming public.[51]

Since long before the Trump administration, there has been bipartisan recognition that overclassification is a systemic problem that is only worsening.[52] Erwin Griswold, who as solicitor general sought to prevent the publication of the Pentagon Papers, acknowledged years later that after the government lost its case before the Supreme Court and the full papers were published, he never saw "any trace of a threat to the national security from the publication."[53] The lesson he drew from this experience was that "there is massive overclassification and that the principal concern of the classifiers is not with national security, but rather with governmental embarrassment of one sort or another."[54] The digital age has only magnified these problems. A leading national security expert, Elizabeth Goitein of the Brennan Center for Justice, has described "the current declassification process" as "wholly inadequate to handle the oncoming wave of classified digital information."[55]

As a first step, President Biden should issue a revised executive order on classification that incorporates the eight recommendations of the Brennan Center, which has studied this problem in depth: (1) establish "a White House-led commission of senior agency officials tasked with narrowing the criteria for classification"; (2) define "intelligence sources and methods"; (3) "declassify or create unclassified summaries of rules or binding legal interpretations"; (4) implement "an auditing system to facilitate accountability for repeated or intentional overclassification"; (5) authorize "the National Declassification Center to declassify records at 25 years without referral to agencies with equities"; (6) create "a system for declassifying information classified for less than 25 years"; (7) establish "an expedited review track under Mandatory Declassification Review for records of significant current public interest"; and (8) establish "guidelines for the next Fundamental Classification Guidance Review."[56]

If the United States is to fulfill Abraham Lincoln's dream of a "government of the people, by the people, for the people," it must provide the public with the necessary tools for participatory democracy. Most prominent among them are statutes like the FOIA, which provide all members of the public with a mechanism to access information by and about their government. But these modes of transparency will be useful only if the Biden administration vigorously embraces the twin goals of transparency and accountability. At the same time, citizens must also play their part to reinstate norms, which begins in the voting booth. Voting, however, is only the start; citizens must constantly guard against complacency and cynicism, and must demand that the government live up to the democratic ideals enshrined in the Constitution and Bill of Rights, as reimagined in the modern era.

## Notes

1. President Barack Obama, in a "day one" memo to all executive departments and agencies, pledged to "work together to ensure the public trust and establish a system of transparency, public participation, and collaboration. Openness will strengthen our democracy and promote efficiency and effectiveness in Government." Memorandum from Barack Obama, President, to the Heads of Executive Departments and Agencies, January 21, 2009, https://obamawhitehouse.archives.gov/realitycheck/the_ press_office/Transparency_and_Open_Government#:~:text=Openness%20will%20 strengthen%20our%20democracy%20and%20promote%20efficiency%20and%20ef fectiveness%20in%20Government.&text=Transparency%20promotes%20accounta bility%20and%20provides,Government%20is%20a%20national%20asset.

2. H.R. 1 and S. 1 detail several such reforms, including enhanced financial disclosures for the executive branch, increased public ethics disclosures, and rigorous database management standards. The Redistricting Reform Act of 2021 would also introduce a requirement to publish a report outlining the selection pool for a Select Committee on Redistricting and further encourages public input on the report. The successor to S. 1, the Freedom to Vote Act of 2021, S. 2747, details enhanced campaign funding disclosures and rigorous database-management standards. It does not address increased executive branch financial disclosures. The redistricting reform provisions of S. 2747 would introduce a requirement outlining the criteria for redistricting and the development of a plan that requires public notice and input, such as through an accessible public internet website and a sufficient number of hearings. See S. 2747, §§ 5001–5008, 117th Cong. (2021–2022), 1st Sess., § 6011, www.congress.gov/bill/117th -congress/senate-bill/2747/text#toc-H9984C28D85CC4B0BA0D1031CE80C45C1.

3. See, e.g., Elie Mystal, "We're Going to Need a Truth and Reconciliation Commission to Recover from Trump," *The Nation*, October 20, 2020, www.thenation.com /article/politics/trump-truth-reconciliation/.

4. Jill Lepore, "Let History, Not Partisans, Prosecute Trump," *Washington Post*, October 16, 2020, www.washingtonpost.com/outlook/truth-reconciliation-tribunal -trump-historians/2020/10/16/84026810-0e88-11eb-b1e8-16b59b92b36d_story.html.

5. For example, according to its annual FOIA report, the Department of Justice received 73,103 requests in fiscal year 2016; that number rose to 95,119 in fiscal year 2019. See Office of Information Policy, U.S. Department of Justice, *FY 2016 Annual FOIA Report: Received, Processed and Pending FOIA Requests* (2017), www.justice.gov/oip

/page/file/920586/download; Office of Information Policy, U.S. Department of Justice, *FY 2019 Annual FOIA Report: Received, Processed and Pending FOIA Requests* (2020), www.justice.gov/oip/page/file/1253771/download.

6. See, e.g., H. Comm. on Oversight and Reform, 116th Cong., *Child Separations by the Trump Administration*, Staff Report p. 34 (Comm. Print 2019), https://oversight. house.gov/sites/democrats.oversight.house.gov/files/2019-07-2019.%20Immigrant% 20Child%20Separations-%20Staff%20Report.pdf.

7. "CREW Requests Records on Federal Police Deployed to States," Citizens for Responsibility and Ethics in Washington (CREW), July 27, 2020, www.citizensforeth ics.org/reports-investigations/foia-requests/federal-police-portland-protests/.

8. FOIA Project Staff, "November 2020 FOIA Litigation with Five Year Monthly Trends," FOIA Project, December 15, 2020, http://foiaproject.org/2020/12/15/november -2020-foia-litigation-with-five-year-monthly-trends/.

9. See, e.g., Nick Schwellenbach and Sean Moulton, "The 'Most Abused' Freedom of Information Act Exemption Still Needs to be Reined In," Project on Government Oversight (POGO), February 6, 2020, www.pogo.org/analysis/2020/02/the-most -abused-foia-exemption-still-needs-to-be-reined-in/.

10. See Complaint for Injunctive and Declaratory Relief, *Government Accountability Project* v. *U.S. Department of State, et al.*, No. 1:2019-cv-00449-RDM (D.D.C. Feb. 22, 2019), ECF No. 1; "CREW on Behalf of Government Accountability Project Sues for Middle East Marshall Plan Documents," POGO, February 22, 2019, https://whistle blower.org/press-release/crew-on-behalf-of-government-accountability-project-sues -for-middle-east-marshall-plan-documents/.

11. Ibid.

12. H. Comm. on Oversight and Reform, 116th Cong., *Corporate and Foreign Interests Behind White House Push to Transfer U.S. Nuclear Technology to Saudi Arabia*, Second Interim Report (Comm. Print 2019), p. 6, https://oversight.house.gov/sites/ democrats.oversight.house.gov/files/Trump%20Saudi%20Nuclear%20Report% 20July%202019.pdf.

13. Ibid., at p. 3. The House Oversight Committee's report describes the severity of the problem as follows: "With regard to Saudi Arabia, the Trump Administration has virtually obliterated the lines normally separating government policymaking from corporate and foreign interests. The documents show the Administration's willingness to let private parties with close ties to the President wield outsized influence over U.S. policy towards Saudi Arabia. These new documents raise serious questions about whether the White House is willing to place the potential profits of the President's friends above the national security of the American people and the universal objective of preventing the spread of nuclear weapons."

14. *Citizens for Responsibility and Ethics in Washington* v. *U.S. Department of Justice*, No. 19-1552, 2021 WL 2652852 (D.D.C. May 3, 2021).

15. "FOIA Update: President and the Attorney General Issue New FOIA Policy Memoranda," FOIA Update 14, no. 3 (1993), Office of Information Policy, U.S. Depart-

ment of Justice, www.justice.gov/oip/blog/foia-update-president-and-attorney-gen
eral-issue-new-foia-policy-memoranda.

16. "FOIA Update: Litigation Review Yields Greater Disclosure," FOIA Update 15,
no. 4 (1994), Office of Information Policy, U.S. Department of Justice, www.justice.gov
/oip/blog/foia-update-litigation-review-yields-greater-disclosure.

17. George Santayana, *The Life of Reason: Introduction and Reason in Common Sense*
(MIT Press, 2011), p. 172, https://santayana.iupui.edu/wp-content/uploads/2019/01/
Common-Sense-ebook.pdf.

18. An audit was conducted by the Government Accountability Office (GAO) in
2019, estimating that federal agencies spent about $13.6 million on Trump's four trips
to Mar-a-Lago in February and March of 2017, but a comprehensive audit representing
a full accounting of such federal funds to the end of his term in 2021 is necessary. See
U.S. Government Accountability Office, GAO-19-178, Presidential Travel: Secret Service and DOD Need to Ensure That Expenditure Reports Are Prepared and Submitted
to Congress (2019), www.gao.gov/assets/gao-19-178.pdf.

19. David Shepardson, "Trump Abandons Plan to Host 2020 G7 Meeting at His
Florida Golf Resort," Reuters, October 20, 2019, www.reuters.com/article/us-usa
-trump-g7-idUSKBN1WZ01E; Tommy Beer, "Ivanka's Trademark Requests Were Fast-
Tracked in China after Trump Was Elected," *Forbes*, September 22, 2020, www.forbes
.com/sites/tommybeer/2020/09/22/ivankas-trademark-requests-were-fast-tracked-in
-china-after-trump-was-elected/.

20. David A. Fahrenthold and others, "Ballrooms, Candles and Luxury Cottages:
During Trump's Term, Millions of Government and GOP Dollars Have Flowed to His
Properties," *Washington Post*, October 27, 2020, www.washingtonpost.com/politics/
ballrooms-candles-and-luxury-cottages-during-trumps-term-millions-of-govern
ment-and-gop-dollars-have-flowed-to-his-propertiesmar-a-lago-charged-the-govern
ment-3-apiece-for-glasses-of-water-for-trump-and-the-japanese-leader/2020/10/27/
186f20a2-1469-11eb-bc10-40b25382f1be_story.html.

21. See *Citizens for Responsibility and Ethics in Washington v. Trump*, 971 F.3d 102
(2d Cir. 2020); *In re Trump*, 958 F.3d 274 (4th Cir. 2020); *Blumenthal v. Trump*, 949 F.3d
14 (D.C. Cir. 2020).

22. John Haltiwanger, "Trump Made $40.8 Million Last Year from a Hotel That
Critics Say He's Using to Illegally Profit from the Presidency," Business Insider, May
16, 2019, www.businessinsider.com/trump-made-millions-last-year-from-his-hotel
-near-the-white-house-2019-5; Walker Davis, "150 Foreign Government Officials Have
Paid Visits to Trump Properties," CREW, October 23, 2020, www.citizensforethics.
org/reports-investigations/crew-investigations/150-foreign-government-officials
-have-paid-visits-to-trump-properties/.

23. David A. Fahrenthold and others, "State Department Signals It Will Keep Most
Details of Its Spending at Trump's Properties Hidden until after Election," *Washington
Post*, October 16, 2020, www.washingtonpost.com/politics/state-department-signals
-it-will-keep-most-details-of-its-spending-at-trumps-properties-hidden-until-after

-election/2020/10/16/83372f30-0f21-11eb-8074-0e943a91bf08_story.html; Nicholas Fandos and Annie Karni, "Trump and His Businesses Sue House Democrats to Hide Accounting Records," *New York Times,* April 22, 2019, www.nytimes.com/2019/04/22/us/politics/trump-sues-congress.html.

24. This section was heavily adapted from an article by the author, "The FOIA Is Broken, But Is It Beyond Repair?" CREW, June 30, 2020, www.citizensforethics.org/reports-investigations/crew-investigations/the-foia-is-broken-but-is-it-beyond-repair/.

25. See Ted Bridis, "U.S. Sets New Record for Censoring, Withholding Government Files," AP News, March 12, 2018, https://apnews.com/article/714791d91d7944e49a284a51fab65b85.

26. Nate Jones, "Public Records Requests Fall Victim to the Coronavirus Pandemic," *Washington Post,* October 1, 2020, www.washingtonpost.com/investigations/public-records-requests-fall-victim-to-the-coronavirus-pandemic/2020/10/01/cba2500c-b7a5-11ea-a8da-693df3d7674a_story.html.

27. See, e.g., U.S. Department of Justice, *FY 2019 FOIA Report.*

28. "FOIA Update: OIP Guidance: When to Expedite FOIA Requests," FOIA Update 4, no. 2 (1983), Office of Information Policy, U.S. Department of Justice, www.justice.gov/oip/blog/foia-update-oip-guidance-when-expedite-foia-requests.

29. Schwellenbach and Moulton, "Abused Freedom of Information Act Exemption."

30. Dino Grandoni and Juliet Eilperin, "Trump Environmental Officials Are Keeping Tight Rein over Stampede of FOIA Requests," *Washington Post,* December 15, 2017, www.washingtonpost.com/news/powerpost/wp/2017/12/15/trump-environmental-officials-are-keeping-tight-rein-over-stampede-of-foia-requests/.

31. On March 31, 2021, the Supreme Court in a 7-2 vote ruled that an agency could rely on the deliberative process privilege to withhold draft biological opinions even though they reflected the agency's final position. See *United States Fish and Wildlife Services, et al. v. Sierra Club, Inc.,* 141 S. Ct. 777 (2021), www.supremecourt.gov/opinions/20pdf/19-547_08m1.pdf.

32. H.R. Comm. on Government Operations and S. Comm. on the Judiciary, 94th Cong. *Freedom of Information Act and Amendments of 1974,* Subcommittee Report (Pub. L. 93-502), 8, 15 (Comm. Print 1975), www.loc.gov/rr/frd/Military_Law/pdf/FOIA-1974.pdf.

33. See, e.g., "The Increase in FOIA Lawsuits Isn't the Problem—It's Agencies Underfunding Their Transparency Obligations," American Oversight, March 17, 2020, www.americanoversight.org/the-increase-in-foia-lawsuits-isnt-the-problem-its-agencies-underfunding-their-transparency-obligations; Jacob Gershman, "'FOIA Is Broken,' Says House Panel Report," *Wall Street Journal,* January 11, 2016, www.wsj.com/articles/BL-LB-52908 (noting that in Fiscal Year 2019, "DOJ allocated about three-tenths of 1 percent of its overall budget to FOIA processing").

34. Jen Psaki, "Biden-Harris Administration Reinstates Visitor Log Policy, Will Be First Administration to Post Records from First Full Year in Office," White House

Briefing Room, May 7, 2021, www.whitehouse.gov/briefing-room/disclosures/2021/05/07/biden-harris-administration-reinstates-visitor-log-policy-will-be-first-administration-to-post-records-from-first-full-year-in-office/.

35. Julie Hirschfeld Davis, "White House to Keep Its Visitor Logs Secret," *New York Times*, April 14, 2017, www.nytimes.com/2017/04/14/us/politics/visitor-log-white-house-trump.html.

36. See, e.g., "CLC Demands Transparency, Submits Series of FOIA Requests to Government Agencies," Campaign Legal Center, September 26, 2017, https://campaignlegal.org/update/clc-demands-transparency-submits-series-foia-requests-government-agencies; "The Travels of Treasury Secretary Steven Mnuchin," CREW, March 15, 2018, www.citizensforethics.org/reports-investigations/crew-reports/the-travels-of-treasury-secretary-steven-mnuchin/. The Freedom to Vote Act does not require reporting of noncommercial, private, or chartered flights by senior political appointees to Congress. See S. 2747, 117th Cong. (2021–2022), 1st Sess., www.congress.gov/bill/117th-congress/senate-bill/2747/text#toc-H9984C28D85CC4B0BA0D1031CE80C45C1.

37. H.R. 1 and S. 1 also necessitate a record of the use of any noncommercial, private, or chartered flight used by any senior political appointee no later than thirty days after use. The bills require the official to submit a written statement to Congress certifying that no commercial flight was available for their travel.

38. There is one area of notable overlap between this chapter and the Protecting Our Democracy Act (PODA). In line with the author's overarching focus on transparency, this chapter includes a recommendation that the Department of Justice publish all Office of Legal Counsel opinions with only classified and personal information redacted and purely legal advice excluded. Similarly, PODA mandates that new OLC opinions be published within thirty days of their issuance and old opinions be published on a retroactive schedule spanning back to 1969 and earlier. These provisions remain unchanged in the 117th Congress's version of the Protecting Our Democracy Act (2021–2022). See H.R. 5314, 117th Cong. (2021–2022), 1st Sess., § 524, www.congress.gov/bill/117th-congress/house-bill/5314/text.

39. *Citizens for Responsibility and Ethics in Washington* v. *U.S. Department of Justice*, 846 F.3d 1235, 1238 (D.C. Cir. 2017). See also Trevor W. Morrison, "Stare Decisis in the Office of Legal Counsel," *Columbia Law Review* 101 (2010), p. 1448 et seq.

40. Alex Adbo, "Selective Disclosure of OLC Legal Opinions Isn't Enough," Just Security, December 20, 2019, www.justsecurity.org/67828/selective-disclosure-of-olc-legal-opinions-isnt-enough/.

41. *Testimonial Immunity Before Congress of the Former Counsel to the President*, 43 Op. O.L.C. (May 20, 2019), www.justice.gov/olc/opinion/file/1215066/download.

42. *Congressional Committee's Request for the President's Tax Returns Under 26 U.S.C. § 6103(f)*, 43 Op. O.L.C. (June 13, 2019), www.justice.gov/olc/opinion/file/1215066/download.

43. Isaac Arnsdorf, "Justice Department Releases Letter Approving Travel Ban,"

Politico, February 2, 2017, www.politico.com/story/2017/02/justice-department-trump
-travel-ban-234561.

44. Annie Karni, "Meet the Guys Who Tape Trump's Papers Back Together," Politico, June 10, 2018, www.politico.com/story/2018/06/10/trump-papers-filing-system
-635164; Vivian Salama et al., "Trump Didn't Deploy Note Takers at Putin Meeting," *Wall Street Journal*, January 13, 2019, www.wsj.com/articles/trump-didnt-deploy-note
-takers-at-putin-meeting-11547419186.

45. Sara Worth, "Trump and the Toothless Presidential Records Act," Media Freedom & Information Access Clinic, Yale Law School, March 11, 2019, https://law.yale
.edu/mfia/case-disclosed/trump-and-toothless-presidential-records-act.

46. Alex Woodward, "What Trump Might Do Now That He's Lost the Election: From Pardoning Cronies to Sabotaging the Transition," *Independent,* November 17, 2020, www.independent.co.uk/news/world/americas/us-election-2020/trump-lost
-election-what-next-b1521183.html. See also Brian Greer, "How to Ensure That Trump Preserves Official Documents," *Lawfare*, November 6, 2020, www.lawfareblog.com/
how-ensure-trump-preserves-official-documents.

47. *Armstrong* v. *Bush*, 924 F.2d 282, 290 (D.C. Cir. 1991).

48. Brady Dennis and Juliet Eilperin, "Scott Pruitt's $43,000 Soundproof Phone Booth Violated Spending Laws, Federal Watchdog Finds," *Washington Post,* August 16, 2018, www.washingtonpost.com/news/energy-environment/wp/2018/04/16/scott
-pruitts-43000-soundproof-phone-booth-violated-spending-laws-federal-watchdog
-finds/; Coral Davenport and Eric Lipton, "Scott Pruitt Is Carrying Out His E.P.A. Agenda in Secret, Critics Say," *New York Times*, August 11, 2017, www.nytimes.com/
2017/08/11/us/politics/scott-pruitt-epa.html.

49. See "Document: Read the Whistle-Blower Complaint," *New York Times*, September 26, 2019, www.nytimes.com/interactive/2019/09/26/us/politics/whistle-blower
-complaint.html#g-page-1; "Full Document: Trump's Call with the Ukrainian President," *New York Times*, October 30, 2019, www.nytimes.com/interactive/2019/09/25/us
/politics/trump-ukraine-transcript.html.

50. Ibid.

51. Mike Giglio, "The U.S. Government Keeps Too Many Secrets," *Atlantic*, October 3, 2019, www.theatlantic.com/politics/archive/2019/10/us-government-has
-secrecy-problem/599380/.

52. See *Too Many Secrets: Hearing on Overclassification as a Barrier to Critical Information Sharing*, H.R. Subcomm. on Government Reform, 108th Cong. (2004), www.
govinfo.gov/content/pkg/CHRG-108hhrg98291/html/CHRG-108hhrg98291.htm; *Examining the Costs of Overclassification on Transparency and Security*, H.R. Comm. on Oversight and Government Reform, 114th Cong. (2016), https://fas.org/irp/congress/
2016_hr/overclass.pdf.

53. Erwin N. Griswold, "Secrets Not Worth Keeping," *Washington Post*, February 16, 1989, www.washingtonpost.com/archive/opinions/1989/02/15/secrets-not-worth

-keeping/a115a154-4c6f-41fd-816a-112dd9908115/?noredirect=on&utm_term=.40e1c0f1 d32c.

54. Ibid.

55. Elizabeth Goitein, "Eight Steps to Reduce Overclassification and Rescue De-classification," Brennan Center for Justice, December 5, 2016, https://transforming -classification.blogs.archives.gov/2016/12/05/eight-steps-to-reduce-overclassification -and-rescue-declassification-by-elizabeth-goitein-the-brennan-center-for-justice/.

56. Elizabeth Goitein and Faiza Patel, "Transition 2020–2021, A Presidential Agenda for Liberty and National Security," Brennan Center for Justice at New York University School of Law, (2020), p. 14, www.brennancenter.org/sites/default/files/ 2020-10/2020_10_LNS%20Transition%20Report_Final.pdf.

# 8

# Restoring Congressional Oversight Authority over the Executive Branch

JARED SCHOTT | COLBY GALLIHER

The Trump presidency simultaneously laid bare both the centrality of government checks and balances in the preservation of the rule of law, and the American system's urgent need for scaffolding. Systemic, decades-long erosion—an executive branch demarcating its own jurisdiction, increasingly enamored with its ability to define those ever-expanding jurisdictional bounds;[1] congressional gridlock; a judiciary less and less insulated from the political fabric underpinning the other branches[2]—accelerated and produced a series of crises. And as the executive branch began to act in increasingly flagrant disregard of norms previously bridging the system's gaps,[3] and the judiciary's caseload of inter- and intragovernmental disputes ballooned,[4] a question emerged as to what extent Congress could and would reassert its legitimate oversight authority.

One early indicator of Congress's response is the Protecting Our Democracy Act. Introduced in the 116th Congress as H.R. 8363 and again in the 117th Congress as H.R. 5314, it passed the House in December 2021 and was transferred to the Senate for consideration. Known as PODA, the act is a collection of reforms responding to the most visceral congressional traumas of the Trump presidency. Across fourteen component titles and nearly 175 pages, the act legislatively broaches many of the subject matter areas and policy reforms discussed throughout this book, and its parts have been discussed in other chapters.[5] At PODA's core, though, is the subject of this chapter: its commitment to reestablishing Congress's oversight authority.[6] In some cases, PODA seeks to rein in attempts by the executive branch to evade existing oversight requirements, as in its provisions limiting the ability of the executive branch to circumvent the Senate's advice and consent on appointments through the strategic use of acting officials.[7] In other cases, PODA establishes entirely new authorities and mechanisms for enforcement. Its common thread, though, is unmistakable. The act represents a holistic attempt to reestablish congressional oversight within American governance.

This approach, of course, also raises questions. To what extent will the reforms underpinning PODA succeed in confronting, or at least eluding, the political impasses and morasses preceding it? To what extent does its unambiguous grounding in the Trump presidency adequately prepare it to address the most salient structural challenges of the next decade in American governance? To what extent does redoubling a commitment to oversight by Congress—a body hardly immune from political dysfunction—simply relocate the potential for mischief? Are these new authorities any less vulnerable to "political repurposing" by strategic actors in this or later Congresses? Lastly, to what extent will the act's proposals pass constitutional muster, "integrat[ing] the dispersed power into a workable government, . . . its branches" constitutionally "enjoin[ed]" in "separateness but interdependence, autonomy but reciprocity"?[8]

The remainder of this chapter looks at four key congressional oversight reforms in the bill, considering them in the context of their post-Watergate predecessors: (1) congressional subpoenas and enforcement; (2) congressional oversight of impoundment and rescission; (3) oversight of emergency powers; and (4) pardon power oversight. Consistent with Brookings policy and the approach of this entire volume, we do not recommend or oppose particular legislative provisions but utilize them as a springboard to discuss key issues and evaluate their pros and cons.

## Enforcing Congressional Subpoenas

Congress's authority to issue subpoenas in support of its legislative functions is well settled; its "power to obtain information, including through the issuance of subpoenas and the enforcement of such subpoenas, is 'broad and indispensable.'"[9] In light of former President Trump's refusal to honor some of those very subpoenas, PODA's Congressional Subpoena Compliance and Enforcement Act (Title IV) understandably prefaces its findings with the above reassurance from Chief Justice John Roberts in *Trump* v. *Mazars* (July 2020).[10] Building on this axiom, Title IV seeks to answer whether and how it might enforce such subpoenas in the event that an executive branch official respectfully (or disrespectfully, in some cases) declines the invitation. While the act's framing deals with Congress's subpoena powers generally, it is plainly and primarily oriented toward addressing the hurdles Congress has encountered in compelling executive testimony. In so doing, the act marks a pathway to judicial enforcement.

Several landmark court cases involving former president Trump and decided during the latter half of his term frame any inquiry about the breadth and boundaries of that path. In July 2020, in the aforementioned *Mazars* case, the Supreme Court, considering four subpoenas issued across three House committees for the former president's personal financial records, reiterated prior court holdings in *United States* v. *Nixon*[11] and *Senate Select Committee on Presidential Campaign Activities* v. *Nixon*[12] in reminding Congress that its subpoenas to presidents must address a "valid legislative purpose" and show a "demonstrated, specific need" for "demonstrably critical" information.[13] On the same day, the court ruled 7–2 in *Trump* v. *Vance* against Trump and the solicitor general's argument that the president is absolutely immune from state criminal subpoenas and that such subpoenas needed to show a heightened need standard.[14] The subpoenas at issue in the two cases, though differing in several important respects, were largely identical; the court noted this in a footnote to its majority opinion in the *Vance* decision, stating that the case's "grand jury subpoena essentially copied a subpoena issued to Mazars in April 2019 by the Committee on Oversight and Reform of the U.S. House of Representatives. . . . The principal difference is that the instant subpoena expressly requests tax returns."[15]

A parallel debate over the House's authority to enforce subpoenas against other executive branch officials worked its way contemporaneously through the D.C. Circuit, with that body signaling support for that authority. In August 2020, the U.S. Court of Appeals for the District of Columbia Circuit *en banc* ruled that the House Judiciary Committee had standing under Article III of the Constitution to subpoena testimony from former White House Counsel Don McGahn about Trump's possible obstruction of the Russia investigation.[16] In a 7-2 decision, the court held that the Judiciary Committee does have standing to sue for McGahn's testimony. The *en banc* decision reversed a previous D.C. Circuit three-judge panel ruling that the House lacked such standing. In its majority opinion, the full Circuit stated that "the ordinary and effective functioning of the Legislative Branch critically depends on the legislative prerogative to obtain information, and constitutional structure and historical practice support judicial enforcement of congressional subpoenas when necessary."[17] On remand, the original three-judge panel (whose ruling had been reversed by the *en banc* decision) interposed a separate barrier to enforcement, ruling that in the absence of express statutory authority (of the kind that currently exists for Senate subpoenas but not House ones), the Judiciary Committee could not enforce its subpoena. The *en banc* court then vacated that opinion pending consideration of the new issue by the full panel, but in May 2021, before the court could rule *en banc* on congressional authority, the House Judiciary Committee and Department of Justice (DOJ) reached a settlement for McGahn's testimony. The testimony has now been taken, concluding the instant matter.[18]

As if the trend of *Mazars* and *McGahn* were not enough, there is a third D.C. Circuit case of relevance to judicial enforcement of Congress's subpoenas: *Maloney* v. *Murphy*, decided in December 2020 by the U.S. Court of Appeals for the D.C. Circuit. The case was appealed to the court by Carolyn Maloney (D-NY) and seven Democrats on the House Oversight and Reform Committee, who in 2017 had requested information from Emily Murphy, the administrator of the General Services Administration. At the heart of the case was the ability of a minority of any congressional committee charged with governmental oversight to have their requests for information from executive agencies enforced by the courts under Section 2954 of Title 5 of the U.S. Code. As Section 2954 states:

> An Executive agency, on request of the Committee on Government Operations of the House of Representatives [now the Committee on Oversight and Reform], or of any seven members thereof, or on request of the Committee on [Homeland Security and] Governmental Affairs of the Senate, or any five members thereof, shall submit any information requested of it relating to any matter within the jurisdiction of the committee.[19]

The court sided with the Democratic appellants, declaring that "a rebuffed request for information to which the requester is statutorily entitled is a concrete, particularized, and individualized personal injury, within the meaning of Article III."[20] The court's decision indicates that the seven-member rule as codified in Section 2954 of Title 5 may serve as an additional pathway by which congressional committees may seek judicial enforcement of their executive branch subpoenas.[21]

While the judiciary's posture on Congress's subpoena enforcement authority has therefore been supportive, it has not been conclusive, and reinforcing this authority has been an early priority of the House during the 117th Congress. The House rules for the 117th Congress now make explicit that committees may issues subpoenas to any president or vice president, whether current or former, in either their personal or official capacities, as well as the White House, the Office of the President, and the Executive Office of the President, including any current and former employees.[22] And in June 2021, the House Judiciary Subcommittee on Courts, Intellectual Property, and the Internet held a hearing entitled "Civil Enforcement of Congressional Authorities," which heard expert testimony on ways to strengthen subpoena authority and sanction noncompliance.[23] At least some of those proposals can be found in PODA.

PODA responds to the court-endorsed idea that Congress may legislate itself into enforcement authority, setting forth an explicit statutory right of action by which Congress can enforce its subpoenas through civil suits. The act directs courts to "expedite to the greatest possible extent the disposition of any such action," while providing Congress the option of requesting a three-judge review, directly appealable to the Supreme Court.[24] The statute makes it clear that courts can impose monetary penalties against noncooperating agency heads, and that any assertions of privilege must be accompanied by thorough privilege logs.[25]

PODA addresses the possibility that officials will simply charge fines to their agencies by mandating that penalties must be paid with personal finances and not with government funds. But what if the officials are so rich that they do not care? A potential vulnerability of the power PODA affords to Congress to enforce its subpoenas is the relative affluence of some agency heads. Cabinet secretaries and other high-level agency officials are sometimes industry executives or other wealthy individuals who maintain substantial personal resources. As such, the threat of a monetary penalty for failing to cooperate with a congressionally issued subpoena, even when compelled by a court, may not dissuade recalcitrant agency heads from noncompliance if their personal means far outstrip the fine in question. PODA falls short of prescribing an enforcement mechanism that can reliably surmount the challenge posed by wealthy officials undeterred by court-ordered fines for noncompliance. Perhaps the solution, as in other litigation contexts, is to allow the court the leeway to set and escalate fines to a level adequate to compel performance.

In its construction, PODA piggybacks off an existing but more limited statutory authorization for the Senate that does not currently encompass the House. The new PODA standard avoids several constraints placed on civil enforcement in the Senate. One such constraint requires, prior to enacting a resolution to pursue a civil action, a report for Senate review on the relevant facts, process, and alternatives to civil enforcement.[26] Even more notably, the Senate statute carves out from court jurisdiction the enforcement of subpoenas issued to executive officials asserting governmental privileges or other grounds "authorized by the executive branch"; PODA does not apply this carve-out to House suits.[27] In thus positioning congressional enforcement authority against the executive branch on an even higher plane than currently exists, the legislation tracks the broad uncodified authority that (prior to the now-vacated *McGahn* decision) had been recognized by courts and experts alike.[28] These authorities determined that separation of powers principles did not forbid enforcement, and PODA reaffirms that.

Congress cannot function without the ability to enforce its subpoenas.

Whether PODA is enacted and survives judicial scrutiny or not, one other parallel vehicle besides judicial enforcement of civil and criminal contempt should be reconsidered. That is Congress's own inherent contempt authority.[29] Congress's power to hold someone in contempt—"essential to ensure that Congress was . . . not exposed to every indignity and interruption that rudeness, caprice, or even conspiracy, may mediate against it"[30]—has not been utilized for almost a century as other remedies have been ascendant. But in the face of executive branch resistance, Congress might find more leverage in imposing fines unilaterally, rather than going through the courts.[31] Rooted in prior Supreme Court opinions holding Congress's contempt powers as analogous to those of the judiciary,[32] Congress could, through legislation or its houses' rules, deduct such fines from official salaries or even use a third-party collection agency for enforcement.[33] Another possibility is that Congress could wield its power of the purse in withholding an agency's appropriated funds;[34] or, in keeping with *Immigration and Naturalization Service* v. *Chadha* (discussed later in this chapter),[35] Congress could instead condition an additional contingent budget to "reward" agency cooperation.[36] Given the uncertain disposition of the judiciary, this may yet prove to be Congress's most direct tool with which to bring the executive branch back to good faith participation in the "hurly-burly" of negotiating subpoena compliance.

### Reasserting the Power of the Purse through Impoundment and Rescission Oversight

The Trump administration earned its reputation—most notoriously, through its withholding of aid to Ukraine, precipitating Trump's first impeachment trial[37]—for unilaterally deciding against spending appropriated funding on agencies and programs it did not hold in high regard. The administration proposed nearly $15 billion in rescissions to program spending appropriated by Congress,[38] to say nothing of its less transparent efforts to, by way of example, "run out the clock" on diplomatic spending[39] or improperly withhold $91 million for clean energy research and development.[40] Of course, there is also the Ukraine matter, where the U.S. Office of Management and Budget (OMB) used delegations of authority to circumvent bureaucratic checks and withhold, for allegedly extortionary purposes, $391 million in assistance to Ukraine appropriated to the Department of Defense and the State Department.[41]

While not unprecedented, rescissions and deferrals such as these became more common, and unabashed, under Trump, harkening back to Nixon's defunding of tens of billions of dollars for programming with which he disagreed.[42] In the waning days of the Nixon administration, Congress passed the Congressional Budget and Impoundment Control Act of 1974, giving Congress greater control over the federal budget, placing limits on the president's ability to avoid spending (that is, to "impound") Congressionally budgeted funds, and unambiguously asserting Congress's "power of the purse."[43] PODA's Title V aims to shore up the very same 1974 Impoundment Control Act (ICA) while adding teeth to the related Antideficiency Act, which dates back to 1884.[44]

PODA would bolster executive transparency by requiring OMB to proactively notify Congress of any noncompliant apportionments,[45] complementing the impoundment oversight of the Government Accountability Office (GAO); requiring OMB to publish any delegations of apportionment authority, informed by the role played by delegation in the Ukraine scandal;[46] requiring presidential budgets to report on expired, lapsed, and/or canceled appropriation balances; codifying reporting requirements for the Antideficiency Act and publication requirements for the DOJ's legal decisions regarding the same;[47] and last but not least, requiring agency heads to report to Congress in response to GAO reports.[48] And if this reporting bonanza alone were not enough to deter misconduct, PODA would also move up the deadline for releasing funding slated for impoundment, in response to the Trump administration's play to "run out the clock" on diplomatic spending. PODA would also statutorily rebut the 2019 OMB guidance that GAO Antideficiency Act determinations are nonbinding[49] and would shorten the waiting period imposed on the GAO before it can bring a civil action to compel the executive branch to make specified budget authorities available.[50]

The sunshine of increased reporting requirements is a welcome deterrent to executives of both parties substituting their prerogative for constitutionally balanced processes. Indeed, the mere reassertion of congressional authority rebalances an out-of-whack situation for the rule of law. And the prospect of enhanced enforcement, too, is a welcome feature, whether in this formation or another statutory scheme. It is too early, of course, to declare the proposed statute a panacea for resolving executive spending decisions that serve as a proxy for political disagreement. Should enforcement, as discussed above in the context of subpoenas, prove elusive or untimely, the myriad reports called for under PODA may end up simply highlighting the budgetary insubordination in question, bringing up continuing questions for court review. It must also be recognized that PODA would extend the reach of congressional dominion in an area in which Congress's exercise of its inherent authority has been afflicted by hyperpartisanship and increasingly teetering legislative processes.

Congress has at times struggled to maintain business as usual in its annual budget duties, "[failing] to adopt a budget resolution nine times since 2001,"[51] and congressional rules have created in the budget process a forum in which the partisan ills of government can concentrate. Appropriators of both parties and in both houses are known for relative cooperation in reaching agreement. Nevertheless, sharp political fights take place through appropriation bills, the only ones to reach the House floor under an open process.[52] In the Senate, budget reconciliation, a product of the post-Watergate Congressional Budget Act, serves as an indispensable vehicle for moving legislation despite the omnipresent abuse of the filibuster (or, to put it differently, the lack of the hard work of bipartisan compromise).[53] Brookings Institution senior fellow Molly Reynolds has written that "as senators' ability to offer amendments on other bills becomes more limited, we should expect them to respond by offering more amendments in the rare chances they are given to do so—like the budget resolution."[54] Increasingly on the lookout for "credit-claiming"[55] opportunities, members may not always play the temperate oversight role envisioned by PODA. Conversely, enhanced enforcement always runs the risk of encumbering good faith attempts by the executive branch to utilize the flexibility to make sound, efficiency-oriented spending decisions later in the appropriations cycle. Still, whether through PODA or otherwise, post-Trump there is a desperate need to rebalance and restore the congressional power of the purse to prevent aggrandizement over spending by the executive branch.

## Reining in Emergency Powers in Process and Substance

Ironically, congressional oversight of the president's emergency powers reached its high-water mark in one way in 2019. It was then that, in response to President Trump's declaration of a national emergency allowing the president to reallocate $8 billion in programmatic funds to pay for the construction of the border wall, Congress twice passed a joint resolution to terminate the emergency.[56] While both resolutions were vetoed by President Trump, it represented the first time since the National Emergencies Act was passed in 1976 that Congress had managed to pass such a joint resolution.[57]

In the United States, congressional oversight of the president's emergency powers, already largely confined to procedural parameters, was dealt a major blow by the Supreme Court in 1983's *INS* v. *Chadha*. In holding that a single-house veto of executive action was unconstitutional, the case precipitated a 1985 amendment to the National Emergencies Act requiring an exceptionally difficult bicameral joint resolution to terminate an emergency.[58] That it took Congress thirty-five years to manage the first such exercise of its authority speaks to the challenges many countries, liberal democracies and autocracies alike, face in constraining the exercise of emergency power. The declarant typically enjoys broad substantive discretion in determining an emergency and the powers invoked in its response, with the judiciary playing a particularly deferential role.[59] Under these conditions, emergencies become "normalized," extending beyond substantive, spatial, and temporal bounds, with emergency powers becoming a "less cumbersome," everyday tool of governance.[60] Notable examples in the United States include, among others, the expansion of the president's economic authority under the International Emergency Economic Powers Act (IEEPA).[61] As of July 2020, presidents had declared fifty-nine national emergencies invoking IEEPA, each of which typically lasts nearly a decade; thirty-five of these emergencies were ongoing as of 2021, including sanctions against continuing flashpoints (Iran), as well as those sanctions lingering seemingly past a region's or crisis's immediate threat to U.S. peace and security (North Macedonia).[62]

Thus, even before President Trump's coterie of informal advisors began to toss about the invocation of a national emergency as a pretense for subverting the 2020 election,[63] Congress had set about in PODA to rein in the president's emergency powers. In addition to new reporting requirements on the use of powers and expenditures based in an emergency declaration, PODA proposes an ingenious way around *Chadha* by flipping the congressional lever: rather than requiring a joint congressional resolution to terminate an emergency, PODA would instead require a joint resolution to affirmatively extend an emergency that would otherwise expire automatically after a shorter period of time.[64] In such approvals, PODA would also give Congress the ability to delimit the president's exceptional authority to specific statutory authorities, even where the underlying state of emergency is extended.[65]

This represents an important and substantial step on Congress's part into an oversight arena where, as mentioned earlier, judicial review has been found wanting, and where cases holding the president's exercise of emergency powers to be unconstitutional are "the exception," as in *Youngstown Sheet & Tube Company* v. *Sawyer.*[66] A fuller review of the 136 distinct statutory powers that become available to the president in an emergency, in her or his nearly unfettered discretion, is warranted.[67] There is an undoubted need to go further in expanding congressional checks on these powers, basing these reforms (and their underlying congressional hearings and legislative record building) upon the outstanding scholarship in this area. Congressional fact-finding should assess each branch's roles, responsibilities, and conduct with clarity. This can raise awareness among stakeholders of both the vulnerabilities and policy tools presented by emergency powers, to solidly ground legislative reforms, and to better equip stakeholders to make difficult decisions when emergency powers are next invoked.

Congress should move beyond procedural checks to review the vast catalog of statutory emergency powers that remain in effect and available to the president after a century of accretion. Congress must determine whether all are still appropriate as emergency authorities, and under what categories and conditions (for instance, which authorities can be unilaterally invoked by the president and which ones are only available pursuant to congressional approval); whether sunsetting these powers is best achieved *en bloc* and/or through context-specific timelines and triggers; whether any laws should be amended to include statute-specific procedural or substantive checks, and whose context-specific tailoring might succeed where broader emergency checks struggle; and whether and where proportionality and necessity standards can be applied, or whether there are more justiciable standards that are preferred. Given the immense powers such laws afford to the president—going so far as the authority to commandeer transportation networks, to redirect telecommunications networks, and potentially to assume control over U.S. internet traffic[68]—emergency powers should not be drafted under the presumption that the chief executive will be deploying them rationally and in the public interest. Rather, oversight authority must be able to account for, and effectively address, the misuse and abuse of such powers, however anomalous.

This introspection is similarly important for the legislative branch. Congressional oversight mechanisms should be made more effective, to be sure, but they also need to avoid the risk of paralyzing critical and bona fide emergency initiatives by subjecting those initiatives to legislative partisanship. For example, consider whether Congress, applying PODA's framework, would have overcome a partisan divide regarding the seriousness of the COVID-19 crisis to extend beyond twenty legislative days the emergency declaration needed by the president to invoke certain provisions of the Defense Production Act. Given the urgent and potentially existential crises in which emergency powers are most needed, reforms need to be carefully considered to ensure that the proposed oversight mechanisms are insulated in practice from the gamesmanship that sometimes afflicts other congressional processes.

### Pardon Reform

Though stopping short of the Rubicon of asserting a preemptive pardon for himself and his family, President Trump's use of his pardon and commutation powers was remarkable[69] insofar as it was wielded more than ever before to benefit persons for crimes allegedly committed in his interest (e.g., Roger Stone[70]), extended family members (Charles Kushner[71]), cronies having connections with foreign interests (Michael Flynn, Elliot Broidy, Paul Manafort[72]), and a number of the most notorious public corruption defendants of the 2000s (Kwame Kilpatrick, Randy "Duke" Cunningham, Duncan Hunter, Rick Renzi, Rod Blagojevich[73]).

Trump, of course, was by no means the first president to invite criticism for his pardons. Bill Clinton and, to a lesser extent, George W. Bush were scrutinized heavily for certain pardons and commutations.[74] But at no time before Trump had the pardon power become so divorced from the moderating advice of the Department of Justice and so rife with clientelism. Allegations circulated that those in the president's orbit were setting million dollar–plus price tags for facilitating pardons,[75] and lobbyists—sometimes with conflicted roles vis-à-vis the White House—descended *en masse*.[76] Perhaps the most salient concern, though, was that pardons would be used strategically to obstruct justice by rewarding associates for noncooperation in ongoing investigations, as was alleged to be the case with Roger Stone and Paul Manafort.[77] In sum, the Trump experience highlighted the severe harm to the rule of law posed by a pardon system guided only by norms and left largely to the president's unfettered discretion.

While the Trump years bore out the inefficacy of norms alone, they do provide a blueprint upon which fencing can be erected around the pardon power. Using the pardon power to protect presidential coconspirators was addressed by the Constitution's framers in their drafting debates, with George Mason, among others, issuing a caution at the Virginia Ratifying Convention in 1788:

> [The president] ought not to have the power of pardoning, because he may frequently pardon crimes which were advised by himself. It may happen, at some future day, that he will establish a monarchy, and destroy the republic. If he has the power of granting pardons before indictment, or conviction, may he not stop inquiry and prevent detection? The case of treason ought, at least, to be excepted. This is a weighty objection with me.[78]

While James Madison's response pointing to impeachment as an adequate remedy prevailed,[79] the language of Article II Section 2—that the pardon power exists "except in Cases of Impeachment"—certainly invites the question as to how strictly that exception should be constructed. There is also precedent for greater transparency in the issuance of pardons: from 1885 to 1932, presidents submitted reports to Congress on pardons and clemencies granted, explaining the decisions, whether such decisions went through proper channels, and to what extent there was disagreement between the president and the attorney general (or pardon attorney) in their assessment.[80] Last, with respect to the president pardoning her- or himself: notwithstanding robust scholarly debate on the matter,[81] perhaps the most authoritative view remains that of the Nixon Justice Department's Office of Legal Counsel (OLC). It issued a memo just four days prior to Nixon's resignation, stating that "under the fundamental rule that no one may be a judge in his own case, the President cannot pardon himself."[82]

PODA builds on these authorities, as well as on ideas in previously proposed pardon reform bills.[83] The act codifies OLC's prohibition of presidential self-pardons[84] and amends the federal bribery statute to expressly criminalize both the offer of a bribe for a pardon and the issuance of a pardon by the president in exchange for something of value.[85] PODA also requires the production of supporting materials regarding the offense and pardon from both the Department of Justice and White House for pardons relating to offenses arising during a congressional proceeding (false statements, obstruction, perjury, witness intimidation) as well as offenses arising from investigations of the president or her or his relatives.[86] In narrowing its scope, PODA forgoes the opportunity for greater transparency as to other pardons posing material conflicts of interest—for instance, investigations of other associates.

Notwithstanding the narrowly tailored nature of PODA's pardon power provisions, they will likely face vigorous constitutional challenge if enacted. In its 1867 *ex parte Garland* ruling,[87] the Supreme Court considered the constitutionality of a law requiring U.S. office holders, as well as "attorneys and counselors of the courts of the United States," to declare an oath of office, under threat of perjury, representing that they had never taken arms against the United States, nor counseled or otherwise supported any such individuals.[88] In reviewing the case of A. H. Garland—a practicing attorney and former Confederate senator who had received a pardon from President Andrew Johnson and now sought to continue his legal practice—the Supreme Court found that the law was an unconstitutional, *ex post facto* bill of attainder in that it extended not only to those engaged in hostilities, but also to those providing "countenance" or "counsel" to those engaged in hostilities—activities not criminal at the time of commission.[89] The court went further in dicta, though, giving additional weight to the pardon that Garland had received and opining more broadly on the president's pardon power:[90]

> The power thus conferred is unlimited, with the exception [in cases of impeachment] stated. It extends to every offence known to the law, and

may be exercised at any time after its commission, either before legal proceedings are taken or during their pendency or after conviction and judgment. This power of the President is not subject to legislative control. Congress can neither limit the effect of his pardon nor exclude from its exercise any class of offenders. The benign prerogative of mercy reposed in him cannot be fettered by any legislative restrictions. . . . It is not within the constitutional power of Congress thus to inflict punishment beyond the reach of executive clemency.[91]

Some later Supreme Court decisions have clarified the very outer reaches of pardon power. In 1877's *Knote v. United States*, for example, the Supreme Court held that a pardon "cannot touch moneys in the treasury of the United States, except expressly authorized by act of Congress."[92] The court has also clarified that a pardon power can be conditioned or otherwise shaped, provided it does not "otherwise offend the Constitution."[93] Taken as a whole, though, the post-*Garland* jurisprudence signals judicial deference, observing that pardons are "rarely, if ever, appropriate subjects for judicial review,"[94] and "reiterat[ing] in most direct terms the principle that Congress cannot interfere in any way with the President's power to pardon. The pardon power 'flows from the Constitution alone . . . and . . . cannot be modified, abridged, or diminished by the Congress.'"[95]

Nevertheless, former President Trump's conduct has created a context in which the outer boundaries of the pardon power are ripe for reexamination, and we assess that the narrowness of PODA's pardon provisions may prove to be their saving grace should they be enacted and challenged in court. While the pardon power is undoubtedly broad, it exists in the context of the Constitution. Self-pardons are inimical to that document's text, structure, history, and purpose, as not only OLC but many scholars and commentators have found.[96] Moreover, the president's pardon power must coexist with the powers of the other branches to perform their functions under the Constitution. Congress's authority over criminal statutes surely includes the ability to sanction a president who corruptly sells pardons, and the courts likewise may adjudicate such charges.[97] The framers would have been astonished at the idea that a president cannot be prosecuted for the corrupt exercise of her or his constitutional powers, and that absurd suggestion is belied by the investigation of President Clinton for such allegations.[98] Finally, requirements of transparency do not limit the exercise of the power; they simply shed light upon it and, as we have noted, do so in a limited fashion.[99]

Other options are also available for reining in a pardon process "of late, [seemingly] drained of its moral force."[100] Following Madison's principle by broadening the aperture of impeachment may be one such path. With the precedent of Trump's second, post-presidency impeachment trial established, the potential extension of retroactive impeachment to improper pardons could yet prove an effective deterrent, where prior congressional resolutions of disapproval, as were passed in the wake of the Clinton pardons, have not.[101] Alternatively, there is a smaller, albeit nontrivial, chance that pardon power could prove to be the rare issue, given the even spread of risks across the political spectrum, capable of garnering enough bipartisan consensus for constitutional reform, where additional checks could be attached, such as abolition of pardons during a president's lame-duck period,[102] or requiring a congressional cosignatory.[103] It is not yet twilight for "clemency as statecraft,"[104] and the pardon power will and should endure. But the harms posed by *carte blanche* pardon authority to the rule of law and public confidence in the U.S. justice system are no longer theoretical. In volunteering congressional oversight as the means by which to mitigate such harms, PODA has offered one solution.

## Conclusion

Two and a half centuries of federal governance and judicial review have moved the United States far from the concern of *Federalist No. 51* of an executive branch so "weak" as to "require . . . that it should be fortified." Faced with long-term trends of a more confident and assertive executive combined with eroding normative guardrails, Congress should seize on a (hopefully) anomalous presidency to establish new and more forward-leaning positions in its oversight authority. PODA is decidedly broad but is not exhaustive in its application of congressional oversight in the service of the rule of law. To take one example, Congress passed the War Powers Act in 1973 in response to Nixon's surreptitious expansion of the Vietnam War to Cambodia,[105] and that legislation would seem to be similarly ripe for statutory clarification, given the steady recoupment by the president of the chief executive's international affairs fiat over the intervening decades. While new oversight vis-à-vis emergency powers may guard against some abuses, ongoing work has identified several areas through which Congress might effectuate a more transparent and accountable use of both war and trade powers, including through a clearer definition of applicable triggers (such as the term *hostilities*), the sunsetting of such powers absent affirmative renewals, and the rerouting of executive decisions through agencies and departments with more robust transparency and accountability mechanisms in place.[106] There is much work to be done across the board to restore constitutional balance between the branches.

**Notes**

1. Ashley Cook, "Kompetenz-Kompetenz: Varying Approaches and a Proposal for a Limited Form of Negative Kompetenz-Kompetenz," *Pepperdine Law Review* 42, no. 1 (2014): pp. 17–34, https://digitalcommons.pepperdine.edu/cgi/viewcontent.cgi?article =2349&context=plr.

2. See Daniel Weiner and Martha Kinsella, "Is the Supreme Court Undercutting Congress' Ability to Check Abuses of Presidential Power?" Just Security, July 10, 2020, www.justsecurity.org/71339/is-the-supreme-court-undercutting-congress-ability-to -check-abuses-of-presidential-power/.

3. See Martha Kinsella, Tim Lau, and Daniel Weiner, "Why We Need to Protect the Rule of Law in the Federal Government," Brennan Center for Justice, October 7, 2020, www.brennancenter.org/our-work/research-reports/why-we-need-protect-rule-law -federal-government.

4. By one count, state attorneys general sued the Trump administration no less than 157 times. Paul Nolette, "Searchable List of Multistate Lawsuits," State Litigation and AG Activity, Attorneysgeneral.org, February 7, 2021, https://attorneysgeneral.org/ multistate-lawsuits-vs-the-federal-government/list-of-lawsuits-1980-present/. This represented a sharp increase over prior administrations (observing that the Obama administration was sued 78 times over its two terms and the George W. Bush admin-istration, 76). Erik Ortiz, "State Attorneys General Have Sued Trump's Administra-tion 138 Times—Nearly Double Those of Obama and Bush," NBC News, November 16, 2020, www.nbcnews.com/politics/politics-news/state-attorneys-general-have-sued -trump-s-administration-138-times-n1247733.

5. Title III of both the 116th and 117th Congress versions of PODA would, as noted in chapter 1, address the Constitution's prohibition on receiving foreign and domestic emoluments. In addition to requiring disclosures on potential emolu-ments, Title III of both versions provides three distinct pathways to enforcement: through the issuance of fines or corrective actions by the Office of Government

Ethics; through special counsel investigation; and by providing Congress a statutory right to bring civil actions concerning any violations. Title VI in both bills relates to chapter 3's discussion on restoring the rule of law in the Department of Justice. As noted in the chapter, Title VI in the 116th and 117th Congress bills requires that communications logs between the department and the White House be shared periodically with the DOJ's inspector general. Titles VII and VIII parallel chapter 2's discussion on building a "moat" around integrity officials by broadening whistleblower rights, including protections against retaliation, and by precluding the president from dismissing inspectors general without cause or notice to Congress. As discussed in chapters 1 and 6, respectively, PODA would further authorize greater enforcement and transparency around Hatch Act violations (Title X in both bills), while also tightening rules and compliance mechanisms around foreign money (Title XIV in both versions) and involvement (Title XI in 116th Congress version and XII in 117th) in U.S. elections.

6. See, e.g., H.R. 8363, § 102, §§ 531-534. These provisions remain unchanged in the 117th Congress's version of the Protecting Our Democracy Act (2021–2022). H.R. 5314, 117th Cong. (2021–2022), 1st Sess., § 102, §§ 531–534, www.congress.gov/bill/117th-congress/house-bill/5314/text.

7. Ibid., Title IX.

8. *Youngstown Sheet & Tube Co.* v. *Sawyer*, 343 U.S. 579, 635 (1952) (Justice Jackson concurring opinion).

9. *Trump* v. *Mazars USA, LLP*, 591 U.S. __, 11-12 (2020).

10. H.R. 8363, § 402. This provision is retained in the same form in the 117th Congress's version of the Protecting Our Democracy Act (2021–2022). H.R. 5314, 117th Cong. (2021–2022), 1st Sess., § 402, www.congress.gov/bill/117th-congress/house-bill/5314/text.

11. *United States* v. *Nixon*, 418 U. S. 683 (1974).

12. *Senate Select Committee on Presidential Campaign Activities* v. *Nixon*, 498 F. 2d 725 (D.C. Cir. 1974).

13. *Trump* v. *Mazars*, at 11–12.

14. *Trump* v. *Vance*, 591 U.S. __, (2020); Julia Solomon-Strauss, "Summary: The Supreme Court Rules in Trump v. Vance," *Lawfare*, July 10, 2020, www.lawfareblog.com/summary-supreme-court-rules-trump-v-vance.

15. *Trump* v. *Vance*, at 2.

16. The editor of this book is a lawyer who worked on the McGahn case.

17. *Committee on the Judiciary* v. *McGahn*, No. 19-5331, at 4 (D.C. Cir. Aug. 7, 2020).

18. *McGahn* (*per curiam*); "Chairman Nadler Statement on Agreement in McGahn Lawsuit," May 12, 2021, https://judiciary.house.gov/news/documentsingle.aspx?DocumentID=4544.

19. 5 U.S.C. § 2954.

20. *Maloney* v. *Murphy*, No. 18-5305, slip op. at 2 (D.C. Cir. Dec. 29, 2020).

21. As of this writing, another important case is underway. In *Trump* v. *Thompson*,

the District of Columbia district court ruled that executive privilege did not stand in the way of the production of Trump administration documents to the January 6 select committee of the House of Representatives. The court found, *inter alia*, that the current administration's determination that executive privilege did not apply overrode the former president's assertion of that privilege. As of this writing, the matter is scheduled for an expedited appeal in the D.C. circuit. See *Trump* v. *Thompson*, Civil Action No. 21-2769 (D.D.C. 2021). Claudia Grisales, "Federal Appeals Court Temporarily Halts Trump Document Release to Jan. 6 Panels," NPR, November 11, 2021, www.npr.org/2021/11/11/1054837174/federal-appeals-court-temporarily-halts-trump -document-release-to-jan-6-panel. Another important precedent just getting underway as of this writing is the criminal contempt prosecution of Stephen Bannon for defying a January 6 committee subpoena. It was the first such prosecution in almost four decades. See *United States of America* v. *Stephen K. Bannon*, Criminal No. 21 (D.D.C. 2021); Pete Williams, "Former Trump Adviser Steve Bannon Indicted by Federal Grand Jury for Contempt of Congress," NBC News, November 12, 2021, www.nbc news.com/politics/justice-department/former-trump-adviser-steve-bannon-indicted -federal-grand-jury-contempt-n1283834.

22. Rule XI, Clause 2(m)(3)(A)(ii)(D). *Rules of the House of Representatives* (117th Congress).

23. Civil Enforcement of Congressional Authorities: Hearing before the Subcomm. on Courts, Intellectual Property, & the Internet of the H. Comm. on the Judiciary, 117th Cong. (2021), https://judiciary.house.gov/calendar/eventsingle.aspx?Event ID=4573.

24. H.R. 8363, § 403; H.R. 5314 § 403.

25. Ibid.

26. 2 U.S.C. § 288d(c).

27. 28 U.S.C. § 1365(a).

28. See Todd Garvey, Cong. Rsch. Serv., RL34097, *Congress's Contempt Power and the Enforcement of Congressional Subpoenas: Law, History, Practice, and Procedure* (2017), pp. 29–30, https://fas.org/sgp/crs/misc/RL34097.pdf; Morton Rosenberg, *When Congress Comes Calling: A Primer on the Principles, Practices, and Pragmatics of Legislative Inquiry* (Washington, D.C.: Constitution Project, 2009), pp. 29–30, https://archive. constitutionproject.org/wp-content/uploads/2009/07/WhenCongressComesCalling .pdf.

29. Grant Tudor, "Avoiding Another McGahn: Options to Modernize Congress's Subpoena Compliance Tools," *Lawfare*, October 16, 2020, www.lawfareblog.com/ avoiding-another-mcgahn-options-modernize-congresss-subpoena-compliance -tools.

30. *Anderson* v. *Dunn*, 19 U.S. 204, 228 (1821).

31. Tudor, "Avoiding Another McGahn."

32. As argued in Kia Rahnama, "Restoring Effective Congressional Oversight: Reform Proposals for the Enforcement of Congressional Subpoenas," *Notre Dame*

*Journal of Legislation* 45, no. 2 (2018), pp. 235–52, https://scholarship.law.nd.edu/jleg/vol45/iss2/4; Tudor, "Avoiding Another McGahn."

33. Tudor, "Avoiding Another McGahn."

34. Todd Garvey, Cong. Rsch. Serv., R45653, *Congressional Subpoenas: Enforcing Executive Branch Compliance* (2019), p. 42, https://fas.org/sgp/crs/misc/R45653.pdf.

35. *INS* v. *Chadha*, 462 U.S. 919 (1983).

36. Garvey, *Congressional Subpoenas*.

37. R. Jeffrey Smith, "Timeline: How Trump Withheld Ukraine Aid," Center for Public Integrity, December 13, 2019, https://publicintegrity.org/national-security/timeline-how-trump-withheld-ukraine-aid/.

38. U.S. Gov't Accountability Off., GAO-B-330828, *Updated Rescission Statistics, Fiscal Years 1974–2020* (2020), p. 3, www.gao.gov/assets/710/708190.pdf.

39. Eric Katz, "White House Pauses Some Diplomatic Spending, and the Money Could Eventually be Cut Off Altogether," Government Executive, August 6, 2019, www.govexec.com/management/2019/08/white-house-pauses-some-diplomatic-spending-and-money-could-eventually-be-cut-altogether/158986/.

40. Emily Cochrane, Eric Lipton, and Chris Cameron, "G.A.O Report Says Trump Administration Broke Law in Withholding Ukraine Aid," *New York Times*, January 17, 2020, www.nytimes.com/2020/01/16/us /politics/gao-trump-ukraine.html.

41. U.S. Gov't Accountability Off., GAO-B-331564, *Office of Management and Budget—Withholding of Ukraine Security Assistance* (2020), www.gao.gov/assets/710 /703909.pdf; David Welna, "The Hold on Ukraine Aid: A Timeline Emerges from the Impeachment Probe," NPR, November 27, 2019, www.npr.org/2019/11/27/783487901/the-hold-on-ukraine-aid-a-timeline-emerges-from-impeachment-probe.

42. Kevin Kosar, "So . . . This is Nixon's Fault?" Politico, October 21, 2015, www.politico.com/agenda/story /2015/10/richard-nixon-congressional-budget-control-act-history-000282/.

43. Staff of the H. Comm. on the Budget, 116th Cong., *The Impoundment Control Act of 1974: What Is It? Why Does It Matter?* (2019), https://budget.house.gov/sites/demo crats.budget.house.gov/files/documents/HBC%20ICA74%20Explainer%202019.pdf.

44. H. Permanent Select Comm. on Intelligence, 116th Cong., *Protecting Our Democracy Act: Section-by-Section* (2020), https://intelligence.house.gov/uploadedfiles/section_by_section_summary.pdf.

45. H.R. 8363, § 502, Title V. This provision remains unchanged in the 117th Congress's version of the Protecting Our Democracy Act (2021–2022). See H.R. 5314, 117th Cong. (2021–2022), 1st Sess., § 502, www.congress.gov/bill/117th-congress/house-bill /5314/text.

46. Toluse Olorunnipa, "White House Official Directed Hold on Ukraine Aid Shortly after Trump's July 25 Call with Zelensky," *Washington Post*, December 22, 2019, www.washingtonpost.com/politics/white-house-official-directed-hold-on -ukraine-aid-shortly-after-trumps-july-25-call-with-zelensky/2019/12/22/7af19ae0-24 d5-11ea-a14c-412f7b9e2717_story.html.

47. See chapter 7, this volume.

48. H.R. 8363, §§ 501–524. These provisions are unaltered in the 117th Congress's version of the Protecting Our Democracy Act (2021–2022). See H.R. 5314, 117th Cong. (2021–2022), 1st Sess., §§ 501–524, www.congress.gov/bill/117th-congress/house-bill/5314/text.

49. Ibid., § 521; Jason Miller, "Should You be Concerned over OMB's Decision That GAO's Antideficiency Determinations Are Non-Binding?" Federal News Network, December 16, 2019, https://federalnewsnetwork.com/reporters-notebook-jason-miller/2019/12/should-you-be-concerned-over-ombs-decision-that-gaos-antideficiency-de terminations-are-non-binding/.

50. The waiting period would be shortened from twenty-five to fifteen days, or none at all if "contrary to the public interest." H.R. 8363, § 504. This provision is unaltered in the 117th Congress's version of the Protecting Our Democracy Act (2021–2022). See H.R. 5314, 117th Cong. (2021–2022), 1st Sess., § 504, www.congress.gov/bill/117th-congress/house-bill/5314/text.

51. Alan J. Auerbach and William G. Gale, "Revisiting the Budget Outlook: An Update After the Bipartisan Budget Act of 2019," Brookings Institution, October 10, 2019, www.brookings.edu/research/revisiting-the-budget-outlook-an-update-after-the-bipartisan-budget-act-of-2019/; Molly E. Reynolds, "Considering the Budget Resolution in the Senate: Challenges and Consequences of Reform," Brookings Institution, May 11, 2017, www.brookings.edu/research/considering-the-budget-resolution-in-the-senate-challenges-and-consequences-of-reform/.

52. Molly E. Reynolds, "What's Wrong with the Congressional Budget Process?" Brookings Institution, November 3, 2017, www.brookings.edu/blog/unpacked/2017/11/03/whats-wrong-with-the-congressional-budget-process/.

53. See Ezra Klein, "The Senate Has Become a Dadaist Nightmare," New York Times, February 4, 2021, www.nytimes.com/2021/02/04/opinion/democrats-senate-reconciliation.html.

54. Reynolds, "Considering the Budget Resolution," p. 6.

55. Ibid., p. 11.

56. "Trump Vetoes Measure to End his Emergency Declaration on Border Wall," Reuters, October 15, 2019, www.reuters.com/article/us-usa-trump-congress-emergency/trump-vetoes-measure-to-end-his-emergency-declaration-on-border-wall-idUSKBN1WV06P.

57. Sarah Binder, "The Senate Voted to Block Trump's National Emergency Declaration. Now What?" Washington Post, March 15, 2019, www.washingtonpost.com/politics/2019/03/15/senate-voted-block-trumps-national-emergency-declaration-now-what/.

58. Chadha.

59. See more generally Oren Gross and Fionnuala Ní Aoláin, Law in Times of Crisis: Emergency Powers in Theory and Practice (Cambridge University Press, 2006); David

Dyzenhaus, *The Constitution of Law: Legality in a Time of Emergency* (Cambridge University Press, 2006).

60. Ibid. See also Jared Schott, "Chapter VII as Exception: Security Council Action and the Regulative Idea of Emergency," *Northwestern Journal of International Human Rights* 6, no. 1 (Fall 2008), pp. 24–80, https://scholarlycommons.law.north western.edu/cgi/viewcontent.cgi?article=1065&context=njihr.

61. Pub. L. 95-223, Title II.

62. Christopher A. Casey, Cong. Rsch. Serv., R45618, *The International Emergency Economic Powers Act: Origins, Evolution, and Use* (2020), p. 2, https://fas.org/sgp/crs/nat sec/R45618.pdf.

63. Gillian Brockell, "Trump Loyalists Harboring Martial Law Fantasies Don't Know Their History," *Washington Post*, December 22, 2020, www.washingtonpost.com /history/2020/12/22/martial-law-trump-flynn-history/.

64. H.R. 8363, § 531 (amending 202(a)(2), 202(b)(2) of National Emergencies Act); H.R. 5314, § 531; H. Comm. on Intelligence, "Protecting Our Democracy Act."

65. Ibid.

66. Elizabeth Goitein, "The Alarming Scope of the President's Emergency Powers," *Atlantic*, January/February 2019, www.theatlantic.com/magazine/archive/ 2019/01/presidential-emergency-powers/576418/.

67. One hundred and twenty-three such powers become available upon presidential declaration, and an additional thirteen become available upon congressional declaration. "A Guide to Emergency Powers and Their Use," Brennan Center for Justice, December 15, 2018, www.brennancenter.org/sites/default/files/2019-10/2019_10_15_ EmergencyPowersFULL.pdf.

68. 47 U.S.C. §§ 308, 606; Goitein, "Alarming Emergency Powers."

69. John Kruzel, "Trump's Pardons Harshly Criticized by Legal Experts," *The Hill*, January 20, 2021, https://thehill.com/regulation/court-battles/535147-trumps-pardons -harshly-criticized-by-legal-experts.

70. "Who Did Trump Pardon?" *New York Times*, January 26, 2021, www.nytimes .com/article/who-did-trump pardon.html.

71. Amita Kelly, Ryan Lucas, and Vanessa Romo, "Trump Pardons Roger Stone, Paul Manafort and Charles Kushner," NPR, December 23, 2020, www.npr.org/2020/12 /23/949820820/trump-pardons-roger-stone-paul-manafort-and-charles-kushner.

72. Ibid. See also Kenneth P. Vogel, "Elliott Broidy Pleads Guilty in Foreign Lobbying Case," *New York Times*, October 20, 2020, www.nytimes.com/2020/10/20/us/pol itics/elliott-broidy-foreign-lobbying.html.

73. Phillip Bump, "With His Last Pardons, Trump Makes Clear His Position on Political Corruption," *Washington Post*, January 20, 2021, www.washingtonpost.com/ politics/2021/01/20/with-his-last-pardons-trump-makes-clear-his-position-political -corruption/.

74. Jessica Taylor, "More Surprises: FBI Releases Files on Bill Clinton's Pardon of

Marc Rich," NPR, November 1, 2016, www.npr.org/2016/11/01/500297580/more-surprises-fbi-releases-files-on-bill-clintons-pardon-of-marc-rich; "Bush Decision on Libby Draws Fire," NPR, July 3, 2007, www.npr.org/templates/story/story.php?storyId=11688269.

75. Martin Pengelly, "Giuliani Associate Told Ex-CIA Officer a Trump Pardon Would 'Cost 2M,'" *Guardian*, January 17, 2021, www.theguardian.com/us-news/2021/jan/17/rudy-giuliani-associate-john-kiriakou-trump-pardon; Peter Stone, "A Million-Dollar Pardon Offer at the Trump Hotel," *Atlantic*, February 10, 2021, www.theatlantic.com/politics/archive/2021/02/corey-lewandowski-allegedly-pitched-more-1-million-trump-pardon/617980/.

76. Beth Reinhard and others, "The Cottage Industry Behind Trump's Pardons: How the Rich and Well-Connected Got Ahead at the Expense of Others," *Washington Post*, February 5, 2021, www.washingtonpost.com/politics/trump-pardons-lobbying/2021/02/05/896f0b52-624b-11eb-9430-e7c77b5b0297_story.html.

77. Norman Eisen, "Unpacked: Presidential Pardons and Obstruction of Justice," Brookings Institution, August 13, 2018, www.brookings.edu/blog/unpacked/2018/08/13/unpacked-presidential-pardons-and-obstruction-of-justice/; Maggie Haberman and Michael S. Schmidt, "Trump Gives Clemency to More Allies, Including Manafort, Stone and Charles Kushner," *New York Times,* January 17, 2021, www.nytimes.com/2020/12/23/us/politics/trump-pardon-manafort-stone.html.

78. See, e.g., D.W. Buffa, "The Pardon Power and Original Intent," Brookings Institution, July 25, 2018, www.brookings.edu/blog/fixgov/2018/07/25/the-pardon-power-and-original-intent/. Quoting from Jonathan Elliot, ed., *The Debates of the State Conventions on the Adoption of the Federal Constitution, as Recommended by the General Convention at Philadelphia in 1787*, vol. 3, 2d ed., (Philadelphia, 1836), pp. 496-99.

79. Ibid.

80. Martha Kinsella and others, "Executive Actions to Restore Integrity and Accountability in Government," Brennan Center for Justice, October 6, 2020, www.brennancenter.org/sites/default/files/2020-10/ExecutiveActionsReport.pdf. Quoting from P. S. Ruckman Jr., "Preparing the Pardon Power for the 21st Century," *University of St. Thomas Law Journal* 12, no. 3 (2016), pp. 475–76, https://pdfs.semanticscholar.org/eb75/7d9ac0a1f0c17736b43be0d9de4e4c86c97d.pdf.

81. Jack Goldsmith, "A Smorgasbord of Views on Self-Pardoning," *Lawfare*, June 5, 2018, www.lawfareblog.com/smorgasbord-views-self-pardoning.

82. Memorandum opinion from Mary Lawton, Acting Assistant Attorney General, Office of Legal Counsel, to the Deputy Attorney General, "Presidential or Legislative Pardon of the President," August 5, 1974, www.justice.gov/sites/default/files/olc/opinions/1974/08/31/op-olc-supp-v001-p0370_0.pdf.

83. See, e.g., Presidential Pardon Transparency Act of 2017, H.R. 3489, 115th Cong. (2017); Abuse of the Pardon Prevention Act, H.R. 5551, S. 2770, 115th Cong. (2018); Proposing an Amendment to the Constitution of the United States Limiting the Pardon Power of the President, H.J. Res. 8, 116th Cong. (2019).

84. H.R. 8363, § 104; H.R. 5314, § 104.

85. Ibid., § 103; H.R. 5314, § 103.

86. Ibid., § 102; H.R. 5314, § 102.

87. *Ex parte Garland*, 71 U.S. 333, 334 (1866).

88. Ibid., at 333–35.

89. Ibid., at 334–35, 377.

90. Dicta are those portions of a court's opinion not essential to the holding, but which, while nonbinding, nevertheless are treated as persuasive.

91. Ibid., pp. 380–81.

92. *Knote* v. *United States*, 95 U.S. 149, 154 (1877).

93. *Schick* v. *Reed*, 419 U.S. 256, 266 (1974); *Burdick* v. *United States*, 236 U.S. 79 (1915)

94. *Connecticut Bd. of Pardons* v. *Dumschat*, 452 U.S. 458, 464 (1981). "Pardon and commutation decisions have not traditionally been the business of courts; as such, they are rarely, if ever, appropriate subjects for judicial review."

95. *Public Citizen* v. *Department of Justice*, 491 U.S. 440, 485 (1989).

96. Memo from Lawton, "Pardon of the President"; Frank O. Bowman III, "Presidential Pardons and the Problem of Impunity," NYU *Journal of Legislation and Public Policy* 23 (2021), http://dx.doi.org/10.2139/ssrn.3728908.

97. "Preventing and Deterring Unlawful Pardons," Protect Democracy, https://protectdemocracy.org/project/preventing-and-deterring-unlawful-pardons/#section-0.

98. David Janovsky, "No Excuse for Corrupt Pardons," Project on Government Oversight (POGO), April 11, 2019, www.pogo.org/analysis/2019/04/no-excuse-for-corrupt-pardons/.

99. See, e.g., chapter 7, this volume, for a fuller discussion of transparency in the federal government.

100. Justice Anthony Kennedy, Speech at the American Bar Association Annual Meeting (August 9, 2003), www.supremecourt.gov/publicinfo/speeches/sp_08-09-03.html.

101. 145 Cong. Rec. H8012-20 (daily ed. September 9, 1999), www.govinfo.gov/content/pkg/CREC-1999-09-09/pdf/CREC-1999-09-09-pt1-PgH8012-3.pdf.

102. Keith E. Whittington, "Time to Amend the Presidential Pardon Power," *Lawfare*, July 14, 2020, www.lawfareblog.com/time-amend-presidential-pardon-power.

103. Budd N. Shenkin and David I. Levine, "Revising the Pardon Power—Let the Speaker and Congress Have Voices," *The Hill*, January 16, 2021, https://thehill.com/opinion/white-house/534441-revising-the-pardon-power-let-the-speaker-and-congress-have-voices?rl=1.

104. Margaret Colgate Love, "The Twilight of Pardon Power," *Journal of Criminal Law and Criminology* 100, no. 3 (Summer 2010), p. 1175; Margaret Colgate Love, "Are Trump's Pardons a Blessing in Disguise?" *Lawfare*, December 29, 2020, www.lawfareblog.com/are-trumps-pardons-blessing-disguise.

105. Andrew Glass, "Nixon Vetoes Congressional Ban on Bombing Cambodia,

June 27, 1973," Politico, June 27, 2017, www.politico.com/story/2017/06/27/nixon
-vetoes-congressional-ban-on-bombing-cambodia-june-27-1973-239903; 50 U.S.C. 33
§§ 1541–1550.

106. See generally "Presidential War Powers: Session 1 of the Congressional Study
Group," Brookings Institution, December 30, 2020, www.brookings.edu/research/
presidential-war-powers/. See also Rebecca Ingber, "Congressional Administration of
Foreign Affairs," *Virginia Law Review* 106, no. 395 (2020), pp. 395, 401–06, www.
virginialawreview.org/wp-content/uploads/2020/12/Ingber_Book.pdf.

# 9

# The Case for Filibuster Reform

JEFFREY A. MANDELL | MEL BARNES
| NORMAN EISEN

The history of the filibuster is a history of modification by senators bent on shaping the tool to their purposes. This procedural obstacle to an up-or-down Senate vote as of this writing requires sixty senators to agree to open debate. While we favor scrapping this outmoded apparatus altogether, enough of today's senators have made it clear (publicly or quietly) that they are not ready to entirely blow it up.[1] It follows that to advance legislation on many of the topics addressed in this volume, the filibuster will need to be reformed, as it has been repeatedly over the institution's history.

The sense of urgency for a next round of adaptations to this procedural tool is underlined by the failure to open debate on voting rights legislation in the Senate repeatedly throughout 2021 after its passage in the House. Perhaps the greatest public outcry as a result has come in the face of the mount-

A version of this chapter was first published as a Brookings report in substantially similar form on September 13, 2021, www.brookings.edu/research/fiilibuster-reform-is-coming-heres-how/. Norm Ornstein joined as a co-author of that report, and the authors here are grateful to him for his many contributions.

ing voter suppression and election subversion activity around the country that chapter 5 of this volume discusses and that S. 1, the For the People Act and its successor version, S. 2747, the Freedom to Vote Act, would address. But the filibuster is equally an obstacle to the ethics, campaign finance, and other reforms of the kind proposed elsewhere in this volume.

In this chapter, we survey the history of the filibuster and catalog today's principal proposals for its modification, enumerating their pros and cons. We include remedies such as reducing the number of senators needed to open debate in the face of a filibuster; obligating the objectors to be present with one of their number speaking at all times during a filibuster; and shifting the burden to them to muster the requisite number of votes required to maintain the filibuster whenever challenged, instead of requiring the sixty who wish to proceed to so vote.

The chapter also includes a remedy that we have previously written about and that we call democracy reconciliation.[2] It is based upon the existing practice of budget reconciliation, which allows purely fiscal measures to have an up-or-down vote and pass if fifty-one senators agree. As the chapter explains, we would craft a similar exception for democracy measures, allowing them a similar opportunity to be voted upon by a majority.

At the time of this writing, we assess that the pressure to effectuate one or more of these proposals is building. As explained below, influential figures inside and outside of Congress have renewed calls for a solution, including a subject-matter exception along the lines of democracy reconciliation.[3] It is hard to understand how the Senate will stand by and do nothing while U.S. democracy is dismantled (and many senators' jobs are threatened). Still, it remains to be seen whether any of the fixes we discuss will be undertaken by the time of publication. Because the filibuster is a perpetual obstacle to reform, and because even if modified it is unlikely to be eliminated, we articulate the full range of reform options. But first, we begin with the history of this controversial procedure.

## History of the Evolving Filibuster

Amid talk about the Senate's illustrious tradition of "unlimited debate," the filibuster can seem to embody a time-honored pillar of American democracy, enshrined in the Constitution and necessary to the structural soundness of U.S. government. The truth is, the filibuster as practiced today would be unrecognizable to the framers, who considered and specifically rejected the idea of requiring more than a simple majority to advance legislation in Congress.[4]

The framers, who had experienced the challenges imposed by supermajority requirements under the Articles of Confederation, were eager to correct that mistake in constructing the Constitution. Frustration with the impasse a supermajority threshold too often created under the previous system led the framers to reserve a requirement that more than a simple majority agree to only the weightiest decisions.[5] Those decisions include overriding a presidential veto, impeaching an officer, ratifying a treaty, and amending the Constitution itself.[6]

This is not to say that the framers were dismissive of arguments that had not yet attracted majority support. To the contrary, the rights of those in dissent were considered at length. The Senate rules were shaped to ensure that such voices were not only heard, but also given sufficient opportunity to persuade colleagues—or, failing that, the voters themselves.[7] Allowing a minority faction to exercise a veto over the wisdom of the majority, however, was considered antithetical to the core principles of the Constitution's design. As Alexander Hamilton wrote in *Federalist No. 22*, "To give a minority a negative upon the majority (which is always the case where more than a majority is requisite to a decision), is, in its tendency, to subject the sense of the greater number to that of the lesser."[8] James Madison expanded upon the danger of giving the minority faction outsized power: "In all cases where justice or the general good might require new laws to be passed, or active measures to be pursued, the fundamental principle of free government would be reversed. It would be no longer the majority that would rule: the power would be transferred to the minority."[9]

The idea that the Senate was designed to be a "cooling saucer" for legislation passed in haste out of the House of Representatives has a kernel of truth, but it has been distorted across time.[10] The framers chose other means to accomplish cooling legislative passions. Indeed, the very existence of a second chamber was a compromise accepted to prevent legislation from proceeding too quickly.[11] Beyond that, the Senate was structured to be slower to respond to political winds than the House by requiring both an older membership (at least 30 years old as opposed to 25) and responsibility to a broader constituency (the full state legislature and, later, an entire state, not just a local district). Staggered six-year terms also insulated senators from political winds, so that the passions of any given moment would settle before the body's membership could be meaningfully altered.[12]

The decision to grant every state equal Senate representation was critiqued at the time as unduly favoring minority interests (even then, population differences across states were significant enough to concern the framers, as they continue to trouble modern observers).[13] But the understanding was that half the states, if not half the American people, would be able to advance legislation, after thorough debate, on a simple majority vote. The prospect that a minority faction could indefinitely, even perpetually, block legislation supported by a majority would have been not only foreign to the framers, but also in direct opposition to their design.[14]

How, then, did the supermajority requirement come to be? The filibuster as it is known today is the result of a long evolution—and at times devolution—of Senate procedure.

The story begins with a suggestion by Aaron Burr. Attempting to tidy up the Senate rules in 1805, Burr suggested removing several unused procedural tools, including the motion for calling "the previous question."[15] At the time, the adoption of Burr's suggestion was unremarkable, as other tools existed to express that debate had passed the point of usefulness. Those tools, however, slowly fell by the wayside.[16]

Decades after Burr brought about removal of the previous question rule, the consequences of his action were first felt. A number of eminent authorities point to 1837 as at least the first "incipient filibuster," waged in connection with the battle over expunging the controversial Senate censure of then-President Andrew Jackson.[17] Another early milestone came in 1841. Recognizing that his Senate colleagues had no formal mechanism for ending floor debate, South Carolina Democrat John C. Calhoun engaged in what might be called a protofilibuster.[18] Previewing a consistent theme underlying the filibuster's evolution, two main forces brought this procedural issue to the fore: an individual senator's desire for personal power combined with an effort to bolster white supremacy.[19]

Calhoun opposed the establishment of a national bank, which he saw as a threat to the economic power of the South and its dependence upon slavery.[20] He convinced a band of Southern senators to take to the floor in succession for days, offering amendment after amendment to the bank bill.[21] Calhoun hoped to run out the clock to the Senate's summer recess, preventing the bill's passage until the following session.[22] Senators were outraged by this unprecedented obstruction, and in the end the bill passed only slightly later than expected, before the summer adjournment.[23] But Calhoun would continue to employ this tactic in the following sessions, invoking the language of "minority rights" while advocating for Southern secession and opposing recognition of an antislavery territorial government in Oregon.[24] Other Southern senators joined him, anxious to wield power disproportionate to their faction's numbers.[25]

Over the following years, senators attempted to end this obstructionist tactic through multiple reform proposals, but filibusters (or threats of filibusters) made procedural change difficult.[26] Efforts to reform the tools of delay were themselves filibustered. Finally, in 1917, the filibuster fever broke. Wisconsin Progressive Bob La Follette and his allies opposed U.S. intervention in World War I. La Follette coordinated a filibuster that blocked a vote on arming merchant ships.[27] In response, President Woodrow Wilson publicly demanded a procedure to force a Senate vote. A compromise was reached: Congress agreed to adopt Rule XXII, known as "cloture," but with a steep supermajority threshold then set at two-thirds of senators present and voting.[28]

Wilson's drive to (somewhat) limit obstruction was finally successful because it was tied to a must-pass policy: protecting national security on the brink of war. Procedure and policy have always been intertwined in the case of the filibuster. That is also revealed by reversals in the positions of leaders in both the Democratic and Republican caucuses in the Senate over the past decade, switching from majority to minority status and back again.[29]

But Wilson had not killed the filibuster so much as forced its reinvention. Resistance to civil rights–era legislation would breathe new life into the filibuster. Extended speechmaking became a vital tool for obstructing the expansion of civil rights protections, delaying federal bans on poll taxes and lynching long past the time when they had the support of a majority of the public, even in the South.[30] Georgia Democrat Richard Russell picked up where Calhoun left off, creatively coordinating Senate delays and consolidating his own power in the process. Unable to completely block reforms, Russell and his "Dixie-land band" of senators delayed popular civil rights legislation for years with filibusters and threats to filibuster.[31] Strom Thurmond (R-SC), perhaps the Senate's most famous segregationist, still holds the record for the longest filibuster in the institution's history: speaking against the Civil Rights Act of 1957 for twenty-four hours and eighteen minutes. The bill passed less than two hours after he finished.[32]

The distortion of the filibuster into a tool that could truly prevent passage of legislation, not simply delay it, occurred more recently, in the 1970s. Two key changes in Senate procedure brought this about, both of which were initially considered progressive reforms aimed at reducing gridlock.

First, in 1975, Senate Rule XXII was amended to lower the vote threshold needed for cloture in most instances[33] from two-thirds of senators present and voting to three-fifths of the full Senate. This lowered the necessary supermajority from as many as sixty-seven senators to only sixty. But it also freed obstruction-minded senators from having to come to the Senate floor to vote against cloture—by simply staying home, they could deny a cloture motion one of the sixty votes it needed to pass. The burden shifted from the minority to the majority.[34]

Second, also in the 1970s, the Senate adopted a "two-track" process for scheduling business on the floor. While allowing the chamber to get more done, this new approach also ended the "talking filibuster" of the kind employed by Strom Thurmond. No longer did blocking a vote require a senator to hold the floor and speak continuously. Instead, any senator could merely indicate an intention to filibuster, and the Senate would proceed with other business while the clock ticked down to the cloture vote. Filibustering senators no longer needed to engage in "debate"—some have even stooped to the level of reading from a phone book—to advance their aim of delaying Senate action.[35]

These changes in the 1970s inverted the burden of the filibuster: ever since Calhoun's innovation, the filibuster had always required active, even extraordinary, performance by the senator seeking delay; but now the objecting senator did not need to hold the floor, or even speak aloud, but only signal an intention to obstruct. The result is that a majority in the Senate is no longer sufficient; legislation often cannot move forward in the Senate until a supermajority, comprising sixty senators, votes for cloture. A minority that opposes a bill generally does not need even to vote against the bill. That minority can block a vote on the legislation from occurring by triggering a procedural maneuver with minimal effort. The result is diametrically opposed to the principled debate the framers sought to guarantee for minority factions.

Once the filibuster evolved to this level of obstruction, passing even the most essential legislation became difficult. Without a supermajority willing to reform or abolish the filibuster, exceptions to its reach became necessary. The Senate has created such exceptions through legislation, like the budget reconciliation process created in the 1970s and refined in the 1980s and 1990s.[36] It has created other exceptions via reinterpretations of the cloture rule: setting new precedents that exempted first executive and certain judicial nominations, and then expanded to include nominations to the U.S. Supreme Court. "Fast-track" legislatively enacted procedures like budget reconciliation and the Congressional Review Act (CRA) were passed to set limits on debate for certain types of future legislation. Supermajority support was, in effect, required to pass the bills that originally established these fast-track pathways (they could have been filibustered although they were not). In contrast, the changes that lowered the threshold to approve executive nominations in 2013 and 2017 were accomplished with a simple majority vote in the Senate.[37] These moves did not pass a new law or amend a formal Senate rule; instead, they overruled precedent—previous interpretations of a Senate rule—to the same effect. Although overruling precedent in this manner has been referred to as "going nuclear," the long history of senators developing and altering the filibuster suggests that description may be overly dramatic.[38] The filibuster's history has been one of periodic evolution.

What is a shocking departure is the level of obstruction the modern Senate has achieved. Even after the end of the talking filibuster and the introduction of the two-track process made delay easier, the use of the filibuster did not skyrocket until the current era of hyperpartisan polarization. The Senate has too often stopped functioning as a great deliberative body—or functioning at all. From January 2001 to the end of 2006, a Democratic minority in the Senate used 201 filibusters to block bills with majority support. In a comparable six-year period, from January 2009 to the end of 2014, Republicans were in the minority and used the filibuster 504 times—more than two and a half more times as often.[39]

For the half-century between the advent of the cloture rule on the eve of World War I and the two-track reform in 1970, the Senate averaged fewer than three filibusters per two-year Congress (measured by cloture motions filed, the best analogue publicly tracked by the Senate). By the George W. Bush administration, that average was up to eighty-five per Congress.[40] Everything changed when the filibuster gained its most recent and innovative champion: Senator Mitch McConnell (R-KY). As the minority leader for most of the Obama administration, McConnell vowed early, clearly, and publicly that his number one goal was ensuring Obama served only one term as president.[41] McConnell would fail by that measure but succeed tremendously in delaying and blocking popular legislation supported by Obama, the majority of the Senate, and majorities of the American public. During Obama's presidency, the average number of filibusters (cloture motions filed) per Congress shot up to 158—nearly double the previously unheard-of record during the term of his immediate predecessor.[42] Correspondingly, fewer bills on average were passed as filibuster numbers increased: from 1950 to 1990, over 1,000 bills were passed by the Senate each Congress; between 2009 and 2018, that average was less than 450.[43] The modern drop in Senate productivity is even more dramatic when examining how many bills passed excluding those passed via voice votes (generally indicative of a noncontroversial bill with broad support, such as a bill to rename a post office). Roll call votes accounted for only fifty-two pieces of legislation passed in the 2017–2018 Senate; the remainder, which accounts for the vast majority of all bills passed in that two-year period, were voice votes.[44]

McConnell's use of cloture and other procedural rules to stall any business in the Senate from his perch atop the minority did not engender an age of great debate. It did not incentivize negotiation among senators with differing views. It merely prevented everything from civil rights advances to the most basic and necessary business of government from proceeding—all in silence and nearly invisible to most voters. Those who say the filibuster promotes legislative compromise are ignoring history. But to the extent that was ever true, it describes a bygone era that has nothing in common with present politics and the modern Senate.

## Proposals for Modern Filibuster Reform

Neither the filibuster itself nor the extreme abuse of its current iteration is a new problem. The current iteration of the filibuster has been obstructing routine governance and a properly functioning Senate for a generation now. Numerous proposals have been developed to mitigate the filibuster's abuse without abandoning the concept entirely. This section recaps the leading contenders, including our preferred approach.

### Talk, Talk, Talk

Perhaps the most common—and most intuitive—reform proposal is to restore the filibuster to its popular understanding: a senator holding the floor and speaking at length to show her or his passionate objection to the policy under consideration. This is the *Mr. Smith Goes to Washington* version of the filibuster,[45] most notably practiced by Senator Thurmond in a futile effort to delay the Civil Rights Act of 1957[46]—and more recently at the state legislative level by Texas state senator Wendy Davis in a successful effort to forestall adoption of restrictions on abortion clinics in that jurisdiction.[47] The basic idea is to restore a talking filibuster so that a senator who wants to slow the progress of Senate business has to do something—and something difficult—to pursue that goal.[48]

Senators Elizabeth Warren (D-MA) and Jeff Merkley (D-OR) have long championed this reform.[49] And Senator Joe Manchin (D-WV) recently signaled that he, too, would favor making the filibuster "a little more painful" to use by requiring a filibustering senator to "stand there and talk."[50] The underlying theory is that if, as filibuster proponents often proclaim, the purpose of the filibuster is to promote debate, then use it to extend debate, not to passively delay legislation in the background while the Senate proceeds with floor business on a separate track.[51]

Proponents of the talking filibuster point to two significant benefits.[52] First, by making it harder for a senator to filibuster, this approach would likely decrease the filibuster's use. It would substantially realign the costs and benefits of any individual senator's decision to filibuster, thereby (at least in theory) deterring those filibusters that are frivolous and leading to a chamber in which filibusters occur only in those instances where senators feel the issue is of significant importance.[53] Second, a talking filibuster would increase transparency, attaching the name, face, and speech of a filibustering senator to the delay imposed by the filibuster. This would (again, at least in theory) require filibustering senators to clearly articulate their reasons for filibustering a particular proposal, generating public attention—and scrutiny—to their positions. Even if the filibustering senators are unable to persuade their colleagues, they may persuade—or at least inform—their voters. An additional point about this approach has received somewhat less attention: it would return the filibuster to a tool of temporary delay rather than one that functions as an effective veto. Recall that, until the combination of the cloture rule and the multitrack Senate floor schedule, a filibuster could forestall legislative progress for only the time that a senator or group of senators could hold the floor; once they yielded, the Senate could—and often did—proceed to adopt the bill under consideration. For example, Senator Strom Thurmond held up the Civil Rights Act of 1957 for more than twenty-four hours (even though the bill had already been weakened to overcome filibuster threats). The bill passed less than two hours after his filibuster ended.[54]

But there are downsides to this proposal. First, the reality is that this reform might not quite be painful enough to truly weaken the filibuster as it is today: senators coordinating a tag-team effort would be required to undertake some logistics but not necessarily hold the floor for even an hour before yielding to the next team member to take up the tactic. On many bills, this inconvenience may be enough, but it is unlikely to offer sufficient deterrence or obstacle when it comes to major policy priorities, like democracy reform. But more consequentially, by restoring the Senate to a one-track schedule—a necessity if a filibuster would last only as long as its sponsor(s) could hold the floor—the talking filibuster would allow the Senate's minority faction to delay not only a particular proposal that one or more of its senators was willing to filibuster, but all other Senate business as well.[55] A filibuster of a major bill, for example, might draw attention to and delay an infrastructure package, but every hour of filibuster would also prevent other essential Senate tasks—whether judicial nominations, treaty ratifications, budget resolutions, or other legislative proposals—from reaching the floor. A talking filibuster therefore expands a tool to block one legislative proposal into a tool that delays all legislative business entirely. That is why one commentator has noted that "the basic reason we don't have talking filibusters is to protect the majority party, not the minority party."[56]

## Your Move, Minority

An alternative would keep the filibuster in place and allow the Senate to continue with a multitrack floor schedule while shifting the onus in any cloture vote to the minority faction. Instead of requiring sixty votes to end a filibuster, this approach, proposed by Norm Ornstein and Al Franken, would require forty-one votes to keep the filibuster going.[57] Even though the filibuster itself would continue to be a theoretical exercise rather than a performative one on the Senate floor, a vote called by the Senate majority to end the filibuster would succeed unless there were forty-one votes to sustain the filibuster. And since the minority faction would merely be voting to sustain the filibuster, the majority could call that vote repeatedly, across time. In any instance where the minority faction did not have at least forty-one votes to keep the filibuster going, the cloture vote would succeed and the Senate could proceed to a vote on the merits of the bill.

Like the talking filibuster, this approach would "require a huge, sustained commitment" by those seeking to use the filibuster, rather than "the minor gesture" that is now sufficient to trigger a filibuster.[58] Moreover, this alternative would not keep the Senate from proceeding with other business during a filibuster. Some critics complain that "the legislative filibuster would no longer be able to prevent the passage of a bill; it could only slow it down, because octogenarian senators aren't capable of staying on the Senate floor round the clock for years on end, no matter the righteousness of the cause."[59] This is an odd criticism given that, for most of American history, the filibuster—which itself was never an intentional feature of the Senate—could, at most, delay Senate passage of legislation. It is only recent changes that have turned the filibuster into "the easily deployed blockade it is today."[60] Others complain that this approach, even as part of a larger package of reform, amounts to nothing more than a tepid half-measure, ill-suited to "solve the problem of polarized parties, separation of powers, and lack of accountability."[61] The reality is that no feasible change in the broader filibuster rule—that is, no change that can likely command fifty votes now—will entirely "solve the problem." But changes like this can remove the use of the filibuster as a casual weapon of mass obstruction, one that is used on minor and major measures alike. This reform would sharply increase the burden on the minority, while shedding much more public light on the use of the filibuster as a weapon of routine legislative obstruction.

## Ratcheting Down

Another oft-discussed reform option is to create a diminishing threshold for cloture, so that each successive vote on an individual piece of legislation ratchets down the number of senators from whom consent is needed to move on to a final merits vote.[62] This has the benefit of allowing for debate—or even a silent signaling of opposition—that presents a real and tangible hurdle, but not the brick wall of the current practice. Establishing a window of debate required by each unsuccessful cloture vote, before another could be called, would slow down the process.[63] It would allow senators in the minority to indicate their strong opposition to legislation. It would require multiple votes before a bill could move forward, with as much attendant public scrutiny as the minority could muster. But it would also create a path forward. By setting the threshold for cloture at sixty senators on a first pass at ending debate, then fifty-seven after a few more days of discussion, then fifty-four, down to a simple fifty-one vote majority, this method would restore the filibuster to the delay tactic (even one painful to the majority) that it was for most of the Senate's history.[64] This option would ensure the majority is truly committed to passing legislation, without maintaining the absolute veto power the minority now wields.[65]

Senator Tom Harkin (D-IA) introduced a version of this reform repeatedly, but it never gained sufficient support in the Senate.[66] To Harkin's credit, he advanced this sliding-scale approach when he sat in both the minority and the majority, from the 1990s into the Obama administration. Even two decades before peak gridlock, Harkin was articulating how drastic the filibuster's evolution had been and how at odds with the tool's purported purpose its modern iteration had become. "The filibusters aren't just against passage, they're also against process."[67] It was 2009 when Harkin said, "We've entered a new era here of outright stoppage at all costs," and even opponents of his reform proposal can't seriously argue that the Senate's functionality has improved in the years since.[68]

## Full-Majority Press

If the sliding-scale or ratcheting-down approach sounds too complex or burdensome, here is a simpler idea: set the threshold for cloture to match the number of senators in the majority in any given Congress.[69] This approach attaches the filibuster to a sliding scale, but a different, more consistent version. Keep in mind this is not going nuclear: in a Senate with even the slightest one-party majority, this would require more than the fifty-one votes needed to actually pass a bill. A fifty-two, fifty-four, or even sixty-member vote would be required to bring a bill to a vote, ending debate. For every senator the majority party could not convince to toe the line, one vote from the minority would be needed. For example, if the majority party held fifty-three seats, then in order to invoke cloture, fifty-three votes would be needed. This would allow the majority to control the agenda and move legislation, but it would theoretically promote negotiation and compromise by requiring unanimity among the majority party (or a minority-party replacement for each holdout) to invoke cloture. This is *de facto* how budget reconciliation works in the evenly divided Senate today. This reform has the benefit (perhaps undesirable to those outside the Senate) of preserving or even enhancing the leverage that any single senator can exercise—similar to the current and historical filibuster.

## A One-Two Punch

Perhaps a more obvious and simple approach than ratcheting down or a majority party numbered threshold is to lower the number of votes needed for cloture. Reduce, for example, the sixty votes currently required for cloture to fifty-five. The result is still a supermajority requirement (55 percent of the Senate's membership), but one that further limits opportunities for minority rule by requiring a larger minority for obstruction. In the current Senate, this may have little practical effect; but in the long term, it puts more negotiated compromises within reach.

Alternatively, the current sixty-vote threshold could be reconceptualized not in terms of a strict number of votes, but as a percentage of those senators present and voting. Recall that until 1975, this was how the cloture threshold worked (though two-thirds instead of three-fifths of the votes were needed at that time). A return to a present-and-voting standard can hardly be critiqued as a dramatic reform when it was in place for most of the filibuster's history. Moreover, the essential fairness of this reform is hard to deny: if the minority wants to block cloture, it at least needs to make sure its members show up. The current filibuster rules allow senators simply to avoid votes that they might not wish to defend on the campaign trail or in the press; they can advance obstruction by absenting themselves, whereas members of the majority must be present to advance legislation over a threatened filibuster. A return to "present and voting" would force senators to put their position on record.[70]

Both these paths have been advanced by Norm Ornstein as options that reform the filibuster while retaining the facets its proponents, Senator Manchin included, value.[71] These options retain minority input, as well as the minority's ability to slow down legislation and extend debate in the congressional "cooling saucer."

These two paths also lend themselves nicely to being implemented in combination: 55 percent of senators present and voting could be the new standard for closing debate. As a pair, this one-two punch of changes offers a requirement of commitment to a particular filibuster—not holding the floor in a *Mr. Smith*-style speech perhaps, but not going home to a comfortable bed either. At the same time, these changes mitigate, without ending, the minority's ability to exert control over the majority. A Senate with a thus-reformed filibuster (55 percent of present-and-voting senators required for cloture) could, with time, look a lot more like the idealized body of great debate enshrined in movies or in politicians' memories.

### Debate Freely

One of the most troubling aspects of the filibuster's current iteration is its consistent use to foreclose not only substantive policy votes, but also procedural votes.[72] A narrower reform could restrict the filibuster to votes on substantive policy—that is, senatorial decisions on the merits of proposed legislation. This would eliminate the filibuster on motions to proceed,[73] which are currently used to prevent even bringing a piece of legislation to the floor for debate. Under this reform, a simple majority could control the agenda enough to open substantive debate on a bill,[74] even if it could not ever force a vote. (Sixty votes would still be needed to invoke cloture and start the thirty-hour countdown to an end of debate and a vote on the bill.)

In reality, this reform would likely be ineffectual, doing little to end the gridlock that plagues the Senate. While it would cut in half the opportunities to filibuster a given bill, the failure of the majority to get sixty votes could still prevent a final vote on any piece of legislation. But proponents point out that, at least in theory, senators will find it more difficult to obstruct a vote on a bill after substantive debate and news coverage of that debate. A more informed public might assign some level of shame and accountability to obstructionism they see as tied to a specific policy. Then again, senators should ask themselves how likely that sounds in the current partisan world and whether it is even worth bringing a reform this minor (and inconsequential) to a vote. At any rate, broader reform of the filibuster can easily include the removal of a higher threshold on the motion to proceed, taking away the "two bites of the apple" delay.

## Democracy Reconciliation

Another solution that two of the authors of this chapter have advocated elsewhere[75] may be termed democracy reconciliation—the Senate creating an exception allowing for a majority vote to accomplish voting reforms, akin to the exception the Senate already allows for legislation known as budget reconciliation. This could be done through passing a statute allowing the exception, as was the case with the creation of reconciliation. The problem of course is that the effort to pass such a statute in the Senate could itself be filibustered. Accordingly, a democracy exception would likely need to be accomplished through the "nuclear option," with a simple majority voting as a parliamentary matter to create such an exception, as we explain more fully below. The nuclear option to create a voting rights exception could be undertaken within and as part of a larger budget reconciliation process, or entirely independent of budget reconciliation, as we also explain.

Because the fast-track procedures of budget reconciliation as an exception to the filibuster were honed by legendary West Virginia senator Robert

Byrd, budget reconciliation's application is now guided by the "Byrd Rule." The Byrd Rule governs which provisions are subject to a fifty-vote threshold and which are subject to a sixty-vote threshold.[76] We have advanced an approach inspired in part by the Byrd Rule, although as explained below, it could be accomplished without legislation and by a simple majority vote of fifty-one senators. Because the approach responds to concerns raised by a current West Virginia senator, Joe Manchin, it could fairly be termed the "Byrd-Manchin Rule." Under this approach, voting-related measures would also be handled separately from the current cloture hurdles.

Indeed, Senator Manchin himself has mused about this possibility. He suggested in an interview that a reconciliation approach might be utilized if all efforts at bipartisanship fail with respect to S. 1 (and he has since suggested an openness to many of the other reforms discussed in this chapter).[77] Representative James Clyburn (D-SC), a close White House ally, has similarly advanced "the idea of creating a carveout to the legislative filibuster in the Senate for legislation that applies to the Constitution."[78] Clyburn stated that President Biden could "pick up the phone and tell [Sen.] Joe Manchin, 'Hey, we should do a carve out.' . . . I don't care whether he does it in a microphone or on the telephone—just do it."

Democracy reconciliation would remove the current supermajority requirement for those legislative proposals addressing issues fundamental to the structure of American democracy, including voting rights, election procedures, and redistricting.[79] They are the core concerns of American democracy. Even more so than the nation's annual budget, these issues are essential if America is to continue having a functional, legitimate, accepted government. Without democracy—the consent of the governed—the entire concept of government of the people, by the people, for the people falls to pieces.[80] These democracy issues, distinct from substantial debates on proper policy responses to a plethora of other pressing problems, are at the root of everything the United States does as a nation, and certainly everything that Congress considers. If the framework underlying U.S. self-governance cannot be maintained, even as it openly falls into disrepair and demands congressional attention, then America itself becomes untenable.[81] Such a path risks endangering the national experiment, the key role democracy plays worldwide, and the notion that democratic government is up to the challenges presented—here and abroad—by a new generation of would-be autocrats.[82]

To meet the challenge and avoid catastrophic decline, the Senate must be able to address these narrow democracy issues on a majority basis. Democracy reconciliation acknowledges the existence of a constituency that accepts, or even strongly favors, the idea that a minority of senators, who can in theory represent less than 12 percent[83] of the American people, is able to block any Senate action. But democracy reconciliation also recognizes that minority rule is incompatible with democracy issues. Even the filibuster's fiercest supporters have to acknowledge the perverse irony of allowing a minority faction to block, repeatedly, proposals to ensure that majority rule within the constraints of the Constitution—the very premise of American government—is effectuated.

Democracy reconciliation can be achieved in two ways, neither of which would require changing statutory language or the text of Senate rules. The first would be to use the nuclear option if a minority in the Senate were filibustering election-related legislation. This approach would not require any change to the text of the Senate rules. During a filibuster on election-related legislation, the majority leader would raise a point of order that cloture on election-related legislation be decided by a simple majority vote, which would be denied by the presiding officer (acting on advice of the parliamentarian). The leader would then appeal the ruling to the Senate, the vote on which, if done in reconsideration of a failed cloture vote, is not subject to debate. The Senate would then vote on the appeal. If the appeal were successful by simple majority, the new precedent of requiring only a simple majority vote for cloture would prevent the filibuster of voting legislation, such as S. 2747.[84] A majority vote deeming the filibuster inapposite to S. 2747 would create the mechanism of democracy reconciliation and would establish it as a narrow exception, not a wholesale change, to the filibuster.

Alternatively, this could be accomplished within reconciliation itself. Election-related provisions could be offered as part of a budget reconciliation bill, and if challenged under the Byrd Rule, the presiding officer would rule the provisions are allowable, disregarding the advice of the parliamentarian. That ruling would presumably be appealed by the minority, but the appeal could be tabled by a simple majority vote, thus setting a new precedent—that election-related legislation can be advanced using the fast-track procedures afforded to budget bills.

Either of these two approaches would allow the champions of tradition to keep their word on not blowing up an institution they find valuable. The Senate, by excepting legislation that addresses voting and elections from the "unfunded-mandate rule," has already acknowledged that democracy issues are unlike any others that come before the Senate.[85] The unfunded-mandate rule prohibits federal legislation from imposing financial burdens on state and local governments without also providing aid to pay for the burdens Congress is creating. This is, generally speaking, a sound practice. But when Congress adopts new laws for elections, states and localities must comply even when they bear the burden of finding the money to do so. This follows from the Senate's sensible recognition that elections are simply too important to be held hostage to disputes ancillary to the merits of the democracy reforms at issue. Voting-rights laws protect the most core constitutional rights, and therefore, states should and must prioritize implementation. By the same rationale, the practice of democracy should also be exempt from any use of the filibuster.

Democracy reconciliation is not without hypothetical risks. Once democracy reconciliation opens the door to majority rule on democracy issues, a future Congress with a narrow majority and a very different policy orientation may walk through that door. While the current Congress might use democracy reconciliation to expand voting rights, a future Congress could instead rely on democracy reconciliation as a tool to restrict voting rights. To give a couple of hypothetical examples, a stringent federal voter ID requirement or a nationwide prohibition on voting by mail would both fall within the ambit of democracy reconciliation and could pass the Senate on a majority vote. These risks should not be ignored, but neither should they be overstated.

A simple truth is relevant here: Americans are proud of our democracy. Voting rights and fair elections are enduringly popular with the electorate. As the nation has expanded the franchise and access to the ballot over the decades, there has not been a successful effort at the congressional level to roll them back significantly. There is little reason to think that Congress could or would do so in the future. Elected officials are more comfortable blocking proposed policies than reversing such policies once they are enacted. Take the Civil Rights Act of 1964 and the Voting Rights Act of 1965 as examples: notwithstanding the extensive efforts to frustrate and delay those bills through the filibuster and other tactics, opponents have not repealed either piece of landmark legislation, even as the composition of the Senate changed across time. To the contrary, Congress repeatedly extended those landmark laws, with the only significant rollbacks resulting from misguided judicial decisions. Thus, the concern that democracy reconciliation could be used against voting rights may be more theoretical than practical. Even if it is not, that possibility must be weighed against the profound danger of taking no action in this moment.

## Conclusion

All of the proposals we discuss for modifying—but not eliminating—the filibuster would preserve the fundamental principles of American democracy without upending wholesale either the Senate's rules or its traditions. And adopting one or more of these proposals would be only the next step in the filibuster's more-than-two-century journey. The filibuster has always been a tool. It evolved from one characterized by epic floor speeches and endurance contests to the present iteration that has imposed regular shutdowns of congressional business with precious little fanfare.[86] One benefit the contemporary filibuster confers upon its patrons is that it exacts no cost; not only does invoking cloture require no effort or action, but the fact that such invocations have become part and parcel of everyday Senate procedure means there is no public attention to, and no cost associated with, any individual senator's decision to block legislation.

Reform would help move the filibuster back toward being a tool in a functioning deliberative body. It would end the antidemocratic blockade that has bottled up necessary reforms to U.S. voting laws, elections, and democracy. By doing so, reform would allow U.S. laws to catch up to the political tactics, the social media environment, the court decisions, and the practical realities that have altered the practice of American democracy— many without any congressional response for far too long, if ever. Realigning U.S. laws with current political practices will restore health to democratic processes and promote public confidence in both U.S. elections themselves and the ability of the federal government to respond to changing circumstances. Better, fairer elections may also yield different results, ensuring that the United States' representative government more accurately represents the will of the people. That is an invaluable end in itself; it may also yield a Senate in which the filibuster would be a less effective tool for evading debate on the topics to which it would still apply.

The worst-case scenario, however, is not a hypothetical future abuse of democracy reconciliation but a failure to act now. American democracy is at a point of inflection, as we detail throughout this volume. To continue with the voting-rights example (discussed in depth in chapter 5), absent federal legislation, some states and municipalities will further restrict the rights and opportunities for voters to participate in American democracy. This is not alarmist rhetoric: we have seen these restrictions metastasize since the Supreme Court struck down large portions of the Voting Rights Act in *Shelby County* v. *Holder*,[87] and now it has further curtailed surviving provisions of that law in *Brnovich* v. *Democratic National Committee*.[88] The past years have seen a sustained, consistent, baseless attack on the integrity of U.S. elections, leading to an armed attempt to seize the U.S. Capitol and disrupt the peaceful transfer of presidential power. And in the period since that insurrection, literally hundreds of proposals have been introduced in state legislatures around the country to make it harder for eligible voters to cast their ballots and have their voices heard.[89]

Worse yet, 2021–2022 is a redistricting cycle. In the absence of a federal legislative solution, gerrymandered state legislatures across the country will likely take all possible steps to perpetuate their own power.[90] These steps include last-gasp passage of unprecedented restrictions of voting rights, as well as a no-holds-barred effort, in state legislatures and courtrooms alike, to enact new, extreme gerrymanders to ensure those in power do not meaningfully reflect the will of the voters.

These present efforts are antithetical to American democracy. Neither any individual politician nor any political party should be able to cling to power without winning the contest of ideas and building an electoral coalition that attracts majority support. But there is a clear trend to invert this most basic understanding of democracy, to change the ground rules of the electoral system to obviate any need to build winning coalitions and to instead exclude voters, limit voting opportunities, enhance opportunities for partisan and racial gerrymanders, and otherwise reject the fundamental premise of American democracy.

The last four years are instructive on how much U.S. institutions—no matter how enduring they may seem—can be tested, and eroded, in a short period of time. Filibuster reform may not be the ultimate solution to some of the challenges facing the Senate, but it is a necessary step; without it, further debate over the alternatives may be meaningless. The filibuster cannot be more sacred or important than the government itself. Whether through some combination of the reforms described in this chapter or otherwise, reforming the filibuster is not an act of escalation; to the contrary, without reform, the Senate will endanger American democracy by choosing inaction. An overly broad application of the filibuster, a tool adapted to support the Jim Crow era and weaponized to distort the Senate's function, cannot be the reason that the United States risks, more seriously than it has since the Civil War, the prospect that American democracy shall perish from the earth.[91]

With the mounting political pressure created by antidemocracy overreach around the country, some change is very likely coming to the filibuster. Institutionalists should pick their path now, before is too late.

## Notes

1. J. M. Rieger, "39 Senators Who Now Support Changing or Eliminating the Filibuster Previously Opposed Doing So," *Washington Post*, June 18, 2021, www.washingtonpost.com/politics/2021/06/18/39-senators-who-now-support-changing-or-eliminating-filibuster-previously-opposed-doing-so/. As of November 2021, four more Democratic senators have signaled a willingness to carve out a voting rights exception to the filibuster: Angus King (King is an independent but caucuses with the Democrats), Mark Warner, Jon Tester, and most recently Senator Tom Carper. See Paul Waldman and Greg Sargent, "Republicans Have Given Joe Manchin the Perfect Reason to End the Filibuster," *Washington Post*, October 21, 2021, www.washingtonpost.com/opinions/2021/10/21/manchin-republicans-end-filibuster/; Steve Benen, "To Protect Voting Rights, Dems Eye Carve-out to Filibuster Rules," MSNBC, November 4, 2021, www.msnbc.com/rachel-maddow-show/protect-voting-rights-dems-eye-carve-out-filibuster-rules-n1283223; Tom Carper, "No Barrier—Not Even the Filibuster—Must Stop Our Obligation to Our Democracy," Delaware Online, November 4, 2021, www.delawareonline.com/story/opinion/2021/11/04/tom-carper-no-barrier-not-even-filibuster-stop-our-obligation-our-democracy/6269169001/.

2. Norman Eisen, Richard W. Painter, and Jeffrey Mandell, "Opinion: The Most Important Exception the Senate Can Make," CNN, March 5, 2021, www.cnn.com/2021/03/05/opinions/senate-filibuster-exception-eisen-painter-mandell/index.html.

3. Laura Barrón-López, "Top Biden Ally Pleads with Him to Scrap Filibuster for Election Reform," Politico, July 10, 2021, www.politico.com/news/2021/07/10/clyburn-biden-filibuster-election-reform-499051?nname=playbook&nid=0000014f-1646-d88f-a1cf-5f46b7bd0000&nrid=00000151-3612-d6a2-a155-ffd2292b0000&nlid=630318. At a town hall meeting in October 2021, President Biden stated that he was open to ending the filibuster on voting rights legislation, as well as other changes to the rule. See Michael D. Shear and Emily Cochrane, "Biden Is Open to Scrapping Filibuster for Voting Rights Bill 'and Maybe More,'" *New York Times*, October 21, 2021, www.nytimes.com/2021/10/21/us/politics/biden-filibuster-voting-rights.html.

4. Sarah A. Binder and Steven S. Smith, *Politics or Principle? Filibustering in the United States Senate* (Brookings Institution Press, 1997), pp. 4, 33.

5. Victor Williams, "Madison, Hamilton, and Scalia: Original—Not Nuclear—Option to End Gorsuch Filibuster," *The Hill*, April 6, 2017, https://thehill.com/blogs/congress-blog/politics/327504-madison-hamilton-and-scalia-original-not-nuclear-option-to-end.

6. Walter J. Oleszek, Cong. Rsch. Serv., 98-779, *Super-Majority Votes in the Senate* (2008), https://fas.org/sgp/crs/misc/98-779.pdf.

7. Judy Schneider, Cong. Rsch. Serv., RL30850, *Minority Rights and Senate Procedures* (2005), https://fas.org/sgp/crs/misc/RL30850.pdf.

8. Alexander Hamilton, *Federalist No. 22*, *The Federalist Papers*, May 28, 1788, https://guides.loc.gov/federalist-papers/text-21-30.

9. James Madison, *Federalist No. 58*, *The Federalist Papers*, May 28, 1788, https://guides.loc.gov/federalist-papers/text-21-30#s-lg-box-wrapper-25493335; see also Alexander Hamilton, *Federalist No. 22*, *The Federalist Papers*, https://guides.loc.gov/federalist-papers/text-21-30#s-lg-box-wrapper-25493335: "The public business must, in some way or other, go forward. If a pertinacious minority can control the opinion of a majority, respecting the best mode of conducting it, the majority, in order that something may be done, must conform to the views of the minority; and thus the sense of the smaller number will overrule that of the greater, and give a tone to the national proceedings. Hence, tedious delays; continual negotiation and intrigue; contemptible compromises of the public good. And yet, in such a system, it is even happy when such compromises can take place: for upon some occasions things will not admit of accommodation; and then the measures of government must be injuriously suspended, or fatally defeated. It is often, by the impracticability of obtaining the concurrence of the necessary number of votes, kept in a state of inaction. Its situation must always savor of weakness, sometimes border upon anarchy."

10. "Senate Created," U.S. Senate, www.senate.gov/artandhistory/history/minute/Senate_Created.htm.

11. Frances E. Lee and Bruce I. Oppenheimer, *Sizing up the Senate: The Unequal Consequences of Equal Representation* (University of Chicago Press, 1999), p. 28.

12. "Senate Created," U.S. Senate.

13. Alexander Hamilton, *Federalist No. 22*, Avalon Project, Yale Law School, https://avalon.law.yale.edu/18th_century/fed22.asp; see also Hendrik Herzberg, "Alexander Hamilton Speaks Out (III): Two Senators Per State, Regardless of Population?" *New Yorker*, January 8, 2011, www.newyorker.com/news/hendrik-hertzberg/alexander-hamilton-speaks-out-iii-two-senators-per-state-regardless-of-population.

14. Adam Jentleson, *Kill Switch: The Rise of the Modern Senate and the Crippling of American Democracy* (New York City: W.W. Norton, 2021), p. 6; see also "James Madison to [Edward Everett], 28 August 1830," Founders Online, National Archives, https://founders.archives.gov/documents/Madison/99-02-02-2138; Binder and Smith, *Politics or Principle?*, pp. 4, 33.

15. Sarah A. Binder, "The History of the Filibuster," Brookings Institution, April 22, 2010, www.brookings.edu/testimonies/the-history-of-the-filibuster/.

16. Ibid.

17. Franklin L. Burdette, *Filibustering in the Senate* (Princeton University Press, 1940), p. 20. Burdette outlines the preparations Jacksonian senators made for a long night of continuous session, including laying in a supply of "cold hams, turkeys, beef, pickles, wines and cups of hot coffee" and speeches by opponents lasting until near midnight. See also Thomas H. Benton, *Thirty Years' View* (New York: D. Appleton, 1854), p. 727.

18. Gail Russel Chaddock, "The Filibuster—A Debate That Has Never Ended," *Christian Science Monitor*, May 5, 2005, www.csmonitor.com/2005/0505/p01s02-uspo.html; see also Sarah Binder, "Mitch McConnell Is Wrong. Here's the Filibuster's 'Racial History,'" *Washington Post*, March 24, 2021, www.washingtonpost.com/politics/2021/03/24/mitch-mcconnell-is-wrong-heres-filibusters-racial-history/.

19. Chaddock, "The Filibuster—A Debate that Has Never Ended." See also Binder, "Mitch McConnell Is Wrong."

20. Benjamin Wallace-Wells, "Examining the Case Against the Filibuster," *The New Yorker*, February 4, 2021, www.newyorker.com/news/our-columnists/examining-the-case-against-the-filibuster.

21. Tony Madonna, "Senate Rules and Procedure: Revisiting the Bank Bill of 1841 and the Development of Senate Obstruction," in *New Directions in Congressional Politics*, edited by Jamie L. Carson (New York: Routledge, 2011).

22. Ibid.

23. Ibid.

24. Ibid.

25. Ibid.

26. Binder and Smith, *Politics or Principle?*, pp. 161–195.

27. Wallace-Wells, "Examining the Case Against the Filibuster."

28. "About Filibusters and Cloture," U.S. Senate, www.senate.gov/about/powers-procedures/filibusters-cloture/overview.htm.

29. Mara Liasson, "Why Possibly Changing the Filibuster Brings Threats of Political 'Nuclear' War," NPR, March 29, 2021, www.npr.org/2021/03/29/981364153/why-possibly-changing-the-filibuster-brings-threats-of-political-nuclear-war.

30. Caroline Fredrickson, "Examining the Case Against the Filibuster," Brennan Center for Justice, October 30, 2020, www.brennancenter.org/our-work/research-reports/case-against-filibuster.

31. Wallace-Wells, "Examining the Case Against the Filibuster."

32. Gillian Brockell, "Note to Mitch McConnell: The Senate's Longest Filibuster Was Definitely Racist," *Washington Post,* March 26, 2021, www.washingtonpost.com/history/2021/03/26/thurmond-filibuster-senate-mcconnell/.

33. Changes to the Senate rules still require a two-thirds majority to invoke cloture and end debate. Once cloture is invoked, only a simple majority is required to agree to the resolution changing the rule. See Molly Reynolds, "What Is the Senate Filibuster, and What Would It Take to Eliminate It?" Brookings Institution, September 9, 2020, www.brookings.edu/policy2020/votervital/what-is-the-senate-filibuster-and-what-would-it-take-to-eliminate-it/.

34. Reynolds, "What Is the Senate Filibuster, and What Would It Take to Eliminate It?"

35. James Fallows, "How the Modern Faux-Filibuster Came to Be," *Atlantic,* April 2, 2012, www.theatlantic.com/politics/archive/2012/04/how-the-modern-faux-filibuster-came-to-be/255374/.

36. Molly E. Reynolds, *Exceptions to the Rule: The Politics of Filibuster Limitations in the U.S. Senate* (Brookings Institution Press, 2017); see also "Budget Reconciliation: The Basics," H. Comm. on the Budget, U.S. House of Representatives, June 22, 2021, https://budget.house.gov/sites/democrats.budget.house.gov/files/documents/Budget%20Reconciliation%20The%20Basics%20-%20Final%202021.pdf.

37. Mark Strand and Tim Lang, "The U.S. Senate Filibuster: Options for Reform," Congressional Institute, September 25, 2017, www.congressionalinstitute.org/2017/09/25/the-u-s-senate-filibuster-options-for-reform/.

38. Ibid. See also "Senate Floor Activity—Thursday, November 21, 2013," U.S. Senate, www.senate.gov/legislative/LIS/floor_activity/2013/11_21_2013_Senate_Floor.htm.

39. Steven Waldman, "Learning to Love the Nuclear Option," *New York Times,* April 5, 2017, www.nytimes.com/2017/04/05/opinion/filibusters-arent-the-problem.html; "Cloture Motions," U.S. Senate, www.senate.gov/legislative/cloture/clotureCounts.htm. Comparable here denotes a president of the same political party as the majority, presumably willing to sign legislation that passed, maximizing the need for the filibuster as a defeat tactic.

40. "Cloture Motions," U.S. Senate; Waldman, "Love the Nuclear Option."

41. Glenn Kessler, "When Did Mitch McConnell Say He Wanted to Make Obama a

One-Term President?" *Washington Post*, January 11, 2017, www.washingtonpost.com/news/fact-checker/wp/2017/01/11/when-did-mitch-mcconnell-say-he-wanted-to-make-obama-a-one-term-president/.

42. "Cloture Motions," U.S. Senate.

43. Sarah A. Binder, "Polarized We Govern?" Center for Effective Public Management at Brookings, May 27, 2014, www.brookings.edu/research/polarized-we-govern/.

44. James Wallner, "Mitch McConnell Said the 115th Congress Was 'the Best,' But It's More Dysfunctional than Ever," LegBranch.org, February 4, 2019, www.legbranch.org/mitch-mcconnell-said-the-115th-congress-was-the-best-but-its-more-dysfunctional-than-ever/.

45. Alissa Wilkinson, "Mr. Smith Goes to Washington Has Become Synonymous with the Filibuster—for Good Reason," Vox, April 8, 2017, www.vox.com/culture/2017/4/8/15168072/mr-smith-goes-to-washington-filibuster.

46. Brockell, "Note to Mitch McConnell."

47. Tom Dart, "Wendy Davis's Remarkable Filibuster to Deny Passage of Abortion Bill," *Guardian*, June 26, 2013, www.theguardian.com/world/2013/jun/26/texas-senator-wendy-davis-abortion-bill-speech.

48. Ryan Grim, "Jeff Merkley Circulates 'Talking Filibuster' Reform Proposal," *HuffPost*, December 6, 2017, www.huffpost.com/entry/jeff-merkley-filibuster-reform_n_2287831.

49. John J. Monahan, "Warren Joins Push to Tame the Filibuster," Telegram, November 15, 2012, www.telegram.com/article/20121115/NEWS/121119715.

50. Zack Budryk, "Manchin Firm on Support for Filibuster, Mulls Making It 'a Little Bit More Painful' to Use," *The Hill*, March 7, 2021, https://thehill.com/homenews/sunday-talk-shows/541993-manchin-unmoved-on-filibuster-keeps-door-cracked-open-on.

51. Aaron Blake, "The Talking Filibuster—and Its Limits," *Washington Post*, March 17, 2021, www.washingtonpost.com/politics/2021/03/09/most-likely-filibuster-reform-its-limits/.

52. Richard Fox and John M. Parrish, "A 'Talking Filibuster' Would Be Better than What the Senate Has Now," *Orange County Register*, February 9, 2021, www.ocregister.com/2021/02/09/a-talking-filibuster-would-be-better-than-what-the-senate-has-now/.

53. Ibid. The following second point is also based on this source.

54. See Robert A. Caro, *Master of the Senate: The Years of Lyndon Johnson III* (New York: Vintage Books, 2003).

55. Henry Olsen, "A Talking Filibuster Will Not Help Democrats as Much as Some Might Think," *Washington Post*, March 17, 2021, www.washingtonpost.com/opinions/2021/03/17/talking-filibuster-will-not-help-democrats-much-some-might-think/.

56. Jonathan Bernstein (@jbview), tweet from March 7, 2021, 3:20 p.m., https://twitter.com/jbview/status/1368657785085378562.

57. Norm Ornstein, "The Smart Way to Fix the Filibuster," *Atlantic*, September 3, 2020, www.theatlantic.com/ideas/archive/2020/09/fix-filibuster/615961/.

58. Ibid.

59. Dan McLaughlin, "Neutering the Filibuster Is Just as Bad as Killing It," *National Review*, September 8, 2020, www.nationalreview.com/2020/09/neutering-the-filibuster-is-just-as-bad-as-killing-it/.

60. Ornstein, "The Smart Way to Fix the Filibuster."

61. Richard L. Hasen, "Why Washington Can't Be Fixed," *Slate*, May 9, 2012, https://slate.com/news-and-politics/2012/05/thomas-mann-and-norman-ornsteins-ideas-wont-solve-washingtons-gridlock.html.

62. Binder and Smith, *Politics or Principle?*, p. 211.

63. Strand and Lang, "Filibuster Reform."

64. S. Res 5, *A Resolution Amending the Standing Rules of the Senate to Provide for Cloture to Be Invoked with Less Than a Three-Fifths Majority After Additional Debate*, 113th Cong., January 3, 2013, www.congress.gov/bill/113th-congress/senate-resolution/5.

65. Benjamin Eidelson, "The Majoritarian Filibuster," *Yale Law Journal* 122, no. 4 (2013), p. 1019, https://digitalcommons.law.yale.edu/cgi/viewcontent.cgi?article=5549&context=ylj.

66. Ezra Klein, "End the Filibuster! An Interview with Sen. Tom Harkin," *Washington Post*, December 26, 2009, http://voices.washingtonpost.com/ezra-klein/2009/12/end_the_filibuster_an_intervie.html.

67. Ibid.

68. Ibid.

69. Strand and Lang, "Filibuster Reform."

70. Letter from Danielle Brian, Executive Director, Project on Government Oversight (POGO), to U.S. Senate, "A Practical Way Forward on Filibuster Reform," June 17, 2021, www.pogo.org/letter/2021/06/a-practical-way-forward-on-filibuster-reform/.

71. Norman Ornstein, "Democrats Can't Kill the Filibuster. But They Can Gut It," *Washington Post*, March 2, 2021, www.washingtonpost.com/outlook/2021/03/02/manchin-filibuster-never-sinema/.

72. Strand and Lang, "Filibuster Reform."

73. Jack Holmes, "Joe Manchin Should Check in with 2011 Joe Manchin," *Esquire*, May 27, 2021, www.esquire.com/news-politics/a36545745/joe-manchin-senate-filibuster-then-and-now/.

74. "Manchin: West Virginians Deserve a Government That Works for Them," Joe Manchin Senate website, January 27, 2011, www.manchin.senate.gov/newsroom/press-releases/manchin-west-virginians-deserve-a-government-that-works-for-them.

75. This section is adapted and borrows substantially from Eisen, Painter, and Mandell, "The Most Important Exception."

76. Ibid. We use "reconciliation" loosely when describing the process we term "democracy reconciliation." It differs from budget reconciliation in numerous regards, except from the most important one of all: voting measures would no longer require sixty votes to advance. We do note, however, that budget reconciliation is

procedurally distinct in that it subjects relevant proposals to a limit on debate, thus obviating the need for a successful cloture vote. See 2 U.S.C. § 641(e)(2).

77. Ben Kamisar, "Manchin Says He Still Supports Filibuster, But May Back More Party-Line Votes on Key Bills," NBC News, March 7, 2021, www.nbcnews.com/politics /meet-the-press/manchin-says-he-still-supports-filibuster-may-back-more-party-n12 59902. See also *Meet the Press*, NBC, March 07, 2021, www.nbcnews.com/meet-the -press/meet-press-march-7-2021-n1259907. The full exchange was as follows:

> Chuck Todd: Well that sounds like, if the Republicans—then what you're saying is if Republicans continue to be unified in opposition and don't have an open mind, then you may change your mind?
>
> Sen. Joe Manchin: Well, I'm not going to change my mind on the filibuster. I'll change my mind if we need to go to a—to a reconciliation—
>
> Chuck Todd: Gotcha.
>
> Sen. Joe Manchin: —to where we have to get something done. Once I know they have process into it. But I'm not going to go there until my Republican friends have the ability to have their say, also. And I'm hoping they'll get involved to the point to where we have 10 of them that will work with 50 of us, or 15 of them that will work with 45 of us. However, you know, we, I just—whatever it takes the majority—and it takes 60 when we are moving it through normal process—I'm for that. You said something about the founding fathers. Why did, why did Washington have bicameral? Why'd he want two bodies? One was supposed to be the cooling saucer, as you will. It takes deliberation, it takes listening to the minority, to make sure that the majority is getting it right.

The senator later suggested openness to other modifications to the filibuster from among those discussed in this chapter. Among the proposals Manchin said he was open to were those that suggest lowering the cloture threshold and shifting the onus onto the Senate minority to maintain a filibuster. When asked about the proposal to lower the threshold to end debate to fifty-five, he said, "That's one of many good, good suggestions I've had. . . . So I'm open to looking at it, I'm just not open to getting rid of the filibuster, that's all. . . . It should be [that] 41 people have to force the issue versus the 60 that we need in the affirmative. . . . Anyone who wants to filibuster ought to be required to go to the floor and basically state your objection and why you're filibuster-ing and also state what you think needs to change that'd fix it, so you would support it." See Lee Fang and Ryan Grim, "Joe Manchin Call with Billionaire Donors Offers Rare Glimpse of Dealmaking," The Intercept, June 16, 2021, https://theintercept.com/ 2021/06/16/joe-manchin-leaked-billionaire-donors-no-labels/.

Although less outspoken than Senator Manchin, Senator Kyrsten Sinema has also indicated resistance to eliminating the filibuster. A close look at her words makes clear that she would not oppose modifications. See Kyrsten Sinema, "We Have More to Lose than Gain by Ending the Filibuster," *Washington Post*, June 21, 2021, www.washington

post.com/opinions/2021/06/21/kyrsten-sinema-filibuster-for-the-people-act/. ("It is time for the Senate to debate the legislative filibuster, so senators and our constituents can hear and fully consider the concerns and consequences. Hopefully, senators can then focus on crafting policies through open legislative processes and amendments, finding compromises that earn broad support.") Moreover, she ultimately joined Senator Manchin in voting for S. 1. and has otherwise been a reliable member of the majority once it makes up its mind. See "Kyrsten Sinema's Voting Records," Vote Smart: Facts Matter, https://justfacts.votesmart.org/candidate/key-votes/28338/kyr sten-sinema. Most recently, on her negotiating process in adopting comprehensive immigration reform, Sinema has echoed her stance on the filibuster and reconciliation process and said, "I am firmly committed to ensuring that the Senate retains its ability to be a place where members who are in the minority have a say." See Ben Giles, "Sinema Says the $1 Trillion Infrastructure Bill Is Proof Her Bipartisan Method Is Working," Fronteras, updated November 9, 2021, https://fronterasdesk.org/content /1731546/sinema-says-1-trillion-infrastructure-bill-proof-her-bipartisan-method -working.

78. See Barrón-López, "Top Biden Ally Pleads with Him."

79. "Annotated Guide to the For the People Act 2021," Brennan Center for Justice, March 18, 2021, www.brennancenter.org/our-work/policy-solutions/annotated-guide -people-act-2021.

80. Michael Sozan, "Momentum Grows for Bold Democracy Reform," Center for American Progress, February 10, 2021, www.americanprogress.org/issues/democracy/ reports/2021/02/10/495607/momentum-grows-bold-democracy-reform/. Abraham Lincoln, "The Gettysburg Address" (November 19, 1863), www.ourdocuments.gov/ doc.php?flash=true&doc=36&page=transcript.

81. Brian Klaas, "The World Is Horrified by the Disfunction of American Democracy," *Washington Post*, June 11, 2021, www.washingtonpost.com/opinions/2021/06/11/ pew-research-global-opinion-us-democracy/.

82. Ezra Klein, "The Rest of the World Is Worried about America," *New York Times*, July 1, 2021, www.nytimes.com/2021/07/01/opinion/us-democracy-erosion.html.

83. World Population Review, "U.S. States—Ranked by Population 2021," Accessed July 12, 2021, https://worldpopulationreview.com/states. The percentage was calculated based on the premise that 21 states (42 senators) would be enough to deny the 60 votes needed. Taking the sum of the population of the least populous 21 states and dividing it by the total U.S population, we arrived at approximately 11 percent. (Note, the total U.S. population includes D.C. and Puerto Rico.) Therefore, we concluded that, technically, senators representing less than 12 percent of the U.S. populations could prevent a bill from coming to a vote. (Several of the small states are Democratic, so that is not what is happening now.)

84. See Senate Rule 20; 2 U.S. Code § 644.

85. Robert Jay Dilger, Cong. Rsch. Serv., R40957, *Unfunded Mandates Reform Act: History, Impact, and Issues* (2020), https://fas.org/sgp/crs/misc/R40957.pdf.

86. Jack Rakove, "The Filibuster May Not Even Be Constitutional the Way It's Used Now," *Washington Post*, February 8, 2021, www.washingtonpost.com/outlook/2021/02/08/filibuster-constitution-madison/.

87. *Shelby County* v. *Holder*, 570 U.S. 529 (2013).

88. *Brnovich* v. *Democratic National Committee*, 594 U.S. ___ (2021).

89. Amy Gardner, Kate Rabinowitz, and Harry Stevens, "How GOP-Backed Voting Measures Could Create Hurdles for Tens of Millions of Voters," *Washington Post*, March 11, 2021, www.washingtonpost.com/politics/interactive/2021/voting-restrictions-republicans-states/. See also Aaron Blake, "A Deeply Cynical Moment in Gerrymandering from the Ohio GOP," *Washington Post*, September 16, 2021, www.washingtonpost.com/politics/2021/09/16/deeply-cynical-moment-gerrymandering-ohio-gop/.

90. Wendy R. Weiser, Daniel I. Weiner, and Dominique Erney, "Congress Must Pass the 'For the People Act,'" Brennan Center for Justice, July 1, 2021, www.brennancenter.org/our-work/policy-solutions/congress-must-pass-people-act.

91. Lincoln, "The Gettysburg Address."

# 10

# Renewing U.S. Leadership on International Ethics and Rule of Law

## JOSEPH FOTI | NORMAN EISEN

The domestic reversals on ethics, rule of law, and democracy that this volume has chronicled were hardly lost on the rest of the world. However imperfect American leadership, including by example, had been in these areas, our allies and adversaries alike had grown accustomed to it. Both in the Trump administration's behavior at home, and in its conduct abroad, Trumpery offered something rather different. Trump's "America First" approach was characterized by "a lack of interest in or concern about violations of democratic norms and rights in other countries, a strong disinclination to prioritize democracy support in U.S. foreign policy, and an admiration for repressive strongmen."[1] That was capped off by the extended refusal to accept the legitimate outcome of an election Trump lost and his incitement of a violent insurrection against his own government. It was the kind of behavior commonly condemned by American presidents but never before practiced by one. It was widely noted around the globe, both by those who had counted the United States as an ally as they fought illiberalism and authoritarianism in their own nations and by authoritarians and illiberals themselves.

In the wake of all that, any approach to reform at home must be coordinated with international efforts if the United States is to recover its badly needed leadership role. Such an approach will need to move on several fronts simultaneously:

- Carrying out comprehensive domestic reform around democracy, ethics, and the rule of law of the kind that this book has analyzed;

- Promoting rule of law abroad through exchange, support, and cooperation; and

- Enhancing law enforcement and accountability for violations of human rights and corruption through implementation of existing U.S. legislation and commitments.

Done well, such an approach could lead to mutually reinforcing outcomes—with international attention raising recognition and expectations for domestic reform, and with domestic reform helping to restore U.S. credibility and democracy promotion abroad.

Fortunately, there is no need to reinvent the wheel. The Biden-Harris administration can recommit to and expand participation in existing multilateral efforts that continued despite the United States' four-year retreat from multilateralism.[2] We offer a few examples in this chapter. They include two multistakeholder partnerships—the Open Government Partnership (OGP) and the Extractive Industries Transparency Initiative (EITI).[3] In addition, there will be critical moments to reengage other national governments, to showcase domestic reforms, and to learn from other countries, such as the Biden Democracy Summit and its follow-up. Finally, robust implementation of new legislation included in the 2021 National Defense Authorization Act (NDAA), namely the Banking Secrecy Act and the Extractive Industry Transparency Act, will contribute to limiting corruption domestically and abroad while also making U.S. leadership concrete rather than abstract.

## The Open Government Partnership

In 2011, the Obama-Biden administration founded OGP with leaders from seven other major democracies and representatives of civil society organizations from around the world.[4] It has since grown to seventy-eight nations and a rapidly growing cohort of cities and local governments.[5] Working with civil society, these governments have collectively committed to over 4,000 reforms through independently reviewed two-year action plans to strengthen transparency, participation, and accountability.[6] One in five of the reforms evaluated have been assessed as profoundly changing government practice, such as helping to reduce corruption and giving citizens a stronger voice in government.[7] OGP brings added international visibility and accountability for domestic reforms, with an independent reporting mechanism and structured exchanges to learn across borders.[8]

A renewed commitment to OGP will work best with investment in both domestic and international processes. During the Obama-Biden administration, the United States used its action plan for major reforms including protecting national security whistleblowers,[9] improving access to justice,[10] enhancing procurement reform in the American Recovery and Reinvestment Act (and beyond) through USAspending.gov,[11] and establishing the highly successful Police Data Initiative.[12] At the same time, OGP's Independent Reporting Mechanism (IRM) documented underinvestment in ethics and underengagement with the legislative branch.[13]

Now is an excellent time to reinvest in these critical areas. What were stress cracks during the Obama administration became fault lines during that of Trump. OGP can serve as a critical means of implementation, as a vessel for regulation and administrative reform stemming from anticorruption legislation, with the passage of the 2021 National Defense Authorization Act and any of the changes stipulated in H.R. 1/H.R. 4 or other ethics- and transparency-related bills.[14] In the absence of legislation, OGP also succeeds as a proving ground for bold new ideas—whether that is developing politically exposed persons databases, restricting money in politics, or moving to limit illicit financial flows to the United States.[15] These recommendations should emerge from the dialogue between the users—watchdog organizations, journalists, civic organizations—and the various agencies with equity in improving ethics, democracy, and rule of law. Importantly, because OGP is a big-tent organization—with its membership using good governance approaches to tackle any number of problems, from homelessness to money laundering and from education policy to civil liberties—it creates a structure within which the White House can encourage agencies to engage with international partners and to innovate.[16] While OGP may lack the standard-setting aspirations of a treaty-based organization, it allows for adaptation and innovation across regions of the world. In 2021, more than 100 OGP members—including forty-nine new subnational members—designed and submitted their new action plans, and the organization celebrated its tenth anniversary in Seoul.[17] Though OGP recently notified the Department of State that the 2019–2022 U.S. action plan, formulated by the Trump administration, did not meet the partnership's minimum requirements,[18] the Biden administration's renewed focus on policy engagement and international partnerships suggests that greater U.S. ambition vis-à-vis OGP is in the pipeline.[19] The current administration's robust commitment to domestic ethics and transparency is a promising step in that direction.

## The Challenge of Leadership in the Extractive Industries

Countries that are highly dependent on natural resources for government revenue are at higher risk for a mix of undesirable outcomes—unsustainable debt, slower industrialization, and higher rates of poverty, conflict, corruption, and authoritarianism—all varying facets of the "resource curse" or the "paradox of plenty." The resource curse not only delays economic and political development, but also weakens national security and global democracy.[20] To combat the curse, resources must be put to good use rather than funneled away by bad actors. Ensuring that theft and bribery do not take place requires transparency of payments made to governments and their intended destinations in national treasuries or in communities. U.S. efforts dealing with transparency in extractive industries revenue are largely focused in two policy areas: the Extractive Industries Transparency Initiative and the Cardin-Lugar amendment to the 2010 Dodd-Frank Wall Street Reform and Consumer Protection Act, formally titled the Extractive Industries Transparency Act, but more commonly referred to as Section 1504.[21]

The EITI is a fifty-five-member global multistakeholder initiative that seeks to address these phenomena with cooperation from governments, civil society, and major extractive companies.[22] EITI aims to make revenue payments along the entire natural resource value chain more transparent in order to lower corruption, raise domestic revenue, and improve the quality of investment.[23] Unlike OGP, the EITI is primarily a standard-setting body, with validation of its members' transparency in oil, gas, mining, and other extractive industries.[24] Countries announce their intention to join, take actions to become "candidates," and are "validated" by an international body of reviewers.[25] The United States committed to joining in 2011 and withdrew in 2017, moving from being an "implementing country" to a "supporting country."[26]

In addition, Section 1504 authorizes the Securities and Exchange Act of 1934 to require all oil, gas, and mining companies listed under the act to disclose payments to any government. The Securities and Exchange Commission (SEC) has issued a third rule to enact the law following the vacating of a first rule by the D.C. Circuit Court[27] and invalidation of a second rule via the Congressional Review Act.[28]

The fate of the international initiative and the domestic regulation are closely intertwined. The two processes are complementary but not entirely overlapping. The EITI is voluntary and was previously governed in the United States by a federal advisory committee, while regulations under Dodd-Frank are legal in nature, with regulatory requirements and consequences for access to capital markets.[29] The rules also vary in terms of coverage. The EITI covers all companies operating in the United States, while Section 1504 covers all companies listed in U.S. securities exchanges, including with regard to their overseas operations.[30]

For the United States to achieve EITI validation should it choose to rejoin, it would need tax payment disclosures from all companies with operations within the United States. The noncooperation of the major oil companies Chevron and ExxonMobil with this requirement is what led to the United States' withdrawal from the EITI in 2017.[31] Without the full participation of the "oil majors," the United States would not have been able to achieve validation. Since that failure, public interest organizations in the United States have filed a grievance letter with the EITI against Chevron and ExxonMobil,[32] resulting in the public censure of the companies (members of the EITI board) by the chair of EITI, Fredrik Reinfeldt.[33]

To rejoin the EITI, the United States would need to credibly lay out a plan for full implementation of the EITI standard. This will prove difficult for two reasons. First, oil majors have continued to undermine implementation of SEC regulations consistent with the EITI standard (see below) and have not signaled their intention to meet the disclosure requirements. In fact, Publish What You Pay USA has filed a complaint with the EITI chair regarding an individual EITI member, arguing that it has actively undermined the adoption of U.S. regulations consistent with the standard.[34]

The second difficulty in rejoining the EITI arises from the fact that the world of extractive industries transparency advanced considerably while U.S. leadership was in retreat. Since the U.S. withdrawal, the EITI has expanded beyond a narrow focus of publishing resource revenue to cover contract disclosure, as well as transparency around resource production, environmental payments, and employment data.[35] This may mean that, should the United States rejoin the EITI, the Department of Interior (heretofore the lead agency for fulfillment of the EITI standard) may need to reestablish the federal advisory committee it created in 2012 and commit to an even more ambitious set of reforms, some of which include disclosures not covered under current U.S. regulations.[36] Even with such an advisory committee in place, it is unclear whether a voluntary process would be able to overcome resistance to disclosure.

Given the likely difficulty in achieving revenue transparency through the EITI, the United States will need to prioritize regulatory approaches based on Section 1504.[37] The law obligates publicly traded extractive corporations to disclose revenue reporting in all operations, domestic and foreign.[38] The third draft of the rule was issued at the end of SEC Chairman Jay Clayton's term in 2020[39] and has been widely panned by transparency advocates in civil society and in Congress.[40] At issue is that the new rule defines "project-level reporting" as aggregate national payments rather than on a contract-by-contract basis. Inconsistent with the legislative history and intent, this hamstrings the usefulness of the data in several ways. It can easily mask illegal or unethical payments for individual projects; obscures public understanding of contract performance and compliance; and renders it more difficult for communities and local governments with revenue-sharing agreements to track whether they are receiving their money.

As a consequence of the weak final rule, the Biden administration, the SEC chair, and civil society groups will need to prioritize robust implementation of Section 1504, to be complemented by secondary, voluntary disclosure processes. The experience of the last ten years has shown that EITI participation cannot substitute for a rule inconsistent with legislative intent and plain interpretation of the legislative text.

Strategic alternatives to Section 1504 regulations may require a variety of approaches. The SEC may withdraw the current regulation or issue a second regulation implementing the law. Anti-corruption advocates among civil society organizations may seek legal challenges in courts. Members of Congress may pursue a second use of the Congressional Review Act. Another option may be to simply wait and then act on disclosures in 2022 so as not to delay release of this critical data. Each of these approaches will have their associated risks. The administration can play a role in listening to the intent of stakeholders (including its own agencies) and signaling its intent early on.

## International Democracy and Rule of Law Forums

The United States has a number of high-visibility opportunities to promote and leverage its values—proving that "America is back" not only through speech, but also through a bold package of credible domestic reforms. Chief among these opportunities is the so-called Biden Summit for Democracy. The White House has stated its commitment to hosting one of two virtual summits in December 2021 that "will galvanize commitments and initiatives across three principal themes: defending against authoritarianism, fighting corruption, and promoting respect for human rights." After one year, "President Biden will . . . invite world leaders to gather once more to showcase progress made against their commitments."[41]

The proposed summit will need to have a "thick definition" of democracy—one that includes elections, but also goes further by embracing human rights, rule of law, and fighting corruption.[42] A U.S.-hosted Summit for Democracy could include political advocacy for policies such as enhanced support to civil society in emerging democracies, beneficial ownership transparency, and digital governance reforms to combat disinformation and undermining of democracy online. Many such summits can be overly focused on definitions of democracy, lists of attendees, international declarations, or establishing new organizations. Rather than spend precious diplomatic resources on these issues, the summit could instead focus on credible implementation for democracy, ethics, and rule of law. Multistakeholder partnerships such as OGP can provide the scaffolding and infrastructure for design, as well as the follow-up and implementation of commitments made on the international stage.

Of course, the Summit for Democracy will not be the only opportunity for reform. A litany of other multilateral events will have some focus on good governance. Future convenings will provide room for enhanced cooperation on specific thematic topics ranging from enforcing and harmonizing the U.S. Magnitsky Act with its new European equivalent,[43] transatlantic harmonization of lobbying,[44] regional and global enhancement of beneficial ownership reporting standards,[45] and other critical democracy and law enforcement areas.

## Beneficial Ownership Implementation[46]

As much as reinvigorating partnerships will be essential, the United States will also need to lead by example in implementing a suite of anti-money laundering efforts. Chief among these will be the beneficial ownership transparency requirements in the 2021 National Defense Authorization Act.

The end of the Trump era brought with it not only damage to America's reputation and institutions, but also a promising new vehicle for their repair: the state-of-the-art anticorruption provisions attached to the NDAA. Fittingly, passing the NDAA required an override of then President Trump's veto of the bill,[47] but its enactment represented the first major act of Congress in the new year and a profound lift to the United States' damaged reputation for fighting corruption. Contained within the legislation's 1,480 pages are anticorruption measures that advocates within and outside of government have championed for more than a decade; with the bill's passage, the United States joins the community of nations working to combat the transnational scourges of shell companies and money laundering.[48]

Since the passage of the Foreign Corrupt Practices Act of 1977, which was the world's first piece of domestic legislation outlawing transnational bribery,[49] the United States has played a leading role in global anticorruption efforts. However, the ease with which domestic and foreign actors alike can create anonymous shell companies based in the United States—a 2019 study found that forming a company requires the disclosure of less personal information than getting a library card in every state in the country[50]—has facilitated a range of malign activity. By not mandating the disclosure of companies' true owners, controllers, or financial beneficiaries—known as beneficial owners—the United States has become a hub for money laundering, terrorist financing, tax evasion, and other forms of corruption.

Fortunately, bipartisan supermajorities in Congress decided to do something about it. Title 64 of the NDAA—known as the Corporate Transparency Act—changes this state of affairs.[51] The measure mandates (with some exceptions) that those seeking to form a company in the United States report their beneficial owners—which the law defines as the global norm of a 25 percent or more ownership stake or "substantial control over the entity"—to the Treasury Department's Financial Crimes Enforcement Network (FinCEN).[52] FinCEN will maintain an "accurate, complete, and highly useful" database of beneficial ownership information, which federal, state, local, and tribal law enforcement authorities can access in the course of authorized investigations (as can financial institutions with customer consent).[53]

The collection of this data and its access by law enforcement agencies will have profound ramifications for financial crimes investigations; beneficial ownership opacity has previously hindered investigations into kleptocratic behavior, drug trafficking, political corruption, tax evasion, sanctions evasion, and more.[54] It will also impede the ability of terrorist groups and other illicit actors to use shell companies to financially support their operations in the first place.[55]

In addition to improving beneficial ownership transparency, the Corporate Transparency Act and other measures of the NDAA strengthen a range of other anti-money laundering provisions. The antiquities trade, long known for its use as a money laundering vehicle, will now be subjected to increased federal scrutiny under the terms of the 1970 Bank Secrecy Act, from which it had previously been exempted.[56] Meanwhile, other provisions improve information sharing among government agencies, create an anti-money laundering whistleblower reward and protection program, and require FinCEN to improve.[57]

Regardless of the specific steps taken, success internationally will more than ever depend not just on what the United States claims to stand for, but also on what it is willing to do to repair its image as a beacon of liberal democracy and rule of law.

## Notes

1. Thomas Carothers, "Democracy Promotion Under Trump: What Has Been Lost? What Remains?" Carnegie Endowment for International Peace, September 6, 2017, https://carnegieendowment.org/2017/09/06/democracy-promotion-under -trump-what-has-been-lost-what-remains-pub-73021.

2. See Anthony Dworkin, "Europe's Fight for Multilateralism: With or Without the U.S.?" European Council on Foreign Relations, October 21, 2020, https://ecfr.eu/ article/commentary_europes_fight_for_multilateralism_with_or_without_the_us/.

3. See Open Government Partnership (website), www.opengovpartnership.org/; Extractive Industries Transparency Initiative (website), https://eiti.org/.

4. Open Government Initiative, "Open Government Partnership," Obama White House Archives, https://obamawhitehouse.archives.gov/open/partnership.

5. Open Governance Partnership, *OGP's Three-Year Implementation Plan* (draft), November 2019, p. 3, www.opengovpartnership.org/wp-content/uploads/2020/01/ OGP_3YP-Implementation-Plan_Draft-for-Comment.pdf.

6. Ibid., pp. 3–4. One in five commitments is found to be credibly implemented and ambitious.

7. Ibid., pp. 4–5.

8. Ibid., pp. 8–10.

9. Samuel Rubenfeld, "Obama Signs Whistleblower Protection Bill into Law," *Wall Street Journal*, November 27, 2012, www.wsj.com/articles/BL-CCB-7424.

10. See Maggie Jo Buchanan, Maha Jweied, and Karen A. Lash, "The Need to Re-build the DOJ Office for Access to Justice," Center for American Progress, November 24, 2020, www.americanprogress.org/issues/courts/news/2020/11/24/493195/need -rebuild-doj-office-access-justice/.

11. *United States Second National Action Plan 2013–15: Increase Transparency in Spending* (US0052), Open Governance Partnership, December 5, 2013, www.opengov partnership.org/wp-content/uploads/2019/06/US-National-Action-Plan.pdf.

12. Megan Smith and Roy L. Austin, "Launching the Police Data Initiative," Obama White House, May 18, 2015, https://obamawhitehouse.archives.gov/blog/2015/05/18/ launching-police-data-initiative#:~:text=Last%20December%2C%20President%20 Obama%20launched,enforcement%20and%20enhance%20community%20engage ment.

13. Independent Reporting Mechanism (IRM) Staff, *United States Progress Report, 2015–2016*, Open Governance Partnership, n.d., p. 15, www.opengovpartnership.org/ wp-content/uploads/2018/01/United-States_Mid-Term_2015-2017.pdf.

14. Jeanne Whalen, "Congress Bans Anonymous Shell Companies After Long Campaign by Anti-Corruption Groups," *Washington Post*, December 11, 2020, www. washingtonpost.com/us-policy/2020/12/11/anonymous-shell-company-us-ban/; "NDAA Includes Historic Anti-Corruption Reforms," Project on Government Over-sight (POGO), December 11, 2020, www.pogo.org/press/release/2020/ndaa-includes -historic-anti-corruption-reforms/; For the People Act, H.R. 1, 116th Cong. (2019),

https://www.congress.gov/bill/116th-congress/house-bill/1. The successor bill to H.R. 1 is the Freedom to Vote Act, S. 2747, 117th Cong. (2021–2022), www.congress.gov/bill /117th-congress/senate-bill/2747/text. In the 117th Congress, H.R. 4 was renamed the John R. Lewis Voting Rights Advancement Act of 2021.

15. Natural Resource Governance Institute, Open Governance Partnership, and World Resources Institute, "Disclosing Beneficial Ownership Information in the Natural Resource Sector," February 2016, https://opengovpartnership.org/wp-content/up loads/2019/05/FIN20OGP20Issue20Brief20BO20Disc1.pdf; "Political Integrity," Open Governance Partnership, www.opengovpartnership.org/policy-area/elections-political -finance/; "Beneficial Ownership," Open Governance Partnership, www.opengovpart nership.org/policy-area/beneficial-ownership/.

16. "Partnerships and Coalitions," Open Governance Partnership, www.opengov partnership.org/about/partnerships-and-coalitions/.

17. Sanjay Pradhan, Open Governance Partnership, "OGP CEO Sanjay Pradhan Addresses the 19th International Anti-Corruption Conference," YouTube (video), December 2, 2020, www.youtube.com/watch?v=nR9P0KmTuqM&ab_channel=Open GovernmentPartnership.

18. "Memorandum on Revitalizing America's Foreign Policy and National Security Workforce, Institutions, and Partnerships," White House Briefing Room, February 4, 2021, www.whitehouse.gov/briefing-room/presidential-actions/2021/02/04/memoran dum-revitalizing-americas-foreign-policy-and-national-security-workforce-institu tions-and-partnerships/.

19. Ibid.

20. See Jeffrey A. Frankel, "The Natural Resource Curse: A Survey," Working Paper, National Bureau of Economic Research (March 2010), www.nber.org/system/ files/working_papers/w15836/w15836.pdf.

21. "Cardin, Lugar Statement on U.S. Withdrawal from the Extractive Industries Transparency Initiative," Press Release, March 20, 2017, www.cardin.senate.gov/ newsroom/press/release/cardin-lugar-statement-on-us-withdrawal-from-extractive -industries-transparency-initiative.

22. "Who We Are," EITI, https://eiti.org/who-we-are#implementing-countries.

23. "Outcomes and Impact of the EITI," EITI, https://eiti.org/outcomes-impact-of -eiti.

24. "Who We Are," EITI.

25. "Guide to Implementing the EITI," EITI, https://eiti.org/guide.

26. "United States of America," EITI, April 28, 2020, https://eiti.org/united-states -of-america; "Extractive Industries Transparency Initiative (EITI)," U.S. Department of State, www.state.gov/extractive-industries-transparency-initiative-eiti/.

27. *American Petroleum Institute, et al.,* v. *Securities and Exchange Commission and Oxfam America, Inc.,* 12-cv-01668-JDB (D.D.C. 2012), ECF No. 51, www.sec.gov/rules/ final/2013/34-67717-court-decision-vacating-rule.pdf.

28. *Disclosure of Payments by Resource Extraction Issuers,* Securities and Exchange

Commission, Exchange Act Release No. 34-78167, 81 Fed. Reg. 49359 (proposed July 27, 2016), www.sec.gov/rules/final/2016/34-78167.pdf.

29. *Disclosure of Payments by Resource Extraction Issuers*, Securities and Exchange Commission, Exchange Act Release No. 34-87783, 85 Fed. Reg. 2522 (proposed January 15, 2020), www.federalregister.gov/documents/2020/01/15/2019-28407/disclosure-of -payments-by-resource-extraction-issuers.

30. *Disclosure of Payments by Resource Extraction Issuers*, Securities and Exchange Commission, Exchange Act Release No. 34-90679, 86 Fed. Reg. 4662 (proposed January 15, 2021), www.federalregister.gov/documents/2021/01/15/2020-28103/disclosure -of-payments-by-resource-extraction-issuers.

31. Kelsey Landau and Norman Eisen, "Unhappy Anniversary: U.S. Withdrawal from the Extractives Industries Transparency Initiative, One Year Later," Brookings Institution, November 16, 2018, www.brookings.edu/blog/fixgov/2018/11/16/unhappy -anniversary-u-s-withdrawal-from-eiti/.

32. Letter from Danielle Brian, Executive Director, Project on Government Oversight, and others, to Fredrik Reinfeldt, Chair, Extractive Industries Transparency Initiative, February 7, 2018, www.pwypusa.org/wp-content/uploads/2018/02/CONFI DENTIAL-USEITI-Grievance-Letter.pdf.

33. Statement by Fredrik Reinfeldt, Chair, Extractive Industries Transparency Initiative, on U.S. EITI Grievance Letter (2018), https://eiti.org/files/documents/eiti_ chair_statement_in_response_to_useiti_grievance_letter_2.pdf.

34. "ExxonMobil Representative Should be Removed from Board of Global Transparency Initiative, Say Watchdog Groups," Publish What You Pay United States, February 17, 2021, www.pwypusa.org/pwyp-news/exxonmobil-representative-should-be -removed-from-board-of-global-transparency-initiative-say-watchdog-groups/.

35. EITI, *EITI Standard 2019*, October 15, 2019, https://eiti.org/document/eiti -standard-2019.

36. Danielle Brian and Tim Stretton, "POGO Opposes the SEC's Resource Extraction Disclosure Rules," POGO, March 16, 2020, www.pogo.org/letter/2020/03/pogo -opposes-the-secs-resource-extraction-disclosure-rules/.

37. Keith Paul Bishop, "Is Coal a Mineral and Why Ask?" *National Law Review* 10, no. 10 (2020), www.natlawreview.com/article/coal-mineral-and-why-ask; Press Release, U.S. Securities and Exchange Commission, "SEC Adopts Rules for Resource Extraction Issuers under Dodd-Frank Act," June 27, 2016, www.sec.gov/news/press release/2016-132.html; Nicholas Grabar and Sandra L. Flow, "Congress Rolls Back SEC Resource Extraction Payments Rule," Harvard Law School Forum on Corporate Governance, February 16, 2017, https://corpgov.law.harvard.edu/2017/02/16/congress-rolls -back-sec-resource-extraction-payments-rule/.

38. Ibid.

39. *Disclosure of Payments*, Securities and Exchange Commission, 86 Fed. Reg. 4662.

40. "Trump's SEC Chair Deals a Major Blow to Global Fight against Corruption,

Publish What You Pay United States," press release, December 16, 2020, www.pwypusa
.org/pwyp-news/trumps-sec-chair-deals-a-major-blow-to-global-fight-against
-corruption/; Laura Peterson, "SEC Extractive Industries Rule: More Disclosure Evasion Hurting Investors," National Whistleblower Center, www.whistleblowers.org/
news/sec-extractive-industries-rule-more-disclosure-evasion-hurting-investors/;
letter from Elizabeth Warren, United States Senator, to Walter Joseph "Jay" Clayton
III, Chairman, Securities and Exchange Commission, December 15, 2020, www.
warren.senate.gov/imo/media/doc/2020.12.15%20Letter%20urging%20the%20SEC%
20to%20delay%20finalizing%20resource%20extraction%20rule.pdf.

41. White House, "President Biden to Convene Leaders' Summit for Democracy,"
press release, August 11, 2021, www.whitehouse.gov/briefing-room/statements
-releases/2021/08/11/president-biden-to-convene-leaders-summit-for-democracy/.

42. Joseph R. Biden, "Why America Must Lead Again," *Foreign Affairs*, March/April
2020, www.foreignaffairs.com/articles/united-states/2020-01-23/why-america-must
-lead-again.

43. Zachary Basu, "EU Adopts Human Rights Sanctions Framework Styled after
Magnitsky Act," Axios, December 7, 2020, www.axios.com/eu-global-magnitsky-act
-sanctions-1853435e-17f4-4bdd-9517-dc30462a7a7a.html.

44. "Setting the Rules for Lobbying," OECD, www.oecd.org/about/impact/setting
-the-right-rules-for-lobbying.htm; "OECD Principles for Transparency and Integrity
in Lobbying," OECD, www.oecd.org/gov/ethics/oecdprinciplesfortransparencyandint
egrityinlobbying.htm.

45. *A Beneficial Ownership Implementation Toolkit*, Secretariat of the Global Forum
on Transparency and Exchange of Information for Tax Purposes and Inter-American
Development Bank, March 2019, www.oecd.org/tax/transparency/beneficial
-ownership-toolkit.pdf; Financial Action Task Force, *FATF Guidance: Transparency
and Beneficial Ownership*, October 2014, www.fatf-gafi.org/media/fatf/documents/
reports/Guidance-transparency-beneficial-ownership.pdf.

46. This section is adapted from Kelsey Landau and Norman Eisen, "A Momentous
Victory for Global Anti-Corruption Efforts," Brookings Institution, January 28, 2021,
www.brookings.edu/blog/up-front/2021/01/28/a-momentous-victory-for-global-anti
-corruption-efforts.

47. National Defense Authorization Act for Fiscal Year 2021, Pub. L. No. 116–283,
H.R. 6395, 116th Cong. (2019–2020), www.congress.gov/bill/116th-congress/house-bill
/6395.

48. "Landmark Anti-Corruption Provisions Included in Annual U.S. Defence Bill,"
Transparency International, December 4, 2020, www.transparency.org/en/press/
landmark-anti-corruption-provisions-included-in-annual-u-s-defence-bill#.

49. Jan Wouters, Cedric Ryngaert, and Ann Sofie Cloots, "The Fight against Corrup-
tion in International Law," Working Paper no. 94, Leuven Centre for Global Governance
Studies (2012), http://dx.doi.org/10.2139/ssrn.2274775; International Anti-Bribery and
Fair Competition Act of 1998, Pub. L. No. 105–366, S. 2375, 105th Cong.

50. "The Library Card Project: The Ease of Forming Anonymous Companies in the United States," Global Financial Integrity, March 21, 2019, https://gfintegrity.org/report/the-library-card-project/.

51. National Defense Authorization Act, Title LXIV.

52. Ibid., § 6403.

53. Ibid.

54. Statement of Steven M. D'Antuono, Acting Deputy Assistant Director, Criminal Investigative Division, Federal Bureau of Investigations, "Combating Illicit Financing by Anonymous Shell Companies," S. Comm. on Banking, Housing, and Urban Affairs, 116th Cong. (2019), www.fbi.gov/news/testimony/combating-illicit-financing-by-anonymous-shell-companies.

55. Jack Hagel, "Defense-Bill Override Paves Way for Overhaul of Anti-Money-Laundering Rules," Wall Street Journal, January 1, 2021, www.wsj.com/articles/defense-bill-override-paves-way-for-overhaul-of-anti-money-laundering-rules-11609542221.

56. National Defense Authorization Act, § 6110.

57. Brett Wolf, "U.S. Senate Passes Defense Bill with New Anti-Money Laundering Measures," Reuters, December 15, 2020, www.thomsonreuters.com/en-us/posts/corporates/defense-bill-anti-money-laundering/.

# Conclusion

## A Cure for Trumpery

From its inception, the office of the presidency has been guided by the public trust,[1] which has dictated the conduct of the president and his appointees. President Trump proved to be an extreme exception, compromising and nullifying this fundamental principle by retaining business interests in pursuit of personal wealth.[2] That made him vulnerable to corruption,[3] and set a tone of disregard for ethics and the rule of law that careened into repeated misconduct by Trump and those around him. He assaulted democracy itself, including by seeking or obtaining assistance from foreign governments to influence the outcome of presidential elections to further his partisan political interests.[4] There can be little wonder that a series of scandals ensued, as did two impeachments of a president for the first time in American history—both involving his efforts to corrupt our election processes.

We have termed Trump's corrupt approach to ethics, rule of law, and democracy "Trumpery." While the fight against corruption is an ongoing process that ebbs and flows in the best of times, the battle against Trumpery was exceptionally challenging during the ex-president's tenure due to a combination of harmful forces. Leadership at the Department of Justice

(DOJ) failed to uphold the rule of law and maintain its independence, opting instead to use the agency's vast powers to further the president's personal and partisan political interests.[5] The current campaign finance system, supported by volumes of cash from special interests whose identities are oftentimes shielded from public disclosure,[6] not only distorted the system of checks and balances established by our framers but contributed to a corrosion of public trust.[7] Trump's incessant tweeting and plethora of public lies,[8] reinforced by a powerful media propaganda machine,[9] too often left the true operations of the federal government insulated from traditional means of public access such as the Freedom of Information Act (FOIA) and meaningful congressional oversight, both of which were met regularly with overwhelming resistance.[10] Those fabrications culminated in one final Big Lie—that the 2020 election was stolen. The former president then openly incited an insurrection against his own government.

The excesses of Trumpery only made more evident what was already apparent to ethics, rule of law, and democracy experts—meaningful reform is long overdue. Executive branch ethics laws enacted during the Watergate era have not kept up with the evolving nature of financial investments and outside influences. Within days of his election, Trump announced that, as president, he could not have conflicts of interest.[11] This statement not only put him at odds with long-standing constitutional limits and ethical norms that governed the conduct of his predecessors, but also forewarned of many ethical and rule of law transgressions yet to come. Trump's failure to divest his business interests was the gateway drug for all that followed. It allowed him to profit from his companies' business dealings with foreign and domestic governments in violation of the U.S. Constitution, as well as from the corrupt influence of special interests and other groups.[12] If the failure to divest his business interests in the Trump Organization was his original sin, his decision to appoint his son-in-law and daughter to senior White House positions was a close second.[13] To help prevent similar abuses in the future, Congress should enact laws that prohibit future presidents from sharing in profits derived from business dealings with foreign, federal, and domestic governments or special interest groups; mandate disclosure of presidential tax returns; and ensure the president is covered by the criminal conflict of interest law and restrictions on nepotism.

Additional needed reforms focus on raising the floor or shoring up gaps in the existing framework for executive branch ethics, including by establishing a range of divestitures for "very senior employees" and "senior employees" whose authority poses heightened risks of conflicts of interests.[14] Congress can significantly reduce the risk of outside influence by enacting restrictions that prohibit or limit the types of payments the employer of an incoming official can make.

Congress should supplement the criminal laws with a noncriminal conflict of interest law that has a broader reach, lighter penalties, and an effective administrative mechanism for enforcement and that would, as a noncriminal statute, likely lead to greater enforcement. Additional reforms should protect the independence of inspectors general and whistleblowers from possible retaliation.

Although most evident during the Trump administration, our experience with DOJ since the Nixon administration raises concerns of politicization under both Republican and Democratic administrations.[15] To restore DOJ's independence from partisan politics and assure its commitment to the rule of law, this book incorporates proposals that would strengthen the independence of the special counsel, U.S. attorneys, inspectors general, and career DOJ attorneys. To ensure greater accountability, Congress should use its power of the purse and transfer some of the oversight responsibility from the Office of Professional Responsibility to the DOJ inspector general.

The 2016 general election showed that foreign powers can reach the American people and influence opinions with the potential to affect the outcome of our elections and other democratic processes.[16] These threats necessitate reform of the Foreign Agents Registration Act[17] (FARA) to strengthen its enforcement, tighten its exemptions, and improve the ability of FARA to deal with the challenges posed by foreign agent activity in today's global climate.

More fundamentally, our election systems must be reformed. As a result of Trump's Big Lie, a new wave of voter suppression and election subversion is sweeping the nation. Hundreds of bills have been proposed, and rogue state legislatures have begun passing them as of this writing. But what the states can take away, Congress can protect. Here, too, strong federal solutions are required to expressly counteract these brazen assaults on democracy, and this volume lays some out.

Although Russia contrived novel ways of interfering in the 2016 election on a relatively low budget through computer hacking and social media propaganda,[18] the infusion of large amounts of principally domestic cash into electioneering communications remains the most prevalent way of influencing who wins American elections and of controlling decisions that winners of elections make once in public office.[19] If we do not enhance disclosure requirements, limit donations, and counterbalance the influence of big money, our representative democracy will devolve into an oligarchy controlled by corporate wealth.

Rather than give in to the cynicism that contributed to the rise of Donald Trump, citizens must play a prominent role in reinstating norms. To do so, Congress must arm citizens with the necessary tools for transparency: a FOIA law that works, record-keeping laws that ensure the preservation of our nation's history, and access to a wealth of data ranging from accurate and current ethics information on public officials to reliable scientific data. An informed democracy demands that the public be equipped with these necessary tools and that its elected officials full-throatedly embrace the twin goals of transparency and accountability.

Part of restoring ethics and rule of law to the executive branch involves empowering Congress to conduct its oversight, investigative, and appropriations duties as prescribed by the Constitution. The Trump years demonstrated just how much the scales have tipped toward the executive branch, often at the expense of the legislative branch. The Trump administration further concentrated power in the White House, rebuffing Congress's subpoenas and actively obstructing its investigations while making broad use of emergency powers and redirecting Congressional funds to unrelated projects. These power-seeking efforts highlighted the need for the restoration of Congress's oversight and legislative roles in the pursuit of rebalancing the three branches of the federal government.

Legislation is required for many of the proposals detailed in this volume. Executive orders are well and good, but statutes are enduring. Yet a minority of just forty senators can, and often does, block the passage of governance reforms. The antiquated filibuster rule that makes that possible is ripe for revision. We have outlined the many good ideas for adjusting it that are in circulation today, including our proposal of creating an exception for democracy-related measures only. We assess that changes are likely—not to eliminate the filibuster but to make it work better.

Finally, an overhaul of domestic ethics and rule of law regulations must be matched by U.S. reengagement with global efforts of a similar kind. Once an international leader on issues of democracy, good governance, and rule of law, the United States largely retreated from this traditional role during the Trump administration. Now, with President Biden vocally committed to reestablishing U.S. prominence in the international ethics and rule of law landscapes, the United States can restore its credibility among its allies by meaningfully committing to good-government initiatives like the Open Government Partnership and the Extractive Industries Transparency Initiative. New opportunities for global progress are also available, including in connection with the Biden Summit for Democracy and its follow-up activities. The reliable presence of U.S. leadership on ethics and rule of law has been sorely missed. Full commitment to these and other international collaborations will vault the United States back to its historical role among the vanguard of reform-minded democracies while accelerating progress on ethics and rule of law back home.

Though sorely tested, our democratic institutions have survived the unprecedented challenges of Trumpery. As in the wake of Watergate, we now have the opportunity to restore the public trust through meaningful and comprehensive reform. If we fail to capture the moment, we run the risk of reversion to the depths of the Trump era. But if we succeed, we can lift American ethics, rule of law, and democracy to new heights. We should seize the chance to bar Trumpery once and for all. Our future depends on it.

## Notes

1. Thomas E. Ricks, *First Principles: What America's Founders Learned from the Greeks and Romans and How That Shaped Our Country* (New York: HarperCollins, 2020).

2. "President Trump's 3,400 conflicts of interest," Citizens for Responsibility and Ethics in Washington (CREW), September 24, 2020, www.citizensforethics.org/reports-investigations/crew-reports/president-trumps-3400-conflicts-of-interest;

"President Trump's Legacy of Corruption, Four Years and 3,700 Conflicts of Interest Later," CREW, January 15, 2020, www.citizensforethics.org/reports-investigations/crew-reports/president-trump-legacy-corruption-3700-conflicts-interest/.

3. Jill Abramson, "Nepotism And Corruption: The Handmaidens Of Trump's Presidency," *Guardian*, March 6, 2018, www.theguardian.com/commentisfree/2018/mar/06/nepotism-corruption-handmaiden-trump-presidency; Norman L. Eisen, Richard Painter, and Laurence H. Tribe, "The Emoluments Clause: Its Text, Meaning, and Application to Donald J. Trump," Brookings Institution, December 16, 2016, www.brookings.edu/wp-content/uploads/2016/12/gs_121616_emoluments-clause1.pdf. Expressly limited to the President, the prohibition in the Domestic Emoluments Clause also was intended to protect the government from corruption. *Federalist No. 73* (Alexander Hamilton): "The legislature, on the appointment of a President, is once for all to declare what shall be the compensation for his services during the time for which he shall have been elected. This done, they will have no power to alter it, either by increase or diminution, till a new period of service by a new election commences. They can neither weaken his fortitude by operating on his necessities, nor corrupt his integrity by appealing to his avarice. Neither the Union, nor any of its members, will be at liberty to give, nor will he be at liberty to receive, any other emolument than that which may have been determined by act. He can, of course, have no pecuniary inducement to renounce or desert the independence intended for him by the Constitution."

4. "President Trump's 3,400 conflicts of interest," CREW; Dan Alexander, "Forbes Estimates China Paid Trump at Least $5.4 Million Since He Took Office, Via Mysterious Trump Tower Lease," *Forbes*, October 23, 2020, www.forbes.com/sites/danalexander/2020/10/23/forbes-estimates-china-paid-trump-at-least-54-million-since-he-took-office-via-mysterious-trump-tower-lease/#106bd06eed11.

5. Devlin Barrett and Matt Zapotosky, "Barr accuses Justice Department of Headhunting and Meddling with Politics," *Washington Post*, September 16, 2020, www.washingtonpost.com/national-security/william-barr-hillsdale-college/2020/09/16/0986da c4-f887-11ea-a275-1a2c2d36e1f1_story.html; Sadie Gurman, "Barr Defends Deploying Federal Agents to Protests in Showdown with House Democrats," *Wall Street Journal*, July 28, 2020, www.wsj.com/articles/attorney-general-barr-to-face-lawmakers-questions-after-string-of-controversies-11595904449.

6. Brian Schwartz and Lauren Hirsch, "Presidential elections have turned into money wars—thanks to a Supreme Court decision in 2010," CNBC, December 20, 2019, www.cnbc.com/2019/12/19/presidential-elections-are-now-money-battlesthanks-to-supreme-court.html; Emma Green, "Local Consequences of *Citizens United*," *Atlantic*, July 2, 2015, www.theatlantic.com/politics/archive/2015/07/the-local-consequences-of-citizens-united/397586/.

7. The Foreign Emoluments Clause was the framers' response to the tactics deployed by foreign sovereigns and their agents to acquire influence over officials by giving them gifts, money, and other things of value. See Zephyr Teachout, *Corruption*

*in America* (Harvard University Press, 2014); Eisen, Painter, and Tribe, "The Emoluments Clause."

8. Glenn Kessler, Salvador Rizzo, and Meg Kelly, "President Trump Has Made More Than 20,000 False or Misleading Claims," *Washington Post*, July 13, 2020, www.washingtonpost.com/politics/2020/07/13/president-trump-has-made-more-than-20000-false-or-misleading-claims/.

9. Sean Illing, "How Fox News Evolved into a Propaganda Operation," Vox, March 22, 2019, www.vox.com/2019/3/22/18275835/fox-news-trump-propaganda-tom-rosenstiel.

10. First Amendment Watch (website), "Limits of Transparency," https://firstamendmentwatch.org/deep-dive/the-limits-of-transparency-and-foia-under-trump/.

11. Isaac Arnsdorf, "Trump: 'The President Can't Have a Conflict of Interest,'" Politico, November 22, 2016, www.politico.com/story/2016/11/trump-the-president-cant-have-a-conflict-of-interest-231760.

12. Walter Shaub, remarks at the Brookings Institution, January 11, 2017: "The [Trump] plan does not comport with the tradition of our presidents over the past forty years. This isn't the way the presidency has worked since Congress passed the Ethics in Government Act in 1978 in the immediate aftermath of the Watergate scandal. Since then, Presidents Jimmy Carter, Ronald Reagan, George H. W. Bush, Bill Clinton, George W. Bush, and Barack Obama all either established blind trusts or limited their investments to non-conflicting assets like diversified mutual funds, which are exempt under the conflict of interest law." In addition to rent and hotel income, the Trump Organization has received at least sixty-six foreign trademarks, the vast majority of which are from China. See "President Trump's 3,400 conflicts of interest," CREW.

13. *Application of the Anti-Nepotism Statute to a Presidential Appointment in the White House Office*, 41 Op. O.L.C. 14 (2017), www.justice.gov/opinion/file/930116/download. The opinion concluded that the White House was exempt from 5 U.S.C. § 3110, the anti-nepotism statute that forbids a public official from appointing a relative "to a civilian position in the agency . . . over which [the official] exercises jurisdiction or control." See also Abramson, "Nepotism and corruption."

14. 18 U.S.C. § 207(c), (d).

15. Sam Berger, "How a Future President Can Hold the Trump Administration Accountable," Center for American Progress, August 5, 2020, www.americanprogress.org/issues/democracy/reports/2020/08/05/488773/future-president-can-hold-trump-administration-accountable/.

16. Abigail Abrams, "Here's What We Know So Far About Russia's 2016 Meddling," *Time*, April 18, 2019, https://time.com/5565991/russia-influence-2016-election/.

17. "Protecting Democracy: Modernizing the Foreign Agents Registration Act," Center for Ethics and the Rule of Law, April 17, 2019, www.law.upenn.edu/institutes/cerl/conferences/fara/.

18. Abrams, "Russia's 2016 Meddling."

19. "Citizens United v. FEC," Federal Election Commission, www.fec.gov/legal -resources/court-cases/citizens-united-v-fec; Ted Deutch, "Supreme Court's Citizens United Mistake Just Turned 10 Years Old. It's Time to Reverse It," NBC News, January 21, 2020, www.nbcnews.com/think/opinion/supreme-court-s-citizens-united-mistake -just-turned-ten-years-ncna1119826.

# Contributors

**NORMAN EISEN** (editor) is a senior fellow in Governance Studies at Brookings and an expert on law, ethics, and anticorruption. He served as special counsel to the House Judiciary Committee from 2019 to 2020, including for the impeachment and trial of President Trump, and was a "critical force in building the case for impeachment" (*Washington Post*). His book about his service, *A Case for the American People: The United States v. Donald J. Trump* (2020), was praised as "tantalizing" (*New York Times*) and "compelling," (*Washington Post*). Eisen's other books include *The Last Palace: Europe's Turbulent Century in Five Lives and One Legendary House* (2018) and *Democracy's Defenders: U.S. Embassy Prague, The Fall of Communism in Czechoslovakia, and Its Aftermath* (2020). From January 2009 to January 2011, Eisen worked in the White House as special counsel and special assistant to the president for ethics and government reform. The press dubbed him "Mr. No" and the "Ethics Czar" for his tough anticorruption approach. He also advised President Obama on lobbying regulation, campaign finance law, and open government issues, helping to assure the most scandal-free White House in modern history. From 2011 to 2014, Eisen was U.S. ambassador to the Czech Republic. He is the co-founder and executive chair of the States United Democracy Center. Before government service, Eisen was a partner in the D.C.

law firm Zuckerman Spaeder LLP, where he specialized in litigation and investigations. Eisen received his J.D. from Harvard Law School in 1991 and his B.A. from Brown University in 1985, both with honors.

**MEL BARNES** is staff counsel at Law Forward, a nonprofit law firm focused on advancing and protecting democracy in Wisconsin. Currently her work is focused on election administration and voting rights, as well as the state redistricting process. She joined Law Forward from Planned Parenthood of Wisconsin, where she was the director of legal advocacy and policy, leading litigation, lobbying, and grassroots initiatives to advance access to health care across the state. In that role, she oversaw development of a groundbreaking case challenging the constitutionality of three Wisconsin laws restricting access to reproductive healthcare. Barnes has worked on political campaigns, with the state legislature, and with a variety of nonprofits on legal and policy issues impacting women and families. Barnes graduated with honors from the University of Wisconsin Law School, where she worked with the Wisconsin Innocence Project.

**VICTORIA BASSETTI** is a fellow at the Brennan Center for Justice and a senior advisor to the States United Democracy Center. Prior to joining the Brennan Center, she was chief counsel and staff director to several Senate Judiciary Committee subcommittees, and for Senators Dick Durbin and Herb Kohl. In addition, she was legislative director for Senator John Edwards. Bassetti is the author of *Electoral Dysfunction: A Survivor's Manual for American Voters* (2012) and a chapter in *This is What Democracy Looked Like: A Visual History of the Printed Ballot* (2020). She helped Senator Chris Murphy write his book *The Violence Inside Us: A Brief History of an Ongoing American Tragedy* (2020) and helped Elizabeth Holtzman write her book *The Case for Impeaching Trump* (2019). Bassetti's works on voting and democracy have been published in *Harper's Magazine*, the *Financial Times*, the *Washington Post*, the *New York Times*, the *Daily News*, *Politico*, *USA Today*, and other outlets.

**VIRGINIA CANTER** is the chief ethics counsel for Citizens for Responsibility and Ethics in Washington (CREW), a nonpartisan organization dedicated to promoting government ethics and accountability. She joined CREW in 2016 after a career in public service, most recently with the Department of the Treasury's Office of General Counsel, which she rejoined in 2015 after serving as the ethics advisor to the International Monetary Fund (2010–2015); associate counsel to President Obama (2009–2010); and ethics counsel to the Obama-Biden Presidential Transition (2008–2009). Canter served in the Obama administration and transition while on detail from her position as associate director for the Office of Foreign Assets Control at the Department of the Treasury (2005–2010). She previously served as senior counsel for ethics at Treasury (2001–2005), general counsel for the National Endowment for the Humanities (1998–2001), deputy counsel to Vice President Gore (2000–2001), associate counsel to President Clinton (1997–1998), and assistant ethics counsel to the Securities and Exchange Commission (1990–1997). She also served *ex officio* as counsel to the Federal Council on the Arts and Humanities (1998–2001). Earlier in her career, she was a government contracts lawyer serving as attorney-advisor to the Securities and Exchange Commission (1987–1990) and the Naval Sea Systems Command, Department of the Navy (1984–1987). Canter received her B.A. and J.D. from the University of Baltimore and is a member of the Maryland State Bar.

**CLAIRE O. FINKELSTEIN** is the Algernon Biddle Professor of Law and Professor of Philosophy at the University of Pennsylvania, teaching there since 2000, and director of the University's Center for Ethics and the Rule of Law (CERL). Her current research addresses national security law and policy, with a focus on ethical and rule of law issues that arise in that arena. In 2012, she founded Penn Law's Center for Ethics and the Rule of Law, a nonpartisan interdisciplinary institute that seeks to promote the rule of law in modern-day conflict, warfare, and national security. Before she began teaching in Philadelphia, she was a tenured Professor of Law at the University of California, Berkeley. In 2019, she was named senior fellow at the Foreign Policy Research Institute (FPRI). An expert in the law of armed conflict, military ethics, and national security law, she is a coeditor (with Jens David Ohlin) of *The Oxford Series in Ethics, National Security, and the Rule of Law,* and a volume editor of its four titles thus far: *Targeted Killings: Law and Morality in an Asymmetrical World* (2012); *Cyber War: Law and Ethics for Virtual Conflicts* (2015); *Weighing Lives in War* (2017); and *Sovereignty and the New Executive Authority* (2018). Finkelstein has briefed Pentagon officials, U.S.

Senate staff, and Judge Advocate General (JAG) Corps members on various issues in national security law and practice. Her prior scholarly work focuses on criminal law theory, moral and political philosophy, jurisprudence, and rational choice theory. She is also the editor of *Hobbes on Law* (2005) and is currently completing a book called *Contractarian Legal Theory*.

**JOSEPH FOTI** is the chief research officer of the Open Government Partnership (OGP). He leads the analytics and insights team, which is responsible for major research initiatives, managing OGP's significant data resources, and ensuring the highest quality of analysis and relevance in OGP publications. He has over a decade of experience leading research and accountability efforts across a range of sustainable development issues. With over thirty publications to his name, he has expertise in environmental policy, impact assessment, justice reform, civic space, and access to information. His most recent major work was as the chief editor of OGP's first global report, *Democracy Beyond the Ballot Box*. Before his current role, he was the founding director of OGP's Independent Reporting Mechanism, which evaluates Open Government Action plans in nearly eighty countries. Prior to his work at OGP, he was a senior associate for the Access Initiative, a network led by the World Resources Institute (WRI). Previously, he worked as a public school teacher.

**COLBY GALLIHER** is a research analyst and project coordinator in the Governance Studies program at the Brookings Institution. Prior to joining Brookings, he worked as a program assistant in the Eurasia Center at the Atlantic Council. He has written on topics including corruption and electoral politics in Eastern Europe, the NATO alliance, and climate- and energy-related issues in the U.S. for Brookings, *Lawfare*, and the Atlantic Council. Galliher received his B.A., cum laude, in politics from Bates College in 2018, where his research and senior thesis focused on state-society relations, national identity, and civil conflict.

**JEFFREY A. MANDELL** is the founder, president, and lead counsel of Law Forward, a nonprofit law firm focused on advancing and protecting democracy in Wisconsin. He is also a partner at Stafford Rosenbaum LLP, where he cochairs the firm's appellate law practice and its election and political law practice. Mandell graduated from the University of Chicago Law School and served as a law clerk to the Honorable A. Raymond Randolph on the U.S. Court of Appeals for the D.C. Circuit. Before moving to Madison, Wisconsin, he practiced at Bartlit Beck Herman Palenchar and Scott LLP in Chicago and Jones Day in Washington, D.C.

**RICHARD W. PAINTER** has been the S. Walter Richey Professor of Corporate Law at the University of Minnesota Law School since 2007. He has served as a tenured member of the law faculty at the University of Oregon School of Law and the University of Illinois College of Law, where he was the Guy Raymond and Mildred Van Voorhis Jones Professor of Law until 2005. From February 2005 to July 2007, he was associate counsel to the president in the White House counsel's office, serving as the chief ethics lawyer for the president. He is a member of the American Law Institute (ALI) and a reporter for ALI's Principles of Government Ethics. He was vice chair of Citizens for Responsibility and Ethics in Washington (CREW) from 2016 to 2018, and a founding board member of Take Back Our Republic, a campaign finance reform organization. He is also on the board of advisors of the Center for Ethics and the Rule of Law (CERL) at the University of Pennsylvania. From 2014 to 2015, he was a residential fellow at Harvard University's Safra Center for Ethics, which funded his work on a book, *Taxation Only with Representation: The Conservative Conscience and Campaign Finance Reform* (2016). Painter received his B.A., summa cum laude, in history from Harvard University and his J.D. from Yale University. Following law school, he clerked for Judge John T. Noonan Jr. of the United States Court of Appeals for the 9th Circuit, with whom he coauthored three editions of a professional responsibility casebook. He later practiced at Sullivan and Cromwell in New York City and Finn Dixon and Herling in Stamford, Connecticut, before entering law teaching in 1993.

**JARED SCHOTT** is an associate general counsel at the Brookings Institution, where he advises the organization on a broad suite of matters, including governance and regulatory compliance. Prior to Brookings, he worked for over fifteen years on a host of prominent governance initiatives globally. His experience includes prior work in the World Bank's Governance Practice on inclusive governance in fragile and conflict-affected scenarios, as well as for the United Nations Department of Peacekeeping Operations on rule of law reform. Uniquely, he has also served in embedded advisory capacities with foreign governments and civil society, including in Kosovo, Palau, and Liberia. In Liberia, he served as a special advisor to the administration of Nobel Peace Prize winner and Liberian president Ellen Johnson Sirleaf. There, he supported cabinet ministries and agencies across a range of strategic, legislative, and governance reforms underpinning economic development, the rule of law, and the preservation of peace and security. Before joining Brookings, the native Angeleno served as the director of international relations and assistant general counsel for LA 2028, the organization overseeing Los Angeles's candidature for, and organization of, the 2028 Olympic and Paralympic Games. He began his legal career in the international law firm of Latham and Watkins LLP, and graduated from Stanford University with distinction and interdisciplinary honors from its Center for International Security and Cooperation. Schott received his J.D. and LL.M. from New York University School of Law, where he was a dean's scholar and junior fellow at the Institute for International Law and Justice.

**WALTER M. SHAUB JR.** is a senior ethics fellow at the Project on Government Oversight (POGO). He served as the Senate-confirmed director of the U.S. Office of Government Ethics (OGE) from January 2013 until July 2017. The OGE director position also entailed *ex officio* roles on the Council of the Inspectors General on Integrity and Efficiency (CIGIE) and CIGIE's Integrity Committee. He served at OGE for a total of nearly fourteen years, in the roles of attorney, supervisory attorney, deputy general counsel, and director. He also served in general counsel offices of the Department of Health and Human Services and the Department of Veterans Affairs. Outside government, he has worked for POGO; Citizens for Responsibility and Ethics in Washington (CREW); the Campaign Legal Center; the law firm of Shaw, Bransford, Veilleux, and Roth; and CNN (as a contract contributor). In 2020, he delivered the Elson Ethics Lecture for the St. George's House Trust of Windsor Castle in the United Kingdom; in 2019, he received the Paul H. Douglas Award for Ethics in Government from the University of Illinois; in 2018, he received the Nesta Gallas Award for Exemplary Professionalism in Public Service from the American Society for Public Administration;

and a Distinguished Alumnus Award from James Madison University. He is licensed to practice law in the District of Columbia and Virginia. Shaub graduated with a J.D. from American University's Washington College of Law and a B.A. in history from James Madison University.

**ANNE WEISMANN** served as chief counsel and chief Freedom of Information Act (FOIA) counsel for Citizens for Responsibility and Ethics in Washington (CREW), a nonprofit organization committed to identifying, analyzing, and deterring unethical government conduct. On behalf of CREW, she has handled a wide range of high-profile litigation, from lawsuits seeking public access to White House visitor records and opinions of the Office of Legal Counsel, to a lawsuit seeking to compel President Trump to comply with his record-keeping obligations under the Presidential Records Act. She previously served as the executive director of the Campaign for Accountability, a nonprofit organization that uses research, litigation, and communication to hold those who act at the expense of the public accountable for their actions. Before entering the nonprofit arena, she served as the deputy chief of the Enforcement Bureau for the Federal Communications Commission and as an assistant branch director at the Department of Justice, where she oversaw the department's government information litigation. She has received numerous honors for her transparency work and is a frequent lecturer on transparency and ethics issues. Weismann received her B.A., magna cum laude, from Brown University and her J.D. from George Washington University Law School.

# Index